ATHENS AND JERUSALEM

ÆR

American Academy of Religion
Studies in Religion

Editors
Charley Hardwick
James O. Duke

Number 49
ATHENS AND JERUSALEM

by
E. G. Weltin

ATHENS AND JERUSALEM

An Interpretative Essay on Christianity and Classical Culture

E. G. Weltin

Department of History
Washington University

Scholars Press
Atlanta, Georgia

ATHENS AND JERUSALEM
An Interpretative Essay on Christianity and Classical Culture

by
E. G. Weltin

© 1987
The American Academy of Religion

Library of Congress Cataloging-in-Publication Data

Weltin, E. G., 1911–
    Athens and Jerusalem.

    (Studies in religion / American Academy of
Religion ; no. 49)
    Bibliography: p.
    Includes index.
    1. Christianity and culture — Early church, ca.
30-600. 2. Christianity and other religions—Greek.
3. Christianity and other religions—Roman.
4. Church history — Primitive and early church, ca. 30-600.
5. Civilization, Classical. I. Title. II. Series:
Studies in religion (American Academy of Religion) ;
no. 49.
BR166.W43   1987   261   87-9873
ISBN 1-55540-143-0 (alk. paper)
ISBN 1-55540-144-9 (pbk. : alk. paper)

Printed in the United States of America
on acid-free paper

To My Family

ACKNOWLEDGEMENTS

I wish to thank Professor Carl W. Conrad, Professor of Classics, Washington University for his invaluable comments and Professor James O. Duke, Professor of Church History, Pacific School of Religion, for his patient and constructive editing. Recognition is also due Mrs. Dora L. Arky for her tireless stenographic labors.

CONTENTS

Citations of Classical and Christian authors, unless indicated otherwise, refer to English translations found in *The Loeb Classical Library* and *The Ante–Nicene Christian Library* or in *A Select Library of Nicene and Post–Nicene Fathers of the Christian Church*, Series 1 and 2. Only when the above texts are not available or an alternate English translation is preferred will the specific location of a citation be given. Christian writings existing only in Greek are generally cited in Migne, *Patrologia Graeca* where the reader has the benefit of a Latin translation.

Abbreviations

ACW	*Ancient Christian Writers*
CSEL	*Corpus scriptorum ecclesiasticorum latinorum*
LCC	*Library of Christian Classics*
PG	Migne, *Patrologia Graeca*
PL	Migne, *Patrologia Latina*

INTRODUCTION

Since Christianity is so clearly of Jewish origin it would be historical folly to attribute any of its features to Classical Greek and Roman influences when they can be accounted for readily as Judaic. Yet it is a commonplace that Christianity was Hellenized within the womb of apocalyptic Judaism during the intertestamental period after 250 B.C. when Jewish covenantal assurances and Greek philosophical speculations were encountering each other in the Holy Land and Alexandria. Though born in Hellenized Judaea, young Christianity quickly leaped over the wall of Palestine, alienated its Jewish parentage, and chose to risk its future among Gentiles in the Classical world of Greece and Rome. The remarkable fraternization between Christianity and Classicism that eventually resulted was clearly not prompted by any compelling natural intellectual or spiritual affinity. Tertullian's famous query "What has Athens to do with Jerusalem?" expressed colorfully enough his conviction that their value commitments were miles apart since they disagreed so basically on their epistemological tools. Just as those Jews who suffered through the Maccabean tragedy had learned that the cities of God and of man did not speak the same language, so Christians were to discover that Caesar and Christ did not readily understand each other either. Nonetheless, their geographical and temporal proximity forced Athens and Jerusalem to communicate. In this intellectual exchange Western civilization was conceived.

Even though young Christianity's converts after 150 were predominantly "Greek," the new religion was quite choosy in its encounter with contemporary pagan values and attitudes: it elected in the long run to adopt some, to compromise with some, and to reject some. Polytheism, while possibly leaving some residue in Christian theology, was of course adamantly resisted. More debatable was the issue whether the New Jerusalem should learn to live with other time–honored Classical commitments like the trenchant "totalitarianism" of the day. Could it afford to ignore Greek rationalism or Roman legalism? How should it deal with Classical "aristocraticism"? Could it, to any extent, accommodate itself to Classical humanism? To reflect on these specific matters in a rather general way is the purpose of this book. Judgment, but also the need for brevity, recommends that we pass over the obvious, ignoring, for instance, discussion of the impact on Christianity of the Classical humanistic love of the artistic. Patent evidences of the new religion's esteem for art—especially for painting and sculpture as early as the third century—witness clearly enough the unmistakable triumph in Christianity of the liberal Classical aesthetic spirit over the artistic restraints inherited from Jewish sources.

The choices Christianity would make in respect to Classical culture were determined fairly early so that a remarkable intellectual synthesis emerged by 450 A.D. to build a bridge between the decaying Classical world and the emerging Christian polity. By 450 pagan theogonies and Greek philosophy had been virtually replaced or absorbed by fresh Christian theological speculation which culminated, appropriately enough, in the representative struggle between Augustine and Pelagius and in the final definitions of Chalcedon. By 450, too, Rome, under the fully developed papacy of Leo, was prepared to pick up the pieces of the western Roman commonwealth being scattered about by invaders. All in all, by 450 the testimony was in that a new civilization was emerging from the cross fertilization of Athens and Jerusalem.

Obviously a study of the new intellectual synthesis cannot be undertaken profitably on the vulgar level since the common folk were inarticulate in the ancient world. Instead, it has to be pursued in the extant writings of the educated. John the Evangelist had already initiated the philosophical rapprochement between Athens and Christian Jerusalem but the movement gained appreciable momentum in the mid–second–century apologies of Justin Martyr who discovered that Greek and Jew, to use Paul's terms, could agree at least on one intellectual tool, reason, and somewhat on one philosophical teacher, Plato. The discovery fascinated, in turn, Clement of Alexandria, the learned Origen, and many of the great theologians of the fourth and mid–fifth centuries who sensed that an historical continuity of learning was crucial to civilization. Although at times obscured by the darkness of barbarian invasion, the work of synthesis went silently on in the remote monasteries of Europe to appear quite well formed in the premature renaissance of Charlemagne. Then, continued by the Schoolmen of medieval universities, it reached a climax in the mid–thirteenth century with Thomas Aquinas who channeled the two streams of Christianity and Classicalism into a strong river capable of holding revelation in partial suspension with Platonic Realism and Aristotelian Conceptualism. But once the turbulence of the confluence slowed, the two divergent streams threatened to siphon away the Medieval blend. One stream feeding the so–called Renaissance tapped the Classical heritage; the other, the Reformation, drew heavily on early Pauline–Pentecostal Christian tradition. The Renaissance, in turn, fed the Enlightenment and subsequent modern age of science, while the Reformation diffused itself into many meandering currents leaving Jerusalem, Moses, and Christ stranded from Athens, Plato, and Caesar. So it stands today.

   Whether the partial Hellenization and Romanization of Christianity was a boon or a disaster depends largely, if one honestly reflects upon it, whether one views it from a Protestant or from a Catholic perspective. The learned Lutheran, Adolf Harnack, grand master of all modern church historians, typically represented the former position for nine-teenth–century Protestantism by declaring that the apostolic Church had been contaminated by Classical sophistication, transforming simple faith into hair–splitting dogma, personal scriptual piety to hierarchical institu-tional formalism, and trust in God to dependence on magical formulas. The Catholic is more apt to view the early Church as a primitive institu-tion amenable to philosophical and theological elaboration through the development of a progressive tradition provided by council, theologian, and pope. The modern Catholic may well conclude from this study that the recent changes in the Roman church can best be understood as a planned toning–down of the Classical influences that permeated early Christianity, influences which Protestantism eschewed long ago. The discarding of Latin liturgy will appear more important as an indicator of these deeper changes than a significant event in itself.

   Hopefully all readers, whatever their ideological proclivities, will enjoy sensing the excitement early Christianity experienced when it tapped into the Classical intellectual consensus in order not only to provide some continuity in history but to empower a new civilization whose split personality provided the need for constant dynamic intro-spection. Some might view this success story as an interesting contrast to modern Christianity's seeming difficulty in defending itself against a resurgent paganism reflecting the likes of ancient Epicurean mechanistic materialism.

CHAPTER I

PLATO AN ATTIC MOSES?

Today's specialization prompts scholars to dismiss terms such as Greco–Roman and Judaic–Christian as indefensible generalizations, mere clichés. To a degree they are. Emphases within the system of Greek and Roman values vary so in time and area that any attempt to telescope them into a single "Classical" pattern necessarily distorts them. The Christian way is equally complex as a progressive product of late Jewish apocalyptic thought expressed in terms of Greek philosophy and Roman law. But if the terms Hellenism and Judaism are merely unintelligible clichés, a great deal of scholarship has been in vain. That Greek and Jew stood for something identifiable and something different was certainly clear to the apostle Paul, who declared that in Christ there was neither Jew nor Greek. Only a few Greek thinkers like the historian Hecataeus of Abdera (c. 300 B.C.), Clearchus of Soli (c. 240) and the Stoic Posidonius of Apamea (c. 100), ever took time to report that Greeks and Jews had something to talk about as philosophical colleagues. Galen was about the only important Classical scholar ever to concede, and very hesitatingly amidst his general condemnations, that Christians might at times display some wisdom. On the other hand, only a few Jews, generally from cosmopolitan Alexandria—an Aristobulus (c. 170 B.C.) interested in Pythagorean, Platonic, and Stoic conceptions, or the elusive author of the Wisdom of Solomon, or the later Philo—were willing to respect Greek attitudes. The disagreement between Greek and Jew was, indeed, fundamental because each assigned a different priority to the basic tools of thought available to man: revelation and observation coupled with reason and mysticism. Given this basic disagreement, Hebraic and Classical civilizations could not come away with anything but divergent answers about what was true or good. Consequently, the value systems of Jew and Greek were largely irreconcilable. The question "What has Athens to do with Jerusalem?" was well formulated.

Yet since Greco–Roman views and Jewish–Christian commitments were mysteriously thrown together in space and time by fate or divine providence, their proponents had to devise some way to get along. Since persecution and slaughter clearly did not solve matters, rapprochement ultimately provided not only a more productive approach but also a more humane one. It came to operate on two planes: on a vulgar surface where the unlettered proletary of the street worked, and on a sophisticated level where the intellectual functioned. From the start, humble converts to Christianity naturally carried over pagan elements into their new faith. Simple believers found it easy to introduce honored magical properties into the new Christian context, to recognize in Christian sacramental rituals efficacious powers once vested in pagan formulas and to transfer the potency of old idols to new Christian sacramentals like the sign of the cross, shrines, icons, and relics. Prodigious miracles ascribed to martyrs like Laurence or Stephen, or to a Protasius or Gervasius, no doubt, seemed quite credible in terms of past pagan wonders and theophanies. Room was found in Christianity for venerable semi–divine beings such as daimons and stars; ancient family rites and pagan festivals all found some accommodation. To the delight of St. Augustine's mother, Christians continued to celebrate *refrigeria*, or toasts to the dead at graves. Quite appropriately, Tertullian found it wise to warn Christians to avoid idols and shows, and even to stop adorning their door posts at festival times lest they seem to be honoring a lingering Janus anxious for recognition and worship.

As interesting as this vulgar synthesis is, our concern is with the accommodation that took place on the more influential learned plane. As we already noted, the interchange began early. Only a short time after Jesus had urged people to believe as little children, John identified Christ as the Logos—divine Reason to the Stoics—a concept which, even if commonplace at the time, involved elusive philosophical complexities dating back to Heraclitus or possibly even to some obscure Oriental sage. Influenced by such texts as the Epistle to the Hebrews, Philo's learned Jewish works, and Middle–Platonist teaching, pioneer Christian apologists like Justin Martyr, Clement of Alexandria, and Origen found ways to strike up some friendship between Christ and Plato. The growing intimacy caused some Christian leaders to worry about a pagan contamination of the Master message almost as much as Classical thinkers began to fear that Christianity would subvert Classical *paideia*. By the end of the first century Rome felt compelled to resort to fire and crosses to bring its contagious Christian dissidents, both humble and sophisticated, back to their Classical sanity.

But persecution, as Tertullian boasted, could not deter the despised Galilean from penetrating either the vulgar camp and army, shop and marketplace, or the subtilized academies and even the imperial courts themselves. In less than three centuries after Jesus died, his cryptic emblem bobbed on imperial standards, a sign that Constantine had made fraternization between Christ and Caesar not only legal but desirable. Within two more generations, Theodosius made the association almost obligatory. Probably at no time in history had a foreign peaceful ideology so quickly and permanently penetrated the mind of a highly–cultivated hostile society.

Among the explanations for this revolutionary phenomenon is the fact that the trend, the incentives, and the agencies were all present to foster and facilitate a brisk interchange of ideas. Actually, the synthesis of Christianity and Classical culture was in many ways the culmination of an already on–going general intellectual syncretism in the Greco–Roman world. The sobering impact of centuries of rational philosophy, growing disrespect for the foibles of the old Classical gods aired so blasphemously by the satirist Lucian, as well as the disturbing incongruity of myriad local national cults in a consolidated Roman empire, all encouraged a subtle movement to consolidate theological and philosophical systems; the trend was probably brought on as much by frustration as inspiration. Inscriptions and writings reveal a growing tendency to telescope superfluous gods by treating their different names as mere synonyms for a single deity or as epithets emphasizing whatever aspect of the divine power a devotee chose to honor. Diana became Isis; Dionysos, Serapis. Mithra helped popularize Sol Invictus, the Unconquerable Sun, who came to outshine other deities in late pagan Rome. Finally, the synthetic solar "monotheism" of the apostate emperor Julian tried to swallow up all the lesser heavenly beings in a grand system by depicting them as emanations or relatives of Helios, who, as the composite Zeus–Mithra–Horus, charged them with appropriate departmentalized jurisdiction over regions and aspects of the cosmos. Macrobius' *Saturnalia,* as well as funereal inscriptions, reveal how attractive this trend toward a composite monotheism was to pagans of the fourth century.

The trend toward a synthetic god worthy of the united empire found further expression in the growing worship of abstractions such as *Concordia* and *Pax* and even such deterministic forces as *Tyche* and *Ananke.* The worship of hypostasized *Roma* eminently served the needs of the far flung empire. A syncretistic composite, the cult skillfully combined Hellenistic veneration of heroes with the primitive Roman household worship of the generative spirit of paternal ancestors. *Roma* became incarnate, so to speak, in the genius of the emperor, the surrogate *pater patriae.*

The syncretism in the air went in other directions as well. Scholars who deal with pre–Christian gnosticism describe it as a complex quasi–mystery–religion of Oriental–Hellenistic components trying to bring together the fatalism of ancient astrology and features of redemptive religion. Be that as it may, popular mystery cults definitely mirrored the general syncretism. Serapis seems to have been a composite god from the start; some mystery cults shared liturgical practices such as the taurobolium.[1] Devotees, if Apuleius and Aristides can be trusted, com-

---

[1] Augustine (*Tract. in Joan.* 7.1,6) records that some pagans wanted to identify even Mithra, the "capped one" *(ipse pilleatus),* as a Christian.

fortably or frantically shopped around for gods. Even Christianity, despite its militant monotheism, could not escape pagan efforts to assimilate it. Although some emperors taunted Christ, others like Heliogabalus and Alexander Severus invited him into the pantheon. Philostratus' life of Apollonius of Tyana contains enough parallels to the life of Jesus to suggest plagiarism. Julian, to make his late pagan solar concoction competitive, deliberately incorporated many of Christianity's attractive features, theological, ethical, and ecclesiastical.

By the advent of the Christian era, Greek philosophy already had been popular among educated Romans for over two centuries; consequently it was ready to be swept up, along with religion, in the general trend toward synthesis. The Stoic Panaetius, founder of the Middle Stoa, was an eclectic who greatly admired Aristotle and Plato, and, via the Academy, even Carneades the Sceptic. An effective popularizer of eclecticism, Posidonius of Syria, Cicero's mentor, was a middleman in the syncretism of the day. Fatigued by Stoic pantheistic fatalism, he became so profoundly attracted to Platonic dualism that he came to exert not only a considerable Platonic influence on late Stoicism but even on later mystical neo–Platonism. Antiochus of Ascalon, contemporary of Cicero, called himself a member of the Academy when he was actually more a Stoic. Declaring that Aristotelians, Platonists, and Stoics taught much the same in ethics, he attempted a synthesis of the three and is largely responsible for leading Platonism from narrow Scepticism into a wide eclecticism. Cicero, taught by both Posidonius and Antiochus, clearly preferred a blended rather than a straight draught of philosophy; he found Stoic ethics a good mixer for Platonic cosmology and Carneadean ontology. Neo–Pythagoreanism became a proverbial hodge–podge; Nigidius Figulus, another friend of Cicero, seasoned it heavily with astrology while Apollonius of Tyana later exploited it as a religion featuring rites of purification, salvation, and transmigration of souls. Roman love poets found ways to accommodate even Stoicism and Epicureanism; in their hands even Epicureanism found meaningful room for gods. The famous Jewish scholar, Philo, strained developing Jewish orthodoxy by platonizing a semi–gnostic Judaism. He and middle–Platonism's Numenius, who called Plato an Attic Moses, were freely drawn upon by the Christian Origen who himself was busy platonizing Christianity as much as Christianizing Plato. Another middle–Platonist, Ammonius, may actually have been a Christian for a time. Such men provided a bridge to later Alexandrian neo–Platonism which finally attempted to construct an all–embracing pagan philosophical system comparable to that which the emperor Julian attempted to build in religion. In the neo–Platonic amalgam Classical Platonism, Aristotelianism, Stoicism, and Pythagoreanism were shaken together in religious–philosophical blenders along with, as some maintain, a generous dash of Oriental thought to reconcile mystical intuitiveness and rational empiricism.[2] The more restrained Alexandrian branch became especially attractive to Christianity; indeed, one of the chief exponents, Porphyry, may have been a Christian. The Athenian school of neo–Platonism, stemming from the Syrian Iamblicus, forced an exaggerated neo–Pythagoreanism to keep close company with everything bizarre in pagan gnosticism hoping to find the effective theurgic rite, the esoteric cabalistic word, which could force divinity into compliance.

Finally, in post–Socratic days the earlier Ionian domains of philosophy and religion became blurred while philosophy, with the possible exception of Scepticism, took on salvific functions.[3] Neo–Pythagoreanism, more and more a profound concoction of magic, religion, and science, paid honor to both observable knowledge and theistic speculation. It is difficult to judge to what extent middle–Platonism was a philosophy or a religion, as Plato's Forms became thoughts of god. Somewhat anticipating Julian, Hierocles, an anti–Christian author–friend of Diocletian, made an especially valiant effort to synthesize religion and philosophy by attempting rationally to reconcile traditional polytheism and philosophical monotheism. He postulated one god, at once both the absolute One and the Demiurge, who shared his power not with one only–begotten son but with many.

The Christian evangelist could readily capitalize on this lively tendency to synthesize and syncretize. Most apologists, possibly Tatian and Tertullian excepted, realized that their proselytism would be more fruitful if they could make the Master speak in terms familiar to the Classical mind. About the time John called Jesus the Logos, Clement of Rome (c. 95) invoked cherished Stoic tenets in order to convince obstreperous Corinthian Christians that the natural rational symmetry of the macrocosm should be reflected in the microcosm of their church. Justin Martyr, who called Heraclitus a "Christian before Christ," considered it the duty of philosophy to speculate on the nature and ways of deity; it was a mere step to call such philosophy "theology."[4] Clement of Alexandria, a second–century Christian of learning and polish, deemed

---

[2] For a brief statement of the composite character of neo–Platonism see M. L. W. Laistner, *Christianity and Pagan Culture* (Ithaca: Cornell University Press, 1951), p. 24. For a general history of this philosophy so important to Christianity see T. Whittaker, *The Neo–Platonists: A Study in the History of Hellenism*, 2nd ed. with a supplement on the commentaries of Proclus (Cambridge: Cambridge University Press, 1918).

[3] W. Jaeger, *Early Christianity and Greek Paideia* (Cambridge, Harvard University Press, 1961), pp. 29–30, notes that already early Classical writers spoke of even the Jews as a "philosophical" race. By the second century A.D. however, the idea of a philosopher as a person interested in God was taken for granted. Justin asks Trypho (*Dial.* 1) "do not philosophers turn every discourse on God? . . . Is it not truly the duty of philosophy to investigate the diety?"

[4] Justin, *Apol.* 1.46.

Christianity, saturated with Platonism, a proper catalyst for the divergent intellectual strains of his day. In the third century, Origen permitted his love of Plato to carry him into heresy, the inevitable result, already noted by Irenaeus, Tertullian, and Hippolytus, of undigested doses of philosophy in Christian revelation. In the East Gregory of Nyssa, attracted to fourth–century neo–Platonic thought, cited even Christian trinitarianism as an interesting reflection of both Jewish monotheism and Greek polytheism.[5] The fifth–century Synesius, pupil of the noble pagan martyr, Hypatia, attached as a condition to his consecration as bishop of Ptolemais the right to temper his Christian faith with three cherished neo–Platonic views. The sixth–century Boethius, often accepted as the last great Christian representative of philosophy in the West before the end of the patristic age, was so taken up with secular learning that he neglected to mention Christ or the Scriptures in his musings *On the Consolations of Philosophy*. He would, almost, it would seem, reverse Tertullian's query by asking "*Quid Hierosolyma Athenis?*"

Not only had the mood to synthesize grown popular but the agencies were at hand to facilitate it. Tertullian colorfully identified some of these agencies when he boasted that Christians, although "of yesterday," had penetrated everywhere among pagans "in cities, islands, fortresses, towns, market–places, the very camp, tribes, companies, palace, senate and forum." The Fathers were so concerned that this familiarity with the world exposed the everyday Christian to contamination and even destruction that in general they agreed that occupations such as office–holding, idol manufacturing, acting, perfume distillation, incense–selling, often soldiering, and pandering should be outlawed. Along with the camp, the bath, the inn, the games and the theatre where the murderous gladiator, the frivolous charioteer and the lascivious actor polluted morality en masse, one needed to avoid as well the Cynic philosopher drumming up business among the unsophisticated on the street corner. With good reason Clement of Alexandria admonished women to walk with their eyes glued to the sidewalk; he felt, though, that male Christians, if they took reasonable care, might be able to act piously in face of it all, even in barber shops.

On the intellectual front the most powerful agency of synthesis was the established educational structure, even though it was geared to propagate a deep commitment to vested pagan institutions. Primary schools owned for the most part by enterprising teachers were found throughout the cities and even villages of the empire. Judging from graffiti and inscriptions in baths, the school system seems to have taught a large percentage of the urban population of the early empire to read and write. Deterioration apparently set in only during the third century;

---

[5] Gregory of Nyssa, *Catech. Magna.* 3.

by the fourth century Cyril of Jerusalem seems tacitly to assume that many of his hearers were illiterate.

Higher education provided by schools of grammar and rhetoric supported by the state or locality, private philanthropy, or individual enterprise, was widely available in the early Christian era to the urban middle and upper classes. Epictetus, however, knew of advanced students who were so poor they had to beg for bread or sell their clothes in order to survive. The upper classes, almost pathological in their anxiety to appear educated and refined, could take advantage of some twenty higher schools of learning in Rome founded over the years by Vespasian, Hadrian, Antoninus Pius, and Marcus Aurelius. Athens, Alexandria, Rhodes, Smyrna, Ephesus, Byzantium, Naples, Nicopolis, Bordeaux, and Autun also enjoyed enviable reputations as hosts to institutions of advanced learning.

Education centered around a broad liberal training based on grammar and rhetoric; dialectics, geometry, music, and astronomy which also formed a traditional part of the curriculum were taught from a theoretical rather than a practical stance. Emphasizing language and literature, Roman Classical *paideia* in the Christian era compounded the fetish of earlier trends for correct diction and for stilted rhetoric generally employed to embellish archaic themes. Everywhere, it appears, there existed a passion for eloquence; the young were taught to look into every metaphor, to evaluate the measure and cadence of every word. Not oriented toward natural science, education, for the most part, relegated mathematics to a jumble of mystical numbers, geography to a picture puzzle of ill–defined pieces, and astronomy to astrology. Never a distinct subject of instruction, history did not learn take serious interest in contemporary events, however world–shattering their import. Fortunately, the Christian Eusebius and the pagan Ammianus Marcellinus record something of the Christian–pagan encounter. Strangely, the cultivated correspondence of the important pagan, Symmachus, is historically colorless; even Pope Innocent's letters completely ignore Alaric.

A resurgent interest in philosophy, especially Stoic and Platonic, set in under the Antonines to greatly shape, in this crucial time of the pagan–Christian synthesis, the mind of pagan statesman and scholar as well as that of Christian bishop and theologian. Only in the latter half of the fourth century, if Jerome is right, did philosophy come to be less and less important in the liberal education of the day.[6] Eventually, just as grammar and rhetoric degenerated into a stilted and enervated study of

---

[6] Jerome, *Epis. Gal.* 3.5 (*PL* 26:428). Since philosophy and theology were closely allied since the second century, the diminished importance of philosophical training by the fifth century may help account for the decline of theology after Augustine. See S. Dill, *Roman Society in the Last Century of the Western Empire* (London: Macmillan, 1910), pp. 410–13.

past literary masterpieces, so philosophy became a pedantic dressing gleaned largely from handbooks available for ready references, allusions, and name–dropping.

At any rate, out of this school system, whatever its merit, came those who would direct the Classical–Christian intellectual encounter. Since Christians erected no primary schools of their own, an amazing fact in its own right, the Classical educational structure provided identical backgrounds for the future pagan philosopher and the potential Christian apologist, for the priest of Jupiter and the aspiring bishop of the Church.[7] Whether one was a late convert such as Athenagoras, Justin, Pantaenus, and Tertullian, or a born Christian, as a little boy he had to study the favorite pagan authors of the past—Homer, Euripides, Demosthenes, Virgil, Horace, Terence, Cicero, Pliny the Younger, and the historian Sallust. Along with his pagan classmates he had to struggle to memorize the names, genealogies, and adulteries of the gods who had done so much for Rome. Some Fathers like Cyprian, Basil, and Augustine began their careers as teachers of rhetoric; others like Lactantius, Hilary of Poitiers, Gregory of Nazianzus, Ambrose, John Chrysostom, and Jerome were trained as orators; John Chrysostom, Theodore of Mopsuestia, and Gregory of Nazianzus were fortunate to be trained by the eminent pagan rhetorician, Libanius, Julians' friend.

The very fact that the Christians, by and large, were indifferent about establishing their own schools suggests that they were not overly anxious to alienate themselves from the scholarly heritage of Greece and Rome. Although some Christian Gnostics maintained schools, only at Alexandria and Nicaea in the third and fourth centuries were any efforts made to provide some sort of instruction in what turned out to be mainline Christianity. While Justin reportedly organized a "school" at Rome, it must have been short–lived because the Eternal City was still vainly planning one as late as the sixth century. It is equally revealing that despite the great number of Christian teachers available—a fact deducible from the restrictive legislation of Julian against Christian educators— few attempts were made to create a Christian literature as a substitute or supplement for pagan educational materials. A certain Juvencus, a priest of Spain, wrote a gospel history of four books in Virgilian verse, and a Proba, wife of a Roman prefect, related in six hundred ninety–four lines of dactylic hexameters various biblical themes such as the creation, fall, flood, and the life of Christ. Apparently, too, Apollinaris hoped to make the virtues of old Classical literary masterpieces available to Christians by composing an epic on Old Testament history, Christian tragedies in the

---

[7] Laistner, *Culture*, chap. 3, pp. 49–73, provides an excellent summary of the higher education of the Christian Fathers through Augustine.

style of Euripides, and Christian odes in the manner of Pindar. But not much seems to have come of the effort.[8]

Christian education, then, had to depend primarily on training in the home and on catechetical instruction and homiletic exhortation in church. A few fourth–century samples of Christian religious instruction are still extant—Cyril's *Catechetical Lectures*, Gregory of Nyssa's *Great Catechism*, John Chrysostom's *On Vainglory and the Right Way for Parents to Bring up their Children*, Augustine's *On Catechizing the Uninstructed*, and the extant parts of a six–book rustic instructional manual written by Niceta of Remesiana for a half–Romanized peasant congregation in Dacia.

It is not surprising that some Fathers, reacting to their pagan training, came to be skeptical about education in general, or that, while admitting the need for formal training for purposes of apologetics, biblical criticism, and theological speculation, they remained anxious about aspects of Classical *paideia*. For almost three hundred years, from the *Didache* to Augustine, Christian scholars carried on a tradition quite censorious of Classical education. Convinced that all significant truth was already available in the Scriptures, the *Didache* expressed little concern for formal instruction. The polemical Tatian indicted Classical education roundly. Theophilus of Antioch conceded that an education, if basically worthless, was at least ornamental. Tertullian, condemning pagan education as immoral and fundamentally irrelevant, professed to trust in the judgments of the innate common sense of the simple folk rather than in sophistries belched forth in the academies. What has Athens to do with Jerusalem except to create heresy? Yet constrained to admit the practicality of formal instruction, Tertullian made the best of the situation hoping that reading Classical foolishness would highlight Christianity's superiority. Epiphanius of Salamis and John Chrysostom condemned philosophy and Greek learning in general as bankrupt. Gregory of Nazianzus, although familiar with Homer, Hesiod, Pindar, the tragedians, Aristophanes, Plato, Plutarch, Lucian, and others, remained, on the whole, more critical than laudatory of pagan *paideia*.[9]

---

[8] Juvencus' work (*CSEL* 24:1–146) reveals Christians' interest in supplying their own educational materials already before Julian's edict. Apollinaris composed his educational literature directly to offset the impact of the edict while Proba (*CSEL* 16:568–609) wrote about 450. See Jerome's *Epis.* 21:13 (*CSEL* 54:122–23) and Basil *Hom.* 22 (*PG* 31:563–90). It remains problematic whether Julian's decree resulted in erection of Christian schools as H. I. Marrou claims in his *History of Education in Antiquity*, trans. G. Lamb (New York: Sheed and Ward, 1956), p. 323.

[9] Tertullian's attitudes appear in *De idol.* 10, *De test animae* 1.5, *De praes. Haer.* 7, *Apol,* 46. For the equivocal views of John Chrysostom and Gregory of Nazianzus see Laistner, *Culture,* pp. 50–55 and p. 130 n. 11 as well as the Appendix to his translation of Chrysostom *On Vainglory and the Right Way for Parents to Bring up their Children,* pp. 85–122. For Gregory of Nazianzus see his *Panegyric on Basil,* 11.

In the West Jerome and Augustine entertained quite stringent reservations about Classical education. Jerome would censor pagan literary materials, especially comedies and mimes, as a corrupting influence on the young. He, like Tertullian, asked, "What has Horace in common with the psalms, Virgil with the Gospel, and Cicero with the Apostle?" Jerome professed to abhor rhetoric as mere display, and although thoroughly saturated with Classical lore and the teachings of Plato and Plotinus, he was, like Irenaeus and Hippolytus before him and, indeed, like his contemporaries Basil and the Gregories, wary of philosophers, especially Aristotle. As the father of rational humanism would not Aristotle want to measure even the Holy Ghost? While declaring on one hand that a lack of education might be saintly and ideal, Jerome rationalized on the other that a state of ignorance was basically selfish since it benefited only the individual and thus made him useless to the group as a defender of the faith. Since he was forced to accept education as essential for daily business and for such scholarly pursuits as textual criticism, he saw fit to institute, at least according to Rufinus, the traditional Classical educational pattern in his monastery in Bethlehem. Augustine, over–reacting to the stilted intellectualism of his youth, remained on the whole quite negative about Classical training even though he himself came to Christianity via Cicero and Plotinus. Holding all intellectualism justifiable only as ancillary to the religious life by expediting contemplation of eternal verities, he considered prevailing instructional materials immoral, idolatrous, blasphemous, contributory to heresy, and conducive to idle curiosity and pomposity. Since when were Christian faith and morals arrived at deductively? Yet, like Jerome, he had to concede that formal training was necessary not only for state functionaries but for the Christian scholar as well. Quite disturbed by the obscurities and perplexities in the Scriptures and painfully aware that his age was removed from direct apostolic inspiration, Augustine fully realized that his theological difficulties would not be solved by sudden charismatic illuminations but only by studious application of the knowledge and methodologies which the scholarly Classical world had been perfecting for over eight hundred years. Language, history, geography, natural history, logic, and philosophy all had to lend their services to unravel the puzzles God deliberately had thrown in man's way to stimulate his talents.[10]

Some Fathers like Justin, Athenagoras, Clement of Alexandria, Ori-

---

[10] Jerome's views can be seen in *Epis.* 22.29 (*CSEL* 54:188–89), *Epis.* 53.3 (*CSEL* 54:447, 14–16), *Epis.* 133.1–2 (*CSEL* 56:241–43). Augustine's general reservations about intellectual curiosity are counterbalanced somewhat by his views in *De doct. Christ.* especially 2.11–42, which endorses intellectual pursuits not only to understand the meaning and transmission of the Scriptures (1.1) but also to establish a Christian culture based on the "liberal arts." Educated basically in the humanities, Augustine remained wary of natural science since mathematics and astronomy had dangerous associations with astrology.

gen and Lactantius were quite appreciative of their Classical education. Justin, as we noted, was precocious among Christians in discovering apologetic merit in ancient scholars; Athenagoras, a converted philosopher, remained pleased with his early training; along with Theophilus he found limited Christian uses for even Aristotle. Clement of Alexandria believed that the true gnosis infused through Baptism should cooperate with dialectics, philosophy, and natural science to further an appreciation of Christ.[11] Only Classical knowledge and critical techniques, he thought, could properly equip the Christian to test the Scriptures like coins and so carry out Christ's reported non–canonical injunction to be a banker able to distinguish the counterfeit from the genuine. The *Recognitions of Clement*, besides presenting Peter as willing to employ the liberal studies of his boyhood to bolster his religious convictions, applied Greek physics to enlighten the nature of God. Origen, after repenting of selling his Classical library, decided to incorporate all Classical education into the curriculum of his school at Alexandria, convinced that ignorance was more a danger than knowledge. "Nothing," according to his pupil Gregory Thaumaturgus, "was prohibited to us, nothing hidden from us, nothing placed beyond our reach."[12] Lactantius, the Christian Cicero, maintained for all good purposes that religion and wisdom were inseparable and that individuals could be rational and critical without surrendering the truth lodged in their hearts. Yet as a product of the day's narrow training in rhetoric, he could be pressed to brand philosophy false and empty and to indict natural science as frivolous.[13]

Among the Christian Fathers most favorably disposed to Classical culture were Athanasius, Basil, and Ambrose.[14] Athanasius, especially appreciative of dialectics, was the product of a solid Classical back-

[11] Justin (2 *Apol.* 8–13, *Apol.* 1.46 and 2,8) like Clement (*Strom.* 6.5 and *Exhort.* 6.7) regarded philosophy a legitimate precursor of Christian revelation. Should not Heraclitus, Musonius Rufus, and Socrates be allowed merit?

[12] *Panegyric to Origen* 3–15. Origen, in turn, urged Gregory to use appropriate parts of Greek philosophy to serve as preparatory studies for Christianity and to avail himself of as much geometry and astronomy as would be helpful in the interpretation of Scripture. See also Origen, *C.C.* 5.52.

[13] Lactantius extolls religion and wisdom, i.e., reason, as inseparable because they are the work of the same God (*Div. Instit.* 2.7; 3.10, 11; 4.3) and praises individual judgment (2.7) but especially for pagans so they could learn about the stupidity of their gods. For Christians Lactantius is not so sanguine; they should hold natural philosophy suspect since it dealt with superfluous methodology (logic and dialectics) and has erred in ethics including even Seneca's moralizing. For Christians, then, philosophy is basically false and empty (3.13–14).

[14] H. A. Wolfson, *The Philosophy of the Church Fathers* (Cambridge: Harvard University Press, 1956), pp. 11–15, explains that the Church Fathers used philosophy for three reasons: 1) to convert pagan philosophers, 2) to defend Christianity against accusations brought by philosophers, 3) to deal with gnosticism. He could well have added the

ground. Basil maintained that pagan learning provided an opportunity for character–building because it required the employment of disciplined judgment and even contained some useful moral instruction.[15] Ambrose's wide education provided him a ready stock of Classical references for his sermons. Even though he remarked that God was not pleased to save his people through philosophy, he wrote his *De officiis ministrorum*, the first manual of Christian ethics synthesizing Stoic and Christian values, with a pen in one hand and Cicero's *De officiis* in the other.

Too close a dependence on the Classical educational fare undoubtedly affected Christianity in important adverse ways. Admiration for Greek and Latin literary masterpieces tempted Christian scholars to slight and neglect other more pertinent materials. Thus an Ambrose strained to learn Classical Greek even though he was content to remain ignorant of Hebrew scholarship. Only a few Fathers like Origen and Jerome exerted themselves to widen their Classical background by seriously studying the language of the Old Testament. The great Augustine, largely ignorant of Greek, resented being at the mercy of Jerome's "playing" with the Jewish scriptures. Moreover, when Classical education became more and more monolingual after A.D. 400, Christian scholars in both the western and eastern halves of the empire worked with a still more limited horizon in a Church rapidly dividing itself into Latin and Greek segments. Had Eusebius read Latin fluently, more would be known about early western church history. And had Augustine been able to read the Greek Cappadocians, the West's unhappy struggle with predestination might have been considerably shortened. Moreover, dependence on monolingual instruction involved theologians in acrid sectional contention over the meaning of Greek theological terms such as *physis, hypostasis, ousia,* and *prosopon* in relation to their uncertain Latin equivalents.

Undoubtedly, too, Classical education hampered conversions among the educated in the upper classes. Many were too apt, remembering the sophistication and charm of the literature they studied as boys in the grammar school, to equate the dullness and inelegance of the Scriptures with the merit of their message. Consequently Arnobius, for one, apologetically but rather lamely, maintained that syllogisms, rhetorical devices, and literary polish were unnecessary in Holy Writ because the force of its

---

fascination Christian scholars found in trying to safeguard Christology and Trinitarianism against Parmenidean dualism and neo–Platonic emanationism.

[15] Basil's attractive treatise *To Young men on how They might Derive Profit from Pagan Literature,* trans. Deferrari (*Loeb,* Basil 4:379–435), often referred to as *Hom.* 22, is representative of Basil's positive attitude toward learning. He would, however prefer to leave the gods' adulteries and amours to the stage rather than pay them heed in literature.

elevated message did not require such artificial support. At times the Fathers had to prod themselves to remember that Paul should rate higher than Virgil; Jerome dreamt about his nagging fears that he loved Cicero more than the word of God. He lamented that bishops trained in the bosom of Plato and Aristophanes were more often interested in tickling the ears of the faithful with flowers of rhetoric than in disseminating the truths of revelation. Again, pagan education often nurtured in Christians seeds of persistent doubts and reservations. At times Ambrose forgot he was not a neo–Platonist when he pondered such questions as pre–existence of souls. Synesius' doubts about created souls, the resurrection of the flesh, and the future destruction of the world never left him. "I can take over the holy office of bishop," he mused, "on condition that I can philosophize at home, mythologize in public." Momigliano charitably judges such a position characteristic of a sensitive but practical bishop offended by what he deemed the naivete and inelegance of Christian thought.[16]

But despite its drawbacks, the uniform educational experience of the pagan and Christian thinker had more salutary effects than deleterious ones. It was all important in facilitating the Classical–Christian synthesis by providing a common ground on which the pagan philosopher and the Christian theologian could build. In view of their identical educational background, it is difficult to defend the assumption that Christian scholars were somehow inferior to pagan thinkers, that the intellectual adventure of the ancient world mysteriously terminated with Constantine. In no respect does a Tertullian need to retire before a Celsus, or an Origen before a Porphyry; nor was a bishop of A.D. 450 necessarily intellectually less able to appreciate *Romanitas* than his noble pagan contemporary. If Christian authors in a shallow way quoted philosophical clichés from doxographers, pagans used such handbooks of learning with equal alacrity and aplomb. When Christians, such as Irenaeus, complacently regarded the phenomena of natural science as best reserved for God's knowledge or viewed the world as a bundle of mysterious symbols, they merely reflected the attitude of an unscientific Classical age which already had abandoned the critical Lucretius for the credulous Pliny. If Seneca thought it impossible or unnecessary to investigate the causes of tides or the principle of perspective, contemporary Christians hardly can be faulted for entertaining the same kind of indifference. If Christian writers such as Arnobius, Lactantius and Gregory of Nyssa made no effort to probe the mysteries of astronomy or were content to use them only superficially for exegetical purposes such as expounding the nature of the "eclipse" at Jesus' death, their narrow

[16] A. Momigliano, *The Conflict of Paganism and Christianity in the Fourth Century* (Oxford: Clarendon Press, 1963), pp. 146–50.

outlook was due more to the limited conventional education of their time than to any anti–intellectualism imposed by Christian sanctions.[17] Augustine was quite at home in a pagan world disinterested in its physical environment when he declared any passion to explore the secrets of nature distracting and presumptuous. Even though Christian historical works such as those of Africanus or Eusebius might be used primarily as biased apologetical tools, contemporary Roman historiography scarcely mirrored an objectivity worthy of Thucydides. If Rome's bishops were notoriously nondescript as scholars so were most of her prefects and senators.

The similarity of the educational fare, not its depth, is the all important consideration in studying the Classical–Christian synthesis. Their common educational experience taught pagan and Christian to think along the same lines, to ask the same questions, to use in part the same intellectual tools, especially reason, and to employ the same arguments which often appear in almost identical formulations. It should be no surprise that they frequently arrived at similar conclusions. Trained basically alike, philosopher and theologian exploited similarities of outlook in their respective apologetics. Celsus, the well–read Classical protagonist, reflecting his typically Roman static view of history, maintained there was nothing new in Christianity. Rather than understanding it as a revolutionary intellectual extension of the Classical mind resulting from the ferment of Judaic thought in the Hellenistic environment, Celsus charged that Christianity had merely plagiarized its wisdom from old honored Classical sources. This argument, *mutatis mutandis*, which Tatian, Theophilus, Clement of Alexandria, Justin Martyr, and Origen turned back on their pagan adversaries with equal enthusiasm by claiming that the Greeks borrowed earlier from older Jewish writers. Africanus developed a chronology to prove it. Christians, in countering charges of embarrassing pagan–Christian similarities, did not hesitate to explain that daimons disseminated them, an explanation which, however absurd in retrospect, was at the time understandable to both parties.[18]

A long list of some twenty–five or thirty apologists prior to Augustine reveals not only the wide range of mutual topics pagans and Christians could profitably discuss but also their basic understanding of each other's assumptions and appreciation for their types of arguments. Sometimes views are so similar that legends grew up explaining, for instance, that Seneca had communicated with Paul or that Epictetus was

[17] Arnobius (*Adv. Nat.* 2.55,56,61) considers it no loss if one does not worry about how big the sun is or if the moon reflects its light. Because Gregory of Nyssa, like Augustine, was greatly influenced by other–worldly neo–Platonism, he too counts it no disadvantage to be ignorant of the "elements of the world" (*Adv. Eunom.* 2). Yet Gregory was too influenced by Origen not to subscribe to the value of education.

[18] E. G. Weltin, "Quid Athenae Hierosolymis?," *Classical Journal* 51 (1956): 153–61.

indebted to Christian moralists. Even when the two systems were in mortal combat after Constantine, the social and intellectual exchange between educated pagans and Christians remained astonishingly free and respectful of each other's position. Augustine dealt freely with pagan prefects such as Volusianus and Longinianus; Ambrose respected Symmachus' political position. Agorius Praetextatus, prefect under the Christian emperor Valentinian in 367—the same who once said he would gladly became a Christian if he could be bishop of Rome—seems equally fair in presiding over the last known official dedication of a pagan monument in Rome and in arbitrating the disputed papal election between Damasus and Ursinus.

Respect of pagan and Christian intellectuals for each other's talents is also reflected in non–apologetic literature. Christian historical works, for instance, seem more interested in portraying a continuity in history than indulging in vituperation. The Chronographer of 354 freely incorporates Classical sources and data into his work. Eusebius sees his straight line of history from Abraham through Christ to Constantine far more disrupted by Mosaic Judaism than pagan Classicism. Jerome, in continuing Eusebius' *Chronicle,* consulted pagan writers such as Sextus Aurelius Victor and Eutropius; his *de Viris Illustribus* honors pagan and Christian authors alike. Sulpicius Severus' work called upon pagan historians along with Christian. All in all it seemed to be left to Orosius, under the tutelage of Augustine, to introduce a vitriolic bias into the historical works of the day.

Apologetic pagan works, of course, attack Christianity steadily from the third century on in the tradition of Celsus. Hierocles and Porphyry thought the new religion so foreign and barbaric that it merited the worst kind of vicious censure. From articulate cities of the East such as Athens and Antioch a stream of literary attacks on Christianity seems to extend to the sixth century. Arnobius and later Ambrose record that a flow of such anti–Christian diatribes continually issued from neo–Platonic sources significantly portraying Christianity as a presumptuously plagiarized and distorted Platonism.[19] For the most part these academic attacks have perished since they apparently were expressed in ephemeral speeches and pamphlets; some scholars, however, profess to find examples in Libanius' pro–pagan speeches and letters.

The strange pagan listlessness in attacking post–Constantinian Christianity seems to be associated with a growing pessimism about the future, a gloominess which sponsored a revival of archaic studies and a

---

[19] Arnobius, *Avd. Nat.* 1; 2 blames Hermetists, Platonists, and *"viri novi."* Ambrose in a lost work attacked neo–Platonists who pictured Christianity as a counterfeit Platonism. See Momigliano, *Conflict,* pp. 152–63 and G. Boissier, *La Fin du Paganisme* (Paris: Hachette, 1909), 2:196.

production of manuals and abridgements. Judging from Macrobius' rather pedantic fourth–century *Saturnalia*, pagan intellectuals preferred to discuss the virtues of Virgil rather than the crisis of Christ. Symmachus, Roman prefect and senator, while declaring love of ancient usage the best guide in choosing one's value commitments still was willing to concede that it was an individual matter. The celebrated Nicomachus Flavianus, praetorian prefect of Italy–Illricum–Africa in 391–92, translator, grammarian, and philospher, apparently did not overly exert himself in taking up cudgels for paganism even at this crucial time. Tascius Victorianus, another of the literary elite, occupied himself editing ancient classics as if nothing much had changed. Pagan historiographers, except possibly Eunapius, seemed quite unconcerned about a possible Christian crisis. The late fourth–century epitomists Sextus Aurelius Victor and Eutropius apparently sensed no great cataclysm in Constantine's momentous conversion; and even the last great pagan historian Ammianus Marcellinus—discerning, intelligent and fair—generally stressed other reasons than Christianity for the obvious ills of his day. He actually deplored Julian's edict against Christian teachers![20]

In the West where the Roman senate, the city prefecture, the provincial aristocracy, and the army brass remained predominantly pagan into the fifth and even sixth centuries, the old forces occasionally found opportunities to rally around the pagan flag. Now and then aspiring revolutionary usurpers of imperial power, such as Eugenius in 392 and the puppet Attalus in 409, who needed support wherever they could get it, dusted off the old gods and propped them up in hastily refurbished temples. But such actions had more to do with political expediency than religious conviction. Even the gods seemed tired. They proved disinterested in honoring an oracle confidently circulated by Flavianus which predicted a calculated doom for Christianity in 394. The gods, along with the pagan literati, seemed content to slip away to ponder old heroic thoughts, satisfied that some of their ancient ways would survive in the new synthesis. The fourth–century Palladas of Alexandria was distraught upon seeing, at a cross–road, a toppled statue of the once heroic Heracles, the brazen invincible son of Zeus. He marvelled at the fallen fortune of a god once confidently invoked but now cast aside and laid low. In a dream, however, the god relieved Palladas' anxiety with a smiling assurance: "Even though I am a god I have learned to serve the times."[21]

---

[20] Boissier, *Paganisme* 2:209 explains that Macrobius never mentions Christianity or that neither Aurelius Victor nor Eutropius alludes to the conversion of Constantine because they haughtily disdained the hated new religion. For Ammianus, see *Hist.* 22.10,7.

[21] *Anth. Pal.* 9.441 in *Greek Anthology,* 5 vols., trans. W. R. Paton, *Loeb.*

CHAPTER 2

THE CORPORATE AND "TOTALITARIAN"

THE CLASSICAL CORPORATE PARADIGM

"The State is the highest of all" . . . Aristotle

Learned pagans like Celsus and Porphyry branded Christians as naive, superstitious, stupid, and illogical. But Christians were crucified not so much because they were stupid and ignorant but because they were contumacious, presumptuously and treasonably offensive to a deeply entrenched Classical political value—veneration of the corporate and the totalitarian.

Above all, as Aristotle said, Classical man was a political animal. Ancient political thinkers were well aware that the state grew naturally out of human needs, that without communal effort there was little hope for security and the kind of stability needed for cultural achievement without which life was not worth living. Both the political Aristotle and the nonpolitical Lucretius were conversant with social evolution because they realized that chronic violence and feuding had forced first the individual and then families, clans, and tribes to surrender sovereignty to a larger corporate authority.

As Fustel de Coulanges has made clear, the ancient city, unlike its modern counterpart, was originally not a composite of individuals but of tribes.[1] Sparta earned some dubious distinction by having her three tribes ignobly dubbed Assites, Swineites, and Pigites by deriders. Classical historical sources provide interesting glimpses of the long and arduous process by which the consolidating polis progressively eclipsed tribal autonomy based on traditional local custody of a vague ancestral basic law. According to Plato this fundamental law, or *nomos* to Greeks, was given to the Cretans by Zeus, to the Lacedaemonians by Apollo, and to the inhabitants of Atlantis by Poseidon. Of divine origin, it yielded only reluctantly to the sovereignty of the encroaching and engulfing polis. Early lawgivers such as Lycurgus, Zaleucus, Diocles, Philolaus, and Draco felt constrained reverently to recognize their stewardship before heaven by retaining sacrilege as a state concern. Draco's code reveals how

---

[1] Aristotle, *Pol.* 1.1,7–9, Lucretius, *De rerum. nat.* 5.925–1161, Plato, *Laws* 3.621. It is significant that many Greek names of cities are plural nouns. Fustel de Coulanges, *The Ancient City* (Garden City: Doubleday, n.d.), p. 128.

circumspectly seventh–century Athens had to move in building its city law in the face of problems arising out of lingering clan and tribal rights. While able to abrogate the right of clans to feud over both non–intentional and over voluntary homicide under provocation, the city could not yet regulate the more basic clan blood–law of revenge in cases of first degree murder. By the sixth century, however, Solon could proceed to interfere safely even in family prerogatives, by limiting fathers' rights over their sons. When Cleisthenes felt it necessary to break the family power of the nobility of Athens by completely demolishing the four ancestral aristocratically–dominated tribes, he yet felt obligated to create ten new artificial ones, each entrusted to a borrowed hero, to act as administrative units in the centralized polis.[2]

Rome's early constitutional history follows a similar pattern. Its mid–fifth–century *Twelve Tables* of law began to encroach on paternal rights;[3] soon the Canuleian law struck down tight tribal lines by allowing intermarriage between aristocrats and plebeians. Yet to the end Romans chose to cite their lineage through their proud tribal name: Scipio was first and foremost a Cornelian. The title "tribune" continued long in usage to designate military and civil office holders. In the last analysis, Rome brought to a climax this process of consolidation and centralization by creating a super–polis embracing not only primitive clans and tribes but whole kingdoms and nations, to create a giant new corporate body. Augustus cleverly saw that he could not rule over this conglomerate as a simple monarch, head of a mere city dynasty, but only as a super surrogate priest and father of the great new corporate family hypostasized and canonized as the goddess *Roma* incarnate in his person. His vestals kept the great sacred household fire alive for all to see.

As the original but persistent tribal consciousness yielded to the inexorable drive toward the larger commonwealth of polis and empire, the individual's consciousness of his meaning and importance became blurred and more remote. Today's assumption that individual rights have priority over communal ones would be a novelty in ancient Greece and Rome; at the very best such rights would be reciprocal. Since no

---

[2] For a translation of Draco's code see G. W. Botsford and E. G. Sihler, *Hellenic Civilization* (New York: Columbia University Press, 1916), pp. 289–92. A more detailed study is M. Gagarin, *Drakon and early Athenian Homicide Law* (New Haven: Yale University Press, 1981), pp. 30–64. Plutarch's *Parallel Lives*, Solon 20–25, reveals the polis' growing power over the individual including women. Herodotus, *Hist.* 5.66 and Aristotle, *Athen. Const.* 20–21 record Cleisthenes' constitution.

[3] The code limits, for instance, the power of a father to sell his sons, a major infringement on strongly entrenched paternal rights. Text and study can be found in *The Twelve Tables*, ed. and trans. Warmington *(Remains of Old Latin, Loeb Classical Library)* 3:424–515; or see E. B. Conant, "The Laws of the Twelve Tables," *St. Louis Law Review* 13 (1928):231–45.

revealed anthropology in Classical thought guaranteed that each individual was a personality of great value, an end in himself, an integral link in a divine economy, an entity destined for individual divine recognition, Classical man was largely forced to equate his meaning, his *raison d'être*, his worth, with the extent to which he was privileged to enjoy participation in the affairs of the whole, generally expressed by service to the polis as the custodian of the public consensus.

The charge that personality was never distinctly conceived of by Classical antiquity is not entirely unfounded.[4] However, qualifications as to time and place need to be made; certainly Greek and Roman psychology are not identical. In early Homeric Greece heroic individualism was a natural corollary of aristocracy. Yet in time this rugged idea of individual selfhood was attenuated by sublimation into service of the commonwealth even though it lingered on to inspire occasional rebels who questioned the sanctity of the corporate selfhood of the citizenry. In order to turn Antigone's unique story of self–assertion into a tragedy, Sophocles had to make Creon a villain. In general the Greek value system extended little tolerance to those who challenged corporate piety or offended the conventional political consensus. Socrates, arch–individualist, paid a heavy price. Plato's *Republic* and *Laws*, far from finding validity in the psychology of the individual or envisioning any unplumbed potential in humanity as a whole, held out no promises for a better self–fulfillment in the future; instead, assertions of identity or self–expression were declared dangerous to the community.[5] Novelty is heresy best prevented by educational censorship; individual emotion is best sacrificed to divine Reason. Even when Classical lyric love poets robustly glorified a degree of personal fulfillment by indulgence in hedonistic liberty, they fell short of advocating a true rugged individualism that would dare to challenge "supra–individual forces." Individuals who presumptuously displayed immoderate ambition and sought novel methods or ends to challenge the Greek commonwealth often ended in disaster—A Pausanias or Lysander in Sparta, an Alcibiades or Cleophon in Athens. Even Miltiades, the hero of Marathon, was told he would be given a crown for his military exploits only when he could fight wars all by himself. Aristotle summed it up well. Always assuming that

---

[4] E. Bevan, *Hellenism and Christianity* (London: Allen and Unwin, 1930), p. 141. J. M. Rist's attempt in *Stoic Philosophy* (Cambridge: Cambridge University Press, 1969), pp. 187–89, to find a concept of personality in Panaetius is not very convincing.

[5] The Prior claims of the state virtually comprise the message of the *Republic*. See *Laws* 5.730D, 731E–732A, 739C, 6.758D, 780A, 7.798B. The citizen, in short, has only one area of independent action: to obey. *Laws* 3.689 compares the state and the human soul; like the warring components of the soul, reason and emotion, the state has its corresponding rational law and its "irrational" people. *Laws* 5.73OD would proclaim a delator a hero of the state, a winner of a prize for excellence.

the whole was greater than the part, he maintained in his *Politics* and *Nichomachaean Ethics* that the state aimed at the highest good, a good far more noble and more divine than self–satisfaction, which was not only subsidiary to the corporate good but was virtually impossible outside its context.[6] If the life of the individual was to hold meaning, if one would live the good life, it would be as a citizen, as one who took part in the deliberative or judicial administration of the state. But Aristotle is quick to add that one who wishes to govern must first be willing to be governed. Since the human animal was fundamentally a political creature, even personal virtue was to be cultivated with the commonwealth in mind. In short, even in Greek eyes, except those of Epicureans, Sophists and hard–line Stoics, the individual found value realized almost exclusively in the context of the corporate.

Students of the Hellenistic world generally proclaim that the notion of individualism came into its own in the post–Alexander past. Here the mixing of cultures, the wide geographical frontiers and extensive opportunities for material exploitation tended to weaken the old corporate allegiances by introducing new selfish motivation. This spirit of individualism supposedly lived on, especially in the East, well into the Roman era.

It is palpably true that architecture in the new Seleucid cities showed a heightened interest in personal display of luxury, comfort, and pleasure, exhibited in lavish palaces, theatres, and libraries. Hellenistic sculpture, admittedly, tended to exaggerate realism by graphically depicting personal physical details, even blemishes, while toning down mythological subjects which were often symbolic of the old corporate polis. That the sciences, especially anatomy, displayed a growing interest in man's bodily composition and welfare is evidenced from the days of Herophilus of Alexandria (c. 300 B.C.) to Galen of Pergamun (c. 175 A.D.). Hellenistic comedy revealed a less restricted status for women; tales of travel such as those found in Strabo and a fondness for biography as evidenced by Plutarch or Diogenes Laertius—all pointed to a heightened interest in the individual's personal concerns.[7]

Yet the question remains how seriously the old Hellenic identification of man's ultimate meaning with that of the corporate body was eroded by new Hellenistic materialistic distractions. Many political treatises written in Ptolemaic and Seleucid days—few are still extant and fragments are difficult to interpret—want to emphasize that human beings, still considered basically a political animal, would find meaning

---

[6] Aristotle, *Pol.* 1.1, 11–12, *Nich. Ethics* 1.1094a25–30; 10.1179b30–1180a25.

[7] Bevan, *Hellenism*, p. 54 would include love of nature, the bucolic, in Greek poetry as evidence of growing individualism. Xenophon comes to mind. See also P. Wendland, *Die Hellenistische–Römische Kultur in ihren Beziehungen zu Judentum und Christentum* (Tübingen: Mohr, 1912), p. 50.

best cultivated under the dominance of new divine kings whose examples of wisdom and virtue were conceived as divinely calculated to awaken the best of human potential. Likewise, when the divine monarchs beneficently bestowed subsidies, rights, and privileges they gave them to political corporate bodies such as cities and colonies, a recognition that such entities were still considered the honored milieu in which human beings could find meaning. Philanthropists, too, by consistently endowing the same political corporate entities, evinced a like conviction that the individual's fulfillment was inexorably bound up, as always, with the corporate welfare. The Ptolemies, more bluntly, made it perfectly clear that each man, noble or fellah, was to know his place and realize that he was not to do as he pleased but only what the good of the whole ordained.

Yet, in the political context, Tarn is rightly impressed by the tendency in the Hellenistic age to establish private associations or clubs of all kinds which offered alternatives to the city's monopoly on the right to explain man's *raison d'être*.[8] Chief among these associations, of course, were religious groups made up of devotees of mystery cults hoping to find meaning and salvation in the blessings and promises of a Dionysos, an Isis, or a Serapis. It is quite possible that such private strivings, coupled with the growing conviction that every man had his own daimon or genius—a sort of individuality—so threatened to detract from the citizen's identification with the whole that Hellenistic monarchs found exploitation of existing tendencies toward divine monarchy a convenient way to prop up the sagging importance of the corporate. Granted the impact of private associations, it remains significant to note in the political context that despite the great outpouring of literature—poetic, philosophical, historical, and scientific—none of the over one thousand known Hellenistic writers composed a sustained introspective work on anthropology, human psychology, or personality.

On the philosophical scene, to be sure, the two dominant Hellenistic philosophies, Epicureanism and Stoicism, basically declared that the human being was no longer a creature of the corporate but an individual trying to stand alone, in need of philosophy to find true selfhood and to regulate private conduct. Epicureanism advocated the attainment of personal tranquility by pursuing an understanding of the true nature of one's environment through one's own sense perception and exercise of reason. Stoics would seek personal indifference or "apathy" toward their surroundings through the same means. Both philosophies advocated aloofness from corporate involvement and tried to honor a free will.[9]

---

8 W. W. Tarn, *Hellenistic Civilization* (Cleveland, Meridian, 1967), pp. 93–95.

9 Wendland, *Kultur*, p. 48 would see Sceptic *Ataraxis*, Stoic *Apatheia*, and Epicurean *Autarkeia* as defenses freeing the individual from the overwhelming communal compul-

Yet, as we shall see, both schools had serious limitations as promoters of individualism.

Early Rome, excessively prone to glorify priorities of the corporate good, loudly extolled such patriotic heroes as Cincinnatus, Coriolanus and Dentatus, who found meaning only in corporate service. Hellenic political thought that postulated such identification with the public good found ready approval in Rome. Did not Greeks wisely hold that any leader who usurped rule by violating the constitution should be considered a tyrant and as such an outlaw? Fortunately early Rome had little need to apply this axiom; the inviolability of the Roman corporate image was so sacred that it could stay the hands of even a Scipio Africanus who, despite his overwhelming popularity as the victor over Hannibal, was yet too respectful of the commonwealth's corporate claims to sabotage them for his own individual advantage. Roughly a hundred years later, however, when Rome witnessed the scourge of private armies belonging to Marius and Sulla, it was obvious that a less tractable generation of individuals was emerging. Like Plato before him, Cicero struggled against great odds to shore up respect for the corporate against the maniacal egocentrism of a Caesar, Antony, and Octavian. He tirelessly maintained that the traditional *respublica,* as the embodiment of true *Romanitas,* worked best for the common good because it was the most trustworthy exponent of Stoic natural law and the chief guardian of Plato's abstract Justice. While he maintained that the commonwealth was the possession of all its citizens and their agency to effect just government, statesmanship to him basically meant balancing the narrow interests of classes or estates rather than serving the aspirations of the individual. His *De officiis* so socialized three of the four traditional Classical virtues that it justified one's private role in the world—even one's personal love for his children, kin, and friends—only if it were subservient to love of country[10] His portrayal of Scipio's dream confidently promised to those who served the community the first claims on eternal happiness, a view Virgil will reiterate.[11] Unlike the pontiff, Cotta, who successfully hid his personal religious skepticism for the sake of the public weal, Caesar permitted his dissembling to get out of hand and exhibit himself as an aspiring tyrant disrespectful of the sacred *mos maiorum.* Augustus, taking advantage of the Hellenistic image of the divine ruler or *soter,* brought classes as well as individuals back again to a sense of respect for the corporate. As we saw, he realized he could best emphasize the old corporate image and its virtues by subduing his own

---

sion. Fustel, *City,* p. 359 also interprets Stoicism as a just reaction against the ancient city's tyrannical power that made it the object of all human labor.

[10] Cicero, *De re publica* 1,21, *De officiis* 1.7.

[11] *Aeneid* 6.660.

personality and by presenting himself as *princeps* or *pater patriae* or even as a receptacle hosting an hypostasized Roman godhead.

In addition to individuals who arose from time to time in the Classical world bent upon using their own egos as canons, a succession of philosophies appeared emphasizing a degree of individual fulfillment not always consonant with the wider established values of the community. Such a message was taught by the Cynics founded by Antisthenes who worshiped the enterprising Hercules and admired Socrates for his ideal of independence. Antisthenes' pupil, Diogenes, hoped to wholly "recoin current values" by living in contempt of politics, art, and amenities. But such a program too rugged for most, prompted general derision. Plato, in his day, felt it necessary to champion the virtuous symmetry of the polis against what he considered divisive individualistic preachments of contemporary Sophists who, by championing the claims of nature *(physis)* over those of law *(nomos)*, seemed to be subjectivising communal values in copious flourishes of rhetoric.[12] As we already saw, in the declining days of Hellenic culture Epicurus appeared with his quietism, and Zeno and fellow Stoics followed with their *apatheia*. Lastly, in waning Roman days, Plotinus and his neo–Platonists arose advocating *ataraxia*. All seemed to seek self–fulfillment apart from the corporate. The self–centered Epicureans were the most serious about withdrawal, but, for the most part, their robustness made them lone wolves crying in the wilderness. Moreover, many Roman Epicureans, ignoring Lucretius, tended to express their individualism in bodily indulgence rather than in scholarly withdrawal from society. Roman Stoicism, in turn, preferred— especially after Posidonius (c. 100 B.C.) who was the last rarefied Stoic philosopher able to resist Rome's practical mentality—to emphasize, at the expense of withdrawal, performance of one's duty in fulfilling whatever obligations one's situation rationally demanded. Admittedly, Roman Stoics supposedly extended the effervescent Hellenistic spirit of individualism by replacing the exclusive claims of the traditional, narrow state– corporatism with a world–wide equal brotherhood of man. By doing so they are said to have opened possibilities for a more individualistic outlook featuring personal introspection of the universal rational godhead within them and for new private adjustments to a fresh cosmopolitan order. At first sight, Epictetus' counsel, "Be desirous to converse in purity with your own pure mind and with god," seems to suggest that man has found within himself an impregnable bulwark of personal worth.

Yet everything considered, individual identity in the Stoic system became more lost than ever in the new colorless, abstract, world–wide human brotherhood in which equality was a key word. Stoic idealism

---

[12] See Plato, *Protag.* 316–20 esp.

tended to teach in the last analysis that man as a type was more real than
the individual; the human being was praised as a microcosm reflecting
the order of the macrocosm. As part of pantheistic Reason one was given
a soul destined only for an eternal impersonal absorption into cosmic
reality. While encouraged to make individual judgments about the
"nature of things," the Stoic actually was making something of a mockery
of individualism by being forced, in the last analysis, to assent, however
rationally, to the dispensation of a fatalistic Destiny or Providence often
revealed through astrology. Emotionally starved, the Stoic was best exercised in discovering the intentions of Nature as god and ordering his life
in harmony with them. While talking much about the "I," the Stoic
tended to find fulfillment in *apatheia*, a negative limiting of desires and
an acceptance of the inevitable rather than in an exploration of the
dynamics of man's untapped positive potential. Marcus Aurelius, a
deeply sad emperor, yet one deserving reverence for his resoluteness
and good will, properly brought the philosophy's influence to a colorless
close. In asserting, in an almost Aristotelian way, that what was not good
for the swarm was not good for the bee and that nothing was injurious to
the part if it advanced the whole, he found himself subscribing to
traditional Classical ethics which would honor first and foremost obligations to the community.

If Stoics lost man in Reason, neo–Platonists lost him in mysticism.
While Plotinus ruggedly disdained the fatherland, he fastened man in an
ascending scale of existence reaching from inert matter on one extreme
to the One on the other. His best advice would encourage man to lose his
unique position in the scale of reality and seek absorption of his personality in the godhead. All in all, it appears that Aristotle alone thought of
some dynamism in each man's psychology by making his mind progress
in individuality in proportion to his personal experiences. At the same
time, his ethics advocated a personal freedom for each man, free from
Fate, to discover his own ethical mean between extremes.

THE CLASSICAL "TOTALITARIAN" POLITY

"Citizens belong to the State" . . . Aristotle

The totalitarian aspect of Classical society follows logically enough.
Once it had digested the family, clan, and tribe together with their
peculiar deities and customs, the victorious corporate state—largely unchecked by any effective school of philosophical individualism—readily
assumed a totalitarian stance. It came to enjoy a full quantitative and
qualitative competence, a *plena auctoritas* founded on unwritten law and
a *plena potestas* based on its own legislation. It assumed as natural the
exclusive right to control every facet of human activity so that no other

sovereignty ever arose to claim a sphere of influence. The term "total-itarianism" as used here requires very careful and attentive definition to distinguish it from that spoken of loosely today. In the ancient context, "totalitarianism" should be regarded as a philosophy of government, not a form. It did not necessarily imply either authoritarianism or dic-tatorship.

To the Classical world, "totalitarianism" was a dispensation so natural and philosophy of government so legitimate that it was accepted without much discussion. It was taken for granted in the Hellenic polis because citizens obviously could not conceive of the ancient *civitas*, theoretically resting on the collective consensus of the body of citizens, as something external or foreign to themselves. Unlike the Hebrew Samuel and some few Christian writers, the Classical man did not confront the state as an extrinsically contrived plot imposed upon him to make him miserable. In the Hellenic mind the state could not be considered apart from the nature of man which regarded all rational controls natural and desirable. In other words, state authority was a legitimate extension of man's own nature designed to express itself in all aspects of human behavior and to work for man's total welfare.[13] The ancient Hellenic commonwealth has been compared to a church whose traditional code of values fulfills its members and commands their inherited allegiance.[14]

Differences in political theory in the Hellenistic past in no major way detracted from the state's monopoly on exercising the kind of traditional Classical sovereignty which claimed supervision over the total human being. Here state sovereignty found expression in divine kingship which maintained overlordship throughout the realm via the local city cult of the demi-god King such as that of a Ptolemy Soter or an Antiochus Epiphanes. The origin of divine kingship need not detain us here. Suffice it to say that Alexander's claim of relationship with the divinized Heracles and his adoption as son of Ammon–Ra in Egypt merely facili-tated implementation of earlier Greek tendencies to divine kingship. What is important is the general Hellenistic acceptance, as a basic idea in political theory, that the king was law incarnate and that as living law he enjoyed the right of rational control over his subjects in all facets of their existence. Had not Pindar early said *nomos* was king of all not only the living but the dead? And had not Plato written that *nomos* was divine and had not Aristotle called it divine Reason? As law incarnate, the king's logos logically ruled as an image, an extension of deity, and as such enjoyed the potentiality to exercise divine wisdom and virtue to provide

---

[13] Cicero, *De re pub.* 22.33. True law is right reason in agreement with nature so that neither senate nor people can abolish it. It is so natural that whoever is disobedient to it flees from himself and human nature. See also *De leg.* 1.6, 18–19.

[14] E. Barker, *The Politics of Aristotle* (Oxford: Clarendon Press, 1946), p. xlvii.

a model for his subjects to imitate. What kind of competitor would conceivably challenge such a monarch for a share of sovereignty? Although historians and writers such as Theopompus, Ephorus, Arrian, and Plutarch clearly oppose as folly any attempt to divinize kings, they are willing to accept the superhuman character of the ruler which qualified him in a special way to be associated with the gods if he dutifully imitated them, ruled virtuously, and brought out the best in man.[15]

Romans, as usual, followed their Greek betters by adopting their political thought. During the Republic they liked to think Rome was an Hellenic polis resting on the consensus of the Senate and the Roman people. During the empire they copied the Hellenistic political example, making the emperor both the receptacle of law and host to the divine *Roma*.

Consequently, ancient political writers, whether Hellenic or Hellenistic, such as a Plato or an Aristotle, Polybius, or a Cicero, did not speculate so much on the scope of government but on the form it should take to carry out rationally its natural function to direct man totally. Classical "totalitarianism," so naturally imbedded in the ancient concept of government, was, then, intrinsically neither arbitrary nor malevolent. It merely maintained that all activities, every facet of life, was subject to political communal control.

The very ubiquity of this natural Classical "totalitarianism" invited considerable speculation about the nature of political science. Although some divine sanction for the government of the Hellenic polis was traditionally and piously assumed, philosophers felt free nonetheless to investigate the nature of authority and various forms of government. Was supervision of any area of human activity reserved by the gods or excluded from state jurisdiction by virtue of some determinism rooted in the very nature of the universe? If the state was not to enjoy total competence what kind of competing institutionalized sovereignty was conceivable? The first question evoked a great deal of speculation; the second involved so foreign a consideration that it was scarcely asked.

Since to the Hellenic Sophists both the providential and the deterministic were too uncertain or complicated to serve in any meaningful way, men like Archelaus, Hippias of Elis, and Protagoras broached the idea of a secular natural law claiming that nature was a truer guide than artificial state legislation. But the influence of the Sophists was enervated by an internal contradiction: they considered moral law open to individ-

---

[15] F. Dvornik, *Early Christian and Byzantine Political Philosophy*, 2 vols. (Dumbarton Oaks Studies No. 9, Washington: Harvard University Press, 1966), 1:205–07 and especially section 2, pp. 241–77.

ual subjective interpretation while asserting, at the same time, that a natural instinct led human beings to form regulating communities. Even in his modern day Pericles opted patriotically to appeal to Athenians' collective reverence for unwritten law. Plato's *Laws*, tempering somewhat the rugged totalitarianism of his earlier *Republic*, conceded that some private rights such as marriage, procreation, and private property rested on unwritten natural law. He maintained that this law could be apprehended through reason and he posited it as the basis of his absolute Idea of Justice. Aristotle, in turn, called basic law divine, pure Reason; did not one who bade law rule bid god and Reason rule?

But it was chiefly the Stoics who expanded and refined the implications of natural law for the state. They declared that law, rooted in the orderly processes of nature, was known intuitively in the form of universal notions. These notions, inherent in the nature of rational creatures worldwide, caused people to order their conduct properly in respect to the cosmos. Chrysippus, believing that man's preconceptions included apprehension of universals arising out of nature, quite logically taught that an instinctive knowledge of virtue was common to all men as equals. Posidonius spoke of a validity of moral principles, of an objectivity of natural norms of truth and virtue, which were discoverable through experience without deliberate thought.

Romans, as we saw, echoed the political thinking of Plato, Aristotle, and the Stoics. The middle–Stoic, Panaetius, was quite helpful to Cicero in his effort to shore up the reeling Roman Republic because the philosopher led the great Roman to judge the existing republican constitution the best exponent of that political life which naturally arose from man's basic rational nature. As a supporter of Plato's *ante–rem* universals, Panaetius also helped Cicero justify the state as the logical guardian of absolute Justice which, reflected in the rational natural order of things, was instinctively known to citizens. True law, conformable with Justice, would itself be right Reason, constant in nature, eternal, and diffused among all men. From it *auctoritas* emanated. Only *potestas*, resting on written law and merely executing what *auctoritas* justified, lay in the dominion of state legislators and magistrates. Since the moral order was thus in principle imbedded in nature and since law was subject to the rational instinctive direction of the general social consciousness, government was really being subject to itself. Thus, in a sense, the state was limited by its own nature; it could not, for instance, undermine human rights because they were synonymous with its own rights. Without becoming irrational, it could not, for example, enjoin immoral conduct or deprive citizens of such fundamental rights as the free investigation of truth, the holding of property, or the making of contracts. In other words, the state logically claimed a natural competence to regulate all that pertained to the rational nature of man and to the imbedded rational intention of nature.[16] If Epictetus is correct in saying that human beings must live in harmony with the demands of Nature, or god's will, which is discernible by universal agreement, it follows that if the state makes such conduct impossible and thus wrongly uses its *potestas* by acting unnaturally and therefore irrationally, its citizens could theoretically appeal to the sovereignty of man's collective conscience.

These are surely liberalizing thoughts. But often they did not help much. Cicero's Stoic–Platonic political musings remained theoretical and had little to do with later Roman politics. Moreover in the Stoic system there is no indictment of statism per se but only the admonition that government act rationally in the larger cosmic context. If Stoicism called the state's attention to its built–in rational limitations, it did not suggest that any facet of human activity be stricken from its control or that a competing sovereignty be instituted to limit its jurisdiction. In addition, it took a while for Stoicism's ennobling concepts to take root, and even then they served more to enlighten individual emperors and to temper the harshness of Roman criminal law than seriously to restrict in practice the total scope of government.

Moreover, the powers–that–were did not always see things through rarefied Stoic eyes. Stoic philosophers were frequently silenced by exile or death for criticizing the irrational controls of emperors. Nero ordered the deaths of his old tutor, Seneca, and two senators, Thrasea Paetus and Barea Soranus; Cornutus was banished on the pretext that he had hinted that the emperor's proposed epic on Roman history would be too long in four hundred books! Vespasian put to death Helvidius Priscus, also a senator; Domitian exiled Dio Chrysostom and Epictetus. With the Antonines, however, Stoicism admittedly had its belated brief day. Trajan spoke eloquently of the enlightenment of his reign and Marcus Aurelius, himself the last great Stoic, professed to make government respect the nature of all men, even slaves. Yet even with his strong subscription to Stoic doctrines, the great emperor would never think of sharing the right to apply any natural rights with a competing institutional sovereignty. One is tempted to see in the third–century Christian Origen the first thinker who realized fully the revolutionary implications of natural rights for determining legitimacy in government.[17]

All in all, throughout the Classical period, the total competence of the state really never wavered. In third–century Rome restraints of noble

---

[16] Cicero puts it well: "We need not look outside ourselves for an expounder or interpreter of true law since it is in agreement with nature itself." *De re pub.* 22.23. See *De off.* 1.45, 2.21 and *De leg.* 1.6, 18–19.

[17] E. G. Weltin, "Origen's Teaching on Natural Law" in *Great Events from History* 9 vols., ed. F. N. Magill (Englewoods, New Jersey: Salem, 1972), 2:801–6.

families, independent senates, and assemblies had long disappeared. Even the fiction of the demi–god as ruler, of the Hellenistic king, needed adjustment to fit the military claims of the so–called barrack emperors. Yet jurists, in compiling their law codes, continued to give assent to the king as the source of law now enforced by a corps of imperial legates, curators, and prefects. Under such consolidation there seemed less and less likelihood that the Roman government would divorce legislative areas from itself and thus relinquish its total control over men. In the ensuing anarchy of the third century the military emperors displayed little interest in debating the nature and rights of either man or government. While in theory they preserved the old fiction that their authority rested on the social consensus of *Senatus Populusque Romanus*, their jurists were operating on the dictum that *"quod placuit principi legis vigorem habet"*—what pleased the king has the force of law.

Today probably few would contest the state's right to control economics. Regulations in this area seemed natural to the ancient state as well, especially after the invention of coinage. Even though the ancient state's control over economics was severely restricted in practice by unsophisticated economic theories, simple methods of exchange and taxation, limited coinage, poor distribution of wealth, a subsistence psychology, and naive banking concepts, the Classical commonwealth was no stranger to economic manipulation. Sparta's total stranglehold on economics was an outrageous basic feature of the "Lycurgan" constitution. The early sixth–century Solonian settlement not only penalized mortgage holders but, by manipulating the currency, made the Athenian world safe for the rising business class. The silver mines of Laurium were public Athenian property; Plato would have made all property communal. To balance erratic budgets, the polis at times resorted to arbitrary policies whenever revenues faltered. The pseudo–Aristotelian *Economics,* for instance, takes for granted that every sort of private property was at the disposal of the state.[18] In Hellenistic times the Ptolemies perfected a draconian royal control over their nobles, operating Egypt as a vast regimented economic holding.

The Roman economic mentality was less naive and reserved than the Greek. Romans of the Republic made no secret of their conviction that the imperial provinces offered legitimate economic playgrounds to be exploited; the government was expected to hold provincials still while its officers fleeced them. The Roman Revolution, in a sense, made the

---

[18] The *Oeconomica* was probably written in the latter half of the third century B.C. Book two is especially interesting as a collection of stories relating how rulers and governments filled their treasuries by robbery and exploitation. J. Hasebroek, *Trade and Politics in Ancient Greece* (New York: Biblo & Tannnen, 1965) finds the monopolizing of economics by the Classical state so tyrannous that all free life was constricted for the government's sake.

world safe for Equestrian capitalism and established firmly the practice of "statesmen" to confiscate private property in such an outrageous fashion that it strains the imagination. Wholesale uncompensated confiscation of private estates and peasant farms to provide bonuses for soldiers was not an uncommon practice. With such ruthless examples of eminent domain in hand and of such nefarious practices as tax–farming, it is not surprising that Jesus spoke as though even the coins of the realm belonged to Caesar! Beginning with the Severi, Rome more and more strangled its middle class with imposed and hereditary liturgies and requisitions. Eventually all generations of workers—oil–suppliers, butchers, fish handlers, bakers, transport and mine workers, and minor government officials—were frozen in their occupations to stabilize taxes and balance the budget. Decurions, now hereditary tax collectors personally responsible for their quotas, could stave off bankruptcy only by fleecing the taxpayer in turn. Eventually the Church had to deny them ordination which they sought as a way to escape their ruinous obligations and bankruptcy. Deserters from their posts of labor were branded with official state identification marks. Cochrane remarks, "in the last phase of its history, *Romanitas* resolved itself into a community in which theoretically everyone was a worker but no one could be said to work for himself."[19] Diocletian's celebrated arbitrary law promulgated in 301 remains a prototype of all legislation fixing prices and wages.

If today such kind of economic control seems tolerable, or even theoretically desirable as a legitimate government function, it is another matter in Classical times when no written constitutions with explicit bills of inalienable personal rights existed to protect citizens, to say nothing of slaves. Sparta was notorious for demanding that its citizens deprive themselves of the ordinary decorums of life. The state determined which infants were to live according to a rigid program of compulsory eugenics, maintained regimented youth–corps teaching Ku–Klux–Klan commando tactics to intimidate and liquidate helots, and expected even the peers of the realm to spend fifty–three years of their lives in government service. Even Plato in his *Republic* saw much good in Sparta's regimented educational system which encouraged the state to regulate children's dutifulness toward parents, hair–dressing, clothing, footwear, posture, and marriage. Even though his *Laws* relaxed some of his extreme positions on statism, Plato left no precedent for statesmen to honor a bill of personal rights. Although Athens, consistently upheld the right of personal property, it early sponsored legislation to control displays of luxury at funerals, markets, and weddings. Quite often it was less tolerant of free speech than classicists like to maintain; it ostracized

---

[19] C. N. Cochrane, *Christianity and Classical Culture* (New York: Oxford University Press, 1957), p. 305.

potentially dangerous demagogues, silenced undesirable speakers, executed those who taught subversive views to youth, and punished those
guilty of sacrilege and even those incompetent as military and naval
commanders. Aristophanes' Old Comedy did not last long,

Rome, like all bona fide governments, naturally extended to its
privileged few citizens, such as Paul, the right of life and limb; application of justice was fitful and perfunctory, however, since no bill of
fundamental rights nor constituted agent of public opinion monitored
it—a fact which Paul himself seems to have found out. Provincial governors were given notoriously wide latitude in administration. If such
minor matters as banquets and litters came under restriction in the
Republic, marriage was regulated atrociously by Augustus through legislation which was not entirely repealed until Constantine. By the Lex
Papia Poppaea males were to wed by twenty–five; women by twenty.
Unregulated delators were in good taste even under Augustus and
treason was made so easy under Tiberius that it included off–hand
criticism of the imperial family. Moreover, it was up to the accused to
prove their innocence. The right of assembly was so supervised that even
fire–department personnel came under surveillance. Unless a guild or
organization was specifically licensed, it was unlawful and subject to
arbitrary abolishment, confiscation of property, and forfeiture of the
right to assemble again. Indeed, Christians, who did not enjoy such legal
recognition, complained that they were persecuted merely for their
name. Even Pliny as governor extraordinary had to consult the emperor
about the status of Christians; Trajan, in reply, referred to the enlightenment of his government as though it was purely personal. By time of the
late Theodosian Code practically everything was regulated, even the
wearing of breeches, long hair, and skins.[20] Fortunately, the very exercise of total competence led Rome in the Antonine period to experiment
with the first serious social–welfare legislation in the West. Food doles,
common in Hellenistic cities, had already been institutionalized in Rome
after the Gracchi, but now support of needy children was undertaken by
Nerva's alimentary system. Eventually chief physicians were appointed
for each of the fourteen districts of Rome.

The lack of modern propaganda tools made it difficult for the
ancient commonwealth to carry out its proclivity to control thought.
State education, never in any sense universal or compulsory, was spotty
in time and place. Sparta, of course, managed to brainwash its citizens
thoroughly through graduated levels of youth movements and military

---

[20] Ibid., 306–8. At first sight it would appear from the Theodosian Code published in
438 that the new Christian polity was as "totalitarian" as the old pagan state. But it must be
remembered that the late Roman government now had to share sovereignty with a
competing power, the Church.

training. But neither Athens nor Syracuse would honor Plato's *Republic* by establishing a rigid state educational system to develop character through a standardized, censored, and even deceitful curriculum. If Athens did establish some sort of scheduled training of youths in 338 during the life of Aristotle it was of such short duration that the great philosopher was left regretful that no public educational structure was at hand to tell citizens what the best life was. Lacking a formal instructional system, the ancient polis resorted to the poet, philosopher, and actor to mold opinion, leaving the Athenian, for example, exposed to a varying set of values represented over the centuries in the old heroic Homer, the pious Aeschylus, the reverent Sophocles, the realistic Euripides and the lampooning Aristophanes. Plato would set up standards in music, dance, gymnastics, dice playing, and the like in order to train character. He would confront the subjective Sophist who claimed competence to teach free from state supervision.

In imperial Rome, advocates of education—men like Tacitus, Plutarch and Quintilian—were rewarded to the extent that the state showed some interest in the matter. As we saw, emperors of the early Christian era went about establishing schools. Vespasian endowed teachers of rhetoric at Rome; Trajan, it appears, subsidized education for five thousand poor boys. Hadrian and others, such as Septimius Severus, built classrooms for poor students and maintained scholarships. Private philanthropy was surprisingly generous to education. Inevitably, state supervision and interference crept in. A mid–third–century law permitting the emperor to remove "incompetent" teachers culminated in Julian's famous rescript of 362 censoring both the content and staffs of schools, forbidding Christians to teach, and ordering instructors to introduce no novel opinion against accepted pagan beliefs. The Christian emperors Theodosius and Valentinian continued the policy of state supervision, making it a penal offense for unauthorized persons to open schools.

Unlike Athens, Rome did not honor the theatre as a privileged educational agency; consequently it came under close supervision from time to time. The *Twelve Tables* already held poets liable and censored the stage, a policy maintained even after the days of Plautus and Terence when the theatre was succumbing more and more to the arena. Both Tiberius and Domitian moved against the pornographic theatre of the day and banished actors. Sometimes the stage was adroitly used as a propaganda tool; Maximinus Daia, for instance, recruited its services to debase Christianity. Apparently the only control over the more and more popular arena was the limit of human imagination. The arena's educational impact was rarely evaluated; Cicero, for one, thought it salubrious because it taught courage and disdain for death, views which all philosophers should cultivate. Seneca, however, denounced the games as pernicious spectacles where the masses, besides being subtly lulled into a political stupor, were allowing themselves to be progressively brutalized as well.

Everywhere in ancient lands from the Nile to the Tiber and the Euphrates, religion and politics were faces of the same coin. From its inception, the Classical city was basically a home for divinity. Every facet of the state reflected the gods' images. Laws and constitutions were gratefully ascribed to deities or their deputies; oaths, vows, sacrifices, and rituals were integral parts of every civic function. The polis subsidized religious expression by building and maintaining temples and sanctuaries as well as supporting priests and festivals. Amphictyonies protected common shrines and fostered religious truces which allowed all to attend official games dedicated to a Zeus or Apollo. In Athens, the king—or his later surrogate, the King Archon—protected the interests of the gods and assured the fertility of the land by hosting a yearly mystical marriage for his queen with Dionysos. The council of the Aeropagus, fundamentally concerned with public expiation of sacrilege, contracted in times of perilous religious crises for the services of expert trouble–shooters in sacred matters. One such was Epimenides imported from Crete during the great fear of 632 B.C. The tyrant Pisistratus, anxious for divine support in mid–sixth–century Athens, extravagantly glorified Zeus at state expense with an immense but unfinished temple, publicly financed the elaborate Panathenaic festival, and presumably provided the poor with public payment of initiation fees into the cult of Eleusis. Cleisthenes, in his turn, did not neglect to dedicate each of his new tribes to protecting deities, and even the secular Pericles set up Athena in her magnificent temple on the Acropolis to watch over her city. Her pop–eyed image and her owl guaranteed her coinage while Apollo protected the integrity of her sacred treasury at Delphi and even lent his shrine–island of Delos as the capital of her league and empire.

Few, except the Sophists, saw anything unnatural, irrational, or oppressive about this political–religious amalgam. Plato, unsympathetic to the growing agnosticism of his day, urged the prohibition of foreign cults and approved of state "heresy trials" to suppress various forms of impiety. His intimate union of religious and civil life made an attack on religion by speech or art subject to a court action which might involve imprisonment, brain–washing, or even death. Even the secular Aristotle voiced no objections. Epicureans found it prudent to withdraw, keeping in mind, no doubt, the exile or execution of such as Anaxagoras or Socrates.[21] Growing secularism, glaring in Pericles' funeral oration and

---

[21] *Laws* 10.909B–D. E. R. Dodds, *The Greeks and the Irrational* (Berkeley: University of California Press, 1964), p. 198, reminds us that about 432 disbelief in the supernatural and teaching of astronomy were made indictable offenses in Athens, and that the next thirty

Thucydides' history, probably saved Athens from fostering the new
Hellenistic religious fancy for divine kings, which began with the worship of Lysander in Sparta. The dour Demosthenes shrugged off the
matter by saying, "Let Alexander become son of both Zeus and of
Poseidon if he wishes." Yet even such religious cynicism never led Athens
to exempt religion from state control.[22]

In Rome the union of politics and religion probably was more
pronounced than in Greece. Nothing was begun, done, or ended without an invocation. From the very beginning and at every step of a
procedure, omens declared the will of the gods in the unfolding divine
drama of Roman history. Aeneas obeyed Venus in the first place by
coming to the Lavinian shore to find the Trojan gods a new home: just as
obediently Romulus, by divine guidance, traced out the sacred boundary
of the *pomerium.* He and his successors, understanding that marriage and
trade rights between cities as well as the making of treaties and con-
federations depended upon mutual recognition of each other's pan-
theons, pressed foreign affairs only as far as the gods allowed. Happy
(felix) was that statesman who was able properly to implement the will of
the gods by correct and pious interpretation of auguries and auspices,
manifestations of divine concern which even the later Cicero thought
incumbent upon the gods. Kings and magistrates who misread, ignored,
or violated divine direction swiftly became victims of divine wrath. The
foreign king, Tarquin, almost like the biblical Pharaoh, was denied
divine gnosis; even his belated and befuddled purchase of the Sibylline
books could not save him from disaster. Expertise in religious matters
was originally entrusted in Rome to kings such as Numa who consorted
in fertility rites with the nymph, Egeria, for the common good. In
republican times the *rex Sacrorum* and public priesthoods, charged with
seeing that things were done properly, reminded even the haughty
victorious consul that, painted in red ochre like Jupiter's old statue, he
must be content to celebrate his triumph as a proxy for god. The oldest
of the religious companies—the *Fetiales,* the *Salii,* and the Arval
Brethren—have largely taken their secrets with them. These bodies were
augmented by the great pontifical colleges such as the *Augures, Quin-
decimviri, Epulones, Vestales,* and *Flamines,* all dedicated to the task of
effecting an harmonious *modus vivendi* between gods and Rome.

Even in Rome's somewhat irreligious age between 250 and 30 B.C.,
when philosophy and foreign "isms" were beginning to take a toll on the

---

years saw "heresy" trials which probably caused Anaxagoras to be fined and banished,
Diagoras and Protagoras as well as Euripides to flee, and Socrates to be executed.

[22] Dodds *Irrational,* p. 93 n. 73 suggests that the nearest approach to an ecclesiastical
organization independent of the city state was the organization of "Directors of Pythian
Studies" to expound Apolline sacred law at Athens.

mos maiorum, the states' identification with religion was not relinquished even though high public officials had little faith in it. Appius Claudius Pulcher was an early deviant who sacrilegiously frustrated the omens by throwing the sacred fowls overboard before the naval battle of Drepana in 241. Public figures like Mucius Scaevola declared the traditional religion of the poet and philosopher futile, superfluous, and downright harmful but supported it as useful in statecraft. In the same vein the learned Varro, though personally convinced that the state religion had nothing to do with truth, thought it good for the masses. As for himself, he could entertain only a purged version laced with Stoic philosophy which he judged more responsive to some verification. Probably more out of circumspection than conviction, the thoroughly conservative Cicero continued to pour out verbal libations to the gods but they were heavily diluted with draughts of Stoicism and Platonism. Cotta, as a Sceptic follower of Arcesilaus and Carneades, believed that the existence of the gods was logically under suspicion; yet, as *Pontifex Maximus,* he served scrupulously and patriotically in the tradition of the great pontifices before him because it was the way of his ancestors.

One can understand why Augustus, at the beginning of the Christian era, considered a revival of the old–time religion imperative. Under his sponsorship Livy's patriotic history ascribed anew Rome's world hegemony to its piety. Virgil's magnificent dactylic hexameters pictured, in Platonic fashion, pre–existent Roman heroes waiting in the wings of the underworld for their divinely appointed cue to appear on history's stage. The emperor himself became an Arval, a member of the revived ancient religious brotherhood which offered sacrifices for the fertility of the ground; he set up *Lares* or guardian gods at crossroads to serve even homeless wayfarers, rededicated himself to Apollo, built temples, sponsored glittering religious games, and tried to legislate on morals. But the cosmopolitanism of the day, the uprooting and mingling of national gods in the empire, required a grander concept of divinity—the cultivation of a universal god, an abstraction which would embody the spirit of the great imperial commonwealth. The association of deified *Roma* with emperorship was an attractive solution conveniently prepared for by Hellenistic political theory and Euhemeristic philosophy. Provincial assemblies were duly charged with supervising the new imperial cult by electing local provincial high priests and providing suitable religious games. Caligula, unhinged by it all, took himself seriously as Jupiter; Domitian liked the title *Dominus ac Deus.*

Despite this total identification of religion with statecraft, Rome was generally tolerant religiously; polytheism almost has to be. Occasionally, however, Roman piety prompted punitive measures against this or that blasphemous or lascivious sect. In 186 B.C., for instance, Bacchic rites were forbidden unless licensed and then only for groups of five. In 58

B.C. Isis was excluded from the capital and, shortly after, her temples were ordered destroyed by the consuls. Augustus tried in vain to check the mystic semi–religious neo–Pythagoreans, and Tiberius resumed persecution of the Isis sect after its restoration. Jews were expelled from Rome as early as 139 B.C.; in imperial days Tiberius banished many to work in the mines. Christians waited their turn.

As active, proselytizing, non–national monotheists, Christians were branded atheists who were contumacious, disrespectful to *Romanitas*, and dangerous to law and order. Violent persecutions broke out, especially after 250 when Decius and Diocletian threw out a dragnet to entrap everyone not displaying a certificate of pagan sacrifice. But the Galilean was to conquer; the blood of martyrs was, as Tertullian remarked, the seed of the Church. Using Stoic arguments, Christians branded Rome's exercise of religious totalitarian control an irrational, and therefore illegal, intrusion on natural law. Constantine, in declaring freedom of religion for all subjects, blasted the first breach in the totalitarian structure of the Classical state corporation, an event so significant that one might see in it the end of the Classical era.[23] Many found it impossible to contemplate the city of god apart from the city of man. The learned Symmachus, for one, simply reasoned that he, like Rome itself, was too old to change; he would follow the traditions of his ancestors.

THE CHRISTIAN ENCOUNTER WITH THE CORPORATE

"Your Faith has saved you" . . . Matthew

Obviously Jesus was not thinking along Classical lines which identified human fulfillment with the corporate good. He seemed, rather, to insist that salvation lay elsewhere: "What does it profit a man to gain the whole world and suffer the loss of his soul?"

In the gospels Jesus shows only restricted enthusiasm for the Jewish corporate establishment of his day; his lone definite remark (Matt. 16:18–19) about founding a Church, an ecclesia or assembly, is so unusual that it has created dispute and schism in the Christian body ever since. Concerned primarily with sharing his "good news" of eternal

---

[23] According to Cochrane, *Culture,* p. 288 Julian's effort to restore paganism "marks a steady drift toward totalitarianism within the fourth–century empire" as though such a movement was something of an innovation. The emperor's action was rather an attempt to restore traditional Classical totalitarianism lost by the Edict of Milan. Fustel de Coulange, *Ancient City,* pp. 222–23, sums up the totalitarian position well: "The Ancients, therefore, knew neither liberty in private life, liberty in economics, nor religious liberty." They could not believe there could exist any rights against the city and its gods.

salvation with his personal followers, he showed no mind to absorb them in any new revolutionary political, social, or economic "ism" or corporate body. Paul urges obedience to existing secular powers more in relation to one's personal salvation than in terms of the corporate good. To him, even the Church was a simple assembly of individuals living according to a divine natural law and faith while sojourning in particular places, be it Rome or Corinth. Significantly, his letter to the church of Rome, as presently preserved, salutes some twenty–five specific individuals rather than an institutionalized structure. While Acts shows an interest in the Church as a corporate entity it does not insist that the yet largely charismatic worshippers lose their personality in an emerging church psychology: Ananias and Sapphira are censured not for neglecting communal interests but for personally lying. Lack of a strong emphasis on the early Church as basically a corporate body is to be expected in apostolic times when the Church daily anticipated its own liquidation in view of the impending return of Christ.

Later, however, since the Christian commitment relegated the Classical political corporation to the status of an agent dealing only with external human affairs and one unable to regenerate them meaningfully, the young Church was almost forced to become itself a corporate body assuming direction in those areas which it demanded the state abdicate. The concept of "Church" readily took on mystical hues since it was a transfer into Christianity of the mosaic idea of the holy nation under God. As such, it was already referred to by Ephesians in symbolic terms and then by the Fathers generally who called it a "Holy Virgin," a "Spiritual Mother," "The Spouse of Christ," "The Heavenly Jerusalem." Such highly metaphorical terms scarcely described the kind of secular self–centered polity that the Classical corporation represented. Yet facing Roman institutionalism with its ingenious concept of the corporation or collegium, the Church could not long remain only a vague mystical hypostasis. Moreover, the distribution of charity, the rise of heresy, and the threat of persecution all counseled more and more centralization; waning hopes for the Parousia needed reassurances from authority.

The early Fathers wrote relatively little in a sustained way on the concept of the Church. Some, however, like Clement of Rome and Ignatius of Antioch, c. 100, already see the Church as a professional organization expecting obedience to its officers. *Second Clement*, c. 150, describes the Church in almost Gnostic terms as something of a pre–existent absolute existing as the end of all creation from all eternity, and presents it as a reality existing apart from, and prior to, its constituents. To Irenaeus, it becomes almost indispensable to its members because only its apostolic sees can safeguard the faith necessary for salvation; its *auctoritas,* based on the testimony of apostolic ancestors, would resemble the authority of the *mos maiorum* which lay at the basis of Rome's jurisdiction.[24] To Hippolytus, the Church is a ship of accomplished saints piloted by Christ, something of a closed corporation. In contrast, Pope Callistus emphasizes the Church's service to the individual as a haven for sinners working on their regeneration. The first significant treatise on the Church, Cyprian *On the Unity of the Catholic Church*, not only discusses its episcopal authority and nature, but states clearly that membership in its corporate body is essential to salvation: Could anyone have God for his father who did not have the Church for his mother? Origen, who like Cyprian maintained that outside the church no one is saved, refers to the Church on one occasion as a visionary construction built on individual "peters" or rocks diffuse in personality, nature, and value.[25] At other times he uses more familiar mystical terms making the Church almost a spiritual and psychological force which, after engulfing the entire world, will dissolve into a kingdom of individual saintly seers. When Christianity became so universal that even the Scythians—generally considered rowdy, trouble–making barbarians—would get the word, each individual would become, thanks to the educative power of the Gospel, almost a Platonic philosopher–prince choosing the Good instinctively, apparently without much churchly guidance.

In the fourth century, in the aftermath of the Constantinian settlement, the Church became more and more legalistic. Gregory of Nazianzus, for instance, upholds the Church as a juridical instrument enjoying authority to construct dogmatic assertions, a view which Harnack would deplore because such a church in legislating truth would oppress individuality by believing for the worshipper. Individual faith, like private charity, has become lost in the corporation. Finally, Augustine, the first ancient author to explore personality in some depth, seems torn between two poles: ecclesiastical magisterium and sacramentalism on the one hand, and divine personal election on the other. Rather enigmatically he suggests that if one must deal with the Church as a hierarchical corporation, it is well to remember that it should not be identified with the city of God. Yet at the same time, as God's trustee of truth, it is obligated to countenance persecution of dissenters.[26]

Obviously there is much in common between the corporate polis or *res publica* of Classicism and the new Christian assembly. Both communities are made up of individuals whose good the corporation professes to serve. Both come to be highly institutionalized in their effort to direct

---

[24] Clement of Rome,*Epis. ad Corin.* 24–25; Ignatius, *Epis. Eph.* 5.2, *Trall.* 7.2; *2 Clement* 14.1–4; Irenaeus, *Adv. Haer.* 3.3.1, 4.17.5–6.

[25] E. G. Weltin, "Origen's Church" in *Studies presented to David Moore Robinson* ed. G. P. Mylonas (St. Louis: Washington University, 1951), 2:1015–1022.

[26] Augustine, *De corr. Donat.* 2.9–11, *Tract. in Joan.* 11.13–15.

people to what is considered the highest end. In the Classical tradition, however, the end is largely the well–being of the community itself to which the individual ideally contributes by subordinating his own individual ends; in the Church the end should be the personal salvation of each member whose importance transcends that of the corporate body itself.[27] The Church was to be an agent serving its members, each of whom had an end independent of the body and higher to it. On the whole, the Fathers rarely forgot that it was the individual to whom eternal life was promised, not the Church. Beyond making the Church an indispensable, albeit well organized, agent to expedite the eternal welfare of the person, the Fathers were largely unprepared to go. Nowhere do they guarantee that Christians will find ultimate eternal fulfillment in serving the Church as an earthly corporation, even if it is disguised in mystical terms. Gnostic attempts to make the Church an eternal divine emanation from the Godhead belonged to the world of heresy.

Romans like Celsus and Pliny were quite disturbed to see the hallowed Classical corporate image subjected to the presumptuous ego judgments of a cult of superstitious ignoramuses who deluded themselves that they were immortal. Had these pagan worthies seriously studied the matter, they might have concluded that the new Christian emphasis on individualism was, in one sense, the logical outcome of Christianity's successful synthesis of Classical, Jewish, and Christian views of man's unique component: his soul.[28] As we shall see in more detail later, the Classical world laid the foundation which made such a synthesis possible. Had not Pythagoras made an important contribution by giving everyone a transmigratory soul which led to the enjoyment of unique, individualistic, even bizarre experiences? In turn, Socrates, probably the most significant contributor to the notion of a personal moral soul in the Christian sense, greatly influenced Plato who then dignified each human being with an individual pre–existent, eternal soul whose rational faculty should patently reveal to man his participation in the divine. Aristotle capitalized on the soul's rationality to provide the world with a famous system of humanistic ethics. Stoics also expected the

---

[27] "The Church has no possessions of her own except the Faith." Ambrose, *Epis.* 18.16 (*PL* 16:1018).

[28] Wendland, *Kultur,* pp. 87–8 calls attention to the late Classical trend toward soul searching and personal religion. J. Danielou, *Theology of Jewish Christianity* (London: Darlon, Longman & Todd, 1964), esp. pp. 357–75 touches on the same psychological introspection among Hellenistic Jews when he discusses the theme of the Two Spirits. Christianity by eliminating the opposition between man and nature fostered a new kind of hero who, relieved of conquering his surroundings, now turned inward to conquer his inner self.

individual soul to make rational ethical choices; yet, while agreeing with its divine nature, they denied it an eternal individual existence.

Judaism added the essential ingredient to turn individuality into personality. After the Maccabean discovery that Jews had a soul with an individual eternal destiny, Pharisaic Jews took the unusual step of letting the human body share in the soul's future. Resurrection from the dead thus guaranteed the survival of the whole man or person, body and soul together. It was such an exciting idea that intertestamental Jews talked much about it. Who, for instance, would be resurrected? Both good and bad? Gentiles as well as Jews? Jews of the diaspora? Jews of the age of the flood? Of Sodom and Gomorrah? Where and how would souls enjoy their blessedness or damnation? Where would they go pending the final judgment? Where would the grand assize of the resurrected be held? Unfortunately, such speculation revealed typical Jewish nationalistic blinders which robbed the chosen people of the opportunity to discover anthropology.

The Jewish idea of the resurrection of the whole person was so novel that it boggled the mind of pagan and gentile Christian alike. Many found it quaint, utterly ridiculous, or downright repulsive. Celsus deemed it so degrading that only fools would have thought it up. Since the body, as matter, was evil or at least resistant to good, what sane person would want to recover it? Was it not, as Plato said, the prison house of the soul or at best a temporary schoolhouse where the individual was condemned to learn something of terrestrial existence through experience? Paul and Origen testify that their respective centuries found the doctrine of bodily resurrection disturbing and unacceptable.[29] The fourth–fifth–century bishop, Synesius, as a condition for his ordination, reserved his right to reject it. No amount of speculation seemed to make it less controversial. Would one's resurrected body be glorified in a docetic way allowing one to walk through doors as Jesus did? Paul would prefer such an incorporeal, glorified resurrected body as best demonstrating that the sting of death was, indeed, frustrated. Origen, too, hoped for a spiritual resurrection partly to obviate Celsus' sharp charge that the earth could not contain all the resurrected bodies nor could nature return all the pieces of flesh eaten by mullets. Or would one's real flesh be revivified so that one could eat Like Jesus did after his resurrection? The Roman creed taught as much by using the term *sarx*, the actual muscular flesh. Justin seemed to avoid all speculation by simply dismissing the doctrine as not impossible. Athenagoras, one of the first to write a treatise on the topic, *On the Resurrection*, simply judged that the idea was neither inconsistent with the power and justice of God nor illogical: if

---

[29] Justin, *Trypho* 80 records that many pious Christians dissented over the issue of bodily resurrection.

the entire person was to be summoned to judgment, was not resurrection of the body necessary? Tertullian, in turn, pronounced it dignified, scriptural, rational, amenable to the power of God, and demonstrable through natural analogies. Worshippers trustfully cited the creeds which promised it; personal tomb inscriptions tempered their sadness by expressing confidence in it. When one reads Gregory of Nyssa's loving remarks recording how fervently his dying sister, Macrina, looked forward to a glorious resurrection, it is difficult to see how an individual could more forcefully express confidence in the existence of his own personality.

While entertaining Classical analyses of the soul and Jewish views of its eschatological association with the body, Christianity had its own singular contributions to make which would raise the value of man to new heights. Now each individual could believe that Providence cared enough not only to redeem the personal soul from any flaws it might have but that God also had deigned to dignify the body as well by becoming incarnate. Furthermore, if the Jews hoped for bodily resurrection, Christ gave assurances of it by his own return from the dead. Since the Redemption and Resurrection gave a new meaning and value to human existence, they deservedly were made the central events of Christian history.

The Christian message declared every person a marvelous creature superior to all else in the universe. The human being was, indeed, more than a microcosm stoically fated to reflect temporarily the beauty and order of the macrocosm and then lose identity. In every soul's unique faculties of memory, intelligence, and will, Augustine professed to see not only the essence of consciousness and rationality but also a token of its spiritual endowment as a miniature trinity, an analogy of the Godhead itself.[30] If the soul was unique in its capability to recognize its own consciousness and to contemplate God, the human body was made to stand erect and to gaze on heaven. If each individual soul, as an eternal image of God, was to enjoy personal immortality and not be diffused after death into the general stuff of the universe, to be lost impersonally in some process of divine fulfillment, so the resurrected body of each saint, as a temple of the Holy Ghost, was destined to share the presence of God. Both body and soul were declared indispensable for personality. Against the Apollinarians, orthodoxy insisted that even the God–man had to have a human soul and will as well as a true, nondocetic body.

---

[30] P. Henry, *Plotin et L'occident* (Louvain: Spicilegium Sacrum, 1934), pp. 96–116, sees Augustine as preeminent in discovering personality especially in the *Confessions* dealing with the psychology of temptation, a topic already broached by Origen and Gregory of Nyssa. See *De trin.* 10.

How else could he be a *persona?* The time was now ripe for Nemesius to make the first serious Christian study of anthropology.

Julian the Apostate astutely realized that if his restored paganism was to be successful, he would have to adopt Christianity's concern for the human body as well as for the soul. Probably the social program of the Church more than anything else convinced the ordinary individual that Christianity made him important. Concern for the poor and unfortunate, for the slave and the gladiator was not an outstanding hallmark of paganism. Thucydides' early remark fairly well sums up the Classical social ethic: to be safe one should face one's equals, be deferential to superiors and moderate to inferiors. Good will took the form of philanthropy rather than charity. Even the Stoic held largely as a matter of indifference whatever affected the body, be it slavery or poverty.

The social program of Christianity is, of course, too well known to delay us here. It is enough to say that its concern touched all classes in all stages of life ranging from protection of the unborn to care for the dead. Barnabas, Athenagoras, Minucius Felix, Tertullian, Cyprian, especially John Chrysostom, and the Council of Elvira early denounced abortion;[31] exposure of children was legally forbidden by Constantine. An equal code of morality for men and women did what it could to protect women from sexual exploitation and to safeguard marital vows from abuses formerly tolerated by a double standard. The Church so lauded women for their chastity and compassion that it pictured itself as a female. Mariology of the fourth century declared a woman the indispensable link between the law of the Old Testament and the grace of the New. That the slave was a person enjoying the same divine dispensations as the free seemed well understood by that slave who exclaimed "I am a slave of the emperor but I am a Christian!" Pope Callistus, a former slave himself, recognized intermarriage between the slave and the privileged, even though it was contrary to Roman law. Imperial orders charged bishops to carry out laws concerning the poor and afflicted. "True worship," said Valentinian I, "consists in helping the poor and needy." Hospitals tended the sick; prisoners were ransomed. The dead were buried to save them from dogs and birds.

The new *arete* became personal holiness pursued for one's own sake rather than to enlist the favor of God on any corporate entity. Virtually all agreed that sanctification of the self required grace, a divine aid meted out as a gift on a one–to–one basis. Although the idea of personal

---

[31] Barnabas, *Epis.* 19.5; Athenagoras, *Apol.* 35; Hippolytus, *Philos.* 9.12; Minucius Felix, *Oct.* 30; Tertullian, *Apol.* 9 and *Ad nat.* 1.16; Cyprian, *Epis.* 49; *Apos. const.* 7.3; John Chrysostom, *Hom. in Rom.* 24; Augustine, *De nupt. et concup.* 1.17 (*PL* 44:423) and *Enchridion* 23:85–6 (*ACW* 3:82–3). See M. J. Gorman, *Abortion in the Early Church* (Downers Grove: InterVarsity Press, 1982).

grace was not entirely foreign to the pagan world especially in mystery–cult circles, it was nonetheless quite an academic subject for Classical thinkers who generally approached the religion of the pantheon as citizens rather than as worshippers. Unenlightened by any pagan studies on the subject of grace—a situation quite different in respect to the soul—the early Christian Fathers were for a while content to accept grace on the assurances of the scriptural covenant without indulging in serious analyses of its nature, types, distribution, or efficacy. When Augustine finally did so, he introduced a controversy which disturbed the Church for centuries. Whether grace is earned through the agency of free will and meritorious works or whether it is given gratuitously solely at God's discretion matters little in our present discussion, since in either case grace was given or withheld on an individual basis and it was up to the individual in some way or other to use or reject it.

Probably there is no better way to demonstrate the personal nature of grace than to note its role in conversion. This "turning–about" to embrace a rebirth into a new way of life was so highly individualistic that it came about in different ways, frequently involving a dramatic and traumatic psychic experience signaling adoption of a personal relationship with Christ. As such, it should be distinguished from a general enlightenment induced through philosophical instruction leading to conviction of some form of truth or other. Philosophy's ability to "turn one around," however, was generally asserted in pagan times by many—Pythagoras, by Sophists who guaranteed instructional results, by Socrates, by Plato who made knowledge virtue, and by Stoics. Plutarch even spoke of instantaneous conversion by philosophy and the neo–Pythagorean Apollonius of Tyana reputedly reformed a Sybaritic youth by exorcising him. In his *Lives and Doctrines of Philosophers* (c. 250 A.D.) Diogenes Laertius recounts stories of converts in paganism so inspired by missionary zeal that they gave away their estates, money, and honors. Christians with very few exceptions chose not to see conversion as a product of paideia culminating in a protracted rational decision but rather as a divine gift, which the word, grace, implies.

That mystery cults could convert in a true sense no one doubts. Even the *Bacchae* has been interpreted as a report of Euripides' conversion by Dionysos. The Eleusinian mysteries surely converted. Lucius in the *Golden Ass* was undoubtedly born again in an experience so intense that for all good purposes in his awesome enthusiasm he became someone other than himself. With out–pourings of love he haunted the temples waiting for visions of Isis to welcome him personally into her sacred mysteries. Asclepius set the psychopathic Aristides beside himself. But mystery cults, however popular, were basically foreign to Classicism and more akin, outwardly at least, to Christianity than Justin Martyr appreciated.

Conversion among Christians was entirely personal and disrespectful of status in any intellectual philosophical circle or high socio–economic class. Clement of Rome, Polycarp, and Clement of Alexandria seem to imply that Christian conversion was also unique in embracing a deep sorrow for personal sin, fear of God, and sincere desire for repentance. Feeling a sense of deliverance from nothingness to meaningfulness, the convert often displayed miraculous and charismatic powers—prophesy and glossolalia and even cravings for martyrdom.

Philosophers, soldiers, and slaves alike were fired to repent and confess Christ in spontaneous, spectacular fashions. Marcellus, a centurion of the Trajan legion, impulsively threw away his military belt during pagan sacrifices and publicly proclaimed for Christ; the pagan actor, Genesius, while ridiculing Christianity on the stage, was suddenly and dramatically moved to conversion on the spot, no doubt much to the perplexity of the audience and the embarrassment of the playwright. Paul himself, once knocked to the ground and blinded on his way to Damascus, felt it incumbent to explain that the inscrutable will of God distributed the grace of conversion differently; Christ called some individuals abruptly, others after probation; for some he made it easy, for others somewhat difficult.

Surely nothing so personal resulted from conversion as martyrdom. Spectacular public passions by such stalwart heroes as Ignatius, Polycarp, Justin, Cyprian, Perpetua, Felicitas, or Laurence inspired others to convert. Fathers like Clement of Alexandria, Tertullian, Origen, Basil, Gregory of Nyssa, and John Chrysostom glorified martyrdom in homily and tract. None saw it as a sacrifice primarily for the corporate Church, even though it might redound to its growth.

Finally, once conversion opened the door for a life of personal holiness and salvation, the mysteries of the Church were at hand to encourage the individual's pursuit of sanctification. In Baptism the initiated, as a reborn person, often received a new name and symbolically was given a drink of milk. Sanctified by a laying–on–of–hands and anointed with oil, the candidate personally subscribed to the articles of the symbol or creed. Infant Baptism, attested to by Irenaeus, Tertullian, Origen, and finally Augustine, even recognized the child as a person. The exorcist was at hand to help the individual energumen joust with the devil; the Eucharist was reenacted to nourish the believer's resolve. If salvation was individual, so was sin. Consequently, the penitential system emerged to forgive sins and set penalties for specific transgressions. However one might decry the formalization of the penitential liturgy, it involved a highly personal and embarrassing experience regardless of whether it demanded private self–accusation before God as urged by Ambrose and Chrysostom, public confession before the congregation as recommended by Tertullian, or an intimate unburdening to a cleric as enjoined in the Basilian rule.[32] Since sin was personal, blanket pardons were not encouraged; excommunication or fixed graduated disabilities had to be imposed on each person according to his or her deserts.

Thus it came to be that the Classical search for fulfillment in the corporate had to make way, more and more, for the Christian's quest for salvation of self, accomplished by individual grace, experienced by personal conversion, and nourished by individual ministrations of the Church. The narrow Classical citizen took on a new role as a person concerned about his own existence as an individual, a conscious, and eternal entity of body and soul.

THE CHRISTIAN RESPONSE TO "TOTALITARIANISM"

"For God and Country"

Once a large number of individuals found meaning outside the corporate, the totalitarian sweep of the Classical commonwealth was threatened. When Jesus remarked "Render to Caesar the things that are Caesar's and to God the things that are God's," he not only enraged the Jews but eventually upset the whole Classical consensus.

Naturally any threat to the monopolistic "totalitarianism" of the Classical polity brought its perpetrators trouble. Christians, still a small minority in the early days of persecution, were of necessity discreet in venting their reservations about the state's attitude toward them. Some silently withdrew from society;[33] others, more boldly aired their objections in apologies; a few were defiant activists. The time would come when thousands would go resolutely to their deaths rather than compromise themselves by sacrificing to *Roma*.

Tacitus, laconically but shrewdly, labeled Christians "haters of the human race," a description merited in the minds of patriotic pagans by Christians' refusal to attend spectacles, to serve as actors, gladiators, charioteers, jockeys, even idol or amulet smiths, sellers of incense or perfume, magicians, conjurers, mathematicians, and astrologers. Almost every patristic writer had his own views about how far a Christian should go in withdrawing from society. Paul was more sympathetic to the existing order than John; Clement of Alexandria more cooperative than Tatian or Tertullian. Origen, unable to justify any double standard, told Christians to forego legion and camp as well as forum and office. Were

---

[32] *Didache* 4.14; Tertullian, *De poenit.* 9; Ambrose, *Expos. in Psalm* 118. 15,30 (*CSEL* 62:346); Chrysostom, *De incom Dei nat.* 5.7 (*PG* 48:745); Basil *In Isaiah* 10.244 (*PG* 30:547) and *Reg. brev.* 288 (*PG* 31:1078).

[33] Fustel de Coulanges, *Ancient City* p. 394 emphasizes Christian withdrawal from society as an important step toward the realization of human liberty insofar as it declared that only a part of man belongs to society.

not Christians, as priests, obligated to keep their hands clean of blood? Would not office holding involve sacrilegious oaths and overt participation in pagan ritual? He half–heartedly rationalized payment of taxes as a way to avoid trouble and to purge oneself of earthly goods which carried a terrestrial seal linking them to the world of Satan.[34] Christians were to serve the state only by praying for it, a concession Celsus thought intolerably condescending, downright treasonable, and not very helpful considering that the Jews, who did a lot of praying, did not fare well against the Romans.

Repetition of conciliar canons restricting cooperation with the pagan world reveals that many of the faithful were not whole–heartedly willing to forsake society. We have Tertullian's word for it, as well. He boasted, as we know, that Christians were invading all walks of life. Many were in the army already in the second century judging from the episode of the Thundering Legion which attributed its relief from drought to the prayers of its Christian legionnaires; Clement of Alexandria urged Christian soldiers to be content with their pay. Third–century conciliar canons in Spain and Asia show unmistakable participation of Christians in municipal affairs. The Council of Elvira, for instance, ordered Christian magistrates of cities to abstain from frequenting church during their tenure of office; the extent of participation by Christians in the Flaminate was punished in degrees. Christians taught in state schools, neglecting not even mathematics despite its astrological associations. The director of the manufacture of royal purple at Tyre was a priest of Antioch.

Some Christians spoke out against the existing order. Apologists like Theophilus, Aristides, and Melito of Sardis were reasonably conciliatory; others scolded the government while politely trying to excuse it: was not its thick–headedness due, for instance, to the machinations of daimons?[35] The most learned and interesting critic was the third–century Origen, a student of Paul, Plato, Stoics, and Philo. Cleverly accommodating Stoic thought on natural law to the Christian situation, he argued in his *Contra Celsum* and his *Commentaries* that the state must necessarily bow to an ethic higher than itself since it was actually a divine instrument whose authority was an extension of Providence's universal natural law. Reason required it, therefore, to identify its positive law with God's natural law to guarantee natural rights such as marriage, procreation, and religious freedom to live by the laws of God. His clinching argument identified natural law with the law of the Gospels, a thesis he learned, *mutatis mutandis,* from Philo. Since the Roman government did

---

[34] For this interesting view of taxes see Origen, *Hom. in Luc.* 35 (*PG* 13:1893), *Comm. in Matt.* 13.10, 17.28 (*PG* 13.1120–21; 1557–59), *Hom, in Ezech.* 13.2 (*PG* 13:760).

[35] Justin, *Apol.* 57, *Trypho* 131; Origen, *C.C.* 8.44.

violence to the Gospel message by supporting false deities and by persecuting Christians, it automatically violated natural law, lost its divine sanction, and became a quasi–legitimate government meriting only limited cooperation. At one point, he seemed to imply discreetly that even rebellion was justified.[36] Clearly in his mind the state did not enjoy a *plena auctoritas* simply by virtue of being itself; subject to a law higher than itself, it could not be a law to itself.

Origen, the only Father to see a revolutionary social message in Christianity, was confident that the higher Christian sovereignty would itself prevail and engulf the Classical polity.[37] Were not Christians already triumphantly meeting in practically every city in conventicles superior in quality to the local popular assemblies? More and more, countless persons were abandoning the constitutions of their native countries to secede to Jesus. Jesus was clearly showing his superiority over all other lords by entering with impunity into their territories to call a new people to himself. Superior even to the old Hebrew theocracy where God was king, the new Christian commonwealth had the potential to evolve into a stateless society, a spiritual utopia, a nation of philosophers in the best Platonic tradition. All Christians, schooled in the natural law of the Gospels, would come eventually to choose automatically what God chooses, a result which would encourage the state with its courts, police, positive law, and armies to wither away in a new day of peace and piety. If Origen's utopia never materialized, his Stoic natural–law concepts, kept alive by Eusebius, Basil, Gergory of Nazianzus, Jerome, Chrysostom, and others, passed on through others in later secular days to become a basic principle of Western political thinking.

If Origen would ask Caesar to abdicate, others would ask him to move over, to give Christians some autonomy. Writers like the author of I Peter, Hermas, Barnabas, Ignatius, Irenaeus, Melito, Clement of Alexandria, and Origen quite frequently referred to Christians as a "new people," the "new Jerusalem," the "city of God," a "nation set apart." According to Tertullian, even pagans struck by the uniqueness of the strange Christian folk, referred to them as an alien "third race" in distinction to Greeks and Jews. Why should not Rome, then, tolerate and make concessions to the idiosyncrasies of the Christians as it did to the

---

[36] See *C.C.* 5.37, 8.26.

[37] No work seems to exist on Origen's projected Christian utopia based on Plato's *Republic* and Paul's teaching on law. Cochrane, *Culture*, p. 195, speaks only of Lactantius' vision of a new Christian humanism. Origen's admiration for the Jewish theocracy could lead him, it appears, to accept the establishment of some sort of Christian theocracy as a step to a final glorified Christian republic where all would become philosophers so nourished on the spirit of the gospels that class distinction, armies, and courts would seem unnecessary. See E. G. Weltin, "The Effect of Christianity on Civil Society as Envisaged by Origen," *The New Christianity* 17 (1951):85–94.

peculiar national traits of other peoples in the empire? As an adopted heir of Abraham, the Christian race was older than Rome itself, or, for that matter, Greece. As the "New Jerusalem," now that the old Jewish temple–state had been laid waste, should it not inherit the traditional rights and immunities granted to Jews by Rome?

Needless to say, there were some Christians who tired of all the talk and turned activists. We actually know the names of a few. During Valerian's persecution a certain Leo gained fame by tearing down lanterns and stepping on the tapers in a temple of Fortune; a certain Romanus at Antioch enjoyed holding up heathen processions. Gregory of Nyssa records that a Theodore of Pontus used the day given him to recant, to set fire to the temple of the Great Mother, an act that pagans doubtless considered an immoderate assertion of individuality.

The estrangement of Christians from society, the failure of dialogue, acts of defiance, all culminated in the persecutions, the final all–out confrontation of the new Christian race with the Classical "totalitarian" commonwealth. How many thousands throughout the empire took the final step to their deaths under patriotic emperors like Decius, Diocletian, and Galerius is uncertain.

After Constantine's indult recognizing Christianity as lawful, the new Christian people, through emperor and theologian, were free and, indeed, obligated to do more than talk about the proper scope of state authority. Hellenistic political theory holding the king as a divine instrument found new and ready expression in Christian Constantinople to put Constantine in charge of church affairs; unbaptized though he be, it was his to plot, along with his successors, the direction the new Ark of the Covenant should take. Should Christianity take advantage of the Classical tradition of political–religious unity to advocate establishment of a theocracy like that of the ancient Jews now that monotheism had prevailed? Origen probably would have nodded in assent. Or could the newly triumphant one God learn to share power with the traditional establishment? Eusebius, historical spokesman for the new regime, reports Constantine's recognition that God had expressly appointed two roots of blessings for humanity: the Roman empire and the domain of Christ. The Edict of Milan indeed shattered the "totalitarian" claims of pagan Rome. But since no precedents existed for the implementation of dual hegemony, the matter had to be resolved by experimentation as revealed in many imperial decrees, letters and laws. An oversimplified version of what happened might divide this experimentation into three periods: one of strong state guidance of the Church between 313 and 361, a stage of separation between 361 and 375, and finally the beginning of church domination between 375 and 395. A century later Pope Gelasius could evaluate the results to provide a definitive statement that two sovereignties did, and should, exist: Church and State.

It is indeed fortunate that Eusebius preserves the actual text of the so–called Edict of Milan. This document, by finally granting all persons the liberty to follow whatever religion they wished, enunciated a doctrine so revolutionary that its full import was not entirely clear even to the emperor. Religion henceforth was to be divorced from "totalitarian" *Romanitas;* there now existed a facet of human's affairs exempt from state control. The decree—shall we call it the first bill of rights in western history?—put the emperor–pontifex–maximus in a paradoxical position. As a political functionary was he no longer to concern himself with religion at all, pagan or Christian? Could he, as pontifex–maximus, desert his numerous pagan subjects who for centuries equated divine bounty with the piety of imperial rule? Would Christ be satisfied and cooperative if the pontifex–maximus merely extended the privileges of pagan priests to the Christian clergy? Eusebius counseled him simply to administer "this world's affairs in imitation of God himself," in accord with prevailing Hellenistic political science which expected kingly rule on earth to reflect the divine rule of the cosmos.[38] Would the emperor, then, have to be a press agent for the true religion and encourage others, even his enemies like the king of Parthia, to convert? Should he decree Christian laws? Build Christian churches as he had pagan temples? Order his armies to pray rather than fight? Would he even have to interfere in the Christian rule of faith?

Practical circumstances helped force decisions. For one thing, peace had to be kept. Discordant Donatists, Arians, and followers of that "little fellow" Athanasius were soon so disturbing both religious and political tranquility that an imperial hand seemed necessary to preserve the integrity of God's Church whose experience in self–administration was obviously inadequate to the demands of its new independence. After an initial disappointment with the ineffectiveness of the Roman bishop to end the Donatist hassle, Constantine, now self–designated as "external bishop," formally called councils at Arles, Nicaea, and Tyre to grapple with his new type of dissenters. To rely on councils or assemblies to solve his problem was an unusually novel choice since effective parliamentary machinery had gone out of style in Roman imperial political practice with the fall of the Republic three hundred and fifty years earlier. Soon, fascination with the wily Arian, Eusebius of Nicomedia, lured Constantine to take a stronger hand in Church matters so that, despite

---

[38] Eusebius, *Orat.* 1.6. In different vein, K. F. Morrison "Rome and the City of God," *Transactions of the American Philosophical Society,* 64 (1964):51, maintains that in the fourth century the Hellenistic concept of emperorship had not yet been Christianized and therefore had not been adopted into the conceptual framework of the Church. Consequently, the king was not automatically expected to head, or even be a trustee of, the Church. Caesaropapism, dependent of Hellenistic ideas of kingship, would, according to this view, develop only later.

Nicaea, he banished "orthodox" bishops such as Eustatius of Antioch, Marcellus of Ancyra, and Athanasius of Alexandria, acts scarcely defensible as mere police actions executing conciliar decisions. Imperial edict followed edict—some sixty of Constantine's are readily at hand—dealing with heretics, church discipline, and doctrinal matters.

Constantine's successors, with such precedents of leadership in church affairs at hand, were not at all scrupulous.[39] The semi–Arian Constantius in the East and the orthodox Constans in the West both exercised a "Caesaropapist" control over the Church between 350 and 361. Constantius not only highhandedly deposed powerful "orthodox" bishops like Paul of Constantinople, Athanasius of Alexandria,and even Liberius of Rome, but also forcefully intruded his Arian minions Macedonius, Auxentius, and George of Cappadocia into strategic sees. In an authoritarian way, he interfered in the conciliar machinery by recognizing the rump Arian synod of Philippopolis and by intimidating the Council of Milan in 355 with a display of his naked sword and the curt directive, "Let my will serve as a canon." Finally, interfering in dogma, he tried to enforce an official creed distilled from the compromising and confusing credal statements forced from delegates of the rival councils of Rimini and Seleucia.

Reaction was afoot. Eventually in accord with the Edict of Milan, Christian emperors would be forced either to abolish the title of Pontifex Maximus or to surrender it to another sovereign head. By 360, in the setting sun of paganism, a candidate for the role was clearly emerging. The conciliar system's failure to establish a workable hierarchy of appellate jurisdiction, its fatal association with Arianism, its tacit assumption that debate can establish divine truth, its production of utter creedal confusion, and its indulgence in ludicrous political maneuvering and horseplay, all served to advance the Roman see, under Julius, as a promising future alternative to the emperor in church government. Displaced and outraged churchmen clustered around the bishop of Rome as a refuge untainted by conciliar entanglements, and then began to agitate for a clearer definition of Church and State jurisdiction. Athanasius, although willing to accept the emperor as legal executor of ecclesiastical decisions, objected strongly to what he considered a current attempt to relegate the Church to a branch of civil government. Whenever, he asked, did a judgment of the Church receive its validity from an emperor? What Fathers ever sought the consent of kings to their judgments? The synod of Milan in 355 accused the emperor of infringing

---

[39] Athanasius' *Apology against the Arians* and his *History of the Arians* as well as the ecclesiastical histories of Sozomen, Socrates, and Theodoret are the chief ancient sources for the period. P. R. Coleman-Norton, *The Roman State and the Christian Church: A Collection of Legal Documents to A.D. 535* (London: SPCK, 1966) is indispensable.

upon the ecclesiastical order by "mingling Roman sovereignty with the constitution of the Church." The venerable Hosius had already warned the emperor out of concern for his salvation not to intrude himself into doctrinal matters: the God who had placed the empire in kingly hands had as surely committed church affairs to the clergy; if the clergy were not permitted to bear rule on earth, the emperor had no right to burn incense. By 360 Hilary, too, was actively denouncing "Casearopapism" in the West. It was to take another hundred years, however, before the emperor's ecclesiastical leadership was to find a serious challenger in the Roman bishop: Even Julius requested the emperor to call an ecumenical council.

Between 361 and 375 the emperors Julian, Jovian, and Valentinian I were willing to oblige the clamor of churchmen for a clearer line of demarcation between Church and State. To be sure, the pro–Arian Valens in the East continued to exile bishops and force the creed of Rimini–Seleucia on the clergy of Antioch. But his tragic death in 378 at the hands of the Goths brought an end to Arian influence. Julian the Apostate, devoted to restoring paganism, cynically gave Christianity freedom from interference hoping ardently that its unpoliced internal feuds would destroy the infamous thing. To hurry that end, he revoked Christian privileges, ordered restoration of pagan temples, forbade Christians to teach, and set up an attractive rival for Christianity in his new syncretistic pagan cult under King Helios. Even pagans must have concluded that Julian's actions, however pleasing to them, were illegal; if a divorce had been issued between religion and politics how could an anachronous Pontifex Maximus legislate in an area declared outside state competence? While the short reign of Jovian quickly restored Christianity to its pre–Julian status, it turned a deaf ear to petitioning Christian factions and sent them away empty–handed. Valentinian I has been styled the last true Roman emperor because, refusing to allow Christian concerns to influence his administration, he operated only on strict secular guidelines.[40] He adroitly excused himself from Christian matters by announcing that it was not right for a layman to examine things of theological nature; did not such considerations, meant for priests, involve him in matters beyond his strength? Churchmen, he declared, "ordained with divine grace and illuminated by its splendor can decide better than I." He refused to exempt Pope Damasus from the jurisdiction of the city prefect, restricted the extent of state cooperation in enforcing papal ecclesiastical administrative decisions, and interfered in

[40] Cochrane, *Culture*, p. 324, in declaring that the separation policies of Valentinian were short lived precisely because they had no religious affiliation, Christian or pagan, judges the new Christian state, like the old pagan one, unable to stand on a strictly secular foundation.

the famous disputed papal election between Damasus and Ursinus only to keep order. Further, he refused to honor Hilary's request for an imperial hearing against the Arian bishop Auxentius of Milan, sensing, no doubt, that the request was inconsistent with Hilary's own avowal of separation.

In the last period from 375 to 395 under the emperors Gratian and Valentinian II in the West and Theodosius in the East, the Church began to lecture the state. While Athanasius, Hosius, and Hilary had argued that the emperor should keep hands off the Church, they did not yet insist that, as a Christian, the emperor was subject to it.[41] Hosius did, indeed, anticipate the idea when he remonstrated with Constantius "out of anxiety" for his salvation but he never threatened to inflict ecclesiastical penalties. But now looming over the orthodox Gratian, Valentinian II, and Theodosius was the towering Ambrose, bishop of Milan (375–97). Since all Christians, he asserted, were members of a kingdom more sublime than that of Caesar, the emperor, as a Christian member of this sacramental kingdom, fell first and foremost under the supreme jurisdiction of its king and the judgment of his ministers.[42] Ambrose also questioned the traditional rights of the Pontifex Maximus over religious properties by arguing that since the emperor was forbidden to lay hands on a Christian altar dedicated to God, he had, by extension, no jurisdiction over the basilica which housed it. Cleverly taking advantage of the old pagan understanding that sacred things belonged to divinity, he refused, in the light of the Edict of Milan, to accept the pagan corollary that their administration fell automatically to the Roman people and the emperor as their representative. Was it not clear that the emperor's position of Pontifex Maximus was untenable?

Before the Church could function effectively as a sovereignty of its own, orthodoxy had to be defined, paganism outlawed, and the high priestship of the emperor terminated. All these programs moved ahead swiftly under Gratian and Theodosius. The decree of Thessalonica, *Cunctos Populos* in 380,[43] repressing the conventicles of Christians at variance with the teachings of the Roman see and of Alexandria, clearly defined orthodoxy and made catholic Christianity the religion of the state. As Gratian withdrew recognition from Arians, many left the empire to evangelize the encroaching German barbarian tribes. Pagans were next to come under the ban. Constantius had already legislated against some heathen practices, had threatened to withdraw civil priv-

---

[41] See K. M. Setton, *Christian Attitude toward the Emperor in the Fourth Century* (New York: Columbia University Press, 1941), p. 107.

[42] Ambrose, *Ser. c. Auxen.* (*PL* 16:1049–52). For an excellent study of Ambrose's relation to the Church see Morrison, "City of God," pp. 40–51.

[43] Coleman–Norton, *State and Church*, 1:353–56 #167.

ileges from pagans in Alexandria, and had removed the controversial pagan statue of Victory from the senate house in Rome. But Gratian's logical and final step of abjuring the office of Pontifex Maximus in 375 was an ominous harbinger of what was soon to come. By cancelling out this political office he withdrew legal support from paganism so that between 382 and 388 the state began to remove subsidies and immunities from pagan temples and priests. Funds formerly spent on pagan cults were transferred to the army by Theodosius. The actual proscription of paganism began in 391; sacrifices were prohibited and temples closed including that of the venerable Vestals whose sacred vows of virginity had honored the gods for over a thousand years. The destruction of the Serapaeum in Alexandria became a celebrated and lamented event of history; armed forces were required to repress pagan opposition at Petra, Gaza, and Heliopolis. The final enactment dooming paganism came in 392 when even private worship of household gods was prohibited.

In this last period, the emperor was induced to kneel before the triumphant bishop. Valentinian II, virtually a puppet of Ambrose, surrendered meekly when he was ordered, under pain of excommunication, to remove again the statue of Victory from the senate house. The great bishop also defied the same emperor's order allowing his mother to attend Arian Easter services in Milan. In a stand–off in front of the church, the emperor's Gothic troops cowered before the defiant Ambrose and forced Valentinian to capitulate complaining, the while, that even his armies would arrest him if Ambrose commanded it. The violent and impetuous Theodosius was not only kept in hand but even humiliated. He scrupulously left the Council Constantinople alone in 381 and dutifully enforced, against dissenters, its Nicene formula now declared the true orthodoxy. To assure religious tranquility he ordered that the same capital punishment meted out for sedition and lese majeste be imposed for disturbing the peace of the Church.[44] Ambrose even refused the hot–headed emperor, as a mere layman, the right to sit in the sanctuary during church services, and demanded that he force the bishop of Callinicum to rescind an order requiring his flock to rebuild a synagogue they had burnt down. Finally, in a famous dramatic finale, Ambrose made Theodosius do public humiliating penance for massacring citizens of Thessalonica. As a Christian did he not know that the king was under the law?

The rest of the story concerning Christianity's triumph over the "totalitarianism" of the Classical corporation is an anti–climax. Wisely the new sovereignty chose to eschew theocracy. Now that the emperor had shown effectively that his will could have the force of law in ecclesiastical

---

[44] Ibid., 1.363 #173, 2:404 #205.

circles, clergy especially in the west deemed it prudent to keep Caesar at arm's length lest familiarity tempt him to exaggerate his rightful claims and try to rule as a theocrat. Church Fathers recalled only too well Constantius' troublesome support of Arianism and Julian's nefarious encouragement of paganism. The Church would wisely be content to be an *isopoliteia:* the emperor would recognize the Church's sovereignty and help execute its judgments; in exchange the Church would recognize the sacred character of emperorship as a divine dispensation. It was a workable bargain; beyond it the Fathers of the fourth century did not wish, or dare, to go.[45]

The Church got the better of the deal: it was destined to play the role of the sun while the empire had to be content with the moon. The emperor even leaned upon the Church to prop up his political authority by declaring violations against his divine imperial constitutions sacrilege. From "Father of his Country" Caesar was demoted to a son of the Church. By this time the interloping emperor Maximus (383–88) had carried out local episcopal wishes to kill Priscillianists. Christians like Augustine grew up expecting the secular arm to give an account of its stewardship by enforcing ecclesiastical decisions. Pope Celestine, a product of the new day, congratulated Theodosius II for his cooperation with the Council of Ephesus and reminded him, in the old–time pagan way, that his government would flourish only in relation to his zeal for religion: "the cause of the faith should be a greater concern than your realm . . . for all things follow propitiously if, first of all, those things which are dear to God are taken care of." Pope Xystus, in much the same vein, praised the wisdom of emperors who devoted themselves to the business of Him who never, in return, would spare himself in concern for the empire. Pope Gelasius addressing the emperor in 495 summed it up clearly:

> There are two chief powers by which this world is governed, August emperor; the sacred authority of the prelates and the kingly power . . . You know, most clement son, that although you are placed in rank above all the race of men, nevertheless you bow your neck in devoted submission to those who are set in charge of matters of religion . . . The leaders of religion themselves obey your laws recognizing that the imperial authority has been conferred upon you from on high . . . With how much greater zeal, then, ought you obey those who are set in charge of the sacred mysteries?"[46]

[45] Morrison, "City of God," pp. 14, 51.

[46] For text and discussion see A. J. Carlyle, *A History of Medieval Political Theory in the West* (London: Blackwood, 1903), p. 191.

CHAPTER 3

THE RATIONAL

THE CLASSICAL RATIONAL IDEAL

"We are Lovers of Wisdom" . . . Paricles

It was one thing for proselytizing Islam to encounter primitive Berbers who washed their hair in rotten eggs and camel urine; it was another for Christianity to cope with the sophisticated rationalism of Classical intellectuals. While Greeks were like all human beings passionate and fanatical, and while Romans were hard–headed, pragmatic, and devoted to tradition, the Greek and Roman world, probably more than any other civilization, prided itself on being a rational society. It assumed that man, as a conscious, remembering, and thinking creature, could abstract what seemed normal and sane from objective observation and deduce what seemed likely even from speculation on the unobservable. It built on the conviction that human beings could innately make classifications distinguishing the particular from the general, the species from the genus, and that they could discern contradictions, make deductions from given facts and established abstract principles, and draw inferences from analogies.

Lacking a systematic revelation, the Greeks learned early to do their own thinking about what they saw and even what they couldn't see. Unlike Yahweh, the Greek gods did not tell people what was what. The oracle at Delphi was never a source of revelation comparable to Mt. Sinai. Since Apollo generally spoke only upon solicitation and mainly to heroes and celebrities to advise them in specific situations, the oracle at no time revealed basic theological or ethical truths or commissioned its devotees to play the role of prophets to fashion a civilization. Nonetheless, it was natural enough for lawgivers, philosophers, and statesmen to claim the sanction of the oracle; its prestige admittedly was great as a national shrine even if its performance was spotty, enigmatic, and not always forthright or even patriotic. Lacking revealed truth enshrined in holy writ, church, or creed, Greeks sought enlightenment from poets, especially Homer, whose works, although hallowed by invocations of the Muses and considered fundamental to traditional Greek moral education, never became sacred books authoritative enough to offer the Greeks an alternative to their self–reliance. As a basically secular people depending largely on their own creative resources, Greeks preferred to choose as worthy intellectual tools only those—among the few vouchsafed humanity—which were within their human competence to operate. Enlightenment through an authoritative extended Revelation was beyond their experience. Observation and reason were seized upon as the tools best fitted to implement and to express their intellectual self reliance in the ultimate form of speculative philosophy and demonstrable science. Even mysticism was not considered totally alien, for many Greeks clearly felt able not only to initiate action which would identify them with the Ultimate Principle but also, to direct the very process of self sublimation, often through graduated steps, involving ascetic practices and contemplation.

The Greeks were such a rational people that, as we saw, they were uncomfortable when they found themselves thinking and acting under the influence of seemingly uncontrollable stimuli. Too often the appetitive or spirited aspect of the soul seemed to dominate. Those strange sudden insights, flashes of cognition, inner voices, feelings of bewilderment or courage, those passionate Medean emotions which so often confounded human rational behavior were explained away in early days as temporary visitations of specialized divinities. Prophetic madness, along with the divine disease of epilepsy, was ascribed to Apollo; orgiastic frenzy was attributed to Dionysos, poetic madness to the Muses, erotic delirium to Aphrodite and Eros. Mental disturbances were consigned to the mysterious realm of Hecate, Cybele, the Corybantes, or Pan. Asclepius was associated with dreams and trances. The legendary Orpheus was called upon to account for inward naggings of guilt, results of a kind of pagan "original sin" which left an imperfection in the soul.

It is important to admit offhand that there existed a persistent mystical strain in the predominately rational Greek mind.[1] Desire for some union with the undefinable godhead or ultimate Reality, however formidable, rare, or fleeting an experience, so intrigued Greeks that they employed at least three different ways to achieve it. The first, eating or drinking of the deity—an act mystical at least in purpose however practical in method—is more an importation into the Classical world than an indigenous tradition. Nevertheless because it is quite rational in concept it enjoyed a wide appeal. Such was the Dionysos–Bacchus approach in which the mystic resorted to sacramental "eucharistic" rites so orgiastic that they taxed the physical endurance of even the most stalwart initiate, and so immoderate that both Apollo and Roman law tried to temper

---

[1] Dodd's *Irrational* is the indispensable work on the "non-rational" side of the Greek mind. In the present instance, see especially chap. 3, pp. 64–101 and 147–56. Quite relevant is J. W. Swain, *Hellenic Origins of Christian Asceticism* (New York: Columbia University Press, 1916).

them. The old Orphics and the Pythagoreans chose a more intellective mystical route emphasizing rites of purification and cathartic effects of asceticism or mathematical gnosis. Fasting, abstinence from certain foods, and sundry disciplinary practices facilitated the induction of an inner light accompanied by hypnosis, trances, dreams, or ecstasy. Platonists of one stripe or another were, however, the most respected exponents of the mystical. Spurning both Bacchic–like "eucharists" and Pythagorean gnostic asceticism, they sought fulfillment in pure contemplation of indescribable Absolutes. Plato himself not only sought to bring his own soul into intimate contact with his highest Idea, the Good, but he also expected his philosopher guardians of *The Republic* to contemplate the realm of the Forms; thus, coming into enlightened contact with true Reality, they could govern well by telling their subjects what was best for them. Even his more seasoned position in *The Laws* never ruled out the importance of intuitive cognition and religious assumptions resting upon them. The amorphous group of middle Platonists, like their successors, the neo–Platonists, sought the ultimate by mental absorption into the One. While the neo–Platonists, like Pythagoreans, stressed the importance of self–discipline and asceticism, they became the greatest advocates of mystic contemplation in ancient times. Through this means, as a purely intellective process, the devotee strove to think away both corporeality and time so that the Self, detached from the body, could soar to the wholly transcendent One. The process was exhausting: Plotinus claimed success only four times; Porphyry only once.

Reason was not only put somewhat on the defensive by mystics, but was at times deliberately abused or even openly attacked by others. In the last half of the fifth century, for instance, the Sophists, commonly accused of excessive rationalism, were additionally charged by Plato with sabotaging the integrity of dialectic, supposedly for the sake of novelty and notoriety, in order to liberate the youngbloods of the day from religious traditions and from any objective moral values. Aristophanes' popular comedies mocked a society which supposedly produced too many rationalistic realists such as Euripides who seemed to dissolve sanity in a flood of sophistic dramatics. Reactionary "heresy" trials in the last half of the fifth century involved several prominent rationalists including the atheistic Anaxagoras and the hair–splitting Socrates; books critical of the traditional hodge–podge of custom were consigned to flames.

Despite these strong mystical strains and occasional anti–rationalistic outbreaks, the hold of reason on the Greeks was so persistent and trenchant that it dominated every field of endeavor in the Classical world. The search for rational government—whether monarchical, aristocratic, timocratic, or democratic—became such an obsession that men like Plato, Aristotle, and Cicero virtually created political science even though it had little if any practical impact. Platonic and Stoic views, extolling Reason as an Absolute and common ingredient of the cosmos, including gods and humans, so influenced Cicero that he repeatedly proclaimed it the root of all law. In the Principate, the Antonines strove to rationalize the law both in spirit and operation. Stoicism, for example, was quite influential in encouraging emperors to temper the spirit of criminal law with equity. Stoics were less successful, as we saw, in their attempts to modify in principle the concept of the *plena potestas* of constitutional law by the injection of restrictive rational natural rights. Nor did Stoic Reason cause an emperor like Marcus Aurelius to lessen the absolute *auctoritas* vested in the person of the king. However, the production of legal codes and improvements in the administrative machinery of justice point convincingly to the impact of reason on law. Balance and symmetry, rather than the bizarre, dominated Greek and Roman sculpture, poetry, and architecture. Historians, in distinguishing occasion from cause and cause from effect, chose to cite human violation of rational moderation, psychological imbalance, excessive human passion—especially greed—and other irrational motivations as the cause of much of history's woes. More and more, history as a serious study of rational causation crowded out theistic arbitrariness. Thucydides, Caesar, Sallust, and Tacitus so ignored the gods—admittedly in contrast to Livy and Plutarch—that for all good purposes divinity did not take charge of history again until the Christian Eusebius in the fourth century turned it over to Christ. Greek science explored human nature as never before. As we shall see in some detail later, practically every Greek philosopher investigated the nature and operation of the human soul. No matter into how many parts or facets they divided it—from three to fourteen—they unanimously declared reason the soul's crowning glory. Reason not only made man man but even allowed him to partake of the divine. In any conflict between Nous and Ananke, reason and constraint, the rational part of the human soul was urged to assume decisive command.

Certainly reason lay at the root of Classical physical sciences. First, by gradually classifying related data into logical demarcated groupings it isolated distinct scientific disciplines. Hippocrates early applied the process to discover medicine, Aristotle zoology, and along with his pupil Theophrastus botany. Then reason dictated formulation of scientific methodology. Hippocrates chose the case study; Aristotle in his *Physics* demonstrated how one should move carefully through definition and deduction to logical demonstration in attempting to give a rational explanation of the natural world. Once under way, science exploded throughout the Hellenistic age to produce a well known galaxy of famous names. Astronomy produced Heraclides of Pontus who discovered that the earth turned daily on its axis, Aristarchus of Samos who proposed the heliocentric system, and Hipparchus of Nicaea whose geocentric system was to have an indirect hand in the condemnation of Galileo centuries later. Medicine produced the anatomists Herophilus of Chalcedon, Erasistratus, and the great Galen. Geometry reached a zenith in Euclid, trigonometry in Hipparchus and Eratosthenes of Cyrene who miscalculated the circumference of the earth by only a few miles.

More important to us, however, is the area of philosophy, virtually a monopolistic Greek discovery. Since philosophy allows reason to soar from the observable to the speculative, to study the indescribable, it, rather than science, brought Christianity into a major intellectual encounter with the Classical mind. Its impact on the early Church was almost overwhelming since it presented attractive, well–thought–out ideas on such fundamental problems as the essence of being or reality (ontology), the origin and nature of the universe (cosmology), the nature and purpose of human beings (anthropology), ethics, esthetics, and even the nature and operation of god (theology). To do all this it had to develop logic and epistemology to formalize reason's use as an orderly and convincing intellectual tool, and to explore the methods, grounds, and limitations of knowledge. Although Parmenides and the Sophists were important in the early development of logic and dialects, Socrates and Plato really began the discipline by making the definition and concept basic in argumentation, tools applicable to both empirical data and abstract speculation. Without the extended syllogism Plato could not have tried to demonstrate his theory of Ideas or prove such basic propositions as the soul's eternity or Reality's transcendence. Aristotle, adamant in his conviction that the proper function of man's unique intellectual nature was to think, deliberate, and supply rational answers, furnished in his so–called *Organon* the formal rules of deliberative procedure. The Classical mind became so fascinated with such basics as inductive and deductive reasoning, first principles, syllogisms, categories,and causes that few philosophers could dare ignore or flaunt them.

To the Greeks philosophy became king because it exercised reason to its fullest, probing both the observable and the speculative. While constituent areas of philosophy are generally not treated separately by ancient writers, three—cosmology, ethics, and anthropology—came to present the greatest challenges to Christian revelation. Since anthropology tends to be imbedded in the other branches of philosophy, it suffices here to say that, in general, Classical thought tended to make man either a material machine, as with the Atomists, or a part of a divine scheme or process, as with Platonists and Stoics. Aristotle, somewhat differently, preferred to see humankind as a unique type, neither wholly mechanistic nor divine, which assumed a close relationship between soul and body. As the body influences the soul by helping it extrapolate Form from the body's sensitive experience, man was driven to fulfill his own appropriate Form as a rational, political animal and even in a sense a divine entity insofar as rationality caused him in his highest activity, the exercise of intellectual virtue, to commune with the divine mind.

Early Greek cosmology could not separate the origins and natures of the gods from that of the universe. Although all cultures in their early stages create mythology to explain an animistic world where all phenomena are divine, Greek reason went on to create theogonies and cosmogonies dealing with the origins of gods and the cosmos making up what later is thought of as cosmology. Theogonic and cosmogonic explanations antedated even Homer who, nonetheless, is considered the first to inject some rational thinking into these obscure matters by making a theomorphic Ocean the beginning of all things.[2] Hesiod's *Theogony* of the early seventh century, relying on observation, logically postulated male–female procreation as the source of all his animistic deities. To Hesiod, the universe, like the nobility of his day, had to have a family tree; and how else than by sexual activity could things rationally come to be? In time, however, reason did not spare even Homer and Hesiod as authorities on cosmology. Hecataeus of Miletus in the sixth century began to find their mythological explanations ridiculous; Xenophanes about the same time thought the whole system immoral and rationally suspect as a product of human presumption: if horses had gods would they not make them horse gods? Was not an "All–One" preferable?

Rationalization soon provided less animistic cosmologies. However simplistic, they were reflective efforts, based of necessity on observation, first to isolate the basic stuff of the universe—water with Thales, air with Anaximenes—then to speculate on the principle of movement as with Heraclitus and to a lesser degree Parmenides, and finally to establish some order in the face of movement as exemplified by Empedocles. His four elements—fire, air, water, and earth—would provide stability; their combinations would accommodate mobility and temporality. Eventually four great rational cosmologies emerged: the Platonic, Aristotelian, Stoic, and Epicurean.

Some Platonic views of the universe have roots going back to the end of the sixth century when Heraclitus declared the essence of the world to be a spiritual governing principle, the Logos, which he embodied in fire to represent the law of inexorable motion in the universe. More influential on Plato was Parmenides of the early fifth century. The first to prefer abstract deductive reasoning to that based on observation, he conceived a

---

[2] Iliad 14.201.246. W. Jaeger, *Paideia: The Ideals of Greek Culture*, 3 vols. (New York: Oxford University Press, 1945), 1:453 n.5, records that Aristotle considered Homer's cosmological idea important enough to make it an anticipation of Thales' watery monism and therefore the beginning of Greek philosophy.

theory of Reality that, like Heraclitus' Logos, was destined to give both
the pagan and the Christian world a great deal of trouble. To him
ultimate Being or Reality appeared to be nothing else but an eternal,
unchanging, immovable simplex. To accommodate motion he made the
domain of the senses a realm of appearances, of non–Being, a world of
temporality, change, movement, and complexity. The universe ran, as it
were, on opposed parallel tracks whose point of junction was hidden in
an intellectual haze.

Plato's school, the Academy, concluded that the only way to deal with
the eternal flux of Heraclitus' Logos and the fixed motionlessness of
Parmenides' Being was to accept a dualistic cosmology of Being and
non–Being. Plato chose to follow his predecessor Parmenides in assigning true Being only to the nonsensible world, to the celestial world of
invisible but real eternal, unchangeable, timeless spiritual essences existing objectively as Ideas or Forms. Knowable only to the soul's reason,
they were, nonetheless, so real that men knew them innately. Non–Being
was the world of inert matter, remote from Being and resistant to it.
Material sensible objects, merely reflections or partakers of eternal essences, speciously existed in transition, as it were, between Being and
non–Being. As mere reflections of Reality, objects were accessible only to
sensation and opinion while the Forms lent themselves to contemplation
as true knowledge. Physical, material things, then, had a recognizable
essence only through participation in Forms; the good man was possible
only because he partook of eternal Goodness and Humanity. How Forms
and matter were actually connected Plato never adequately explained,
although in some degree he attempted to do so especially in the *Timaeus*.[3]

Even though the visible world was only an imperfect changing "expression" of the objective eternal order, Plato viewed it as the work of a
quite perfect being, the Demiurge or creator, who providentially, but
with difficulty, arranged pre–existent matter by imposing the Forms
upon it. The human soul, as part of the world soul created by the
Demiurge, was so entrapped in its material body that it had its wits
dulled to such an extent that it could enjoy only vague recollections of its
pre–existence in the higher world of Reality where the Forms existed.

Aristotle, Plato's pupil, modified his master's conception of cosmology significantly. While keeping Plato's eternal Forms he denied
them existence in a distinct and isolated realm. Forms were eternal
qualities, efficient and final forces, capable of impressing themselves
upon matter which, not completely inert, had the potentiality to be

---

[3] *Timaeus* 27–30C tries to establish a connection between Forms and Matter through
action of the demiurge. His creation, the World Soul, is pictured as struggling against
Necessity to span the hiatus between the Ideas and the corporeal world.

influenced by them to bring different material types to their fullest expression of their own Forms. Forms were grasped not by the soul's recollection but by man's rational power to synthesize abstractions from his observations. To Aristotle Reality existed in the sensible object as a combination of both matter and Form. The cosmos, made up of eternally moving matter under the guidance of an unprovidential unmoved Mover, operated nonetheless with something of a teleological purpose: a totality resulting naturally from the different natures of things. Cycles of specific kinds of being simply followed repetitive developmental courses to the end of their cycles. The unmoved Mover, an independent being, an immortal essence, was pure Form and intelligence, supreme activity, unfathomable although possibly knowable through intellectual contemplation.

The Stoic cosmos, conceived by Zeno of Cyprus as a materialistic pantheism, was synonymous with the world functioning as a necessary mode of divine self–fulfillment.[4] The Logos of Heraclitus furnished the divine fiery generating substance of the universe. While being an evanescent, yet materialistic breath, a divine hydrogen, as it were, that made up the cosmos, the Logos was none other than pure Reason itself, almost another name for hypostasized Nature. Parts of the cosmos became differentiated by the degree to which the rarefied generating substance, or Logos, was congealed by tension into the various relative densities of fire, air, water, and earth spoken of earlier by Empedocles. Cleanthes began to adulterate this Stoic cosmic monism with a dash of dualism. His elevating *Hymn to Zeus,* which honored the Father of the Gods as providential Reason, tended to grant the Logos a personal existence of its own; rather than being the cosmos, Zeus as the Logos permeated it. Although Roman Stoicism toned down interest in cosmology in favor of ethics, its code of conduct remained firmly based on the traditional Stoic cosmology. To the Stoic, in short, Reason, far from being merely an epistemological tool, became a deterministic providential self–fulfilling essence embedded in the cosmos and rationally relating and ordering everything in it.

---

[4] To make definitive statements about Stoic cosmology and ethics is quite presumptuous considering the six-hundred year history of the philosophy, its modifications in the general philosophical synthesis and the paucity of its surviving literature. Even Diogenes Laertius in his *Lives of Eminent Philosophers* written about A.D. 200 feels uncertain about the old Stoic school of Zeno, Cleanthes, and Chrysippus despite the fact that he reported some one hundred sixty works by Chrysippus alone. Fragments of Old Stoicism have been collected by J. Arnim, *Stoicorum Veterum Fragmenta,* 3 vols. (Lipsiae: Teubner, 1921). Fragments of the Middle Stoic, Panaetius, are available in M. VanStraaten, *Panétius, sa vie, ses ésrits, et son doctrine* (Amsterdam: H. J. Paris, 1946). Fragments of the Middle Stoic, Posidonius, have been assembled from sixty manuscripts in *Posidonius, Fragments,* ed. L. Edensten and I. G. Kidd (Cambridge: Cambridge University Press, 1972).

The fourth chief cosmological system of the ancient world was the Epicurean. Anaxagoras somewhat anticipated Epicurus' atomic system by teaching that a countless number of "seeds," unchangeable in quality, combined and separated to account for the diversity and temporality in the universe. His mechanistic system, while in a deistic way allowing a nous to set the cosmic process in orderly movement, rejected all traditional religious preconceptions as meaningless. Indeed, Anaxagoras was exiled for impiety because he insisted the sun was not a god but only a lump of burning rock larger than the Peloponnesus. The immediate forerunners of the Epicurean school, however, were Leucippus and Democritus who also held that indivisible particles moved in infinite space to form various combinations and appear as sensible phenomena. Working with this theory of "atoms" Epicurus and his Roman exponent, Lucretius, turned the cosmos into a giant machine of which man was a part. This ancient mechanistic, deterministic materialism so threatened alike gods, Providence, and eventually Christ that even the secular eighteenth–century Enlightenment found it inspirational.[5]

These four rationally conceived cosmologies were accompanied by corresponding ethical systems. Denied moral illumination by their gods, Greeks sought knowledge of human nature and behavior by observing what men did naturally and then adjusting this conclusion to fit the particular cosmological system they entertained. In early days, Homer generally portrayed both gods and men as honoring a pragmatic honesty–is–the–best–policy ethic when it was not expedient to operate on a more natural might–makes–right basis. Rational refinements were clearly in order.

Sophists, along with Socrates, first took ethical speculation seriously and professed ability to teach men how to act rationally in the perplexing but orderly cosmos philosophers were fashioning. Against the Sophists, who preached an ethic which pitted the laws of nature against those of the polis, Plato gave the polis unqualified support as the best guarantor of mankind's ancient consensus concerning virtue. To Plato, Justice, Temperance, Piety, Bravery and such like, were Forms unchangeable and universal. As such they were not inventions of sophistry but instinctively known objectively to all human beings capable of communicating with Reality or identifying with the Good through an arduous educational program involving Socratic dialectic. In his early writings Plato leaned toward Socrates' view which equated virtue with knowledge so that evil became an error. Since he could not envisage a rational creature willingly choosing a lack of knowledge, it was difficult for him to

---

[5] P. Gay, *The Enlightenment*, 2 vols. (New York: Knopf, 1966), 1:100 remarks: "no propagandist ever conducted the battle of science against religion more exuberantly than Lucretius nor won it for science with such simple means."

envisage anyone electing evil. Later in his life Plato became more pessimistic and made evil almost tantamount to a disinclined will, the legacy of a diseased soul benighted by its association with matter. Punishment became corrective so that the rational function of the soul could learn to take charge of its appetitive parts. Finally, instead of knowledge and punishment as a corrective for evil, Plato saw that for man to achieve his end, a resemblance to god, he would have to detach himself from corrupting earthly existence by contemplation and finally by death to allow the soul to reattain the original purity and knowledge it once knew in its pre–existent state.[6]

Later Platonism tended to overemphasize this or that aspect of Plato's ethics. Taking to heart Plato's restriction of true knowledge to the world of Being, Sceptics led by Carneades despaired of ever attaining any certainty in the sensible world where only appearances and opinion were possible. Thus in daily life they were restricted to operating in a world of probability alone. Middle Platonists and Alexandrian neo–Platonists of the second and third centuries A.D. emphasized Plato's late religious strains centered in his repugnance for matter. Consequently, they sought a life which would mystically abandon the sensible world in progressive degrees so that they could see god. While the neo–Platonic school of Athens became, within the confines of reason, more and more religious, the school of Syria headed by Iamblicus fell overboard into a sea of theurgistic humbug. Iamblicus, an ultra mystic of unlimited credulity who lived in the twilight of paganism under Constantine, vainly tried to rally the old gods. In his syncretistic system, humanity completely retreated before the divine; gods were multiplied and divided; no concept was not hypostasized; no miracle doubted. Efficacy of actions lay in the magical power inherent in symbols comprehended only by the gods so that theurgy, divination, and numerology all figured in this school bewildering to pagans and Christians alike.[7]

No ancient writer has left such a clear account of his ethical system as Aristotle in his popular *Nichomachean Ethics*. Happiness, as the highest good, was attained as a creature approached the perfection of his Form, that is, fulfilled the function nature had assigned to his type. A horse was "happy" when it did what came naturally: acting like a horse. Since man's

---

[6] The change in Plato's attitude toward evil becomes noticeable in the *Gorgias* (477A–C) where human evil results from a diseased soul rather than from ignorance; virtue is not thought of in terms of knowledge.

[7] For a more sympathetic view see Whittaker *Neo-Platonists*, pp. 123–31. Whittaker prefers to stress Iamblicus' *Protrepticus* as a worthy treatise of Platonic, Aristotelean, and neo-Pythagorean elements rather than to emphasize Iamblicus' association with magic and theurgy. Iamblicus himself made no claims to a personal absorption into the godhead. The same kind of widely divergent interpretations that are given to Iamblicus apply also to Proclus, virtually the last of the neo-Platonists.

function was noble activity of soul in obedience to reason, human fulfillment came through a rational choice and cultivation of both intellectual
virtues such as prudence and wisdom, as well as moral virtues such as
courage, temperance, and liberality. Despite his unprovidential cosmology, Aristotle maintained that the intellectual virtues not only involved humankind in the exercise of its true excellence, the use of its
reasoning powers, but also that they were indeed divine gifts relating
men to the divine mind itself. Human reason could be trusted to identify
the content of the moral virtues by determining a rational mean between
two extremes of conduct. Noble birth and economic independence were
virtually necessary for the attainment of virtue since it required leisure
to cultivate good habits, an impossible program for those handicapped
by mercenary distractions or social dependencies which hampered free
exercise of the will.

Since Stoicism assumed that divine Reason was identical with—or
infused within—nature, man's ethical obligation was to grow morally by
rationally cooperating with this divine, "fatalistic" arrangement. Since all
things in the universe were pantheistically related, Stoicism called upon
each individual to make his or her own proper rational association
between things in all situations so that one could act harmoniously with
the universe according to the dictates of Reason embedded in it. If a
Stoic assumed, for example, that a rational relationship existed between
human beings and stars, then living under astrological dictates was
proper for him; so with the gods, and suicide. Epictetus enjoined his
readers over and over to "make the right use of the appearances of
things" and "to live according to nature," to know what was in their
power, to accept that which was not. In doing so they would reach
apatheia or freedom from passion and desire. "Sin" was an improper
identification of the indifferent, the good, and the bad; indulgence in
passion was a misjudgment. The chief ethical contribution, especially of
late Stoicism, taught that all human beings were associated by a natural
law, were equal in essence, and shared a common brotherhood under
the fatherhood of God. Roman Stoicism, in a practical way, emphasized
cooperation with one's duty as determined by the circumstances of his
life. Thus Cicero, even though his *De officiis* reveals his deep commitment to Stoic ethics, had to temper his pursuit of indifference or *apatheia*
because it was not consonant with the demands of energetic statecraft.
The moral tone of Seneca's letters, Epictetus' *Discourses,* and Marcus
Aurelius' *Meditations* reveals a resolute and pious commitment to live in
accord with the intentions of Providence.

Epicureans, as mechanistic materialists, trusted only sensation. The
gods, if they existed, were irrelevant. Epicureans found no teleology in
nature; human beings could find no salvation in the mechanical atoms.
In rationally interpreting the universe, the Epicurean used a mind which

also was constructed of material atoms but ones of exceptionally fine and subtle nature. By introducing an unpredictable "swerve" into the motion of mind atoms, Lucretius, like his mentor Epicurus, apparently hoped to preserve some place for freedom of will in an otherwise deterministic system. Pleasure, ideally intellectual, was the greatest good leading to happiness, to *ataraxia,* or freedom from passion, calmness against such vain anxieties as superstitious fear of the gods and of death. Death, as merely the painless disintegration of man's atomic structure, was robbed of its sting. Tranquility at its best also demanded that Epicureans isolate themselves from worldly pursuits, and be content to enjoy the intellectual stimulation of a small nexus of friends.

In retrospect it would appear that human rationality in building these four ethical systems dealt man interesting destinies. Platonism translated him into a spiritual being; Stoicism strove to give him temporary dignity in the face of a divine fatalism; Aristotle extolled human rationality in a world where virtue was its own reward; Epicurus begrudged his followers free will in a world of mechanistic determinism. It proved difficult for ancient philosophy to conceive of other rational options. At the very sunset of the pagan day, Julian the Apostate could still discover no better ethical advice than the time–honored recommendation that man strive to realize that which was best and noblest for him: a life of reason. For Julian, as for his pagan mentors, it was at the same time the proper way to worship Zeus.

If rationalism created sophisticated sciences and philosophies replete with cosmologies, anthropologies, and ethics, it also concerned itself with a quest for god, or theology. To the ancients the line between philosophy and theology was thin. If Protagoras and Epicurus repudiated the gods, most philosophers did not. The versatile Empedocles believed in divine spirits, an Orphic "fall," and transmigration; Plato trusted daimons, honored the demiurge, and practically made his highest Form, the Good, god; Aristotle equated theology with something of a divine metaphysics; Stoics prayed to Providence, and neo–Platonists contemplated their trinity in hopes of ecstasy.

It is obvious that the same rational mind that doted on philosophy did not necessarily see religion as irrational. Indeed, considered historically, and in the light of Aristotle's final cause, religion can be seen as an eminently logical pursuit which man deliberately uses to modify his environment, whether internal or external, corporate or individual. As such it competes with two logical rivals, magic and science.[8] If the

---

[8] Celsus (Origen, *C.C.* 4.80) adroitly senses the rivalry of religion and "scientia" when he makes contact with the gods relative to the degree of knowledge existing at any given time. In the beginning of the world's existence men sought greater assistance from the gods than they do later when progress in understanding the environment and the invention of the arts advance human independence. Lucretius, of course, would have agreed.

ordered universe suggests the existence of gods, it would be illogical not to study them or not to communicate with them through words and gifts. Who can blame the magician for assuming a wrong sympathy between two phenomena or for falsely connecting an act imitative of a desired result with the result itself?

Only two Greek philosophies, Pythagoreanism and neo–Platonism, might be called basically religious. Even early Pythagoreanism prior to 450 B.C. had a strong religious strain. For its cult members it advocated purification from an Orphic "Fall" through renunciation of the earthly and the employment of ascetic practices.[9] Cardinal to the system was the doctrine of transmigration of souls. Later neo–Pythagoreanism was an amorphous jumble of Platonic, Aristotelian, and Stoic cosmological ideas bound up in a strong religious format featuring miracle–working, prophesy, and gnostic omniscience. Yet both old Pythagoreanism and neo–Pythagoreanism had the marks of true philosophy. Both sought a rational expression of the harmonious order of the universe in mathematical formulas based on serious intellective exertion. And if humanity has to cope with evil who can say that Pythagorean reincarnation is not a rational solution? If neo–Platonic mystics, in turn, indulge in other–worldly contemplative strivings, they are yet employing a disciplined intellective path to god. If man's consciousness suggests a lofty component within him, a soul, would it be illogical to try to bring it to its highest fulfillment? It is significant that the great neo–Platonic mystic, Plotinus, remained to the end a loyal defender of Greek rationalism against gnosticism. Admittedly, however, neo–Pythagoreanism and especially Syrian neo–Platonism show how readily philosophies could turn into a religious shamanism.

Greek philosophers, then, as part theologians, did not object to prying into the psychology and intentions of the divine, to sit in judgment, as it were, over the gods themselves. The results were interesting and diverse. Just as modern science nourished a "god–is–dead" strain of liberal intellectuals, so ancient philosophical rationalism did the same. Anaxagoras, himself indicted for impiety, taught Pericles not to let the gods bother him much. Protagoras rationally concluded that since nothing could be known of the gods, theology was not worth the effort. Thucydides, as a realist historian, reported that neither prayers nor temples tempered the plague at Athens. Euripides, living in a particularly iconoclastic age, cast the gods in a controversial mold. As he used them in his plays, they appeared to many as mere props, ridiculous puppets, or even machines commanded to solve hopelessly entangled

---

[9] Pythagoras is known to us largely through Diogenes Laertius' work. Pythagoreanism is reconstructed from frequent remarks by Plato but especially by Aristotle in such works as *De caelo, Physics,* and *Metaphysics.* It is refreshing to read Dodd's candid reservations about Orphism, pp. 147–49.

plots. Or were they meant as shameful personifications of human emotion? Did not only Athena seem to escape Euripides' censure for lust and injustice? In the *Bacchae* the dramatist seems even to parody the rationalization of religious experience as folly.[10] Epicureanism, of course, ignored the gods, while Stoic rationalism could accept the traditional pantheon or leave it. In Alexander's day, Euhemerus, a native of Messana, "undivinized" the gods entirely. Taking a cue from Hecataeus of Teos, who earlier said the gods of Egypt were simply deified benefactors of humanity, Euhemerus reduced the Classical divinities to deified heroes. Introduced into Rome by Ennius' translation of the *Sacred History*, Euhemerus' theory drew the censure of Cicero as atheistic.

At the hands of reason, religion in Rome fared the same as in Greece. Already after 150 B.C. with the introduction of Greek philosophy, Roman religion was turning into a perfunctory political expression. By Pompey's day augurs had long been grinning at each other as dissemblers. *Pontifex Maximus* or not, Caesar seems no more inclined than Cotta, his predecessor in office, to take the gods seriously in his private life. Cicero in his *Nature of the Gods* so veils his own convictions that it is difficult to decide where he stands. What seems to be a positive Stoic attitude toward the divine might well be nothing more than a calculated assertion of religious patriotism.

When Epicureans like Lucretius openly denied meaning to deity, it is understandable that Augustus in the early Christian era should encourage the revival of patriotic religious sentiment emerging in the aftermath of the great Roman Revolution. Almost as Jesus was born, Virgil and Horace were singing eloquently of a renewed ancient piety in epic and ode; yet, about the time of Antoninus Pius, Lucian, the ancient Voltaire, was doing everything he could to sabotage the revival. As a rational reviler of religion, he became a controversial figure: to some he was the Blasphemer, the Slanderer, the Atheist; to others a crusader against superstition, a martyr to rationalism. Either way, he did Zeus' image no great service by portraying the great god as an indecisive buffoon unsure how to cope with troublesome Epicureans. All the while, the growing popularity of fatalism and astrology was drawing ever tighter threads that would bind even the gods.

On the whole humankind, mindful of mortals' limited understanding, is more inclined throughout history to give gods, even defeated ones, the benefit of doubt rather than to abandon them. Reason, the same tool which nurtures Epicureanism, produces religious apologies. From time to time deeply religious Classical thinkers, yearning for a

---

[10] The "recantation" theory interpreting the *Bacchantes* as a record of Euripides' old-age identification with a personal religious experience, is rejected by many such as Jaeger, *Paideia*, 1:355, who sees the drama as merely the product of the tragedian's fascination with the psychological effects of futile human religious hypnotism.

deity worthy of reverence, felt the need to refurbish the immortals, to remake them in man's growing enlightened image and rational ethical idealism, to whitewash them, as it were, of their scarlet immoralities, irrational imperfections, crude passions and foibles. In a sense, reason restrained the gods from the beginning. In early Greece Hesiod kept them orderly by telling them who they were and by making them obedient to classification and to cause and effect. Xenophanes by 500 B.C. found the traditional gods so beyond redemption as a clique of anthropomorphic thieves, adulterers, slanderers, and deceivers that he opted for a new rationally clean amorphous deity who, unlike mortals, would have neither body nor human mind. Solon and Theognis as poets of the sixth century so moralized myths and purged them of their grosser nature that a scrubbed–up Zeus began to emerge as a sublime chief ruler of the universe. Even Pythian Apollo strove to become respectable as a champion of fairness, balance, and moderation.

Later Greek thinkers continued to reform the Immortals. Aeschylus cleaned up the immoralities of the gods on the stage and presented Zeus as a righteous character who gave up irrationally punishing people out of stupid jealousy. At the same time, Sophocles criticized the gods for their vindictiveness in order to humanize them. Herodotus in his history of the Persian wars rationalized the heavenly powers as agents of Greek justice; righting wrongs, they humbled the presumption of Xerxes who irrationally dared to scourge Poseidon. Aristophanes exposed the foibles of the gods by lampooning them mercilessly in good theatrical fun, logically assuming that they had a sense of humor and could take a joke. Plato, to give the gods some respectable educational value, would censor poetry which immortalized their vices and passions. By the mid–third century, Cleanthes' famous *Hymn to Zeus* salutes the great god of Reason as a merciful providential father.

On the Roman scene it is significant that Octavian took advantage of the on–going religious revival to sponsor a campaign against human vice and corruption. Chastened by association, the gods emerged as a respectable, providential, almost virtuous, lot in Virgil's epic. In contrast to revivalists like the neo–Pythagorean Apollonius of Tyana, who were trying to emotionally evangelize the days of Domitian, pious Plutarch fretted over the renewed decay of traditional religion and did his utmost rationally to exonerate the old deities. Unlike others, he found no reason to allegorize away their vices because he maintained they were fictitious in the first place. Malicious semi–divine daimons had deliberately misled the poets to ascribe bad habits to the gods and generally tell lies about them.[11] Any gods who would earn the respect of men like Dio

---

[11] Plutarch was an avowed enemy of superstition; his conviction that atheism was preferable to credulity had an impact on even the eighteenth-century Enlightenment. His attempt to rationalize and purge the gods, rather than to overthrow them in the manner of

Chrysostom and Maximus of Tyre, or even the monkish Cynics, would have to be associated with virtue. Probably no one so desperately applied reason to the old pantheon as the Emperor Julian who so scrubbed up the ancient gods in his belated effort to resell them that they appeared almost as hypostasized virtues: Reason, Prudence, Wisdom, Courage, and all the rest. Completely classified and ordered, they took their respective places in a rationalized hierarchy of powers each assigned specified jurisdictions. To offset Christianity's ethical appeal, Julian pictured the gods as so vitally interested in morality, piety, and charity that they supposedly were insulted by every beggar neglected in the streets. But by Julian's time it was too late; so many Christians by now were employing Classical reason to ridicule and lambast the pantheon that ancient polytheism was turned into a charade.

While pagan thought to the end remained quite indifferent to a clear concept of monotheism, rationalism's progressive cleaning up of the gods' anthropomorphic limitations might be interpreted as one indirect way of servicing an old recurrent vision of a single spiritual godhead. Already early philosophical efforts to isolate a common element, or elements, in the makeup of the physical universe seems to have seeped into the supernatural sphere by osmosis. Lack of detail makes it totally unjustified, however, to envisage as successful forerunners of monotheism such early postulations as Anaximander's "Infinite" or "Boundless," and Xenophanes' "One Mind." In Heraclitus, at the end of the sixth century, however, one might find a clearer and more influential exponent of a single deity, since his Logos can be conceived of, at least metaphorically, as a supernatural pantheistic force moving the universe from within, a view attractive to later Stoics. Plato is quite equivocal. The popular gods, to be sure, are demoted in favor of more universal conceptions. Is his supreme Idea of the Good, the climax of intelligibility, god? Is it the god of the *Laws* which Plato asserts is the measure of all things?[12] He never says so. At other times, he speaks of god as the demiurge providential, rational, but limited in power. Aristotle's *Metaphysics,* albeit in something of a secular scientific way, postulates a transcendental, theological, but yet unprovidential unmoved Mover. Stoics, who turned Reason into an ultimate principle permeating and governing the universe, tended to make belief in a host of deities less compelling.

In Rome, as in Greece, any trends toward monotheism are smothered by the polytheistic structure. Cicero's theoretical skepticism

---

Lucretius and Lucian, is among the most sincere in Classical antiquity. See especially *De def. orac.* 425F–426A, 417B–F, 414F, 415A–C, 416C, 416F. Also *De Iside et Osir.* 460F, 361E.

[12]*Laws* 716C–717F. Positive Classical trends toward monotheism are discussed in M. Hengel, *Judaism and Hellenism. Studies in their Encounter in Palestine during the Early Hellenistic Period* (Philadelphia: Fortress, 1981), I:261–67.

and circumspect religious patriotism probably explain why he did not raise the question of monotheism. Admittedly the syncretism of the day focused more and more attention on abstractions such as *Roma* who became viable in the emperor's person. We have already noted, too, the rational move to telescope the national deities of the empire by calling the same god different names or to demote them to an inferior status such as daimons or stars or to the role of deputies of a higher being; both these rational devices are found in Plutarch. Add to this the late popularity of an all–encompassing Sol Invictus and the attraction of a more and more rarified, and transcendental middle and neo–Platonic god who, as absolute Being, the One, eternal and unchangeable, dissolved, as it were, everything within himself in an ascending or descending scale. Finally, Emperor Julian's rational hierarchical order of subaltern gods virtually established a solar pseudo–monotheism under King Helios.

How lethal was the impact of this rational reevaluation of the old pantheon? It is difficult to tell. The gods might have died harder than we usually think. Temples were still being built well into the Christian era, the greatest of all to Zeus at Baalbek. Enough objects survive to attest to the Immortals' influence on art motifs into the seventh century. The excavations under St. Peter's reveal that c. 200 A.D., Apollo, Castor and Pollux, Orpheus, Hercules, Proserpina, Dionysos, and Isis were still courted by the upper middle class, a group not generally known as the most religious element in society.[13] But most significant is the continued indictment of polytheism by late apologists from Athanasius through Arnobius, Eusebius, and Orosius to Theodoret of Cyrus whose work, *The Cure of Pagan Maladies,* largely ended the apologetic era. It is difficult to believe that such Fathers were tilting at windmills.

The Olympians could be chastened by reason, but they could not be made to serve as personal deities. True, reason had, to some degree, changed Zeus into a kind and responsive father somewhat attentive to the ethical strivings of his worshippers. But at the same time, reason was at work melting down Zeus' image along with those of his colleagues. By stripping away their characteristic anthropomorphisms, reason tended more and more to dissolve the gods into cold allegories at the very time when many people were seeking identity and assurance in warm personal deities. To this demand the mystery cults were always quick to respond with an attractive package of conversion, regeneration, resurrection, and individual immortality. To be sure, Greeks were long acquainted with this kind of religion; ages ago they had Hellenized old Minoan gods and goddesses at Eleusis and adjusted Zeus to Cretan

---

[13] E. Kirschbaum, *The Tombs of St. Peter and St. Paul,* trans. J. Murray (London: Secker and Warburg, 1959), p. 31.

cultism. But after 200 B.C. unclassical Oriental deities like Cybele, Serapis, Isis, and Mithra began to knock at the temples of the Olympians. It is irrelevant here to discuss the origins, nature, and spread of these cults. Our concern is whether even they are compatible with the Classical rational outlook. The crucial consideration would be: what kind of correspondence between ritual and result did the devotees postulate? Did they consider an imitative liturgy efficacious, but not compelling, in an ex opere operato way because of some magical power hidden within it, or did they hold certain actions effective in persuading a god because of a contract with the deity? Absence of sufficient mystery–cult literature makes an answer impossible. Nevertheless, in either case the devotee seems to act rationally. One can act responsibly any time one is confident that one's ancestors' reflective powers have put one in touch with reality. In regard to magical operations it is well to restate that the cause and effect relationship established both in magic and science are logically conceived. Only hindsight reveals that magic operates with an erroneous connection between cause and effect. Liturgy based on it is wrong, possibly credulous, but not illogical. If devotees of mystery religions operate under the assumption that their cult gods have promised results under a contract, they are operating rationally and legally if they have reasonable assurance the contract exists. There is, however, no existing evidence that either Classical gods, or mystery–cult deities, bound themselves by a solemn revealed covenant to honor observance of enjoined ritual. Only Yahweh and Christ seem that thoughtful.

THE CHRISTIAN ATTITUDE TOWARD THE RATIONAL

"Unless you are like little Children" . . . Mark

Such was the sophisticated, overwhelmingly rational Classical world of philosophy and science with which Christians would have to contend. Would they have to abandon the Master's injunction to be as credulous as little children, to become "experienced bankers" able to tell the spurious from the authentic[14] or to become as cunning as serpents? To the Classical mind of Celsus, Christians appeared an ignorant, stupid, but haughty lot claiming allegiance to an unsociable and unheroic god who, they claimed, gave them a belated monopoly on truth through an extended special revelation, a medium, to pagans, strange in nature and irrational in content. Were not Christians actually "haters of the human race" and "worms crawling in a dungheap," all the while boasting a

---

[14] This noncanonial "saying of Jesus" appears three times in the *Clementine Homilies:* 2.51, 3.50, 18.20. Clement, Justin, and Origen also use it.

special enlightenment which entitled them to claim the whole world was made for them, even the stars and the very Roman empire itself? Christians were censured for arrogance not only by pagans but by Jews as well. The new "third race" was not at all apologetic for asserting the right to inherit the whole Classical world or for appropriating ancient Jewish covenantal guarantees along with Jewish sacred literature. Already the anti–Jewish so–called *Epistle of Barnabas* (c.130) casually but brazenly set the mood by explaining that Jewish writings were meant for Christians from the beginning—"The Lord himself gave them to us"— since the Jews were unworthy and never understood the Scriptures anyway. Were the Scriptures in their hands not a deception? Aristo of Pella presumed to explain the "Old Testament" to a prospective Jewish convert in a work no longer extant. Justin in his *Apology* and *Dialog with Trypho* echoed the same theme that the "Old Testament" was truly the property of Christians.

But already before 200 it was becoming clear that the new revelation would include not only purloined Jewish scripture supposedly dating from Moses and the prophets, but also a new corpus attributed to Paul and the evangelists. The very fact that Paul's letters were eagerly distributed among churches, and that oral, as well as written, versions of synoptic materials were prized and zealously circulated among local Christian communities, attests to the desire of early Christians to have some guiding word in addition to the Jewish background story. Synoptic content was yet flexible, subject to the influences of local versions, and to elaboration or diminution in transmission. Consequently, quotations by early apologists from our Synoptics, or parallel variants, are loose and uncertain. Even Justin (c. 150), while using our Synoptics, is free with the text. Even so both he and Athenagoras, converts from philosophy, could so marvel at the super merits of the new "good news" in implied comparison with philosophy, that they declared matters so profound and sacred as those being imparted to Christians could be known only through the divine Spirit—the Logos as Justin called it—who inspired the words of the prophets and the "memoirs" of the apostles alike. Clement of Alexandria declared, to the dismay of the Classical world, that Christianity's revealed truth was clearly of higher credibility than Greek philosophy; had not six–hundred years of scientific observation and philosophical casuistry led the Greeks only to confusion and despair?

By 200 the Fathers' concept of an emerging "New Testament" was such as to discourage them from altering texts spontaneously. But now that revelation, basically Pauline and Synoptic, had become an accepted source of truth among Christians, an epistemological problem arose. By 200 the converted Christian, even the born Christian, and above all the prospective convert, were predominantly "Greeks" who had inherited an ingrained intellectual tradition of free investigation exploiting observation, logical definition, and rational philosophical speculation. Such an intellectual heritage made it difficult to accept a commitment based solely on a divine fiat. Since the specter of two Latin–Averroist–type truths, that of revelation and that of reason, seemed rationally intolerable, the new "good tidings" would have to accommodate themselves to the demands of rational thinking if they would take hold in the Classical world. The early simple manual of Christian instruction, such as the *Didache*, would have to give way to the rhetorical apology and reasoned exegetical tract.[15] The *Recognitions of Clement* (c. 220) admits as much. Expressing emphatically the need of the Christian for reason, it represents Peter as saying that faith cannot exist without it. Reason must fortify beliefs because mere assent without proof wanes; only the believer chained by reason will not be torn from faith.

To harmonize revelation and the dictates of reason, a new professional Christian body had to arise equipped with both Greek scholarship and Christian piety. Since theologians—the term was applied to Christian thinkers by Hippolytus of Rome about 200—might be required, in a brash un–Jewish way, to psychoanalyze God himself, their task would be a demanding one requiring both learned and devout circumspection. Gregory of Nazianzus pointed out that it did not behoove everyone to philosophize about God nor to do so before every audience, nor at all times, nor on all points. The deep things of revelation, he added, would yield only to such as devoted themselves to careful study with great pain and zeal.[16] Clement of Alexandria, Origen, Jerome, and Augustine all thought that the requisite equipment of the theologian should include, besides humility and piety, a charisma of learning: languages, geography, natural history, chronology, a science of numbers, dialectics, ancient philosophy, music, history, and grammar. Jerome in his practical way added that library, secretaries, leisure, and silence would also be helpful. Patently this was all more than Jesus had commissioned; nor had Paul spoken of a charisma of scholarly authorship.

Christianity was but one hundred years old when Justin stepped out of his pagan background to offer some sort of Christian accommodation to Greek metaphysics. He was the first Father to insist that scrutiny must enlighten blind faith; the latter, he claimed, was actually the hallmark of the pagan. In trying to divorce Greek philosophy from pagan religion in

---

[15] E. Hatch, *The Influence of Greek Ideas on Christianity* (New York: Harper, 1957), p. 49, summarizes the issue: "it is impossible for Greeks, educated as they were with an education which penetrated their whole nature, to receive or to retain Christianity in its primitive simplicity."

[16] Gregory of Nazianzus, though ordained against his will, came to be known as "The Theologian." For his views on theologizing, see *Orat.* 27.3–5 and *Sermon* 32 *(De moder. in disput.)*, *(PG* 36:174–211).

order to ally it, in an eclectic way, with Christianity, he, rather than St. John, may have popularized the Logos theology. Clement of Alexandria soon followed, reminding Christians that logic was not invented by the devil. At times even the legally trained but.anti–Classical Tertullian would admit that acknowledgment of Revelation did not necessarily cause a believer to think less logically or scientifically than a philosopher. Indeed, Minucius Felix boasted that Christian belief and pagan philo-sophical reason were so compatible that philosophers of old were really Christians in disguise.

The anxiety to harmonize faith and reason had gone so far by 225 that it produced in Origen's *De principiis* the first manual of dogma. As a "doctor" of the Church equipped with a treasure of learning and with a finely tuned rational mind, he felt constrained to set forth the body of Christian truth in an organized fashion agreeable to reason. By 400 Jerome knew the names of so many outstanding Christian scholars that he could compose the first patrology, his *De viris illustribus*. In fact, Gregory of Nazianzus had already bewailed theology's excesses; it had become, in his mind, too elaborate, artificial, and far–fetched. Was it not a new Scepticism, couched in an antithetic style, infesting the Church to such a degree that babbling too often was paraded for learning? Au-gustine, likewise reacting somewhat against unbridled theologizing in his day, tried to reemphasize as basic the prior claims of faith. Conclusions arrived at by reason had to agree not only with Scripture but also with the "settled authority of the immovable Church."[17] One cannot know without first believing. Clement of Alexandria should be given some credit for anticipating Augustine's insistence on the primacy of faith when he contended that since assumptions were the beginning and foundation of all pagan philosophy, Christians should not be faulted for believing so they, too, could understand. Augustine put it better. His

---

[17] Gregory of Nazianzus, *Orat.* 21.12. Jerome, *Dial. con. Lucif.* (*PL* 23:165) complains that many bishops ordained in his day from the literate class, from the bosom of Plato and Aristophanes, are not concerned about extracting the marrow from Scripture but about tickling the ears of the people with flowers of rhetoric. Gregory of Nyssa (*Con. Eunom.* 12.5) mentions the same kind of over–sophistication. He accuses Eunomius of constantly bring-ing up Aristotelean divisions of things, and of elaborating on genera and species and of advancing all the technical language of the Categories "to the injury of our doctrine." Although Augustine (*Epis.* 143.4) maintains that reasoning never supplants Scripture, he does (*De doct. Christ.* 2.31–32) hold that "the science of reasoning is of very great service in searching into and unraveling all sorts of questions that come up in Scripture." He maintains that "the validity of logical sequence is not a thing devised by men for it exists eternally in the reason of things and has its origins in God." In other words, the processes of reason so correspond with the divine mind that assertions of theologians, if based on reason, correspond with reality. See also *Epis.* 118:5.32 where he expresses the need to have the agreement of the immovable Church. For *credo ut intellegam*, see *Ser.* 43 (*PL* 38.372) and *Epis.* 120.2 (*PL* 33.453).

"*credo ut intellegam*" would become a pithy slogan evermore for those trying to solve the epistemological problem of faith and reasoned knowledge. Faith was a *sine qua non* if one would know. Was not the knowledge one acted upon based originally on belief and trust in authority? While authority must, of necessity, precede knowledge, it was to be accepted as a way ultimately to understand. As a Christian, the theologian should believe in order to know, but at the same time should he not ask, as a "Greek," whether he should not seek to know in order to believe?

The theologian's first step in trying to harmonize faith and reason was to identify the areas he personally found difficult to rationalize. Then he could expect automatically to recognize the intellectual problems which spawned heretics and finally be able to foresee the rational objections of prospective Christian converts.

Although Christian scholars ardently revered the Scriptures and were horrified to hear pagans, such as Celsus and Porphyry, declare them a pile of nonsense, more than a few expressed a selfish need to allay their own discomfitures over Holy Writ. Many found the sacred books inadequate, obscure, inconsistent, irrational, and inelegant. A strange lack of divine concern about the completeness of Jewish "background" revelation was detected by John Chrysostom. Some prophetic books, he opined, were lost before and during the time of the Jewish captivity. Even Deuteronomy barely escaped destruction in a dunghill. Other commentators were puzzled, as well, by the tantalizing incompleteness of the new Christian Scriptures because of the many silences on what appeared to be fundamental questions. While Irenaeus warned that application of reason to areas where Holy Writ was silent provided a fruitful source of heresy, Cyprian and Novatian felt it was the province of reason to teach especially where revelation was mute. Origen, Gregory of Nazianzus, Cyril of Jerusalem, and Basil all puzzled over the silence of Scripture on such cardinal matters as the birth of individual souls, the nature of the Holy Spirit, and the generation of the Son from the Father.[18] Basil was concerned whether he should brashly deal with what the Scriptures left unsaid or more humbly just quote what was there. He decided not only that the Holy Spirit did not want to be left alone, but had waited for him, Basil, to declare his proper divine nature.

Many Fathers, in turn, considered revelation deep and dark, mysterious, obscure. Origen, first–rate biblical scholar, declared the prophesies filled with enigmas and dark sayings, and the Gospels—to say nothing of

---

[18]Omission in Holy Writ seem to perplex the Fathers as much as Scriptural contradictions. See Gregory of Nazianzus, *Orat.* 31.5.21; Basil, *Epis.* 160.3; Cyril, *Cat.* 11.12; Origen, *De prin.*, preface 4. Basil particularly is disturbed by the paucity of Scriptural references to the Holy Spirit.

the unspeakable mysteries of John's Revelation—so profound that they required the grace of St. Paul to decipher them. According to Jerome, the Jews found Leviticus, Numbers, the ending of Ezekiel, and the commencement of Genesis so obscure that they dared not study them until they were thirty years of age. John Chrysostom, with a human touch, complained that obscurity of the Scriptures caused much inattention in church. Augustine found mysterious clouds and shadows darkening many parts of the Bible; certain psalms puzzled him, as did subjects like the Antichrist and Jesus' descent into hell. He pronounced the Scriptures so profound that even one who began to study them in boyhood could never hope to exhaust them. "Behold oh Lord," he exclaimed, "how many things we have written concerning a few words— how many I beseech Thee! What strength of ours, what ages could suffice if all thy books were handled in this manner!" If God, who said: "I will open my mouth in parables," had only explained them, Christians would not have to toil so. As matters stood, they had to eat their bread in the sweat of their faces. Seemingly almost in desperation, Augustine declared: "Indeed, I would not believe the Gospel unless the authority of the catholic Church moved me to do so," [19] an early reminder that the Church presided over the Scriptures and not the Scriptures over the Church. To Augustine, tradition, miracles, apostolic succession, and a universal consensus of faith all had to lend assurances when the Scriptures failed.

Other Fathers discovered seeming inconsistencies and errors in Holy Writ. Origen, as the first great biblical scholar trained in Hebrew, found not only the character of God in the entire Old Testament incompatible with that in the New, but also troublesome variances in the latter's genealogies appearing in Matthew and Luke. Again, the different sequence of events in John and the Synoptics forced Origen to conclude that an intelligent Christian would have to reject one or the other version or else give up any attempt to accept them as literal. He was willing, he wrote, not to condemn the evangelists if they had a purpose in dealing freely and loosely with history by saying that things happened in a different manner, place, or time than they actually did. Inaccurate proper names and place names could be overlooked. At times he actually thought Scripture deliberately falsified matters. Had the Hebrew Old Testament purposely omitted the virgin birth so that Jews would not punish Mary or take offense generally? Seemingly, to screen the event, Matthew assigned the genealogy of Joseph to Jesus and to conceal the matter still more Luke had Mary say, "Thy father and I have sought thee

---

[19] Augustine, *Confess.* 12.32, *Epis.* 137.1.3, *Psalm.* 78.4. For *"Ego vero evangelio non crederem nisi me catholicae ecclesiae commoveret auctoritas"* see *Contra Epis. Mani. quam voc. funda.* 5.6 (*CSEL* 56:197).

sorrowing." For the same reason the evangelists failed to mention the virgin birth to the shepherds and called James and others "brothers" of the Lord. Augustine, too, found problems of accuracy in Scripture; he believed, for example, that Matthew had been inspired, for some reason, to attribute sayings to the wrong people. Hilary of Poitiers admitted that he would support the Septuagint even if it made mistakes.

Origen found certain parts of the Scriptures irrational, especially laws and commandments in the Old Testament which enjoined things disagreeable to reason. In fact, he said, the laws of Rome, Athens, and Sparta were more elegant than those of God unless one was expected to dignify them by employing allegorical interpretation. If one took literally the purging of the temple, it recorded an undignified action by Jesus. Was it not stupid for Matthew to take delight in describing details of Jesus' entry into Jerusalem, if he meant them to be taken on the surface?

Finally, the Bible's inelegance of style troubled the Classical mind trained in grammar and rhetoric and skilled in reading Homer and Virgil. The rusticity of the Scriptures led men like Jerome, Arnobius, and Lactantius to apologize for it. Jerome felt guilty because he preferred the style of Cicero. Arnobius, as we saw, tried to rationalize the problem by arguing that the Scriptures discussed such profound matters that concern for charm of rhetorical display was irrelevant. "How is the truth of a statement diminished if an error is made in number, case, in preposition, particle, or conjunction?"[20] With a similar argument Lactantius tried to counter charges made by literati that Holy Writ was incredible because it was unpolished: God simply willed his simple and undisguised truth to be clear; his message was such an ornament in itself that it would only be corrupted if embellished. Did not falsehood, on the other hand, have to please by a splendor not its own?

Much scriptural confusion, of course, stemmed from the open–endedness of the canon. Although this problem was especially distressing in dealing with heretics, it was a source of personal perplexity to more than one Father. Not even the content of the Old Testament was settled. Origen pondered over Tobit and Judith. Should the story of Susanna and the Song of the Three Children included in the Septuagint be part of *Daniel*, or be labeled pseudepigraphical as Africanus argued and Jerome later advocated much to Rufinus' dismay? Augustine hardly could be totally satisfied with his judgment that only canonical books were free from error and that all others must be judged in their light, when he himself was disturbed by Jerome's Old Testament emendations, the differences between the Septuagint and the Hebrew canon, and his own concern about the Old Testament apocrypha such as Enoch, along

---

[20] Arnobius, *Adv. Pag.* 58–59 (ACW 7:104–05).

with the Wisdom of Solomon, and Ecclesiasticus. The last two books, as well as Baruch and I and II Maccabees, disturbed Jerome; Ambrose was not sure which version of the Old Testament he should use. The "New Testament" was even more at loose ends than the Old. How could one solve theological problems with a revelation that was indefinite? As more and more "sacred" books—Acts, Apocalypses such as those of Peter and of Paul, Epistles like Peter and Jude, Gospels like James—clamored for equal recognition with Paul and the Synoptics, the canon came to be identified differently in time by an Origen, Eusebius, and Athanasius. Tertullian never heard of Hebrews as Pauline, an ascription doubted already by Barnabas. Dionysius of Alexandria wondered if the totally incomprehensible Revelation of John was not the work of the heretic Cerinthus.[21] Indeed, instruction by theologians on the Scripture must have been either extremely ineffective or hopelessly confused into the late fourth century, judging from John Chrysostom's remark that many of the brethren did not know the names of the sacred books, including the Acts of the Apostles, that many rejected some as useless, even the entire Old Testament, and again that others pruned away parts of the New.

Until the canon would reach a high degree of standardization by some general consensus, the theologian would continue, of course, to have personal problems over the content of Holy Writ. The matter was more urgent, however, for the general Church faced with heretics who thrived on Scriptural loose ends. Although dissidents within Christianity existed from the beginning, by the mid–second century deviants were assailing the Church from right to left; in one sense the early heretic was a theologian who let his personal confusion over the canon get the better of him. Clement of Alexandria was one of the first to note the association between the state of the Scriptures and heresy; Tertullian in his logical way accepted the connection as inevitable. Origen, like Clement earlier, noted that heretics not only interpreted Scripture to suit their ends but claimed as inspired whatever suited their purpose. To improve things, Tatian (c. 160) wrote his own composite version of the gospels, the *Diatessaron,* which was used as the standard text of the New Testament in Syrian churches down to the fifth century. Marcion early rejected the whole Old Testament and retained only Luke and ten epistles of Paul in the New; even these he edited to excise what he didn't like. The gnostic Marcosians, according to Irenaeus, introduced apocryphal books and spurious writings almost at will. Valentinians rejected the greater part of Holy Writ as not worthy of credibility and claimed manuscripts had been

---

[21] Already in the early Church, John is the target of extended and sophisticated biblical criticism. See Dionysius, *Book of Promises* frag. 3.4.6–7; Eusebius, *H. E.* 3.39, 4–8; Jerome, *De vir. illus.* 9.

corrupted; to suit their own schemes they read out of context and dressed up passages. Augustine made similar charges against the Manichaeans.

There were, of course, other inducements to heresy besides scriptural uncertainty. Much of the off–beat Christian teaching was due to imperfectly digested draughts of Greek philosohy that discomforted the body of faith. Hippolytus in his *Philosophumena* linked Greek philosophy with thirty–three different heretical schools: Simon Magus was influenced by Heraclitus, Valentinus by Pythagoras and Plato, Basilides by Aristotle, Marcion by Empedocles. Origen was too fond of Plato; Arius courted neo–Platonism; Pelagius supposedly favored Stoicism. The Artemonites, led by a certain Artemon (c. 250) in Rome, were carried away, in quite a modern fashion, by their attempt to accommodate Christianity to science. Eusebius describes them magnificently as a presumptuous lot who altered the Scriptures and abandoned the ancient rule of faith to form their opinions according to the subtle precepts of logic. He charged them with neglecting the science of the Church for the study of geometry and with losing sight of heaven while they engaged themselves in measuring the earth. Euclid was perpetually in their hands; Aristotle and Theophrastus were the objects of their admiration, and they expressed an uncommon reverence for the works of Galen. Their errors, Eusebius continues, were derived from the abuse of the arts and sciences of the infidels corrupting in the process the simplicity of the Gospel by the over–refinements of human reason.[22]

Probably no Greek philosopher caused as much trouble as Parmenides, dead since 456 B.C. The Parmenidean and Platonic dilemma of Being and Becoming in one way or another never ceased to wrack the Church with heresy. How could God rationally be ultimate unchanging Form and yet be, as it were, in process which automatically entails change? Could God rationally embrace contradiction as the Old Testament seemed to assume? The errant Jewish theologian, Philo, who struggled with the problem early in the Christian era, was something of a harbinger of a famous lot of Christian gnostic heretics of the second century who tried to discover a rational way to associate the immovable eternal Father with creation of movable and temporal matter. As we shall see later, gnostics like Basilides, Valentinus, and later Mani tried to span the abyss between God and matter by theorizing that the eternal One created a ladder, as it were, of emanated pairs of eons, logoi, or intermediary hypostasized divine beings in a way quite reminiscent of the pagan Hesiod. Generally one female eon, often Wisdom, went astray

[22] The Artemonite heresy suggests the life of the circle of philosophies in the eighteenth–century Enlightenment which judged traditional Christianity unsophisticated and intellectually inadequate. Eusebius, *H. E.* 5.28,13–16.

through pride or accident to fall from the divine sphere and eventually, through her bastard progeny, produce the evil demiurge who created the world and man. Thus divine particles, sparks of divinity, were scattered throughout matter to create a monstrosity awaiting the redemptive action of another eon, Christos, united to Jesus. The Parmenidean problem did not affect only Gnostics in relation to soteriology. Athanasius, for example, felt that God almost had to become incarnate to restore the divine image in man lost through his transgressions. How could God logically permit his original blueprint for creation to be changed and frustrated by human action? Augustine, too, in a sense is involved in the Parmenidean dilemma: how could one logically harmonize God's antecedent will to save everyone with his subsequent will to limit salvation after the Fall?

The heresiarch, Arius, too, had Parmenidean trouble. He wanted to know how, when Being is immovable, the Son or Logos could be begotten, a process implying time, and yet be of the same timeless substance as the Father. For two hundred years from Lucian of Samosata, who was called the most learned man in the East, to Eunomius, Arians employed impeccable Aristotelian logic to make their point. Gregory of Nyssa clearly saw that, to the injury of orthodox doctrine, Arians were making the Son a creature, non–substantial with the Father, a copy of the derivative Nous of the neo–Platonists who were trying to shade down Plato's rugged duality.

How could God and man, the Immovable and the moved, the Eternal and the temporal, the Unchangeable and the changeable, the One and the many, Being and becoming live side by side in Jesus–Christ? Were the two contradictory natures separate or blended? How could his divine nature redeem, not being subject to suffering? How could his human nature atone when it could make only a miniscule offering to satisfy for an infinitely grave offense? Heretics abounded with suggestions. The Docetists, including to a degree even Clement of Alexandria, depreciated the humanity of Christ making it easier for divinity to associate with attenuated matter. At the same time, by making Jesus' body something of a phantom whose physical sufferings were more apparent than real, they hoped to safeguard the impassibility of divinity. Apollinarius of the mid–fourth century, following earlier leads, maintained that the divine nature of Christ replaced the essence of humanity of Jesus; the divine Logos took the place of a human soul in the God–man. In this monstrosity Jesus' body was entirely "caught up" in the nature of the Logos; his fleshly nature had to become divinized if it were to redeem humanity. Nestorius, patriarch of Constantinople, by insisting that Mary could not rightly be called "Mother of God," tended to separate the two natures of Jesus–Christ too much. Eutyches opposed Nestorius so vigorously that he was accused of confounding the two natures and thus denying that the humanity of Christ was consubstantial with ours. The indirect father of modern Monophysitism, Eutyches lives on today in his teaching that there is really only one nature in the incarnate Christ, the divine. Parmenides would have enjoyed all these discussions.

Trinitarianism, which completely confounded Greek reason by trying to combine unity and plurality, aroused all kind of opponents. By 300 so–called Monarchians, anxious to preserve the united majesty or monarchy of the Godhead, were impinging on the divinity of the second person of the Trinity. So–called Rationalists, they scandalized the faithful by their excessive devotion to logic, geometry, and medicine. One group thought of Christ as divine only in the sense that he was adopted. The Modalists, often identified as Sabellians, in a very attractive rational way concluded that God simply revealed himself under three different modes, manifestations, or disguises. The Father was the Son or the Holy Spirit on different occasions in history; all three could not appear at the same time. In turn, questions were raised about the position of the Holy Spirit in the Trinity. The Scriptures were unclear. Already Origen, in middle–Platonic style, thought the Spirit quite subordinate to the other persons of the Trinity especially in the sense that he owed his existence, however eternal, to the Son. The Council of Nicaea's curt mention of the Holy Spirit at the end of its creed apparently assumed his divinity needed no elaboration. Yet within forty years the issue became a major one, engaging the attention of Athanasius, the Cappadocians, Didymus the Blind, Jerome, and Basil, in opposition to the so–called Pneumatomachians or Macedonians who arose in the 370s denying full godhead to the Holy Ghost. Many Parmenidean dilemmas were at hand. Could the Holy Spirit be true Being and yet somehow be produced? Was he, or even she, generated or begotten? As a second son of the Father? Or a grandson through the Son? How could the so–called third person of the Trinity be generated at all without being inferior to his generators as a creature? For their trouble the Pneumatomachians were condemned by Pope Damasus in 374 and the Council of Constantinople in 381.

In identifying his own problems with Scripture and his philosophical difficulties with Christian beliefs, the theologian came to understand that the roots of heresy lay deep in intellectual reservations rather than simply in some supposed ill will of dissenters. The same was true of the complex attitudes of prospective educated converts. Besides being patriotic and loyal to old commitments they, too, entertained rational philosophical convictions which kept them at odds with Christian revelation. Early critics of Christianity, like Tacitus and Epictetus who were unacquainted with developing Christian "Scripture," were content to condemn Christians as haters of the human race or as naive people entertaining a childlike disdain for death. But after the end of the second century when pagans could learn more about Christians the indictment of the new religion increasingly emphasized intellectual rational reservations. Galen, possibly from personal experiences, on one occasion proclaimed Christians strangers to logic and rational demonstration, a brash credulous lot operating without using evidence. In the case of Celsus' *True Word* Origen discovered an attack by a learned pagan well–read in the Christian literature of the time. Book VIII of the work fairly well summarizes Celsus' position; his greatest annoyance with Christians, besides their unpatriotic behavior, was their stupidity and irrationality. Erudite and sincere, proud of his country, his philosophy, and his gods, Celsus decried Christians as dangerous dissenters and unthinking worshippers of a crucified sophist who unreasonably delayed saving people until lately. Christians naively demanded blind compliance with faith at the expense of common sense, a stance befitting an uncultivated lot of confused people who followed an unheroic charlatan interested only in unlettered commoners, slaves, women, and children. They stupidly contradicted themselves claiming to be monotheists while worshipping two gods, a Father and a Son. Furthermore, they operated on the philosophically irrational principle that an immaterial God could at the same time be a mortal substance. Since they were good at plagiarizing from their betters, why did they not learn from Plato that God was unapproachable, nameless, incapable of creating matter and evil? Even the learned Origen was strained to make replies. Porphyry's later attack on Christianity, no longer extant, appears to have been extremely erudite and trenchant, criticizing among many things the absurdities of Church history and the gullibility of Christians who tolerated egregious inconsistencies and historiographical errors in the Scripture. Was it not obvious that the Book of Daniel was misdated?[23]

If Origen thought he successfully met Celsus' objections to Christianity, some Fathers actually record their failure to meet the argument of prospective converts. Minucius Felix's *Octavius* furnishes, in the character of Caecilius, a good example of an educated pagan who walks away unconvinced. Not surprisingly, the pagan's chief resistance to Christianity was philosophical; as a Platonist and Sceptic, Caecilius denied that truth could ever be certain. There was in his mind no sane point in postulating revelation since the confusion and disorder of the world logically argued against the existence of a single God or creator. To him Christians were an ignorant and immoral people who yet pre-

---

[23] Prophyry's astute doubts about the date of Daniel in the twelfth book of his *Against the Christians* was but one, among many, accusations which brought condemnation and burning of the book in 448. Porphyry's treatment of Daniel disturbed Methodius and Eusebius among other Fathers and rivaled the studies of Jerome. See A. B. Hulen, *Porphyry's Work against the Christians*, Yale Studies in Religion, No. 1 (Scottdale: Mennonite Press, 1933), p. 46.

sumed irrationally to discuss supernatural matters clearly above their competence. Everything considered, Caecilius thought it preferable to follow the religious dispensations of the past which had given Rome world–wide empire.

A similar example of an unconvinced prospective convert is displayed in Justin's *Dialog with Trypho,* an account of a two–day discussion between a Christian apologist and a cultivated Jew which probably took place at Ephesus. Justin's answers to Trypho's Scriptural arguments were so effectively parried one by one that Trypho went away unconverted. One wonders why such failures in proselytizing were recorded.

Christian problems largely stemming from the uncertainty of the Scriptures and from Classical rational postulations were easier to identify than solve. How could the inadequacies of Scripture be explained, first of all, to the theologian's own personal satisfaction, then be clarified to obviate the heretic, and be rationalized to attract the convert?

Theologians realized that conviction, like charity, must begin at home; they must solve first for themselves the mystery of Scriptural perplexities. Origen tacitly admits that personal inquisitiveness motivated him to theologize; indeed, one wonders how many Fathers were satisfying their own confusion when they prepared tracts for others to read. One feels that such might be the case, for example, with Basil in his effort to demonstrate the consubstantiality of the Holy Spirit. At any rate, two rationalizations emerged to shed light on the reasons for scriptural inadequacies. One argued that far from being introduced to restrict knowledge of God or to make God more mysterious and inexplainable, scriptural difficulties were actually intended as incentives to cause Christians to seek enlightenment. Origen early declared over and over that the very stumbling blocks and impossibilities forced Christians to pry deeper to learn things more worthy of God than those suggested literally. The very mysteriousness was intended to stimulate search and to strengthen spiritual insight. Did not the legislative portions of the Old Testament enjoin commands of such uncertain utility and record such seeming impossibilities that the more inquisitive would have to apply themselves to investigate? The very obscurity was a challenge, a stimulant to exercise talents in order to prevent acquiescence from introducing a stifling static satiety. Christians must become experienced "bankers" by God's command to extract the spurious from the genuine. John Chrysostom, in a colorful way, wrote that the condition of the Scriptures made Christians dive down into the sea, as it were, to pick up pearls. Cassian explained that the Holy Spirit purposely reserved for human meditation certain veiled passages of Scripture so that logical proofs and valid conjectures would be applied to them. To Augustine scriptural obscurities, far from being intended to deny truth to him, were an incentive for him to exercise himself in knocking. In his inscrutable way

God even helped by pointing out where to knock. Repeating an argument used earlier by Tertullian, Augustine declared that God used heretics, produced by Scripture, to prod the orthodox, to arouse the faithful from sleep, so they could make progress toward understanding the holy words. Christians must not always be nourished with milk and remain in senseless infancy. Only when heretics threatened, when revilers were permitted by God to trouble the hearts of believers, would Christians put away the things of the child and nourish scholars to defend revealed truth, individuals who otherwise would say nothing. Only when diligence constrained Christians to reply to heretics would the Scriptures reveal their meaning. Tertullian would have approved Augustine's rhetorical outburst: How many senses of Holy Scripture concerning Christ as God have been vindicated against Photinus? How many concerning Christ as human against the Manichaeans? How many concerning the Trinity against Sabellius? How many concerning the catholic Church against the Donatists and Luciferians? Was the Trinity perfectly treated before the Arians snarled at it? Or was repentance sufficiently dealt with before the Novatians?[24]

A second related, but rarer, rationalization of the confusion of Holy Writ held that its vagueness was intended to throw a veil over the minds of the godless in order to convict them. Tertullian thought that the Scriptures were divinely ordained both to create and to expose heretics like Marcion and Valentinus. Once exposed, however, they should be denied use of the sacred writings lest they further corrupt and exploit them. Pseudo–Clement suggests that the devil added certain false chapters to Scripture so that those who heeded these unworthy passages would be convicted of sin; naturally the righteous would not listen to them. Everything considered, it was thought best, however, to keep silent about these additional passages lest the unlearned be confused.

Such were the ingenious arguments deduced by theologians to rationalize the reasons for Scripture's inadequacies. But in addition to a need for personal conviction there were heretics to confront, a task made difficult by the absence of an accepted corpus of sacred writings. Only when such a body of authoritative literature would emerge could the "true" texts of individual books eventually be established and the meaning of difficult passages be discussed in context with other parts of an entire corpus.

When the heretic Marcion published his version of Scripture (c. 140), it became obvious that some "orthodox" alternative was desirable, even urgent. To build a canon of Scripture—the word is first used by Origen—would prove to be such a long gradual process of sifting out

---

[24] For these and similar remarks of Augustine, see *Enar. in Psalm* 147.10, *Ser.* 1.2, *Tract. in Joan.* 36.6, *in Psalm.* 68.36 and 55.21.

"inspired" books from a larger body of proto–canonical literature that something of a final product had to await the fifth century. The role of local usage, the influence of such great sees as Alexandria, Ephesus, Antioch, and Rome, and the very vagaries of transmission, all obscure the conscious role of the theologian in the process of canon formation. Only in the late second century can some agents in the on–going selection of canonical material be identified. Nonetheless it is obvious that the theologian is important in the selection process because the canon congeals—or expands from the early Pauline–Synoptic corpus—in proportion as theology is refined and "orthodoxy" discovered. Men like Irenaeus, Tertullian, and the author of the Muratorian fragment (by Hippolytus c. 200?) apparently all seem to envisage the day when a full theological consensus will warrant even a closed canon. At times, the work of a particular theologian proves quite definitive in forming the body of Scripture. Such influence is seen in the case of the thirty–ninth *Festal Letter* of Athanasius and especially in the translations of Jerome commissioned by Pope Damasus. Many other theologians such as Irenaeus, Clement of Alexandria, Origen, Eusebius of Caesarea, Gregory of Nazianzus, Epiphanius, and Ambrose subtly influenced the canon at least by reporting how far the selection process had gone by their day.

The grounds of selection, insofar as they are rationally planned, were discussed already by Irenaeus who maintained that any Christian book aspiring for acceptance as inspired should be of apostolic authority, at least indirectly. It should also be vouchsafed by one or more leading churches, and should record a message not contrary to the existing rule of faith.[25] The Muratorian Fragment is also interested in supporting apostolic provenance hoping, apparently, to make the works of the primitive Church classics. Rarely does one find evidence of a conscious authoritative institutional will creating the canon. Origen, however, reports that in his mind the Church had already defined the Old Testament so authoritatively that it should not be tampered with. Harnack sees the inclusion of *Acts* in the canon as a deliberate decision made presumably by the church of Rome.

Irenaeus' suggestions outlining grounds for canonical selection proved quite insightful. So many other theologians shared his concern about the provenance of sacred materials that by the mid–fifth century the contents of Scripture had been looked into thoroughly. By applying both external and internal criticism theologians verified the history, the origins, and transmissions of various Old Testament versions and had come to impugn the apostolic integrity of sundry Christian treatises, letters, gospels, acts, and apocalypses. Origen, equipped with both Greek

[25] Irenaeus, *Adv. haer.* 3.2.2, 3.4.1, 3.3.1–3, 1.10.1–2.

and Hebrew, judged Jewish materials of Septuagintal origins authentic enough to warrant acceptance as inspired literature despite their absence in Hebrew texts. Augustine held the same view later. Jerome, also skilled in Hebrew, was less sure. Consequently he labeled such works as I Esdras, the Song of Solomon, and Ecclesiasticus "ecclesiastical" in distinction to canonical. Clement of Alexandria and Origen held different views about the transmission of "Paul's" Hebrews. About 175 the Epistle of James is first mentioned by Origen; the same Father tried to identify the author of *The Shepherd* with the Hermas in Romans.

Internal criticism, as an indispensable adjunct of external criticism, became a favorite tool of theologians as they checked the contents of books to scrutinize historical references, expressions, grammar, vocabulary, disposition, ideology, and tone hoping to determine authorship as well as the time and place of composition. As Origen remarked, the task required critics to follow the "correct method" of scholarship involving logic and much learning. He was so expert at the work that, according to Chadwick, Porphyry would be justified in calling Origen a crook who stole Greek tools to rationalize a crude barbaric superstition.[26] He argued most learnedly, for instance, for the authenticity of Susanna, Bel and the Dragon, and the Song of the Three Children as parts of Daniel against Julius Africanus who, for reasons of language, style, and vocabulary doubted their genuineness. To do his work effectively as an internal critic of Old Testament materials, Jerome not only studied Hebrew but acquainted himself with Jewish history, customs, geography, and even general topographical materials. He was the first to distinguish Old Testament apocrypha as a group; some of these books he rejected outright while he remained skeptical of others such as I and II Maccabees. Yet he accepted Daniel whose supposed sixth–century date had already been questioned seriously by the neo–Platonist Porphyry. Dionysius of Alexandria early anticipated modern criticism by noting the differences in thought, style, and grammar between Revelation and the Gospel of John. However, Irenaeus and Tertullian, failing to notice the discrepancies in vocabulary in Timothy and Titus on one hand and the letters of Paul on the other, declared both epistles authentic. Many of the New Testament apocrypha condemned themselves internally by the crudity or frivolity of their message. The *Shepherd of Hermas* and others came, in the long run, to offend against the rule–of–faith requirement mentioned by Irenaeus.

---

[26] H. Chadwick, *Early Christian Thought and the Classical Tradition* (New York: Oxford University Press, 1966), p. 103. Origen's remarks (*De prin.* preface 10) are quite to the point: everyone, he says, must enlighten himself with knowledge if he would desire to form a connected series and body of truths agreeable to reason and would form a body of doctrine by means of illustration and arguments discovered in Holy Scripture or deduced by closely tracing out consequences and following a correct method.

Even though Athanasius' *Festal Letter* of 369, which outlined the present New Testament canon, received recognition outside Alexandria gradually throughout the fifth century, many questions about the contents of Scripture lingered on as a result of assiduous application of both external and internal criticism by theologians. What should be thought finally about Paul's Hebrews displaying a style which could assign it to Barnabas, Luke, Clement of Rome, or a secretary of the Apostle? What of John's Revelation whose stylistic differences from his Gospel raised eyebrows so early in the Church? Should one agree with Origen who considered II Peter authentic despite its differences from I Peter, itself hardly written in the style of a fisherman?

Besides helping inject some rational criteria into the selection of canonical books, theologians had to concern themselves with determining the "true" texts of inspired works, a task entailing laborious collation of manuscripts. If one was to associate salvation, even in a minor degree, with faith in the Scriptures, was it not rational to want to know exactly what they said? While Hippolytus should not be forgotten for his interest in textual verification, the two outstanding biblical scholars were Origen and Jerome, both of whom, as we saw, studied Hebrew to check original manuscripts. Latin texts of the Old Testament were grossly unsatisfactory, causing Jerome to find some seven to eight hundred lines of the Book of Job missing. Several Greek variants of the Old Testament were available: the Septuagint, of course, composed in the third century B.C., the literal translation of Aquila, the free rendering of Symmachus, and the moderate version of Theodotion, all from the second century A.D. Origen struggled twenty–eight years composing his *Hexapla* to establish the text of the Septuagint by collating it with the Hebrew canon and its Greek versions. His redaction, accepted into common usage, was later checked against the original Hebrew by Jerome. In the case of the New Testament there were almost as many discrepancies as there were Latin versions. With unsurpassed scholarship, Jerome at the command of Pope Damasus compiled a standard version of the New Testament from some Greek manuscripts and the many Latin variations. To do their textual work, both Origen and Jerome had to make a science out of manuscript study, interpreting scholia, investigating erasures, questioning rewritings as possible interpolations, watching for quotations out of context. Both employed similar diacritical symbols, the asterisk and the obelus (* and − or ÷) to mark off critical areas. The former indicated words found in Hebrew or some Greek translations but not in the Septuagint; the obelus identified terms found in the Greek but wanting in Hebrew.

Textual emendations were often quite disconcerting to the faithful. Some were bewildered by manuscript changes; some expressed suspicion of the critic's honesty or ability. Rufinus, for instance, bewailed the erasure of Susanna and the Song of the Three Children from the Old

Testament: "We have all sung the hymn of the three children in church; has truth come four hundred years late?" It was all very distressing to Augustine who had instinctive reservations about man's intellect checking up on God. Although he was too rational to deny that texts of canonical books should be corrected where needed and that translations should be verified, he was much opposed to Jerome's "tinkering" or "playing" with the inspired Septuagint. What did Jerome mean by saying that we should "amuse" ourselves with the Scriptures? Should he not confine himself to translating the Septuagint and leave the Hebrew alone? How could he be finding new material in Hebrew manuscripts at this late date? Sometimes he thought Jerome was wrong. But who could check his work? Indeed, at times Augustine was disturbed enough to wonder if Jerome was collaborating with Manichaeans. If one admitted that one Scriptural statement was untrue, how could others stand?[27] Would not even the old classics—Plato, Aristotle, or Cicero—be put in jeopardy if this kind of scrutiny prevailed? Others of the faithful sought to allay the dismay by offering explanations for manuscript inconsistencies. Justin, for instance, suggested that the Jews deliberately left out some of the Scriptures such as parts of Esdras, Jeremiah, and some psalms because they were too symbolic of Christ. Jerome, too, thought the Hebrews out of hatred of Christ might have changed texts and that the translators of the Septuagint deliberately passed over in silence passages reflecting the Trinity to satisfy King Ptolemy that they were not polytheists.[28]

Even acceptance of a book as canonical and some agreement on its text did not end the theologian's critical work. The problem still remained: what did its passages mean? Origen boasted to Celsus that Christians were too critical–minded to accept things blindly. Too intelligent, for sure, to take things always literally. As we have seen, Origen and others thought that the biblical texts contained not only indifferent materials pertaining neither to morals nor doctrine, but also offensive crudities unworthy of God. Impossible things contrary to science or history were reported: how could one rationally speak of morning and evening before the creation of the sun? Some statements, if not contradictory to fact, were partially irrational: why should one unreasonably blame the right eye and throw it away when both were guilty of looking at a woman? Only application of the "best methods" could elucidate such passages; that meant they could not be taken literally. It did not escape

---

[27] For these and similar remarks: Augustine, *Epis.* 71.2–5, 82.1.2, *De morib. eccles.* 29.60 (*PL* 32.1335).

[28] Deliberate Jewish manipulation of the Scriptures is a recurrent theme: Justin, *Trypho* 71; Jerome, *Apol.* 2.25 (*PL* 23: 469), *Epis.* 32; Augustine, *De doct. Christ.* 2.14, *Epis.* 82.5.34.

the well–read Celsus that when Christians were ashamed of anything they took refuge in allegory. This convenient device was, however, such a time–honored Greek literary tool—it dated back at least to the mid–sixth century when Theagenes of Rhegium applied allegory to Homer—that Celsus could not object to its use on principle. Christians came by it legitimately enough not only through Classical authors but also through Hellenistic Jewish exegetes such as Aristobulus and Philo. Justin and Irenaeus, together with Clement, felt free to use it as a matter of course; Origen could not have remained a Christian without it. For him Holy Writ contained three possible senses: a bodily, historical literal one; a psychic or moral one; a spiritual, intellectual, anagogical, symbolical, mystical one. Many texts, Origen contended, had no literal sense at all. Eusebius so admired Origen's method that he advised those unable to understand the obscure bare letter of the Scriptures to follow the stronger mind of the great Alexandrian. Cassian, in turn, found four meanings: the historical or literal, the moral, the symbolical, the mystic. Augustine, very fond of allegory too, also supported four meanings in interpreting the Old Testament.

The question of the literal versus the allegorical interpretation became so fundamental in Christian exegesis that two schools crystallized. The school of Antioch, quite Aristotelian, sought the obvious or literal sense first. Even evident metaphors and parables were to be subjected to a commonsense meaning judged in the light of relevant Greek and Hebrew practice in literature. Theodore of Mopsuestia who wrote a book now lost, *On Allegory and the Historical Sense,* was one of the typical representatives of this school, as was his friend, John Chrysostom. The Alexandrian school, more Platonic, was convinced that Scripture was a storehouse of truth not patent to simple minds; only the spiritual reader could discern its symbolic import. To this school belonged such eminent theologians as Clement, Origen, the Cappadocians, Ambrose, Jerome, and Augustine. Athanasius was something of an exception; he would desert the obvious meaning of a passage only after careful consideration of all circumstances prompted him to do so.

Augustine, like Origen, maintained it was intellectual slavery to think only in a literal sense. Book II of his *De doctrina Christiana* is a strong defence of allegory indebted somewhat to Tyconius' *Liber Regularum* which recommended seven rules for interpreting Scripture. Augustine used allegory copiously, sometimes in a bizarre manner, in speaking against Faustus, in interpreting *Genesis,* in explaining crimes imputed to Old Testament characters, and in resolving differences between the Hebrew and Septuagint. In the New Testament, such episodes as the marriage feast of Cana, the expulsion of the buyers from the temple, and the story of the five barley loaves and two fishes all received allegorical treatment. Just as Origen and John Chrysostom saw mystic meaning in names, Augustine assigned extravagant interpretations to numbers and their combinations. In his mind, they were used in the sacred writings to convey instruction under a figurative guise; ignorance of the import of such numbers, like the mystic six and forty, could shut out the reader from proper illumination. In short, to those of the Alexandrian school, the search for the hidden became almost frantic. Even the most trifling minutae were thought to contain some secret divine wisdom. Basil took no preposition for granted; Jerome felt so strongly that every word, syllable, and accent was packed with heavenly meaning that he wrote whole epistles on the significance of individual words. In general, his letters and his work against Pelagius outline in scholarly fashion the principles by which he thought the Scriptures should be interpreted.

Allegory, which could be applied to both testaments, could not accept passages literally. Thus the parable of the Good Samaritan, for example, would take on a deeper significance than the obvious. The traveler was really Adam, Jerusalem the heavenly city from which he fell, Jericho was his resulting mortality, the thief was the devil, the traveler's wretched condition was that of sinful humanity. The priest and the Levite signified the ineffective ministrations of the old law. The Samaritan was Christ; the Inn the Church. Allegory itself should be distinguished from typology, a Christian tool of exegesis used especially by the Alexandrian Fathers, to determine meanings of the Old Testament only. It accepted all Old Testament events as literally and historically true so they could be seen as types, prefigurements, anticipations of New Testament events. Thus the Ark of the Covenant was a prefigurement of the Church; Moses' outstretched arms anticipated the cross; his shining countenance foreshadowed the Transfiguration of Christ; Melchizedek anticipated Christ.

If allegory and typology were employed to suggest rational solutions to scriptural puzzles, tradition was called upon to elucidate Holy Writ where it was silent. Irenaeus and Tertullian early advocated that scriptural interpretations, like heresy, itself, be checked against the "fixed" rule of faith preserved in apostolic churches. Basil explained scriptural silence on the Holy Spirit by arguing that great mysteries were too sacred to parade around in written documents. It was safer to trust unwritten tradition to preserve knowledge of such dogmas; through this medium they would be kept intact and uncontaminated, thanks to the multitude's oral familiarity with them. Augustine fell back on tradition to support such practices as infant baptism about which the Scriptures were silent. Infant baptism, in turn, became an argument for Original Sin. In the final analysis, for Augustine the magisterium of the Church must arbitrate: "I would not believe the Gospel unless the authority of the catholic Church moved me to do so."

By 450 tradition had so developed that it meant not only the unwritten deposit of faith in principal churches, but canons of councils, decretals of popes, and the accumulated writings of the theologians. Theologians became sort of "authorities" for all the great writers of the fourth century. Basil put it well: if a court of law uses witnesses when it is at a loss for documentary evidence, why should not the Church? In such manner he justified his citation of such "authorities" as Clement and Dionysius of Rome, Dionysius of Alexandria, Irenaeus, Origen, Africanus, and Gregory Thaumaturgus. Jerome admitted he learned much from the "Church's most famous writers" and proudly referred to Christendom's long list of famous scholars. Augustine not only quoted the authority of past authors but looked forward to enlightenment from future theologians.[29] The Emperor Theodosius, in a legal way, used "ancient interpreters of the Scripture" to identify heretics.

One interesting sidelight in the development of tradition is the question whether theologians considered themselves agents in progressive revelation. That revelation was progressive seemed reasonable to many Fathers. Origen, for instance, felt that the evangelists had expected persons with expertise to examine into the grounds of their statements and that the future teaching tradition of the Church would clear up questions about the transmission of individual souls, and about angels, and devils. Gregory of Nazianzus explained that God's self–revelation had always been gradual; "lights," as it were, broke upon theologians to guide them in not proclaiming things too suddenly nor keeping things hidden unseasonably. Did not the Savior say that many things could not be borne in the time of his disciples? Gregory of Nazianzus, it appears, considered himself an agent in extending tradition: to the Jews the Father was revealed, to the Christians the Son, to his time—and largely through him—the Holy Spirit.[30] Jerome proclaims: "I must call upon the Holy Spirit to express his meaning by my mouth" in regard to the virginity of Mary.[31] Augustine apparently thought of theologians as divine agents when he judged those who had explained away obscurities in the Scriptures to have earned, in the eyes of the Church, an esteem close to, if not indeed equal to, that of the sacred writers of the canon.[32] Vincent of Lerins thought doctrine grew as

---

[29] Cyprian and Athanasius seem almost alone in allowing no place for progressive tradition. For Augustine's opposition to Cyprian's denigration of "custom" in the Church (Cyprian Epis. 62.17–18) see De bapt. con. Donat. 2.8. Athanasius welcomes tradition only negatively as a way to condemn new doctrine and to help understand the true sense of Scripture. See De decret. 6.25–27, Orat. 1.8.10 (PG 26:28), De syn. 4, Epis. 59.3.

[30] Gregory of Nazianzus, Orat. 31.26 (PG 36:161). In Orat. 41.5 (PG 36:137) Gregory says that those who hold the Holy Spirit as divine tend to keep quiet about it.

[31] Jerome, Con. Helvid. 2 (PL 23:194).

[32] Augustine's remark (in psalm. 119.18) is interesting in this connection: "but in this most profound question I dare not define anything."

naturally as children; old dogmas were polished, fortified, and expanded.

It early became apparent that great confusion reigned in determining heresy and orthodoxy because there was no corpus of precise and universal theological terminology. Since the Scriptures failed to offer one, it became the theologians' task to invent, and tradition's role to pass on, a standard theological vocabulary by which to distinguish heretic from orthodox. It seems best to illustrate the difficulty as minimally as possible. The council of Nicaea, in adopting a non–Scriptural word to define Christ's divine essence as *homoousios* with the Father not only created a problem for those who wanted *homoiousios* but also failed to designate a word for Christ's personality. The term *hypostasis* caused a great deal of trouble. Meaning "objective reality" or "basic foundation," it was used by early church Fathers as synonymous with *ousia*, "being" or "reality." But *hypostasis* also came to mean "individual reality" or "person." Great confusion resulted in western theology where *hypostasis* was translated as *substantia* or "substance." Eastern theologians who spoke of three *hypostases* in the Godhead seemed to be heretically supporting three substances in the Trinity. The Cappadocian Fathers in the fourth century did most to clarify and standardize usage: the Trinity was described as three *hypostases* in one *ousia*. The western church, using Tertullian's terminology, grasped the problem when *essentia* came into usage to express *ousia*. Basil, in turn, opposed the western word *persona*, which he translated as *prosopon*, because it was a theatrical term meaning a person who played a role, a concept that might lend itself to Sabellianism which thought of the Trinity in terms of modes.[33] Quite clearly, Christianity, in the face of Greek rationalism, did not remain simple enough for the minds of children.

Growing canonical standardization of Scripture clarification of its wording through textual criticism, and discovery of its meaning through such devices as allegory and typology and through a growing tradition with a standard vocabulary, all served somewhat to contain heretics or at least to identify them. But since heresy, as we saw, was bloated with undigested Greek philosophy, the theologian had to deal with that difficulty as well. Hippolytus was one of the first to take it upon himself— although he realized the labor would be great and the research long—to identify heresy by exposing how misappropriation and distortion of Greek philosophy had produced no less than thirty–three heretical groups. Clement of Alexandria pointed out one way to proceed. Greatly influenced by Platonic metaphysics, Stoic ethics, and Aristotelian methodology, he magnanimously held that philosophy was providentially

---

[33] This convenient resume is largely taken from the *Nicene and Post-Nicene Fathers*, series 2, vol. 8, p. 355, n.a.

given the Greeks to aid later Christians not only to understand the faith but also to unmask the attacks of heretics as illogical. Obviously theologizing, as akin to philosophizing, would have to honor the methodological tools of philosophy itself. Speaking especially as an Aristotelian and a Stoic, Clement urged the true Christian gnostic to make use of dialectic to distinguish genera from species, "for the cause of all error and false opinion is the inability to distinguish in what respect things are common and in what respects they differ." Irenaeus found logical alternatives useful in confounding Gnostics: if in a dualistic way they separated God from the world, did they not limit deity? If in a pantheistic fashion they confused God with the world, did they not make the world's imperfections God's? Tertullian's philosophical and legal mind delighted not only in analyses of relationships, definitions and logic, but also in hyperbole and paradox. Parmenidean–Platonic axioms served him well in refuting Marcion and Hermogenes who would see a dualism in the divine nature represented by the God of the Old Testament and that of the New. "The Great Supreme," said Tertullian, "must be unique by having no equal and so not ceasing to be the Great Supreme." Praxeas, the modalist, no doubt was taxed not only to counter but even to understand Tertullian's assertion that the relationship between Father and Son in no way destroyed the divine monarchy because it was not by division that the one differed from the other but by distinction. Did not Praxeas perceive that the Father, Son, and Holy Spirit are three, however, "not in quality but in sequence, not in substance but in form, not in power but in aspect?" Yet they are of one substance and one quality and one power because there is one God from whom these sequences and forms and aspects are reckoned out in the name of the Father, the Son, and the Holy Spirit." Even Aristotle might have difficulty with such a proposition. Minucius Felix's *Octavius* is among the earliest writings to employ extended dialectic. Origen operated on the principle that clear statements should be made on Christian topics arrived at by illustration, analogy, and deductive argument. Such was part of the "correct method." Athanasius' *On The Incarnation of the Word* is a logical gem. Disputing with Eunomius, Gregory of Nyssa and Basil made telling use of the syllogism. Basil's *On the Spirit* discusses Aristotle's causes trying to establish the nature of the third person of the Trinity. Augustine freely availed himself of learned argumentative devices in his challenging work, *On the Trinity;* where logic had to fail, he capitalized on the use of analogy and arguments from silence, dwelling not only on all that could be said about the nature of God but also on what could not be said about it. Rational sophistication of this sort was probably more than Jesus had in mind when he spoke in simple parables to his fishermen.

Since it is obvious that the Christian theologian would give no quarter to polytheism the indictment of the gods need not long detain us. Logical dogged Christian attacks on pagan idols and gods were so persistent and trenchant that it would appear the old deities were not as decrepit as is often maintained. They were lampooned, derided, branded as inane, weak and infamous by the apologist Aristides; Theophilus of Antioch gleefully pointed out contradictions in Homer's and Hesiod's treatments of the gods. Tatian in his *Discourse against the Gods* claimed by the use of logic that when pagans spoke of the origin of their deities they declared them mortal. Clement and Tertullian relegated the gods to the status of daimons, not exactly of the kind Plutarch knew, but to demons or fallen angels in the Jewish sense. Origen in his *Contra Celsum* continued the onslaught. Cyprian in the *Idols are not Gods* and Lactantius in the *Divine Institutes* both capitalized on Euhemerus to declare the Immortals nothing but former kings or apotheosized heroes. Eusebius' *Praeparatio Evangelica* and Athanasius' *Against the Heathen* continued to expose the obscene and shocking stories of the pantheon even into the fourth century.[34]

Since the gods were completely unacceptable from the standpoints of both reason and revelation, any perplexing similarities between their myths and rituals and Christian beliefs and practices had to be explained away. Justin found that it was sometimes easier to exploit the differences between pagan and Christian than to explain the correspondences. The pagan explanation for similarities was a strong one: stigmatizing Christianity as a new religion, it simply accused Christians of plagiarizing ideas and rituals. The Fathers countered, as we saw, by turning the argument around and by blaming daimons for the confusion. The latter was a clever and appropriate retort considering that both sides accepted the existence of these spiritual intermediaries, both beneficent and maleficent. A sort of in–between tricky and pesky type, which seemed particularly anxious to confound divine and human affairs, was held responsible by Plutarch for confusing pagan religion by individually masquerading as deities or purposely misleading Classical poets to misrepresent godly conduct. Christians again turned the argument around. Justin held that the daimons, arrogantly taking advantage of stolen information about God's plans, promulgated an unauthorized, premature, and distorted revelation. Portions of truth, torn from context, were circulated as counterfeit religions by these daimons to embarrass Christianity when it should come upon the scene. No wonder that Christianity reflected stories of such gods as Persephone, Minerva or

---

[34] The persistent and common attacks on the Classical gods (e.g. Cyril *Cat.* 12.27; Augustine, *Civ. Dei.* books 4, 6, 7; Gregory of Nazianzus, *Orat.* 39.4–5) should demonstrate, unless the Fathers are poor judges of their times, that textbook pronouncements of the demise of the old pagan deities are greatly exaggerated.

Bacchus, and employed rituals such as the Mithraic use of water and wine.

It might be argued that veneration of saints, as something of a compromise, did much to soften the blow to polytheism. However, the vindictive *contra Vigilantium*, generally ascribed to Jerome, tried rationally to put the record straight and to justify the honoring of saints, a practice long growing since the Decian persecution. Jerome asked reasonably enough: if holy men were effective as friends of God when they were on earth, why should they not be so with him now in heaven?[35] Despite the allurements of polytheism orthodox theologians, especially Cyprian, Tertullian, Ambrose, Chrysostom, Jerome, and Augustine, castigated popular tendencies to translate saints into gods. It is significant that the development of any cult of divinized martyrs was fought off and that no unique formal liturgy for saints' commemorative days ever developed to compete with the eucharistic service. The best a Saint could expect was the inclusion of his or her name in the Preface. Human beings the saints were officially to remain; heroic in a new unclassical way, they became popular enough to help put the old gods to rest without serving as gods themselves.

If rational dialogue with pagan gods could not take place it certainly was not ruled out in the case of philosophy. We have already seen in discussing the Fathers' attitudes toward Classical culture that only a few, like Tatian and the Montanist–converted Tertullian, berated it actively. Although Hippolytus objected to the misuse of philosophy by heretics, he nevertheless countenanced its use to confound them. Lactantius, while discounting philosophy as only a secondary cause of heresy, concluded, at the same time, that it was of limited value to Christianity because of its contradictory nature. Most Fathers, however, following Justin and Clement, took it for what it was: a brilliant product of human reason, a unique treasure of the Classical mind containing partial truths of revelation, and useful tools of scholarly investigation. As such, if eclectically used, it could be quite supportive of Christianity. With Epicureanism, of course, there would be no positive dealings at all.

Already by 200 Tertullian feared that Christianity might succumb to the blandishments of philosophy to become a mottled mess of Platonism, Stoicism, and Aristotelianism. To be sure, even Platonism, by all accounts most attractive to Christianity, could become a source of heresy if mis-

---

[35] On veneration of saints: Jerome. *Con. Vigil.* (*PL* 23:354–367) and *Epis.* 109 (*CSEL* 55: 351–56); Tertullian, *De cor.* 3; Ambrose, *Epis.* 22 (*PL* 16: 1062–70); John Chrysostom, *Hom.* 1.17; Augustine, *Civ. Dei.* 8.27 and 22.10, *Epis.* 29.9, *Con. Faust.* 20.21. Theodoret of Cyrus in the eighth book of his *The Truth of the Gospel Proven from Greek Philosophy* reports the consternation of pagans over the conversion of former temples into shrines commemorating saints. Here "God's blessed heroes," unlike the gods of old, are honored chastely and soberly.

used by such as Origen. At the outset, Justin, former Stoic, Peripatetic, Pythagorean, and finally Platonist, in a pioneer way considered pagans who lived in harmony with the Logos really true Christians. As he saw it, his old master, Plato, was precocious about many things: both his and Christ's kingdoms were not of this world; he had rightly ascribed transcendency to god making him incorporeal, indescribable, and providential; he had properly spoken of a human free will, had expressed interesting ideas of creation in his *Timaeus*, and had entertained correct views about the soul except that its immortality was not self conferred as pre-existent and that it was not subject to transmigration.

Clement and Origen, the famous "Platonists of Alexandria," did more than any others to make Plato the intellectual catalyst between Christianity and Classical culture. Although they do not always agree nor stress the same features of Plato, their concurrence on several general points reveals the fundamental attractiveness the Platonic outlook could offer early Christian thinkers. Assuming with Plato that knowledge was virtue, both Clement and Origen were limited Christian gnostics, men of faith and reason, who yet believed that full communion with God demanded knowledge in addition to faith. While faith and holiness were always basic to the higher life of the Christian gnostic, they should be augmented, perfected in a way, by knowledge and rational conviction. To Clement Christ was the Instructor; Origen was more anxious to be considered a doctor of the Church than a presbyter. Further, Plato's dislike of the body encouraged Clement to entertain slightly docetist views of Jesus' flesh. Both he and Origen were, therefore, critical of bodily resurrection except in some possible glorified fashion.

Origen, however, was the Christian Platonist par excellence. He so approved of Plato's views of the soul that he accepted, along with its immortality, its pre–existent and transmigratory nature. Furthermore, not always distinguishing between Plato's god and the demiurge, and with Genesis doubtless in mind, Origen reasoned that Plato made creation the result of God's eternal goodness and that God's immutability forced him to remain in a state of "genesian" activity. Consequently, eternal creation of a succession of worlds was inevitable, a view servicing transmigration and amenable to Stoic cyclical history. Again, Plato's strong antithesis of spirit and matter encouraged the Alexandrian school to support free will as Plato's way to absolve the Good from evil. In addition, Origen, like Plato, considered evil a negation; since it originated from man's association with matter, it had no true being and was not eternal. Therefore, the Good would prevail, a belief that reinforced Plato's teaching that punishment was corrective, and that suffering was an educative purgative. In consequence, the Alexandrians envisaged Christ as the great Physician who, especially for Origen, would eventually heal everyone even the devil. Obviously both Clement and Origen subscribed to Plato's ineffability and transcendence of God. However, reflecting Plato's trinity in the soul involving the rational, the spirited, and the appetitive—or if one prefers, the later middle–Platonic trinity of the One, the Nous, and the World Soul—Origen made the Christian Trinity subordinationist,[36] as Epiphanius and Jerome claimed. At times he spoke of the Father as absolute Truth, alone to be prayed to; the Son was relative Truth; of the exact nature of the Holy Spirit he was uncertain. In a unique way even Plato's *Republic* influenced Origen; alone of all church Fathers he envisaged Christians as the potential new philosopher kings who would eventually create an earthly utopia. Finally, both Clement and Origen, directly influenced by the Platonistic Philo, were enamored of Platonic symbolism. They found Plato's teaching that the visible world was a mere reflection of invisible Reality a ready suggestion that the written word could be a symbol of something other than its obvious self. Did not Plato, who held that sensible knowledge was only opinion, spur one all the more to look for the true hidden spiritual, symbolical meaning in the words of revelation? It is easy to understand why the Alexandrian school became a fervent promoter of allegory.

Platonism, generally becoming more mystical and "religious" in its middle and neo–Platonic stages, did not lose its attraction for Christian thinkers. Ammonius Saccas might have abandoned Christianity for it. Gregory of Nyssa, for instance, found Plotinus very attractive for his view of God featuring a divine graduated relation to created things. Gregory, as well as Augustine, consequently found Plotinus' reflections on the mystic ascent enlightening. In fact, Plotinus and Porphyry were greatly responsible for Augustine's conversion by teaching him that the true nature of philosophy was to lead to the possession of God as happiness. For such an approach to God the mind would need to be purified by degrees so that, gradually learning to deal with eternal things, it would ultimately come to understand that all beings were realizations of the Ideas of God and all knowledge was a participation in his thought. By 350 neo–Platonism had become so esteemed in Christian theology that imperceptibly it came dangerously close to heresy in a person like the super–rationalist Victorinus the Rhetor, a forerunner in a sense of the later John Scotus Eriugena. Victorinus practically converted neo–Platonism into a semi–Stoic pantheism envisaging the world as God unfolding himself in an on–flowing emanation and then returning to unity. Creation itself was but the expanding emanation of the deity. In this unfolding of the divine nature Christ was pictured as burdened, in a typical Platonic way, with his humanity. Finally, Synesius of Cyrene, the "Platonist with the mitre," insisted on keeping his Platonic views to the last. He agreed to be made bishop in 410 by popular demand only if

---

[36] Origen, *C.C.* 8.15, *De prin.* preface 4.

he could retain his questionable Platonic beliefs in the pre–existence of souls, the eternity of creation, and an allegorical interpretation of bodily resurrection. He is reported even to have carried a marked strain of neo–Platonic mysticism into his religious hymns, reportedly sung in church accompanied by the cithera.

Tertullian warned that Stoicism no less than Platonism might become a danger. In fact, its pantheistic cosmology led even him to believe that the soul was material. It certainly enticed Origen into cosmological difficulties. It did, however, readily furnish cogent arguments for the existence of God based on the order and harmony of the universe. Clement of Rome in 95 urged Corinthian Christians to mirror the harmonious gradations of the macrocosm in their church's organization. In fact, Christian appropriation of the argument of cosmic harmony became so common—Gregory of Nyssa, for instance, used it in his sermon on the Beatitudes and many others in commenting on Genesis— that it remained a stock apologetic proof for the existence of Providence until Darwin introduced the idea of struggle and disorder into the universe.

Stoicism had more to offer, however, than a type of argument. Christian Fathers were zealously partial to Stoic ethics as a way to offset Classical addiction to the heroic, to Aristotelian super-humanism, and to Epicurean hedonism. Moreover, Stoic ethics were quite in line with the general direction contemporary ethics were taking in pagan religion which more and more emphasized that moral action, rather than bloody sacrificial liturgies, pleased the gods. The Cynic philosopher—a lowbrow Stoic in reality—was virtually a Christian monk if Epictetus' description is correct. Epictetus himself taught that god within man was pleased with a pure heart and a right judgment which directed him to cooperate with providential Reason. The Stoic brotherhood of man under the Fatherhood of God and Stoic reverence for natural law were attractive to Christian theologians from Tertullian to Augustine.

The Christian Platonists of Alexandria also were quite partial to Stoicism. Clement of Alexandria liked its emphasis on inner moral virtue and considered its axiom to live according to nature pleasing to God. For him, the first state in mystical ascent to God was *apatheia*, freedom from passion, a Stoic concept. His *Exhortation*, advocating a high code of ethics, reflects Cleanthes, Chrysippus, and Posidonius; his *Tutor* seems to borrow from Musonius. Origen, in his turn, knew Stoic logic and ethics through Chrysippus, Musonius, and Epictetus. Views of Chrysippus, of Cicero, of middle–Platonists imbued with Stoicism, and of Philo, all combined in Origen to make him the greatest exponent of natural law among Christian theologians. His system posits basic human equality, the rationality of man, human freedom, natural rights, limited government authority, and the validity of natural moral notions as the foundation for a just order of society that derives all its authority from God. His enormous influence is felt in Eusebius, the Cappadocians, Chrysostom, and Jerome.

One can see the continued influence of Stoicism on the Fathers in such works as the *Octavius* of Minucius Felix which appears much indebted to Stoicism's Seneca and in Cyprian's *De mortalitate* which suggest Stoic thoughts in connection with the meaning of death. Novatian, known as a Christian Stoic, greatly admired the school's dialectics and syllogistic methodology. While others, like Gregory of Nyssa, wrote a generous amount of Stoicism into their ethics, Ambrose modeled his *De officiis* directly on Cicero's work, featuring such basic Stoic hallmarks as the distinction of reason and passion, and relative and perfect duties. The Stoic influence culminated in Pelagius, the heretical adversary of Augustine, who supposedly was led astray by Stoicism's strong insistence that one could by unaided effort live according to Providence without benefit of grace or Church. Although the extent of Stoic influence on Christian ethics remains a matter of dispute, Jaeger, for one, considers it so extensive as to contend that Stoic morality in the long run overshadowed the "impractical" Sermon on the Mount and the anti-humanistic spirit of St. Paul.[37] Certainly Christian ethical teaching was far more specific, objective, and legalized than that of the Stoics. Hence it could call forth sermons and treatises on every sin—even new ones like vanity—and every virtue—including new ones like humility and virginity.

Aristotle's influence, which Tertullian also feared, entered Christianity chiefly by way of methodology; it was a contribution welcomed by all Fathers who sought to be logically persuasive. Some of Aristotle's concepts, however, did become stock–in–trade for Christian intellectuals. Already Aristides the apologist used Aristotle's argument of motion to prove God's existence and referred to the Aristotelian concept of potentiality and the postulation of causes. Citations such as these will continue through Christian literature; for instance, Basil, in dealing with the nature of the Holy Spirit, calls attention to the importance of prepositions as media through which the operation of Aristotle's causes is expressed. Yet Aristotle's secular, scientific outlook could readily foster agnosticism and heresy, as it did among the Artemonites. In general, Origen's objections to Aristotle's views were common among Christians: the philosopher made happiness depend too much on physical well-being and external circumstances rather than God's law; he taught no providential God, nor accountability in an afterlife; he denied the crea-

---

[37] Jaeger, *Early Christianity* p. 16, remarks that the system of Christian virtues emerging already in Clement of Rome is closer to Stoic moralism than to the spirit of Paul's letter to the Romans.

tion of the world and the immortality of souls. Such indictments effectively safeguarded Aristotle from Christianization until Thomas Aquinas out-foxed him and dragged him into church in the thirteenth century. All in all, it should be obvious that Christian appropriation of Classical philosophy did much to take wind out of pagan sails. Theodoret's twelve–book work (c. 450) finally becalmed the last pagan philosophical breeze; it was entitled *The Truth of the Gospel Proven from Greek Philosophy!*

But establishing compatibility between Greek philosophy and the new Christian thought held out dangers. Although Justin gladly boasted, "We teach the same as the Greeks," he felt simultaneously the need to explain why. While pilfering of Christian truths by daimons served to explain pagan–Christian religious similarities, more sophisticated explanations arose to account for the intellectual affinities between Greek philosophy and Christian thought.[38] Generally two arguments emerged; one was ingenious and learned, the other generous and enlightened. The first adroitly turned around the common pagan charge that Christian wisdom was plagiarized from Classical sources; Christians counter–charged that Homer and subsequent pagan thinkers borrowed from older Jewish sources, sources now appropriated as Christian. Was it not generally known that some early Greek writers had admitted that the ancient "philosophy" of the Jews was admirable? Justin, Tatian, Theophilus, Clement, Tertullian, and Origen all set the stage by pointing out that pagan borrowing from Jewish sources was possible; did not Moses live before Homer? Already the Jew Aristobulus, as well as Philo, had argued so. Clement thought the biblical statement, "All before me were thieves and robbers" seemed clear enough. Plato, of course, was declared the chief collector, because he appropriated Jewish ideas from all over— Egypt, Babylonia, Thrace, and Israel. Egypt, significantly, was singled out as the logical place where most of the larceny took place. Plato was indeed "Moses speaking in Attic Greek." So extensive was this pagan borrowing from Jewish sources supposed to be that Clement wondered in a straight face if Miltiades had not stolen his strategy at Marathon from Moses!

Naive or not, this thesis of plagiarism called forth remarkably learned efforts to establish the first systematic universal chronology ever attempted in the ancient world. The remarkable early third–century pioneer effort of Julius Africanus was continued by Eusebius, Jerome, and finally by Dionysius Exiguus in the sixth century who decided, for all time, that Christ would be the central point from which all chronology would henceforth be reckoned.

---

[38] For a discussion of three arguements Christians used to discredit similarities with paganism see E. G. Weltin, "Quid Athenae Hierosolymis?", *Classical Journal* 51 (1956): 154–61.

The second argument concerning philosophical–theological affinities was a truly enlightened one that eternally should redound to the credit of Clement of Alexandria. He posited a divine economy in which Greek philosophers were enlisted to play a legitimate preliminary role in revelation as colleagues of the Jewish prophets. Say he: "The one and only God was known by the Greeks in a gentile manner, by the Jews in a Jewish way, and in a novel and spiritual manner by us" Christians. Since "a rational work is accomplished through God," Greek philosophy proceeded from God. Thus many philosophers, even poets and dramatists, were scheduled by Providence to anticipate parcels of Christian theology. It was a forward–looking solution. While both the pagan Celsus and the Christian Clement were anxious to preserve the integrity and continuity of history, Celsus, as an antiquarian, would disavow any possible new Christian contributions worthy of incorporation. Clement in a positive and generous way viewed the Classical background admirable and essential. In an enlightened manner he beckoned the Classical past to share in the new Christian future, to take an honored place in the continuity of western intellectual experience. Without such views western civilization would not have been born.

Even Greek science entered at times to create among some Christians intellectual impasses that only faith could surmount. One such area was provided by the creation story in Genesis. Very early Justin and Clement promulgated, in defiance of all Greek knowledge, the biblical proposition that the cosmos was created by divine fiat, *ex nihilo*. Against Plato's doctrine of the demiurge, the new cosmology envisaged no antagonistic duality or resistence between the spiritual and the material; against Aristotle's observations it declared that something could come from nothing; against Stoicism it denied that the cosmos was the natural fulfillment of a pantheistic world soul, and against the Epicureans it refused to accept the universe as the product of a mechanistic determinism. This Jewish view of creation was so foreign and incomprehensible to the Classical rational mentality that Christian writers felt called upon to compose commentary upon commentary, or *Hexamera*, on the subject. Theologians like Basil and Ambrose even incorporated, as best they could, the imperfect Greek science of the day to make the strange six-day creation story plausible. Gregory of Nyssa, it seems, was never quite able to put aside the subtle difficult questions he found in the biblical account.

Despite Christianity's overwhelming endorsement of Classical rationalism it did not rule out the legitimacy of mystical experience so long honored in the Platonic tradition of the ancient world. Distinguished here from a sudden unsolicited visitation by a god, mysticism is taken in the Classical sense to mean a process which a devotee initiates to identify himself with the divine. Whether induced or assisted by eucharistic communions, ascetic practices, or contemplation, at some point the process is expected to transcend mental control so that the practitioner, as it were, rises above himself. The nature of mysticism is complicated in the Christian dispensation by the supposed intervention of grace, especially if, as a totally gratuitous ingredient, it is distributed entirely dependent on God's will rather than as a boon earned by human effort.

Generally speaking, one could say that outside of monastic circles only a few writers, such as Paul, Gregory of Nyssa, and Augustine might qualify as important mystics before 450. Paul's strange interpretation of faith as at most a self–renouncing attitude of receptivity to Christ immediately sets him apart from matter–of–fact Christians who equated faith with simple belief or trust. By identifying himself with Christ, by becoming one with him, by dying and rising with him, Paul felt himself raised to a point of liberty at which formal law, which served only to convict him of sin, was no longer necessary. Experiencing Christ, Paul would reap Christ's conquest over the tyrants of sin, death, flesh, and the devil. Once one's old self had been crucified with Christ, the Christian lived in Christ and Christ in him; he had "put on" the lord Jesus Christ. Some have argued that these Pauline views would be better understood by a mystery–cult devotee than by a Classical mystic since Paul's mystical experience of dying and resurrecting with Christ seems in his mind not a product of his own willing or exertion but of an undeserved election from the outside, the product of grace, a notion known to unclassical cultists but only vaguely to Plato. As we shall see later, there remains the serious question how deeply Paul's gratuitous born-again experience struck roots in the rational Greek and legal–minded Roman.

Ignatius of Antioch is often cited as one of the few Fathers who echoed Pauline mystical overtones. He seems anxious to combine Paul's idea of union with Christ with John's concept of life in Christ. To Ignatius the best way to imitate Christ is to undergo his passion and death by martyrdom. Indeed, Ignatius speaks about the divinity of Christ dwelling in Christians' souls, about Christians being in Christ or in union with him. But he may be thinking as much about membership in the community of Christians functioning as a liturgical ecclesiastical body in union with its bishop, as about Pauline personal mystical encounters. Since Ignatius dealt hardly at all with individuals striving through progressive contemplative stages toward loss of their identity in God, his commitment to mysticism remains quite controversial.

Clement of Alexandria, too, is rather loosely cited as a mystic. For him, resistance to temptation, mortification, and resignation led to *apatheia*, a Stoic–like freedom from passion, as the basic step to higher mystic plateaus. The final gnosis which transforms the Christian into a close friend of God comes as an intuitive experience suddenly leading him into hidden mysteries. Clement, it would appear, seems more interested in being privy to a charisma of knowledge than in enjoying a pure ecstasy in God.

Origen's mysticism is much debated. A good Platonist, he believed that once a Christian realized he was living only in transit, he would seek the good by imitating God in performing works, battling passions, and practicing asceticism. For those who could not imitate Christ to the point of martyrdom, a spiritual death of mortification had to suffice culminating as it would in visions, illuminations, and a mystical marriage between the Logos and the Christian soul. The normal dowry arranged for man by God—the natural law, rationalism, and free will—would be supplanted in this divine marriage by one of mystical kisses of the Word of God each accompanied by revelation of hidden meanings. The question whether such descriptions reflect Origen's actual experiences of rapture in God or are merely artificial constructions has led some to wonder whether the great Christian Platonist is more a would–be mystic than an actual one. His awareness of mystical union, his deep respect for it, and his knowledge of the right terminology may well be more rhetorical than experiential.

Gregory of Nyssa is widely accepted as the greatest post–apostolic mystic in the early Church. For him the mystical vision clearly compensated for the deficiencies of human reason and knowledge. Because it is possible only for like to approach like, it is only the divine element in humanity, the cleansed divine image in the soul, that enables one to see God, one's natural desire. Thanks to this internal image of God, man is possessed of reason, free will and God's friendship; if he himself adds purity, freedom from passion, and alienation from evil in general, intuition of God follows. Gregory's *Life of Moses* allegorically portrays the Jewish leader as the symbol of the mystic wanderings and graduated ascensions of the soul to God.

By the time of Gregory of Nyssa mysticism was flourishing among the so-called Desert Fathers of Eygpt and Pontus. Such was to be expected since, in some sense, monasticism arose as a protest—however emphemeral—against the growing rational sophistication of Christianity fostered so actively in Alexandria. Ammonas, a disciple of the famed Antony the Hermit who died in 356, reveals in his letters an ardent desire to approach heaven in a simple, sincere mystical way, devoid of artificial steps and regulations which will characterize later monastic mysticism in rules such as those of Pachomius and Cassian. The *Spiritual Homilies,* questionably attributed to Macarius the Egyptian (c. 375), have proved to be an inspiration to many later Christians including John Wesley. Evagrius of Pontus, supposedly influenced by Origen, has been called the founder of monastic mysticism in the East. However, it is Cassian, abbot of St. Victor c. 410, who first treated ascetic monastic mysticism formally. His treatises, the *Institutions* and the *Conferences,* based on actual interviews with the Desert Fathers, tried to establish guides outlining the proper way to pursue the mystic path to perfection. It is especially significant that Cassian saw the necessity of reaching some understanding of the relationship between Grace and Free Will in mystical experiences. For his trouble he became, as we shall see, *persona non grata* to Augustinians.

Augustine's mysticism is rooted in Plotinus. Neo–Platonism, quite instrumental in his conversion to Christianity, made him finally aware of the priority of the supernatural and the soul's need of fulfillment by ascending toward the Ineffable to which the entire cosmological existence strove instinctively. His own experience contributed to his conversion by convincing him that it was a serious retrogression for a soul to abandon its proper satisfaction in God to become engrossed in the here and now. For the soul to escape its earthly infatuation and come to desire the Fountain of Wisdom all external things—sense perception, and reasoning processes struggling for material truth—would have to be replaced by insight into the divine. Augustine's *Commentaries on Psalm xli* and his *Confessions* reveal his deep mystical yearnings; as the hart panted after the water of the brook, so his soul would pant after God. The soul could not rest till it rested in God. The stages of ascent were progressive. First one would seek knowledge and sight of God through his creatures, heavenly bodies, the human body, and then the soul. Then one must struggle to ascend higher by seeking a God more inward to oneself than one's most inward self, a God higher than the highest. Finally, one would arrive at the dwelling place of God himself where, as it were, a heavenly music of love ravished the aspirant with sheer inner delight.

It seems fair to remind ourselves that despite Christianity's effort to become rationally respectable, the early centuries of the Church were credulous ones even for the literati. Just as the pagans ascribed seemingly irrational impulses and experiences to the interference of gods so Christians continued to explain theirs as supernaturally induced by the divine or the demonic. Already Paul and Acts record that several kinds of charismatic gifts were vouchsafed Christians: prophesy, clairvoyance, speaking in tongues, interpretation of dreams, and the like. Justin and Ireaneus rejoiced that in their own second century prophetic gifts and glossolalia yet graced the Church. Even Cyprian, level-headed administrator of the third century, reported knowing several bishops who continued to recieve new revelations and of prophetesses who did marvelous deeds in stages of ecstasy. Gregory Thaumaturgus believed his *Exposition of the Faith* was a direct revelation. The most dramatic charismatic movement in the early Church, of course, was Montanism in its heyday about 200. Prophesy, asceticism, and dream interpretation, all were hallmarks of the movement well exemplified in Montanus' two ecstatic followers, the prophetesses Prisca and Miximilla. The group trusted in sudden outpourings of the Holy Spirit and expected the immediate establishment of the final Jerusalem in Phrygia. But Classical rational moderation was to have its way. Already Paul was disturbed by charismatic displays; if prophesy and glossolalia were unintelligible, how could they edify? Montanism—whether construed as a reaction against the rationalism of Gnosticism and therefore a veiled attack on the intrusion of Greek philosophy, or viewed as a protest against ecclesiastical institutionalism—was a conscious attempt to keep alive the primitive charismatic spirit already flagging in the Church. It is significant that the movement was disowned by orthodoxy and eventually smothered as a schism. Yet for a long time it inspired isolated followers creating an enraptured child here, a visionary prophetess there, and even one robust devotee who offered to create the New Jerusalem by herself and to add an earthquake or two if needed for dramatic effect.

Belief in dreams was universal; both Old and New Testaments honored them as divine visitations. Origen considered them a legitimate incentive for conversion; others credited them with causing important crises in the spiritual life of their hosts. Dreams often favored devotees watching and waiting in shrines of saints just as they did those of old who attended Asclepius. The tough–minded Cyprian and the learned Gregory of Nyssa both attested to the validity of dreams; the Emperor Theodosius consulted John the Monk because of his unusual gift of prophesy attained through dreams. Augustine, too, told of a monk adept in the same way. Synesius dreamt hoping for divine revelation and Cassian believed that in the stupor of sleep most secret meanings of Scripture could be revealed. Not much would be done in early Christian days to dispell such notions. Were dreams not to be considered manifestations of Grace?[39]

Fatalism and astrology, especially popular in the late Roman empire, held a great attraction for Christians. We shall see later that a concerted and vigorous learned effort on the part of church Fathers, such as Origen and Gregory of Nyssa, tried desperately to discredit such beliefs and practices as irrational, ridiculous and blasphemous.

Immoderate asceticism became almost theatrical among early desert hermits; they lived in boxes, or stood perpetually; they chained and flagellated themselves and often found imaginary beasts and demons to fight. Whatever their explanations, such antics would automatically be immoderate and therefore irrational to the Aristotelian mind. But again, it is significant that the Classical axiom of the mean triumphed in the

---

[39] One of the few indictments of the efficacy of dreams is made by Peter in *Clementine Homily* 17.14. He feels that "he who trusts in apparitions, visions, and dreams is insecure" because he does not know whom he is trusting. Instead of coming by divine grace a dream may be the work of an evil demon.

moderate monastic rules of Pachomius, Basil, and especially Benedict of Nursia.

Belief that miracles are possible is rational enough; gullibility in accepting them is another. Just as Cicero, a rational man if there ever was one, felt that divine theophanies and omens were incumbent upon the gods, so Augustine considered miracles necessary to help establish the authority of the Church, to confirm truth, and to confound heretics.[40] Whatever their justification, their presence is widely documented. Irenaeus reported all kinds, including healings and raisings of the dead. Origen rejoiced that Christians, unlike the Jews, were still able to prophesy and work miracles, some of which he apparently witnessed. Gregory Thaumaturgus, the Wonderworker, friend of Origen, attracted a wealth of legends including one crediting him with moving a mountain and drying up a swamp. Cyprian related how unworthy recipients of the Eucharist were punished by God immediately and publicly; one had her hands wither in the sight of all. Gregory of Nyssa, like many others, ascribed wondrous cures to the wood of the cross. The sober Ambrose recorded the popularity of miracles of Sts. Gervasius and Protasius once the location of their bodies was revealed to him in a dream. Augustine was impressed with a miracle of these saints he witnessed in Milan; he regretted that so few people knew of the seventy or so authenticated miracles which were worked over a two–year period at the African shrine of St. Stephen. Even more occurred, he reported, in the district of Calama. Why, he asked, did Africa have no shrines to 'ocal saints where miracles were performed? Sulpicius boasted that Martin of Tours worked great wonders not in private, as monks did, but in the midst of crowds even among quarrelsome clerics and jealous bishops; his power to perform these miracles, however, seems mysteriously to have waned when Martin himself became a bishop. Monks were legendary as prolific miracle–workers. One, the Egyptian monk Macarius, was exceptional. Sozomen, at the end of our period, duly noted that the power of sacred words still could cause such wonders as cleaning stone walls.

Yet credulity did not run unchecked. It is interesting, indeed, to hear from Augustine that miracles were being "authenticated" after investigation and that they were even published.[41] The practice may well have been more general than we know.

Chief among the seemingly irrational phenomena ascribed to demonic influence is, of course, possession by the devil. The impotence of logic to explain the reason for, and the antics of, the *energumen*, and the unpredictable effectiveness of liturgical exorcism proved to be something of an embarrassment to the rational Church. Consequently, as we

---

[40] Augustine, *Con. epist. Mani.* 1.4, *De util. cred.* 17.35, *Con. Faust.* 13.5 (*CSEL* 25:383).
[41] Augustine, *Civ. Dei.* 22.8.

shall see, later efforts succeeded to some extent in making even exorcism legally and institutionally respectable.

In summary: even in twilight zones rationality tried to shed light. Church institutionalism smothered the charismatic movement; canon law and monastic rule curbed the extravagance of asceticism; officialdom scrutinized and authenticated miracles; liturgy corralled even exorcism. That the triumph of reason was not complete is not surprising. If the cross once sharpened axes during the Diocletian persecution, the stars are still busy in this modern scientific era shaping the daily destiny of the credulous.

CHAPTER 4

THE LEGAL AND INSTITUTIONAL

THE CLASSICAL DEDICATION TO LEGALISM AND INSTITUTIONALISM

"The Law is Right Reason" . . . Cicero

Classical legalism and institutionalism is fundamentally Roman. Its impact on early Christianity, like many historical relationships, is circumstantially obvious but rarely explicitly acknowledged by contemporaries. Unlike the impact of Greek rationalism, which was openly praised or condemned by Fathers such as Clement of Alexandria or Tertullian, the subtle penetration of Classical legalism and institutionalism was unheralded precisely because it was so natural and pervasive. Besides, the familiar legalistic and institutionary aspects of the Classical world were reinforced for Christians by the covenantal structure of Judaism inherited by the infant Church through the Old Testament. Heralded or not, the impact of legalism is second only to that of rationalism among the most decisive Classical forces molding primitive Christianity.

The Judaic influence on Christianity's legal and institutional experience is, of course, congenital. That Yahweh laid down the law all Jews and Christians knew for sure; in principle it was detailed and peremptory as the revealed incontrovertible will of God even if it was observed differently by such as hellenized Jews—those, incidentally, most subject to Christian conversion—who did not trouble themselves greatly about the dietary rules. Institutionally, the concept of "church" must also be conceded as Jewish. Largely the work of Nehemiah and Ezra, the revived temple cultus offered daily worship in the name of the entire Jewish nation whose exclusive membership under the covenant was uniquely defined and restricted. Its high priest and supreme boule or Sanhedrin claimed a title to a legal divine indult, a Scriptural charter, to operate a temple state so nationalistically oriented that it experienced difficulty in sharing power with Rome. In turn, the development of the synagogue for Jews of the diaspora featured a learned churchly professional personnel together with a standardized liturgy, and provided ready-made fora for early Christian proselytizing and models for emerging Christian assemblies.

In short, any attempts to guide young gentile Christianity into something of a non-legal and non-institutional mystical anarchy would be doomed from the start. Its strong inheritance of Jewish legal-minded-ness was too readily reinforced by an engulfing Classical ethos which for over half a millennium had debated the priority of nature and state law, had cultivated sophisticated concepts of justice, and had experimented with almost every conceivable form of constitutional law.

From their beginnings, Greeks and Romans alike venerated an in-herited general law, *nomos* or *lex;* wide in content, it was a composite of religious taboos, ancient legal usages resting on custom, tradition, opin-ion, beliefs, and common-sense judgments which seemed best to identify behavior proper to living things. Hesiod attributed it to the wisdom of the son of Chronos; Plato and Aristotle later praised it as a dispensation of divine Reason.[1]

In the work-a-day world such an idealistic concept of law required more specific expression and implementation in state positive laws or *nomoi,* especially after the seventh century B.C. when trade, class strug-gle, and colonization began to introduce pressing complicated problems. At one time or another, celebrated lawgivers arose throughout Greece to promulgate civil and constitutional bodies of law: Zaleucus of Locri, "Lycurgus" of Sparta, Charondas of Catana whose code became some-thing of a model, Diocles of Syracuse, Draco and Solon of Athens. Of these, except for a few laws of Solon, only some sentences remain. In time factionalism arose contending the degree to which subsequent legislation, issued by local assemblies or councils, should be restricted by the ancient divine *nomos* or the formulations of particular historical lawgivers. The iconoclastic Epicurus, for instance, regarded the matter pragmatically by advocating that state legislation be grounded in the demands of worldly expediency or The Golden Rule. Sophists argued endlessly that nature's dispensations should take precedence over stat-utory law: *physis* as against *nomos.*[2] Plato feared that such expressions of advancing secularism would lead to a constant making and un-making of laws which would advance a pernicious relativism and obfuscate the more important inherited ethos of general righteousness safeguarded by the traditional sacred *nomos* of earlier days. In his mind, this basic, conservative, unwritten consensus alone could make citizens obedient to state laws. Like Solon two hundred and fifty years earlier, Plato and even Aristotle sustained the tradition that positive law must inculcate and preserve traditional virtues such as temperance, courage, and justice, divine *Dike* herself, in order to safeguard the status quo and protect the corporate polis as man's most valuable expression of his *raison d'être.*

In time Roman Stoics, as we saw, would champion a concept of law

---

[1] Plato, *Laws* 4.713, 12.957D derives nomos from nous. Aristotle *Pol.* 3.1287a4.
[2] Plato, *Laws* 10.908D.

based on human nature and applicable to all humankind.[3] In a way, Heraclitus had early anticipated such a concept by claiming that the eternal, immutable rational principle or Logos embedded in the universe was the foundation of all law. Plato, too, contributed something to the idea of universal law by asserting that Justice, like all virtues, was an Absolute, eternal, unchangeable, and universal. Alexander's conquest, however, with its expanded geographical horizons up to the Indus river made untenable older values centering narrowly around the inviolability of the parochial polis. How could old values stand in the face of strange people—reportedly even umbrella-footed ones—and in the face of new curious customs such as drinking date wine and leading fat children on leashes? The new world called for a fresh awareness of world-wide unity and for a wider natural law which could accommodate it. Although the views of early Stoics are little known, it is clear that men like Zeno and Chrysippus, in line with Heraclitus, spoke of the Logos as the common nature diffused throughout all things, including human beings. However, only when a combination of Platonic-Stoic views, emphasizing the universality of both Justice and of the Logos as Reason, were carried to Rome by such as Posidonius was the importance of natural law transferred more exclusively to men. Consequently, late Roman lawyers identified the *jus naturale* with that law obtaining in the pre-political state of man. This law was identical for the entire human race, identifiable by reason and virtually synonymous with it. What else but reason, the common ingredient of God and man, could better identify what humans universally understood as proper?

Characteristically, the Greek mind found it more interesting to discuss philosophical, educational, and moral aspects of law than to create a scientific, disciplined practice of jurisprudence. Greek court procedure, as we know it mainly from Athens, reveals no fetish for the professional. Often more unruly than orderly, court trials generally were expected to end in twenty-four hours, and Athenian juries, impaneled from the lower classes as something of a welfare project, were hopefully immunized from bribery by their huge size. Acceptable evidence included compurgation and melodramatic witnessing which often resorted to forensic tricks of logic and theatrical character portrayal.

Aristotle's *Politics,* indeed Greek history in general, shows that in the field of constitutional law Greeks experimented with all kinds of government: monarchy, aristocracy, tyranny, timocracy, and democracy. Even though their political experience was punctuated by a maze of revolutions and counter revolutions, they struggled to discover a rational form

---

[3] For a succinct article with bibliography, see "Stoic Concept of Natural Law" in *Great Events from History* 9 vols. ed. F. N. Magill (Englewood Cliffs: Salem, 1972), 1:388–392.

which would allay class struggle, provide stability, and advance virtue and the arts. Plato admired the educational system of the Spartan totalitarian, aristocratic system which inculcated respect for authority and values even if it produced little else than an arrested and stunted society. Aristotle's *Constitution of Athens* reveals the development of a saner system deserving the earlier eulogy of Pericles in his funeral oration. If Solon can be credited with establishing the first rational state, Cleisthenes a hundred years later provided the constitutional machinery to make it work by inventing virtual proportional representation of the citizenry in the *Boule,* a device which, by successfully minimizing class rivalry, provided stability through the ordeal of the Persian wars. Pericles some sixty years later reaped the honor of it all, unable himself to devise a constitution suitable for his own grandiose imperial ambitions. More of a dismal failure yet was Plato's attempt to establish a utopia in Syracuse along the lines of his *Republic.*

Since in early Rome, as in all primitive societies, religion and law were in a totalitarian way one and the same, it is appropriate to think in terms of "sins" against the dispensations of the gods *(fas)* as much as of crimes against public law *(jus). Fas,* much like Greek *nomos,* was made in heaven but in a Roman one less interested in the theoretical and philosophical than the ceremonial and regulatory. It seems important to emphasize here, in view of later Christian developments, that practice of religious law, like early civil law, demanded formal and punctilious performance in using the proper words and actions in all sacrifices, libations, and transactions. Pliny's *Natural History* declares it imperative to use the same correct ritual, the same proper fixed phrases *(certa verba),* the same scrupulous repetition of rites which had been found effective for eight hundred and thirty years. But neither Pliny nor any other respected Classical writer blasphemously implies that in some magical way correct procedure or extended repetition of liturgy forces a god to act or that repeated correction of ritualistic slips and errors, thought to dishonor the god, automatically assures success. The gods, by general consent, cannot be compelled; nor does any evidence exist revealing that gods bound themselves by a solemn oath to perform if there were no slip-up in the ritual.[4] They were expected merely to respond reasonably as responsible gods of Rome especially if matters were done properly according to ancestral custom, that of the "greater ones" *(mos maiorum),* preserved by the piety of the state priestcraft. Romans, like children,

---

[4] Pliny, *Nat. Hist.* 28.3–4. Plotinus, *Ennead* 2.9.14. See W. W. Fowler, *Religious Experience of the Roman People* (London: Macmillan, 1911), pp. 188–89. *Laws* 10.901D makes it quite clear where Plato stands. However, C. Bailey, *Phases in the Religion of Ancient Rome* (Berkeley: University of California Press, 1932), pp. 37–39, 73, records examples of coercing spirits in early Roman religion. Iamblicus might, in the last analysis, be the only exception believing magic can force divinity. See Dodds, *Irrational,* p. 287.

came to learn that certain time-tested pleasing liturgical formulas were more likely to nag their betters, including the gods, into compliance.

Although little is known about the functioning of early Roman law, interpretation and operation of *fas* in the two-hundred-and-fifty-year regal period of Rome (753–509) was most likely monopolized by patrician pontiffs who alone knew when and how to sacrifice and how to consult the auspices to determine what the will of the gods had in store for the community. At the same time, patricians applied the sanctions of *fas* to the *jus quiritium*, or law of citizens, as a matter of pragmatic piety, hoping to keep at a minimum public disabilities incurred by sacrilege or impiety involving violation of oaths and vows, disrespect for family and ancestral gods, breaches of hospitality and such like. Sanctity of the patrician family was protected by strict religious sanctions dealing with adultery, adoption, establishment of landmarks, and property contracts. Non-conformity meant outlawry. Private household enforcement was in the hands of heads of families who as fathers enjoyed absolute power *(patria potestas)* over their children, and as husbands complete control over their wives whom they held "in hand" *(in manu)*. Creditors enjoyed much the same absolute power over insolvent debtors.[5] What communal actions were necessary to execute the demands of *jus* were seen to by the patricians organized in groups or *curiae* composing an assembly of citizens *(comitia curiata)*. A select few, as members of the senate or consistory of the king, dealt with the immediate conduct of the city. Patrician control of the growing non-noble population was exercised through clientage, a sort of vassalage which attached plebeian families to patrician houses. Details of administration during the regal period are non-existent, but it is clear that *auctoritas* was based on ancestral custom, the *mos maiorum*, the custom of the greater ones, "greater" by virtue of time.

The rigid formalism of primitive Roman *fas* characterized *jus* or non-sacred law to such an extent that civil proceedings were oblivious of will or intent; an action correctly consummated literally, even if objectionable, wrong, or fraudulent, was a transaction settled. Procedure according to the letter of the law was always considered preferable to uncertainty. Such static formalism came natural to the Roman mind whose concept of anthropology tended to envision a human being not as a unique personality with singular potential but as a recurring representative of an unchanging type. Roman historians think the same way. Livy's characters are almost mannequins; one Appius Claudius or Cato is like every other one. Rome, like man himself, does not evolve or progress: Romulus founded all its institutions full blown; the only growth is

---

[5] The interpretation of the twelve tables allowing dismemberment of a debtor's body by his creditors has been the object of some study. See M. Radin, "The Early Roman Law of Execution against a Debtor," *American Journal of Philology* 43 (1922): 32–48.

quantitative. Was it not axiomatic that Rome would be eternal? Even Tacitus' perceptive historical works, by stressing the recurring interplay of individuals and temporary circumstances, emerges basically as a chain of biographies chary of deeper historical analysis and devoid of teleology. Change is suspect. Quite characteristically, Celsus chided Christians for their naive notion that something new could also be true; to him, as to Cicero, history was the arbiter of truth. Such reverence for the past was bound to make good lawyers of Romans.

While King Servius Tullius' constitution of the late regal period responded to the need for a more structured government in the face of social and military demands, there is little evidence of an accompanying effort to modernize the rigid formal character of civil law procedure. However, his constitution recognized plebeians or non-nobles as citizens entitled to voting privileges and military obligations according to wealth. By doing so, it outmoded the older noble term, *jus quiritium,* in favor of the expression *jus civile,* the law peculiar to Rome and all its citizens including plebeians. But the innovations were purely constitutional and quantitative, not civil or qualitative. That the traditional formalism of early Roman law continued on even into the early Republic, despite the pressures of new liberalizing forces and problems, is clear from the famous XII Tables of the mid-fifth century, the first code of laws in part extant. It abolished no older procedures based on absolute technical imperatives and its vaguely implied recognition of oral business transactions based on faith gives but scant evidence of a growing concern for intent.

In the last half of the third century B.C. imported Greek philosophical rationalism and analytical thought was at work stimulating Romans to interpret formal legal phraseology more liberally, to resort to the use of analogy and to recognize will and intent. Romans belatedly were coming to appreciate what Aristotle had noted earlier, that it was better not to ignore intent in favor of the letter of the law, that moral purpose was more important than the act.[6] At the same time, an indigenous Roman development began to encourage a resort to equity. This employment of common sense rather than stereotyped precedent found expression in a new branch of law, the *jus praetorium* or *jus honorarium,* that is, the law made by the office (honor) of the praetor or judicial officer. In 242 a new praetor *(praetor peregrinus)* was commissioned to handle suits between aliens and citizens of Rome; lacking precedents, he and his successors were forced to work out their own standards for judgments. At the

---

[6]There is no evidence that Aristotle's precocious concept of equity (*epieikeia* in *Rhet.* 1374b) had any effect on the ancient legal mind. Roman equity emerged more from Roman practical sense in the face of empire than from philosophical enlightenment Aristotelean or Stoic.

beginning of his year of office each foreign praetor issued a written edict stating the principles, generally based on simple fairness, which would dictate his legal decisions. Naturally, praetors sent to govern foreign provinces found it reasonable to follow the *praetor peregrinus* in this freer interpretation of law so that eventually another new corpus of law, the "law of the peoples" (*jus gentium*) emerged to be fully recognized by the imperial jurist, Gaius. These new departures in turn influenced the city praetors in their dealings with Roman citizens. The whole development was given legal recognition in 67 B.C. when every praetor was required to follow the principles of his own edict during his year of office. Straight-laced procedures, rigid terminology, irrational formalism had to yield. Another innovation recognized as early as 125 B.C. allowed litigants under praetorian supervision to draw up their own *formulae*, or instructions, to guide the judicial procedures for their cases. By 17 B.C. the formulary procedure became virtually compulsory.

Roman law had come a long way. By Cicero's time form had largely given way to content, phraseology to intent, and the abstract to the particular. He himself states that the ancient XII Tables which he studied as a young law student had been replaced for law students with readings of praetors' edicts. Taught by Plato and the Stoics, as well as by the cosmopolitanism of the empire, Cicero envisaged Justice as absolute, common to the cosmos, to the gods and to men, eternal and universal. Law was right Reason itself implanted in nature to command what ought to be done and what should be avoided. Since true law must reflect the rational nature of man it could not morally reject or restrict it.[7]

It is important to realize that during the early Christian era Roman law reached new heights of development. While the old *jus civile* of the Republic continued on mostly as criminal law, the *jus honorarium* stagnated because centralization of imperium under the Caesars brought a decline and virtual suspension of inventive authority exercised by independent magistrates. Instead, Roman Stoics talked more and more about natural law in relation to men. Concerned with *pietas* and *humanitas*, with the brotherhood of man under the fatherhood of god, and emphasizing innate rights independent of state imperium, natural law did much to humanize rights of fathers and husbands, and of masters over their slaves. Romans tended to blend this *jus naturale* with their *jus gentium* to represent the law of man in his pre-political state. At the same time, Roman law in general came to fuller maturity through the advance of legal professionalism, centralization, and standardization, movements heralding an age more devoted to digesting and organizing past achievement than to creating and improving procedures.

Professionalism entered law as never before. Since elective political

[7] Cicero, *De leg.* 1:6.18–7.23, *De re pub.* 3.22.

office declined under the Caesars, public-spirited men came to seek opportunity through the study of law. For a short time even professional law schools grew up and vied with each other; an eminent jurist, Gaius, conveniently compiled the *Institutes* as a popular primer for law students. Promising legal careers became more and more the road to success. Career jurisconsults were patented already by Augustus to submit answers to questions sent in by the empire's far-flung judges. Charged with giving concrete advice, these official jurists were naturally conservative rather than liberal, more interested in uniformity than novelty. Hadrian so skillfully used these professional jurisconsults in his privy council that he created what amounted to a supreme court. Moreover, imperial offices, prefectures especially, were more and more entrusted to legal experts such as Papinian, Paulus, and Ulpian who, along with Modestinus, flourished in the so-called classical age of Roman law under the Severi in the first half of the third century.

The demise of legislative assemblies, imperial domination of the Roman senate after Domitian, royal appointment of legal experts, and the abolition of praetorian courts under Septimius Severus progressively centralized legal initiative and execution under the Caesars and their appointees. Indeed, from the very outset of the Principate the emperors issued constitutions or orders having practically the force of law. Soon they were proclaiming laws more openly as edicts *(edicta)*, issuing rulings on existing law in the form of decrees *(decreta)*, and submitting clarifications *(rescripta)* on points of law sought from the chancellery. While such centralized imperial pronouncements became the most important source of law during early Christian centuries especially after Hadrian, after Diocletian they became the exclusive source of law since even the *responsa* of patented jurists had become a thing of the past. The new order came to be recognized frankly by Papinian: "The will of the emperor has the force of law."

Standardization inevitably followed. Already in the fourth century B.C. lawyers began to analyze the law scientifically, to catalog materials, and to establish principles by classifying cases under common denominators. Cicero was trained in such an atmosphere by the eminent Quintus Mucius Scaevola, himself the son of an equally illustrious jurist of the Republic. In the imperial period, however, codification went on apace. Hadrian ordered Salvius Julianus to collect as an *Edictum Perpetuum* all useful edicts of past praetors. Since jurisconsults had more and more cited imperial orders, these too became available as a collection of imperial constitutions by the time of Constantine. In the era of the Christian emperors, Valentinian III and Theodosius II issued the famous Law of Citation limiting the legal canon to the writings of Gaius, Papinian, Paulus, Ulpian, and Modestinus. In case of a tie citation, Papinian was to prevail. Eventually, all came together in the famous

Code of Justinian to live on as something of a model for Napoleon. While the Roman penchant for order, clarification, and practicality finally brought ancient law to its zenith, it unfortunately induced stagnation as well since the closed canon dictated that future decisions by jurists and emperors should be determined by authorities recruited from the dead.

Outside of standardizing the law, legal contributions by Christian emperors were not substantial although some new jurisdictional regulations were introduced and new matters made subject to legal cognizance. For instance, bishops by indult of Constantine were empowered to act as judges if both litigants in a case requested it; Augustan marriage legislation was repealed to accomodate virginity; edicts regulated church property, supervised episcopal handling of charity and guardianships, defined orthodoxy and disabilities for heretics, abolished crucifixion, penalized divorce and exposure of children and in general honored the humane spirit Stoicism had introduced into Roman law.[8]

If the impact of the Roman spirit of *fas* and *jus* on the early Church was indirect but momentous, the influence of Roman constitutional experience was decisive. Like Roman civil law, constitutional law went through an inventive period especially in Republican times, then settled down to a professionalized, centralized, and standardized system under the emperors.

From those mythical days when the wolf-suckled twins founded the Eternal City on the banks of the Tiber in 753 B.C. down through the centuries, Rome displayed an aptitude for civilizing and governing peoples unparalleled in the ancient world. Virgil proudly boasted that while other peoples did better molding brass and charting the heavens, Romans knew how to rule men by law. In 509 the Republic inherited a workable forty-year-old constitution from King Servius Tullius, quite similar to Solon's earlier one in Athens. Readily modernized by making all major offices elective rather than hereditary or appointed, the Republican constitution retained the assembly *(comitia centuriata)* arranged according to "centuries" as voting and military units, replaced the king with two yearly elected executive and military consuls, and arranged that the senate, no longer a royal consistory, should be recruited in the future from emeriti consuls. To be on the safe side with the gods and traditional

---

[8] An excellent idea of the extensive compass of imperial edicts dealing with religion under the early Christian emperors can be studied in the two volumes of Coleman-Norton, *State and Church*. Again it seems useful to remember that if these detailed, comprehensive, and sometimes draconian imperial laws seem to be introducing a new Christian governmental totalitarianism, the state is now recognizing, besides its own interests, the demands of a new coexisting sovereignty, the Church, which temporarily is shaping state policy since the third quarter of the fourth century. It is, rather, Julian who would reintroduce the old monist structure.

totalitarian concepts, the constitution retained the title *rex sacrorum* for a perfunctory king in charge of religious affairs. A corps of officials made up of aediles, censors, quaestors (basically financial officers), and praetors (primarily judicial officials), was adapted and expanded over the years to run the government and accomodate demands of the class struggle and expansion. Ideally the last two magistracies, the quaestorship and praetorship, led an aspirant to the consulship after designated time lapses, thus completing the "course of honors" *(cursus honorum)* which for the most part was monopolized by patricians. When plebeian clamors for more security and wider rights became chronic within a generation after the creation of the Republic, the patrician establishment displayed a clever inventiveness which did more to protect its class interests than to advance statecraft.[9] A sort of second-track administration was designed to quiet plebeians by creating plebeian officers or tribunes who originally enjoyed only negative limited veto powers, and by recognizing a second assembly *(comitia tributa)* representing regional units or "tribes" rather than levels of wealth. In this clumsy system both assemblies passed laws although the older *centuriata* retained the right to elect major officers.

Since the constitutional experience of Rome had a lasting impact on Church government it is well to recall at some length salient events in its development. Even after all offices were opened to plebeians by the Licinian-Sextian law of 367 patricians continued to monopolize them. Demagogues arising through the plebeian tribunate began to promise quick fixes to the many problems becoming chronic after the second Punic war c. 200 B.C. The more or less conscientious administration of the Republic before the Gracchi (c. 130) gave way to devastating sets of civil wars between uncontrollable revolutionaries such as Marius and Sulla (c. 80), then Pompey, Crassus, and Caesar (c. 50), and finally Antony, Lepidus, and Octavian. All ended in 31 B.C. with the triumph of Octavian over Antony and Cleopatra at the battle of Actium where

---

[9] Creation of plebeian tribunes with consular imperium is generally regarded as a response to heightened military demands. But several considerations make the establishment of the office appear more an episode in the class struggle between patricians and plebeians. The obvious complex awkwardness of a dual executive system suggests a compromise rather than constructive statesmanship. Furthermore, the years in which consular tribunes were chosen prior to 400 B.C. coincide with years of plebeian-patrician disturbances recorded by Livy in 444, 432, 421, and 410. The fact that Plebeian tribunes were not allowed to celebrate triumphs suggests class prejudice. Moreover, when the plebeian tribunate ceased in 367 no attempt was made to add new military officers to the returning two-consular arrangement. Besides, the demand that one consulship be reserved in the future for plebeians is further evidence of class rivalry. At any rate, the consular tribuneship, even though not permanent, was an important step in eventually breaking down the monopoly of patricians on offices controlling religion such as the colleges of pontiffs and augurs.

Republican forces collapsed. Cicero had labored in vain to preserve his cherished Republic which he idealized in his *Republic* and *Laws* as the ideal Classical polity based on natural law, universal Reason, and Justice. Christians, to the consternation of Celsus, would claim the collapse was providential: had not the Prince of Peace arranged it so that he could be born in an era of peace?

During 29–28 Octavian assumed quasi-dictatorial powers while deliberating how he might "restore liberty" to the Roman people. In January 27 B.C. he announced an ingenious compromise which retained the old republican machinery disguised under an enlightened despotism. Profiting from the lessons taught by Pompey and Caesar how republican offices and extraordinary commands could be centralized in one man, Octavian assumed at one time or another most of the old republican titles of consul, tribune, and Pontifex Maximus. At the same time he created new executive agencies of his own. While pro-consular *imperium* allowed him to control all the provinces of the empire, he wisely allowed traditional "republican" senatorial governors to exploit a few old safely Romanized areas where dangerous armies could not be justified. Interprovincial services were centered in new imperial procuratorships. The Roman assemblies still met to pass laws and elect officials but only after perfunctory face-saving deliberation respectful of imperial pressure. The senate, expediently treated with honor for the time being, was awed by its new superior who chose to call himself "chief of the senate," *princeps senatus*. Die-hard republicans were puzzled by this strange hybrid; was it a temporary dispensation to hold the Republic in escrow until it could recoup its strength? Or was it a prelude to monarchy? When Tiberius was handed the purple by family arrangement they had their answer. Many, like Tacitus, complained about the subterfuge for years.

Since no effective power base or bodies existed to check the inevitable centralization of authority under the Caesars, the government was honed into a centralized absolutism. The law and its lawyers fell before it. As we saw, Octavian immediately began to issue orders; more and more *rescripta* and *edicta* emanated from imperial palaces arising on the Palatine. Patented jurists decided legal questions in the emperor's name, recorded imperial constitutions, built codifications under royal direction. With the ancient republican aristocracy decimated by the civil wars, the old order provided no entrenched hostile bureaucracy, no conciliar machinery able to check the royal advance. What parliamentary councils the emperors erected could do little more than thank imperial Roman governors for their administration, tattle-tale to the emperor, and present petitions. Tiberius without ado cancelled out the Roman assemblies; the senate, temporarily used by Tiberius to direct election of magistrates, watched its decline with acquiescence. If Vespasian courteously consulted

it, Domitian soon snubbed and degraded it. Cowed, it took the hereditary kingship so for granted that it mounted no serious effort to seize
power after the assassinations of Caligula and Domitian. While the
Antonines of the second century A.D. enlisted the senate's moral prestige to enhance their autocracy, its few remaining rights, the election of
some magistrates and the operation of some allotted provinces were
curtailed and finally terminated by the Severi. Under Diocletian the old
senate became merely the local council of the city of Rome. The new
senate established at Constantinople by Constantine was, like his new
capital, a creation of the emperor from the start. Its members did not
need ask who their master was. Provincial councils originally instituted
by Octavian to supervise the imperial cult had little prospect for advancement under Christian emperors; they had to remain content to
inform and advise but never rule.

Since the old patrician families were virtually depleted by the time of
Vespasian—characteristically the first non-Roman, non-patrician emperor—he and his successors had the opportunity to strengthen their
support by ennobling new families recruited from the wealthy equestrian order which were anxious to oblige as parvenus without cohesion
or tradition. The few remaining old noble families often found themselves passed over by emperors who preferred to have grateful equestrians or even freedmen in their bureaucracies. Finally no independent
corporate "church" was at hand to gainsay the emperor in the totalitarian
system. Far from it. Since 12 A.D. had he not been Pontifex Maximus
and even a receptacle of the goddess Roma herself?

Lest the new order perpetuate the city-state mentality of the Republic whose course of honors provided more a political playground for
the aristocracy than a professional civil service, the emperors introduced
an air of competency into their world-wide government by establishing
new bureaucracies staffed with paid civil servants in graduated programs.[10] While such an innovation helped solidify the power of the
emperors, it should not be overlooked as a rationalization of the administration to temper the dangers of kinright rule evinced in Caligula,
Nero, and Domitian. Octavian, to enlist the support of the moneyed-
class, set up a two-track imperial administrative system featuring new
prefectures to supplement provincial governorships inherited from the
Republic. Generally dealing with services and monopolized by equestrians, such prefectures supervised the vital grain supply and commanded the praetorian guard, the personal shock troops of the
emperor. Tiberius, contrary to republican practice, retained his provin-

---

[10] For the social, economic, and administrative history of the late Roman empire see A.
H. M. Jones, *The Later Roman Empire 284–602*, 2 vols. (Norman: University of Oklahoma
Press, 1964), 1:321–766 esp. On councils, 1:762–766 and 2:1316 n. 120.

cial governors in office as career men as long as they were effective. Christians well remembered one such: Pontius Pilate who probably is the most daily-mentioned Roman of them all.[11] Claudius upset tradition by using even freedmen to staff his new departments of government which took care of imperial correspondence, the treasury, judicial correspondence, petitions and such.

Second and third century emperors continued to run a tight ship. Trajan employed imperial executives, curators or legates, independent of the senate, to supervise towns and combinations of provinces. One such was the enlightened Pliny known only too well to some Christians of Bithynia.[12] Hadrian gave his consistory, liberally composed of professional patented jurists, virtual constitutional status. The fiscus became so professionalized that it was possible to secure refunds of overpaid taxes.[13] Diocletian's reorganization of the administrative districts of the empire opened additional careers for thirteen imperial vicars as heads of his new dioceses and for additional governors to staff his one hundred and one provinces. By the time of Constantine every official was appointed at the emperor's pleasure so that artificial class distinctions became bewildering in the administrative maze. We have already seen that all through the era of the Christian emperors some thirteen thousand major military and civil officers were appointed by suffragium, by recommendation of the emperor's cronies, often eunuchs.

Unfortunately, the emperors had difficulty arranging their own succession. Kinright had produced under the Julio-Claudian and Flavian dynasties rulers of more than dubious excellence. Yet adoption, employed by the Antonines, proved unable to permanently dislodge the claims of inheritance. Naked military force, in turn, served to induce civil strife so that between 68–69 four candidates were backed by their legions as imperial contestants. Again between 193–197 four more aspirants fought it out bringing on the military monarchy of the Severi between 193–235. Between 235–285 so great was military anarchy under the "barrack emperors" that some sixty pretenders claimed the throne beginning with Maximinus, a giant Thracian peasant and common soldier who was said to seek distinction by consuming eight gallons of wine

---

[11] The Nicene creed recited over and over daily throughout Christendom significantly has Jesus crucified *sub Puntio Pilato*. A work, *The Acts of Pilate* is mentioned by Justin (*Apol.* 1.35.48); such fictitious accounts of Jesus' trial before Pilate were used by the emperor Maximinus to compromise Christianity. In the present form *The Acts of Pilate* are probably of fourth-century provenance.

[12] Pliny, *Epis.* 96 and 97.

[13] Especially Trajan expressed concern that abuses of the fiscus be curtailed to show that he followed "a principle of fairness" during his reign. See J. Biegelsen, *Workings of the Fiscus in the Second and Third Centuries* (M. A. Thesis, St. Louis: Washington University, 1942), esp. chap. 6, pp. 64–84.

and forty pounds of meat a day and by breaking horses' legs. The need for some reorganization, reform, and standardized process for choosing emperors was obvious. Fortunately Diocletian between 285–305 proved able to shore up the government with needed military reforms to thwart invasion, with an absolute control of economics to balance the budget, and with an orderly harassment of Christian dissenters to curtail internal sabotage. He so successfully organized imperial succession procedures and rebuilt the provincial administrative divisions of the empire that Rome was given a new lease on life even beyond its so-called fall in 476. Of immense significance would be his division of the empire into two great administrative districts each under an Augustus: an eastern section with its capital at Nicomedia in Asia Minor, a western division with its capital at Milan. Each Augustus in turn chose an understudy, a Caesar, who was scheduled to succeed his Augustus after twenty years and perpetuate the system by himself choosing a new Caesar. One, Constantine, would be so important to Christians that Eusebius put him on a line with Abraham and Christ. He was, indeed, the inheritor of a long distinguished legal tradition, civil and constitutional, which would do much to mould the infant Church.

THE CHRISTIAN RESPONSE TO CLASSICAL LEGALISM AND INSTITUTIONALISM

"Christianity is the New Law" . . . Justin

The complex influences impelling Christianity to become a legalized and institutionalized movement proved decisive in church history. Yet Christianity's immediate background seemed to militate against such a development. Admittedly, Jesus enjoined his disciples to bind and loose but he drew up no formal instructions how to do it. Moreover, in the Beatitudes he made it clear that righteousness derived more from pious dispositions of the heart than from obedience to rules. Since the spirit vivified and the letter killed, the Pharisees were declared spiritually dead in spite of their laws. Then, too, Jesus' apostles were simple followers rather than officers and the groups Jesus spoke to were motley crowds rather than organized societies. If he entrusted his assembly or Church to Peter he did not specifically order him to appoint successors.

In trying to assess the influences propelling Christianity in the direction of the legal and institutional, it might prove useful to distinguish a period before 150 A.D. and one after that date. In the earlier period paramount Jewish influences naturally would instill the idea that the "New Jerusalem" should be a legal and institutionalized establishment. After 150 Classical influences worked more to reinforce and implement the consensus.

Classical influences certainly would not be decisive in the period before 150. Gentile converts raised in a fluid polytheistic background would find a concept of religion as law strange because it presupposed the existence of a religious orthodoxy and authority unknown to them. Who among them had heard of canons, creeds, or church? For centuries *fas* had been dissolving into *jus*. The official priesthoods of Rome were far away and were more political sinecures than oracles of religious authority; all could see that priestly duties in local temples were more custodial than juridic. Even the mystery cult in a polytheistic setting could make no rational claim to binding truth resting on a revealed *auctoritas* and therefore scarcely could propagate its beliefs as a true covenantal arrangement or consider itself, however well organized under *archgalli*, anything but one optional group among many.

Clearly any early impetus in Christianity toward the legal and institutional would come largely from the Jewish background. Admittedly, Paul promulgated an antipathy to religious law in his letters and addresses, declaring that such law was not only irrelevant to justification but that it actually convicted one of sin. Yet few believed him; the influential gentile churches of Christendom were not to be his. Once Jewish writings were accepted as indispensable to Christianity—already Clement of Rome cited them as authoritative—the legal and institutional seemed equally indispensable. In dealing with the disciplinary problems of the Corinthian church, Clement of Rome repeatedly called attention to the hierarchical clerical order honored in the Old Testament, an order which he assumed the apostles rightly imitated and prescribed. Soon Justin was to ask: is not Christianity the new and eternal law based on the transitory old one? Marcion found himself excommunicated in 144 for expounding a Christian theology which would make the Gospel one of love to the total exclusion of law.

Yet it is important to realize that Jewish religious influences were not necessarily irresistible, for even in Paul's time Judaism was not the legal monolith that is often assumed. In practice a clear and coherent conception of Jewish orthodoxy scarcely emerged prior to A.D. 100 even in respect to the Torah; both the Mishnah, as an influential collection of Jewish oral law, as well as the Talmud largely belong to an age after Christians and Jews had parted company. Even Jewish temple-state institutionalism received a devastating blow with the destruction of Jerusalem in A.D. 70. Nonetheless, even if both Jews and Christians were not totally certain what the Jewish law was and what Jewish institutionalism should be, it was clear enough that Yahweh was a legal-minded God. And it appeared reasonable enough for early Christians to assume that a legalistic revelation by a monotheistic deity demanded recognition of a new kind of objectivity standing in need of some official support so that contradiction could not flourish to impune divine Reason and sincerity. And would not the word uttered by a sole God constitute an unimpeachable inescapable basis for *auctoritas*? Was not God's covenant a legal binding? Had God not dictated historically even the constitutional dispensations his people were to follow from the early days of the monarchy, through the high-priest government of the Maccabean period, even to the late government of the Sanhedrin which operated his temple state? Was not even its destruction possibly providential in opening a way for a new religious institutional construction?

In addition to the Jewish legal and institutional tradition so familiar to the early Fathers, Christianity had its own peculiar incentives to transform itself into a closer knit legal organ. The tendency is already evident in such later "New Testament" books such as Ephesians, Titus, and Timothy. The delayed Parousia condemned the Church not only to perpetuate itself but also to learn how to defend itself against assailing dissenters. If beliefs were to be important in opening an unerring path to salvation, it was logical that they would have to be defined and emphasized; ethics would need to be clarified and possibly legislated, and liturgy formalized and standardized. Then, too, the specter of persecution, begun already in the mid-sixties when Christians were yet a tiny minority, introduced mutual troubles and threats which fostered a need for cohesion and determination if Christianity's esoteric saving message was to survive. Already I Peter had to galvanize the courage of the brethren of Asia Minor who were facing persecution; soon thereafter Clement of Rome, referring probably to the Neronian and some "Domitian" harassment, told his Corinthian readers "we are all in the arena." On his way to martyrdom Ignatius of Antioch wrote letters to the churches of Asia Minor urging cohesiveness and stalwartness under their bishops in the face of persecution. Moreover, the distribution of charity, so basic to the Master's teaching, required some evaluation of "orthodoxy," however simple, and some organization. The establishment of the diaconate seems directly related to the issue. Some modern authors have cited the need to keep the Eucharist undesecrated as the major incentive for developing a responsible administration. Protection of property, especially cemeteries, became urgent enough in Rome to require supervision by Callistus before 200. The Fathers, as we saw, constantly credit heresy with forcing creeds, canons of scripture, and church discipline. While something new and irrational to a polytheist, orthodoxy became a logical and important issue once a gentile subscribed to the revelation of a monotheistic God whose word had to be properly understood and protected from adulteration if it would be of any practical value as a way to salvation.

After 150 the all pervading Roman penchant for law and order became crucial in directing church development. Law, as right Reason long identified with deity, had to be associated with the true God now that he had identified himself. Never burdened in a polytheistic system with a religious law officially controlling faith, ethics, and liturgy to such an extent that it involved one in "sin," the gentile convert inherited no Pauline disillusionment with the merits of religious legalism. In fact, a pagan proud of Rome's legalistic and institutional experience found it difficult to understand how any movement could prosper without definition and discipline. It is significant that, along with the "Old Testament," Clement of Rome cited the discipline of the Roman army as something Corinthian Christians should emulate. Even apologists like Tertullian, confessors, and martyrs do not berate in principle the very Roman law that persecuted them. Rather they assign their misfortunes to a misapplication of Roman law sometimes blamed on mischievous daimons or angry Jews who riled up the Roman legal machinery against them. Even Jesus was declared put to death "under" Pontius Pilate not "by" him. Apparently Christians understood they were being treated, however unfairly, in a legal manner normally enlightened both in principle and procedure, as revealed in the famous letter of Trajan and the transcripts of the trial of the Scillitan martyrs in Africa.

Of course it is not new to propose that the gentile Christian's acquaintance with local Roman legal and institutional bodies found expression in the organization and operation of the Christian Church. Among familiar societies, for example, were *collegia* founded already in republican times as products of the Roman legal genius which discovered the corporation. These local societies, regulated by the central Roman government, originally were composed of artisans who united to arrange, through a corporate effort, for religious rites and for burial costs, health insurance, and social entertainment for their members. As corporations licensed under state charter by Octavian, they held their own communal property—generally their guild hall and burial depositories—charged fees and dues for their own treasury, and operated under their own officers. In the second century A.D. they included trade associations for merchants and shippers and came, in fact, to embrace all kinds of vocational, professional, religious, funereal, and social groups. Always under supervision as possibly subversive, they were already disbanded for a time by Julius Caesar; the emperors restricted their meetings and activities quite closely. Some scholars contend, more with imagination than evidence, that early Christian churches actually incorporated as *collegia* to be able to hold property especially their buildings and cemeteries.[14]

Considering, then, the Jewish background, peculiar Christian needs, and the traditional Classical respect for the legal and institutional, Chris-

---

[14] W. M. Ramsay, *The Church in the Roman Empire* (London: Hodder & Stoughton, 1907), pp. 430–31.

tianity could scarcely long remain a mystical body of Christ advocating a Pauline society honoring only an unwritten natural law and the promptings of grace.

In the prevailing legalistic atmosphere Paul's teaching on law became an early casualty. It was difficult for the Classical mind to understand that faith, as normally understood, could make formal obedience to law obsolete as a way of justification, or to believe that law itself was a tyrant convicting man rather than guiding or even rewarding him.[15] Consequently, it is not surprising that some of the evangelized mistakenly judged Paul something of a libertine or that later Gnostic antinomians such as the Cainites and Carpocratians should be declared anathema. Early Christian patristic literature shows that no writer promulgated Paul's anti-legal theme except Marcion the heretic. Even the Epistle to the Hebrews interprets the Gospel as a new covenant of both law and grace. Everywhere law is extolled.[16] Matthew sets forth law as an absolute to be observed in its intention and its letter. Clement of Rome assumed that fulfillment of God's commands was basic; the *Didache*, Theophilus, Irenaeus, Clement of Alexandria, and even Origen conceived of Christ as a lawgiver who came to establish a new law, not to abrogate rules and regulations. Even if Origen looked forward, in a Pauline utopian way, to the distant future when the Gospel's salutary precepts would so transform men as to make law superfluous he cer-

---

[15] Paul's views on law and works are largely ineffective in the development of theology before the third quarter of the fourth century. Tabulations constructed by J. B. Lightfoot, *The Apostolic Fathers* (London: Macmillan, 1891) and by a committee of the Oxford society of historical theology in *The New Testament in the Apostolic Fathers* (Oxford, Clarendon Press, 1905) reveal the paucity of Pauline citations in the early Church. Polycarp, who is preeminent in quoting Paul, did so only nine times, thirteen at most, while citing Old Testament passages two hundred eighty-five times and the gospels sixty-five. In fact, Polycarp's statement (*Phil.* 3.2) "neither I nor anyone else like me can follow the wisdom of the blessed and Glorious Paul" records one of the very few times the Apostle is mentioned by name in the apostolic fathers. Old works like A. C. McGiffert, *A History of Christianity in the Apostolic Age* (New York: Scribner, 1901), pp. 443–51, and R. Seeberg, *History of Doctrine in the Ancient Church*, 2 vols., trans. C. Hay (Philadelphia: Lutheran Publishing House, 1905), pp. 79–80, together with G. P. Fisher, *The History of Doctrines* (New York: Scribner, 1901), pp. 42–44, recognize Paul's limitations albeit reluctantly. Fisher, for instance, merely states that in the apostolic fathers generally a strain of thought prevailed which may be styled legalism and that Pauline justification is seldom brought out in deference to a view of salvation through works of obedience. It is interesting that J. Pelikan, *Development of Christian Doctrine* (New Haven: Yale University Press, 1969) mentions Christianity as the New Law (1:17–18; 38–39) but does not elaborate on the Pauline ramifications.

[16] One exception would be Polycarp who quotes with approval Ephesians 2:8. Early citations impinging on Paul's view of law would include among others: Barnabas, *Epis.* 19.10; the *Didache* 2; Clement of Rome, *Epis.* 50.5; Hermas, *The Shepherd* parable 1.1, 5.3, 5.6; Justin, *Trypho* 11.18.45.95, *Apol.* 14; Irenaeus, *Adv. haer.* 4.14,1, 4.16,4; Tertullian, *De monag.* 7.8; Clement, *Strom.* 1.5, 1.27, *Paid.* 3.12, *Clementine Hom.* 3.3; Origen, *De prin.* 4.1, *C.C.* 3.7; Cyprian, *Epis.* 6.2.

tainly did not consider it a negative, almost sinister, device. Tertullian, of course, knew no way of attaining salvation other than through obedience to law; he envisaged the relationship between God and man as one in which Christ acted as man's lawyer and advocate before a stern God who zealously guarded his rights and dues. Striving mightily to carry the legal perspective into all his theology he provided Christianity with a workable legal terminology so it could function properly. Tertullian would have agreed with Basil's endorsement of civil court procedures as a proper precedent to determine dogma by using witnesses where scriptural documentary evidence was lacking.

One view accompanying Paul's concept of law, that of generic sin, was largely lost sight of until Augustine emphasized it in connection with his interpretation of Original Sin. Already early Christian writers, beginning with the author of the *Didache* and Justin, do not emphasize sin in Pauline fashion as a general indwelling sinfulness, a qualitative infection, a proclivity, a predisposition to evil which was revealed by law; rather sin became more a quantitative evil made up of single acts, sins, personal transgressions which, like individual crimes in civil law, could be atoned for and blotted out. In like manner, Christian faith did not remain a mystical Pauline receptivity to an indwelling of Christ; it became instead a simple trust, a practical motive to endure, an incentive to obey the law, to do what God had commanded in order to attain salvation. Paul's mystical concept of the Church did not dominate except as a metaphor nor did his weak legal and institutional views of sacramentalism and sacerdotalism prevail.[17] Even Augustine, virtually the first Father to take Paul seriously about the priority of faith and election over obedience to law, reinforced the Apostle's doctrine of free grace with a legalistic sacramental ecclesiastical system.

Career ecclesiastics, often theologians and administrators at the same time, were greatly responsible for injecting the Roman legal outlook into the Church's mentality. By 200 it appears that an appreciable number of clerics versed in Roman law were at hand to carry their expertise into ecclesiastical circles. Although the evidence seems to show that only a relatively few bishops came from the senatorial class—Ambrose was one such, the son of a praetorian prefect and provincial governor—lawyers became so common in clerical ranks that even some of their names have been preserved. An early representative, of course, is Tertullian, priest of Carthage in the late second century. During the third century the number of lawyers drawn into orders must have grown

---

[17] None of Paul's churches played a major role in ecclesiastical history. Thessalonica became important only as a papal vicarate; Antioch was considered Petrine and Ephesus Johannite. Most great gentile churches such as Alexandria never saw Paul and no effort was made to mount a Pauline primacy in the Church.

considerably so that Constantine felt safe early in the next century to give bishops judicial power to adjudicate disputes between consenting Christian litigants. Shortly thereafter, the Council of Sardica actually laid down rules for the acceptance of lawyers into episcopal ranks by requiring them before consecration to spend specific periods of probation as readers, deacons, and priests in the developing ecclesiastical *cursus honorum.* Pope Innocent in the early fifth century had to ban bishops who continued to conduct legal actions after their installation. Apparently the legal profession became the avenue to success as much in the Church as in the imperial bureaucracy. Clerics so trained readily envisaged Christianity and the Church as a divine legal dispensation responsible before a heavenly bar where Christ, as judge, upheld the new law of the Gospels being codified on earth into a closed canon of Scripture and more and more implemented by conciliar rules and papal decretals. Lying at the heart of the whole development was the Church's anxiety to attach a legalistic efficacy to its major liturgical functions. To do so it adopted an ingenious juridical synthesis employing the stereotyped formalism characteristic of early Roman sacred and civil law, and the covenantal principle of the Old Testament.

A formal definition of "sacrament" had to wait for the Donatist controversy to stir the interest and analytical talents of men like Optatus and of especially Augustine who began to speak much about sacramentalism in his letters and commentaries on psalms.[18] The term "sacrament," however, appears already before Tertullian to denote a liturgical mystery of the Church, a phenomenon in which what was seen was other than what was understood. The hidden action of certain of these mysteries, especially Baptism, the Eucharist, and Ordination were declared automatic and efficacious by some virtue of their formulas which employed "correct" words and actions as an outward sign attesting to an inner accomplishment. The core liturgy of a sacrament was often embellished with inspiring background typological references to past events of the Old or New Testament; Baptism, for instance, recalled to mind the passage through the Red Sea or the washing in the Jordan, appropriate references suggestive of deliverances from an evil or inadequate condition to a virtuous one. But, significantly, as formalism grew after the days of Acts and the *Didache,* efficacy was not posited in these varying sacred typological citations but in a set core of pithy standardized phrases and actions which resembled the *certa verba* and *actiones* so familiar in the formulas of early Roman legal procedures. Thus Basil, Gregory of Nyssa, and Optatus, among others, insisted that the trin-

---

[18]Optatus, *De schis. Donat.* 5.1–8; Augustine, *Epis.* 138.7, in *Psalm* 74.1, *Hom 3 in Epis.Joan.* 12 (see *Nicene and Post-Nicene Fathers* 7:480, n.11), *Tract. in Joan.* 26.11.

itarian formula exclusively must be used in Baptism; Basil especially contended that grace hardly could be expected if the Holy Spirit, the dispenser of grace, was left out of the action. The Eucharistic formula became surprisingly stylized as early liturgies attest. Cyril, however, still felt obliged in his day to warn that no one must tamper with the Eucharist by omitting the wine.

Yet, while approving strict liturgical formulas, the fathers from Justin on declare that no magical ingrained efficacy should be imputed to the words or actions themselves. Assertions made to claim the contrary must exploit patristic statements pulled out of context—such as the casual references of Cyril of Alexandria and Gregory of Nyssa to imitation as efficacious—or single out rare instances such as Origen's unique fascination with the power of words correctly spoken especially in relation to exorcism.

The Christian sacramental system, then, would go beyond the practice of early Roman religious and civil law which posited an ingrained efficacy in the fixed phrase, the correct action, approved by ancestral usage, by the *mos maiorum*, the custom of "the greater ones." The Christian ritualistic formula drew on a more binding guarantee, a non-magical divine, legalistic covenant, a contract as it were, which Jesus stated for all to see in a kind of revelationary document which only Jews could understand. How could an omnipotent God not assure efficaciousness to the very liturgies he commanded his followers to perform? Did Jesus not order them to baptize and to celebrate the Eucharist in his memory? God has delivered to us, says Justin, what was enjoined in the celebration of the Eucharist; Basil speaks of the "covenant" of Baptism. Clement of Alexandria rejoices that the Logos, as a high priest, clearly invited men, indeed commanded them, to share his mysteries. Gregory of Nyssa reminds his readers that God promised to be with his followers when they called upon him. If he operates in the self-effective power of procreation, in the development of the embryo or in the functioning of the universe when he is not invoked, how much more would he respond and endow acts with power when he is called upon by agreement? The peripheral citations of various appropriate miracles which accompanied sacramental formulas were used to remind the faithful that God has not only promised to respond but had the power to do so. Tertullian, Cyril of Jerusalem, and Gregory of Nyssa added their assurances as well. Only God was capable of sanctifying baptismal waters to endow them with a cleansing grace, or of imparting a quickening force or efficacious virtue to the oil of exorcism. Cyril pointedly advised one to pay no attention to the mere nature of the baptismal waters since salvation came through the operation of the Holy Spirit.

The very choice of the word *sacramentum* is itself significant, pointing up the fact that the contractual nature of certain liturgical functions was well understood. The term appears before 200 and became widely adopted thereafter to replace the word *mysterium*. Literally it signifies a deposit of a sum of money as a bond in civil suits, an oath guaranteeing a mutual understanding, hence a military oath. Appropriately in the Christian context it entails an understanding or agreement obligating God as a free covenanting party to guarantee the efficacy of human actions by endowing human words or substances, such as water, wine, and oil, with a grace or virtue foreign to their natures.

This legalistic guarantee of sacramental efficacy constitutes the decisive difference between Christian liturgies and those of mystery cults which operated, as far as evidence goes, without benefit of a covenantal arrangement between gods and men decreed in a revelation. Rather, in view of the popularity of astrology and the prevalence of animism, it seems safe to infer that mystery cult devotees assumed that liturgies released power through cosmic sympathies triggered by imitative magic while they vicariously relived some drama in a deity's life.[19] It is very interesting in this connection to note that while the Christian offering of bread and wine is often understood, as in the anaphora of Serapion, to be a repetition of Christ's living sacrifice, no Christian liturgy follows a sequence which attempts to identify scenes in the passion, death, and resurrection of Christ. If the ordinary worshipper did not distinguish the covenantal arrangement from magic, church thinkers did. Justin Martyr already understood the difference: were not the wicked devils vainly causing Mithraic worship to imitate the Christian Eucharist? They should have known their incantations were only forgeries since Christian power to work mysteries came from above. Gregory of Nyssa, too, clearly understood the magical distortions to which Christian formulas might be subjected when he complained that some worshippers remained doubtful because they regarded only the outward and visible sign, as if that which was operated corporeally occurred not without the fulfillment of God's promises. This contractural legalistic view endowed the sacraments with an ex opere operato efficacy, with a capability to release an instantaneous power through divinely guaranteed formulas which often wrought a permanent result and acted heedless of the character of the minister or, in some cases, even the intent of the recipient.

The question arose seriously in the case of Baptism whether the minister's character affected the validity of the sacrament. Some synods

---

[19] S. Angus, *The Mystery Religions and Christianity* (New York: Scribner, 1928), p. 249 calls the alliance between mystery cults and magic, "the bastard sister of religion," a dangerous ally. A. D. Nock, *Early Gentile Christianity* (New York, Harper & Row, 1964), pp. 132–33 notes the different vocabulary used by the pagan mysteries and Christian liturgy. Interestingly, Cyril of Jerusalem (*Cat.* 3.3) seems to grant a defiling efficacy to invocations made in the name of pagan idols over heathen sacrifices.

in Asia Minor and the great Cyprian of Carthage clearly advocated rebaptism of those washed by heretics. How, Cyprian asked, could such persons impart the Holy Spirit if they themselves were not receptacles of the Spirit? But such views were not to prevail over those advocated by Pope Stephen of Rome in his dispute with the worthy African prelate over the Donatist controversy.[20] Were not the sentences of a corrupt judge legal? Was a law valid only when its advocates were virtuous? The Council of Arles in 314, too, pronounced Baptism by heretics binding as well as ordination by traditores who in time of persecution had shamefully surrendered the sacred books. The verdict was virtually unanimous in both West and East. Just as Ambrose in Milan urged one not to consider the person of the minister, so Gregory of Nazianzus cautioned one not to ask for credentials of the baptizer. He and Cyril of Jerusalem both maintained that the baptismal candidate was stamped with an eternal seal, a witness as it were to a legal action and that this mark was imprinted regardless of the moral character of the minister. Baptizers, Gregory added, might use different meal ring mountings holding the seal but the seal imparted was the same. Augustine's sacramental mentality led him to join with the general consensus that Baptism by schismatics was indeed legally binding even if it was not fruitful; it was valid but profitless.[21]

Some aspects of Christian sacramentalism dutifully reflected the assumption in early Roman religious and civil law that the question of intent was overpowered by the efficacy of a rote recitation of the *certa verba*. Frequently the divinely guaranteed efficacy of a sacramental performance disregarded, or even overruled, the intent of the recipient. As reported by Sozomen, Alexander, Bishop of Alexandria, held after due reflection that rebaptism was unnecessary for boys who had administered baptismal rites to each other in play. In their simplicity, Alexander asked, had they not been judged worthy of divine grace? Pachomius, a monk of Serapis, obviously accepted his forced Christian baptism as valid. Cyril of Jerusalem, too, thought that Baptism was valid without the proper intent on the baptized's part. Had not Simon Magus, he argued, come to the laver without his mind properly on the matter? Nevertheless, baptized he was even if he was not enlightened. Ambrose would have disagreed; while holding the minister's character irrelevant,

---

[20] Cyprian's view of the subjectivity of sacramental operations (*Epis.* 69.3, 71.1, 72.12) seems almost unique in the African church. Augustine later will completely endorse the legalistic view in *Epis.* 89.5, *De bapt.* 4.17–24, 3.4–6, *Ser.* 49.8, *Tract. in Joan.* 12.4. No doubt, Stephen's position that a sacrament can be valid outside the Church greatly encouraged the concept of ex opere operato sacramental efficacy.

[21] For Augustine's distinction between validity and salubriousness of schismatic Baptism, see *Bapt. con. Donat.* 1.2 also 3.10–13, 7.53–102, 5.33, *Con. epis. Petil.* 3.40. Augustine's distinction is shared by Cyril of Jerusalem (*Procat.* 2).

he believed nonetheless that a wrong faith invalidated a sacrament. Augustine, though, considered the question of intent in Baptism so worthy of serious investigation that he hoped the matter would somehow be settled by future theologians. As a strong sacramentalist, he was anxious to hold that all, even boys at play, were baptized, regardless of place or minister, if the ministration was performed with the proper formula.[22]

That candidates could receive Baptism without any degree of faith was assumed in the case of infant Baptism, a practice prevalent in the early days of the Church and specifically vouched for by such as Irenaeus, among others. Both Tertullian and Gregory of Nazianzus approved of the practice in principle but advised some delay in the administration of the sacrament. The latter recommended a three-year waiting period. Gregory of Nyssa, however, opposed any delay at all, a position Cyprian had advocated years before. Traditional usages in the matter so impressed Augustine that he deemed endorsement of infant Baptism by church tradition a strong argument for the existence of Original Sin. He struggled somewhat unsatisfactorily with the problem of sponsors by convincing himself that they possessed the same regenerative spirit which the child was about to receive and that they in some telepathic manner were able to impart it through their wills to the infant candidate.[23] Apparently a canon of the synod of Neo-Caesarea sought to put limits on vicarious Baptism by declaring that christening a pregnant woman did not baptize her child. Likewise, vicarious baptism for the dead, which had been already mentioned in I Corinthians 15:29, never materialized in orthodox circles.

If Baptism imparted an instantaneous and permanent seal, the eucharistic rite also, by general agreement, effected some sort of automatic and lasting change of, or in, the bread and wine. Soon after Paul told Corinthians that if they ate and drank the body and blood of the Lord unworthily they drank judgment to themselves,[24] Ignatius spoke as though the Eucharist were a sacrifice of Christ himself. Justin's emphatic statements about the change of the elements are, of course, classic. Cyprian, saying much the same as Justin, attests in a dramatic way to the awe-filled power of the Eucharist. Had it not withered the hands of a person who touched it unworthily and had it not worked deadly effects on a girl too young to receive it? Curiously, an extant inscription does record the death of an eighteen-month infant in Sicily who was unwisely given the Eucharist. The list of witnesses attesting to the ex opere

[22] Augustine, *De bapt. con. Donat.* 7.53–101.102.

[23] Augustine, *Ser.* 174.8, 176.2; *Epis.* 98.2.

[24] See E. Fuchs, *Das urchristliche Sakramentsverständnis* (Bad Cannstatt: Müllerschön, 1958), p. 12.

operato mystery of the Eucharist includes Ambrose, who clearly vouches for the change of the elements, and Gregory of Nyssa, who informs us that the bread is not changed gradually by eating but immediately by means of the Word. The recipient is united with the Immortal Man who, by his own independent action, transfuses himself through the vital organs of the communicant.[25] John Chrysostom graphically emphasized the realism of the Eucharistic change by resorting to language suggestive of cannibalism.

Clearly, too, the eucharistic change is not only instantaneous but permanent as well judging from ample evidence for the reserved Eucharist. Justin, along with others, states that it was transported as *viaticum* to the sick; Dionysius of Alexandria records that a boy thoughtfully soaked the elements before offering it to a sick man. We hear of the Eucharist carried in wicker baskets, in vessels of glass according to Jerome, kept at home and carried into the desert according to Basil, paraded before catechumens and even heathens according to Athanasius. Throughout, it is clearly understood that the ex opere operato change is wrought by the power of God in response to a covenantal, legalistic command and as such has nothing to do with any occult virtue of the formula or even, as Chrysostom asserts, with the character of the minister.

Ordination, too, was automatic and permanent even when conferred upon reluctant and frightened victims and, according to Augustine, even when performed by a minister who himself was not "clothed in righteousness" since he gave not what was his but God's. For various reasons, numerous priests and bishops were ordained or consecrated against their wills and even in absentia. Sometimes such actions were instigated by governments to shelve dissidents, or demanded by popular tumult, or insisted upon by strong-willed metropolitans. Thus Basil was tricked into ordination by John Chrysostom, who blithely defended his deceit by claiming ends justified means. One Dracontius swore he would run away if he was ordained; a certain Nilammon chose to die rather than accept a bishopric. A monk, Ammon, after vainly cutting off an ear to forestall ordination, threatened to cut out his tongue as well. One Ephraim acted like a madman so his abductors would turn him loose. Epiphanius ordained Jerome's brother against his will after a little roughing-up and gagging made him more cooperative. Gregory of Nazianzus was much aggrieved at being ordained; an act of tyranny he called it. Theodoret was consecrated Bishop of Cyrrhus against his will and Martin of Tours was torn from his monastic cell and ordained under guard. Augustine was hard put to avoid being forced by a mob to ordain

---

[25] Gregory of Nyssa, *Cat. Mag.* 37; Cyril of Jerusalem, *Cat. Myst.* 4.1–6, 5.20–22 has the idea of the real presence completely stated.

a terrified and uncooperative Pinianus; on another occasion Augustine
promised an Alypius he would not ordain him against his will despite the
clamor of the populace; doubtless he remembered how he himself was
dragged weeping before his bishop when his ordination was demanded.
The emperor Majorian in the mid-fifth century felt inspired to legislate
against such robust legalistic practices.[26]

Even exorcism was not immune to the allurement of legalism. Endorsed far more often by Jesus in the Scriptures than the Eucharistic
rite, it is everywhere in evidence in the early Church, attested to by
among others Justin, Irenaeus, Tertullian, Athanasius, Cyril, Lactantius,
and Augustine. The rite, however, proved to be something of a problem
for an increasingly legal-minded Church whose sacraments operated in
an ex opere operato manner. Exorcism resisted being wrapped up in a
neat legalistic package because, unlike Baptism, the Eucharist, and Ordination, its effectiveness could be tested visually. It was all too evident
that some devils were recalcitrant and defied whole handbooks of formulas and frustrated the efforts of even worthy divines, often with the
most interesting side remarks. Although no one formula seemed to
assure immediate or final results, exorcism in the name of the God of
Abraham, of Isaac, and of Jacob seemed most effective. Yet reports had
it that some devils could be shrivelled up by the name of Jesus alone. By
180 a way was discovered which could honor exorcism's divine endorsement and yet tame its unpredictable nature. We read in Hippolytus that
it was made, in part, an adjunct of the baptismal ceremony. Cyril of
Jerusalem, too, speaks of it in this connection. In this case, not dealing
with true *energumens,* the potency of exorcism could be assured through
standardized formulas and declared ex opere operato effective in assuring an inward invisible action which supposedly loosened a vague hold
by the devil on baptismal candidates. By the mid-third century exorcists
became an institutionalized corps of minor clergy; by 450 Theodore of
Mopsuestia could finally cast baptismal exorcism in legal terms as a quasi
lawsuit against the devil who, thanks to Original Sin, had possession of
the unbaptized. By divine verdict, conceived in proper legal terminology, the devil is forced to manumit his slave. The older type of
exorcism, dealing with the obviously possessed, continued on in a clos-
eted sort of way; never able, like the liturgy of healing, to guarantee
automatic results, it was to be denied the dignity of a sacrament.[27]

[26] Parents sometimes forced ordinations of disliked sons in order to disinherit them.
See Jones, *Later Empire,* pp. 914–16, 1383.

[27] Virtually no literature exists on the development of the two types of exorcism as a
way to safeguard the ex opere operato operation of sacramental liturgy. See Hippolytus,
Apos. Trad. 20.3.8 and 21.7.8.10 also Cyril *Cat.* 20.3, *Procat.* 9. For Theodore of Mopsuestia's *Ser.* 3, see translation in E. C. Witaker, *Documents of the Baptismal Literature*
(London: SPCK, 1960), pp. 46–48. See also *Apos. Const.* 7.42 and John Chrysostom, *Cat. ad
illum.* 1.2.

Finally, the legalistic nature of ecclesiastical functions affected penance. Even though it was less formalistic than Baptism and the Eucharist,
forgiveness of sins was commonly assumed possible by virtue of a covenantal arrangement, the power of the keys, which invited as time went
on more and more legalistic expression. Basic to any development of
penitential discipline was the understanding, championed by Tertullian,
that sin was an individual act which, like a civil crime, could be repeated
and, like a criminal act before the law, could be forgotten after satisfaction and reconciliation.

This is no place to involve ourselves in the dispute whether the early
Church generally held four sins—idolatry, apostasy, sins of the flesh, and
murder—beyond the pale of forgiveness, thus making Pope Callistus
and Cyprian innovators in pardoning adultery and apostasy. Nor shall
we tarry over the question whether sins committed after Baptism could
be forgiven only once even though such a harsh view would strengthen
our legalistic thesis because it would endow penance with a one-time
efficacy so permanent that, like Baptism and Ordination, it could not be
repeated. At any rate, by the mid-third century such restrictions have
disappeared making sins of all sorts subject to the power of the keys—as
indeed Justin, Irenaeus, and Origen had maintained all along—and
allowing sins to be forgiven more than once. All was made operative
through confession and reconciliation after some sort of satisfaction.

The confession requirement, however, because of its deep intimacy,
fought off formal institutionalization quite effectively. Public confession
before the congregation, distasteful and embarrassing to slave and emperor alike, disappeared in the West by the time of Leo the Great. The
embarrassment of public confession and the reluctance of the Church to
forgive sins over and over caused many to sidestep the entire penitential
matter by delaying Baptism until death hoping to shed at the last minute
their sin-poxed skin once and for all, a prospect the pagan Celsus
thought at once astonishing and presumptuous. Nor was confession to a
cleric popular judging from Socrates' statement that the office of the
official presbyter of penance appointed to hear confessions of the laity in
Constantinople was abolished by the time of Nectarius at the end of the
fourth century. Auricular confession, however, the normal practice in
monasteries, continued as an option open to the laity as did personal
confession to one's self or to another layman.

The requirement of satisfaction, in contrast, succumbed to detailed
legal regulation, especially in the East. For example, Gregory
Thaumaturgus of Pontus advocated graduated stages of public penance:
weepers were forbidden to enter a church and were condemned to beg
prayers at the door; hearers could listen at the door only through the
homily; kneelers or prostrates could enter the church but also had to
leave before the canon; standers could remain during the service but
were denied the Eucharist. Finally one graduated to the rank of the

restored. Cyprian of Carthage introduced a similar system of graduated satisfaction commensurate with the degree of guilt incurred by an apostate during the Decian persecution. The Council of Elvira listed some twenty sins—mostly of the flesh—which incurred excommunication; communion at death was allowed for others; fixed years of penance were assigned for still others (including those who played at dice), and finally discretion, in certain cases, allowed the bishop to alter the time period assigned to the different grades of penitential satisfaction. The latter action, for instance, was applied to mitigate the punishment of women who married actors. The Council of Ancyra of 314 spelled out in detail the number of years a sin would cost in each stage of satisfaction. Ten years of expiation were demanded for abortion; twenty years were levied against those younger than twenty years who lay with beasts. If they continued to enjoy this sin after they were twenty and were married, thirty years were required. The Council of Nicaea, which also appointed years and degrees of penance for the lapsed, permitted *viaticum* to be given those who died before satisfaction was completed. The Synod of Hippo of 393 merely enjoined the bishop, or the priest with consent of the bishop, to proportion penance to the greatness of the sin. It is interesting that the Russian Orthodox Church legislated penitential satisfaction in terms of years down into the seventeenth century. Reconciliation in most cases seems to be automatically granted without resort to any liturgical formula once satisfaction had been made although Tertullian in his *De paenitentia* and Cyprian in the case of the lapsed required that a cleric attest to formal reconciliation.

While several of the Church's liturgical functions were taking on a pronounced legalistic nature, ecclesiastical governmental machinery progressively mirrored the constitutional experience of Classical Rome. Ecclesiastical synods or councils—agencies of church government coming into vogue especially after 200—modeled themselves on the Roman senate. Although its legislative power had been extinguished in the early empire and although it was demoted to the status of a local council for the city of Rome itself after 285 when Milan became the chief capital city of the western empire, the influence of the Roman senate lived on since it had served as a model for provincial city councils since Julius Caesar's day. Like Rome, all enterprising towns boasted a senate or curia generally made up of one hundred influential citizens, although some municipalities, to enhance their image, prided themselves on senates composed of six hundred or even a thousand members. Each city, like Rome, also had an assembly of citizens which as late as the second century still elected what magistrates were necessary to carry on local business and to meet obligations imposed by the imperial government. Quite interestingly, Origen's unfavorable comparison of these assemblies to the congregations of local Christian churches attests to their declining reputation. As assemblies more and more lost their elective rights and forced the appointed city curia to select officials, citizens found themselves privy to local governmental affairs only when officials occasionally chose to punctuate the excitement of the games with a public announcement.

Christians were well acquainted not only with city councils but also with provincial ones made up of delegates from regional towns. Some of these councils dated from the late Republic but most were established by the early emperors primarily to organize and oversee the religious operation of the state cult of Rome. Since they were never allowed to exercise any political *imperium,* their competence, supervised by provincial governors, was only deliberative and hortatory though they often petitioned governors with great success especially concerning matters of taxation. Under Diocletian attendance of members at provincial councils was made compulsory and hereditary; at the same time new larger diocesan councils were created. Continued by subsequent emperors, these diocesan councils persisted late in Roman history; one of the most successful was that composed of the seven provinces of Gaul which met at Arles.

Since provincial councils traditionally dealt with pagan religious matters some Classical precedent existed to cause Christian bishops, already conveniently residing in Roman capital cities, to consider synodal or conciliar meetings proper media for the discussion of church affairs. And since all conciliar machinery existed by indult of the emperor, Constantine alone could call an empire-wide meeting to deal with the Church's Arian problem. Bishops officially invited to attend were extended the customary use of the imperial post so they could scamper, much to the consternation of pagans, to this or that city to supervise the smooth operation of the cult of Christ newly endorsed by the Pontifex Maximus.

With the hoary parliamentary procedure of the Roman senate as an example, Christian conciliar deliberations were conducted according to established rules of order; first came the presentation *(relatio)* of the proposal, then the ranking of opinions *(sententiae),* debate, recording of acclamations, and statement of conclusion. All was duly recorded in stenographic minutes. Hamilton Hess maintains that the tone of Christian conciliar statements or canons, especially those of the fourth century, accurately reflects the restrained accent of pronouncements characteristic of the humbled Roman senate of the day.[28] These conciliar canons, which Hess calls the *placuit* type (it pleased us), more express mutual agreement of conciliar members on a subject than promulgate a binding legal command, a tone quite in keeping with the suppressed advisory character of the *senatus consulta* during the first three centuries

---

[28] H. Hess, *The Canons of Sardica* (Oxford, Clarendon Press 1958), pp. 37–40.

of the empire. However, the advisory nature of provincial councils in the empire should also be considered in explaining the conciliatory tone of church synods.

Christian synods and councils, though limited in a sense by the fundamental law of the Scriptures, dealt with a wide range of administrative, disciplinary, and doctrinal issues: qualifications, translations, and disciplining of bishops as well as interpretation and enforcement of orthodoxy. That conciliar actions often received a mixed reception and qualified support should not be surprising; the early type of *placuit* canon itself reflects convincingly the contemporary assumption in the Roman world that parliamentary procedures enjoyed no juridical competence. Sometimes canons, even those issued by ecumenical councils like Nicaea and Constantinople, were recorded carelessly or were selectively ignored. Rome, for instance, seemingly without much concern or reverence, recorded canons of Sardica as Nicene and chose to reject until 1439 the ranking of sees promulgated at the Council of Constantinople in 381. Moreover, the Nicene Creed, far from being automatically known and accepted, enjoyed a mixed reception. Some, like Cassian, considered it comparable to the Scriptures which had been fashioned under the direct authority of God by prophets and evangelists; others such as Hilary of Poitiers, even as a bishop, did not learn of the original Nicene symbol for thirty years.[29] One hundred years would elapse before Peter the Fuller, Bishop of Antioch, would introduce the creed of 381 into the Eucharistic service. Curiously, Augustine did not cite the Nicene Creed in his *De trinitate* even when dealing with Arians; his *De fide et symbolo* recognized the pre-conciliar Apostles' Creed as standard.

By the fifth century, according to Hess, conciliar canons could no longer be ignored. Once canons were deemed more than hortatory by the great sees of Christendom, interest in constructing bodies or codes of canon law began to appear in imitation of the trend carried on by Roman jurists in civil law. One of the earliest is the late-fourth-century so-called *Canons of the Apostles;*[30] by 418 the African and Roman churches were already at odds over the accuracy of their respective canonical collections involving the decrees of Nicaea and Sardica.

Ecclesiastical conciliarism in copying Roman political experience inherited both its assets and liabilities; while borrowing advanced parliamentary procedures from the secular conciliar tradition, the

---

[29] Cassian, *De incar. dom.* 6.4; Hilary of Poitiers, *De syn.* 91. Confidence in councils as agents of the Holy Spirit grew apace after Nicaea whose supposed number of bishops, 318, was later proclaimed symbolical of Christ himself. See Socrates, *H.E.* 1.9, 4.12; Sozomen, *H.E.* 1.20; Basil, *Epis.* 114; Leo, *Epis.* 105.3, 119.5, 124.1; Athanasius, *Epis.* 52.1–2. For an early, more skeptical, view of synods see Dionysius, *Book of Promises*, Frag. 2.

[30] Hess, *Canons*, pp. 40, 110.

ecclesiastical conciliar machinery, as we saw, also inherited the lack of *auctoritas* characteristic of contemporary Roman parliamentary bodies. Everywhere the Roman political establishment was succumbing to centralized absolutism as the Roman emperorship moved through the benign Principate of the Julio-Claudians, the enlightened despotism of the Antonines, the authoritarianism of the Dominate, and the naked military control of the third-century Barrack Emperors. Yet the fifty or so important ecclesiastical synods and councils between 250–450 might have been able to escape the influence of this constricting absolutism in the secular sphere if they had been able to establish an acceptable reputation for themselves by an unusual display of efficiency and probity. Unfortunately their deportment was not all it could have been. Party politics, imperial pressures, betrayals, and horse-play too commonly marred conciliar deliberations. Even before Nicaea met, worthy bishops enthusiastically tattled on each other to Constantine and at the venerable meeting itself some members stuffed up their ears in a remarkable display of closed-mindedness lest they be persuaded by what they heard. At the Council of Tyre a severed hand was solemnly but fraudulently passed around so that delegates could see at first hand how brazenly Athanasius had mutilated a priest. At another time a prostitute was smuggled into the bed of a venerable prelate to discredit him; the perpetrators seem to have forgotten he was over eighty years old! The emperors had to dissolve the Council of Ephesus in 431 because of uncontrollable dissention. Moreover, rival councils, rump councils, partisan councils, all vied with each other to produce what Socrates called a "labyrinth" of creeds bewilderingly contradictory and unclear. Long creeds, dated creeds, several of Sirmium, four of Antioch, all laid councils open to charges of heresy or of subservience to intimidating caesaropapist emperors.[31]

More disastrous for the future of conciliarism was the nagging lack of contemporary secular conciliar competence which denied the Church precedents for running an authoritative parliamentary system. The ecclesiastical venture was hopelessly frustrated by its inability to devise, at a crucial juncture c. 340, a workable order of appellate jurisdiction.[32] The

[31] Athanasius, *De decret. 21* maintains that true councils, even though using non-scriptural terms, only rediscover or interpret the ancient faith provided by Holy Writ. Therefore he saw with dismay the confusing conciliar pronouncements after Nicaea (*De syn.* 26–32). Leo, *Epis.* 124.1 thought any announcements made by councils were additions only to the "confession" of the Church and not to the faith itself. Socrates lists some ten creeds made between 325–360. Hilary of Poitiers complains (*Ad Const.* 2.4,5) that every year, nay every moon, Christians were making new creeds to describe invisible mysteries and then explained them just as arbitrarily. See also Hilary, *De syn.* 62 and Socrates, *H.E.* 2:8.10.18.19.30.

[32] Councils growing up spontaneously in response to emergencies interfered in a bewildering way in the affairs of almost any area. Even Nicaea's Canon 5 seemed to plan no

Council of Nicaea had merely advised that affairs of each province be settled by its own synodal machinery. Yet did it not assume by its very convocation that local resolutions were subject to review by general councils? Thanks to inexperience with parliamentary machinery, church leaders did not think to ask how the work of general councils should be reviewed. By larger councils, thus making truth commensurate with the number of debaters worrying it? Moreover, if the macrocosm of the universe supervised by a divine monarch in heaven was to be reflected, in a Stoic way, in the microcosm of the Church, was parliamentary procedure proper at all? At any rate, when the semi-Arians, fearing revision of the Council of Tyre, refused to attend an ecumenical meeting which they had urged Pope Julius to call, the system showed a fatal vulnerability.[33]

The long developing monarchical trends of the times, coupled with the patent inexperience and incompetence of conciliar management, fostered the growth of an alternative form of ecclesiastical government in the person of the monarchical bishop of the old apostolic see of Rome. Failure of parliamentary machinery to deal adequately with heresy, especially Arianism, convinced many that, as Irenaeus had long ago contended, religious deviation could best be detected and silenced by the theological purity supposedly residing in the traditions of apostolic sees especially that of Rome. Christian Rome, like Classical Rome, claimed twin founders in Peter and Paul, recapitulations as it were of Romulus and Remus, and it assumed, therefore, that it enjoyed a unique Magna Carta in the famed Matthean passage, "Thou art Peter and upon this Rock I will build my Church." Rome's succession of bishops from the prince of the apostles was considered impeccable by contemporaries.[34] Moreover, Roman bishops fortunately were untainted with attendance at any council. All considered, it was not ambition or duplicity on the part of Rome but the frustration of "Nicene" bishops of East and West, who had taken refuge in Rome against the Arianizing caesaropapism of emperors like Constantius, that pushed the Roman see into the limelight as a new contending pilot of the Church tossed in a sea of conciliar confusion. While the term "pope" was occasionally applied to any eminent bishop in the early Church, the concept of the papacy as a working institution emerged uniquely in Rome under Pope Julius in the mid-fourth century. The intended ecumenical council which both eastern

---

review system. See Hess, *Canons* p. 8. Augustine, seeing plenary councils as supreme, did not regard lower councils as irreversible (*De bapt. con. Donat.* 2.3,4). See also H. E. Symonds, *The Church Universal and the See of Rome* (New York: Macmillan, 1939) p. 110.

[33] Hess, *Canons* p. 114.

[34] Important documents with a connected account dealing with the rise of the papacy are conveniently found in J. Shotwell and L. Loomis, *The See of Peter* (New York: Columbia University Press, 1927) and in Coleman-Norton, *State and Church.*

and western prelates urged Pope Julius to call—the first such summoned by an ecclesiastic—degenerated into a basically western synod after eastern semi-Arians declined to attend. The resultant Council of Sardica in 343 accomplished what the conciliar caesaropapist structure could not: the establishment of an appellate jurisdiction over all synods. The Roman see was granted the right to hear all bishops who wished to appeal indictments or convictions by local ecclesiastical tribunals. Pope Damasus lived to hear the faith of Rome and Alexandria proclaimed official by the emperor; in addition he was given a limited right to enforce orthodoxy by calling upon imperial troops. Pope Siricius, in the manner of emperors, began issuing *decreta;* one pointedly warned bishops—now referred to more and more as "honored sons"—that they were "not at liberty to ignore the decisions of the Apostolic See" any more than "the venerable decrees of canons." Reminiscent of the Roman emperors of old whose genius hosted the indwelling of the divine *Roma,* the popes spoke of responsibility to Peter mystically dwelling within them; as prince of the apostles he laid upon them the burden and care of all the churches. Pope Innocent, in imperial style, responded with *rescripta* to what he chose to deem *relationes* or referrals sent to him by bishops of the empire. Both Boniface and Celestine, much to the consternation of Augustine, sent *legati* to interfere in matters of the African church now tottering sadly on the eve of its destruction by the Vandals. With almost its last breath it accused Rome of imitating the pride of the imperial court by sending such representatives *a latere.* Since when, they asked, had some ordinance of the Fathers deprived African bishops of the right to settle their own affairs? By Leo's time the West knew it had its own ecclesiastical foreman in Rome; the East was not so compliant.

Diocletian's jurisdictional division of the Roman empire in 285 indeed was to have a momentous impact on the Church. If pagan Nicomedia and Milan, as new capitals of the empire, each boasted its own Augustus, Christian Constantinople and Rome now vied with each other for the primacy of their patriarchs. Rome would base its claim of *auctoritas* on apostolic tradition, a principle suggested by Irenaeus of Lyons as early as 170 or indirectly enunciated by Clement of Rome already in 95; consequently it ranked itself, Antioch, and Alexandria in order as the prime churches of Christendom. Constantinople's Council of 381, echoing Nicaea, made it clear that it would associate ecclesiastical authority with imperial jurisdiction. Was it not the New Rome? Up to 350 the issue of primacy remained largely academic; Pope Julius, for instance, in no way at that time disputed the imperial prerogative to operate the Church through councils called from Constantinople. Pope Damasus (c. 375), however, ominously found it more and more a hopeless prospect to keep control, through his papal vicar at Thessalonica, of the territory of Illyricum which was under Eastern political authority.

While Valentinian III and Marcian recognized Roman "primacy" in 445, for all good purposes they restricted its operation to the West. The debate will continue forever whether the "disdainful" Damasus helped pry East and West apart by his apathy in responding to the pleas of eastern Nicene bishops to settle credal differences in their churches, or whether Leo, saluted by emperors as "preeminent in the episcopate," widened the gulf between Constantinople and Rome by ignoring the emperors' request to call a general council in 450. At this council, that of Chalcedon, finally summoned by the emperors, Leo's representatives were to play a prominent role. Yet when Leo refused as late as 453 to honor Chalcedon's administrative canon reaffirming Constantinople's rival primacy, the future schism of East and West was on its way, a division to a great extent a legacy of pagan Rome's constitutional arrangement.

If the government of the Church universal responded—both East and West—to the contemporary Roman monarchical atmosphere, local and regional churches also found their administration more and more ordered by a kind of professionalized career personnel that a Roman could appreciate. The laity, progressively squeezed out of church affairs, was admonished already by Clement of Rome and by Ignatius of Antioch to be obedient to the established clerical order. Should not passengers in a ship heed the captain and pilot? By 230 the great lay doctor Origen had to submit to ordination to be able to continue in service to the Church. Soon, the laity could find a niche[35] only by joining a monastery where they could exploit opportunities to annoy the organized clergy; Jerome, Athanasius, and Gregory of Nazianzus record how lay monks enjoyed sneering at the clergy when they dealt with married women or even pelting them with rocks during services. But even the vexatious monasteries, the last redoubt of the laity, eventually would have to submit to progressive regularization.

The movement toward professionalism of the clergy already was so pronounced by the end of the second century that the Montanists arose as a strong, but vain, protest to the growing institutionalized sacerdotalism in the Church. The monarchical bishop, already in evidence in Rome and Antioch by 100, had by the mid-third century everywhere crowded out whatever early presbyterial boards that once might have governed local churches such as Alexandria.[36] After Constantine, presbyters were more and more appointed as episcopal agents with limited

---

[35] The Council of Laodicea (c. 360?) by canon 59 forbade introduction of songs by private persons; all church hymns were to be authorized.

[36] In the absence of any serious evidence of a presbyterial form of government attached to the Roman church, it seems reasonable to argue that if the monarchical bishop is already known in Antioch by 100 the Roman church would even earlier reflect the monarchical principle established in the empire's capital since 27 B.C. Clement of Rome's

liturgical powers to serve the many rural churches springing up in abandoned temples. Again by the mid-third century a regular ecclesiastical *cursus honorum* was at hand to provide a graded and somewhat trained personnel. Tertullian mentioned minor orders even earlier; by 250 Pope Cornelius revealed that the ranks of porter, lector, exorcist and acolyte were accepted preliminary steps to higher ordination. While this course of ascent in office generally prevailed by the fourth century, some laymen were known to have been consecrated bishops without lower orders as late as the sixth century. Even the great metropolitan sees did not escape being ranked; as we saw, Rome and Constantinople long disputed the pecking order: was it Rome then Constantinople or Rome, Antioch, Alexandria, Constantinople?

To assure an ordered corps of full-time ministers, it became common, especially by the latter half of the third century, for bishops and local synods to subject ecclesiastical personnel to closer control. Ordination not only was made more and more contingent upon completion of specified periods in preparatory minor orders but was sometimes ordered delayed until a candidate was thirty years old, or was forbidden entirely by impediments such as castration, curial status, or this or that marriage status. In the East, for instance, priests could marry before ordination but not after; bishops could not remarry after the deaths of their wives. In 386 Pope Siricius required priests to be continent; mutual vows of continency by man and wife were required before a married man could be ordained. Efforts were made to assure orderly nominations of bishops by clergy rather than by popular clamor; other attempts were made to restrain ambitious prelates by supervising translations from one see to another. Regulations even sought to restrict non-professional activities of bishops; one such limited their economic endeavors by forbidding them to huckster goods from one market to another. Such attempts of bishop and council to regularize the clergy paid high dividends. For one thing, the program provided the Church during the fourth and fifth centuries with a staff of professional theologians, "experienced bankers," so illustrious as to be unequalled for many centuries. Such "men skilled in the mysteries of our religion," as Eusebius called them, kept the development of Western Civilization on course by struggling to harmonize revelation and reason, to discover the limits of rationalism in explaining the ways of God. High dividends from tighter church control were forthcoming in another way as well. However presumptuous, over zealous, and resented at the time, Rome's attempt to

---

epistle should be read in the light of Ignatius' letters: *Ephes.* 6, *Trall.* 2, *Phil.* 3, *Smyrn.* 8,9. Irenaeus, *Adv. haer.* 3.3 knows no other Roman tradition. By 250 Cyprian (*Epis.* 68.8) can confidently remark: the bishop is in the Church and the Church in the bishop. If anyone is not with the bishop he is not in the Church. Also *Apos. Constit.* 2.20.26.

defend or discipline clergymen—men like Apiarius, Antony of Fussala, and Hilary of Poitiers come to mind—instilled a needed sense of ecclesiastical authority without which the western Church might well have collapsed in the impending Dark Ages of barbarian invasions.

From the days of Papias and Justin, who early venerated the "memoirs of the apostles," up to the issuance of Athanasius' Festal Letter of 369, the persistent effort by theologians to define a final authoritative corpus of revealed truth seems strangely similar to the activity of Roman jurists of the second and third centuries trying to establish a closed canon of Roman law. Tertullian certainly would have agreed to the comparison for he always saw Scripture as something of a legal instrument, a true title, a charter, conferring full legal rights on doctrines which derived from it in much the same way as state positive law followed from basic *nomos* or *lex*. Just as Roman jurists struggled to constrict Roman law to definitive authoritative codifications such as the *Edicta Perpetua* or the *Law of Citations* from which only dead men spoke, so scriptural scholars moved to establish a final closed canon of revealed truth precluding God from speaking authoritatively to those alive after apostolic days. Theologians rightly puzzled over the question whether conciliar canons, papal decretals, theological speculations were mere refinements, amplifications of the closed messages or whether they were means of continued divinely inspired enlightenment. On the one hand, Augustine, like Athanasius, was willing to endorse a canon so closed that its sacred content could never be subjected to review, doubt, disputation or change; as in Roman law, basics would be guarded by the classic dead. Current epistles of bishops or pronouncements of councils, as supplementary or ancillary, would be subject to review. Yet somewhat inconsistently, on the other hand, Augustine would brook existing scriptural confusion and inadequacies as temporarily tolerable only because ultimately they could be subjected to the judgment of the magisterium of the Church.

Another demonstration of the legal and institutional trend invading Christianity was the lively concern for fixing credal formulations. Lacking Jewish precedent in this case, Christian creed-making, fixing of declared dogma in concise form, well reflects the Roman spirit which prized legal clarification to stifle dispute and appreciated simplification of complex matters in manuals and handbooks. Pope Damasus was a man of this type. It is, of course, not our intention here to speculate on the origin and development of the so-called Apostles' Creed or to debate the working model for the Nicene symbol. The very plethora of doctrinal statements—some twenty Arian ones alone within seventy-five years—indicates almost a frenzied effort to reach definitive statements of belief. More than just partial summaries of faith to assure the faithful, creeds became actual legal instruments used to test and guarantee the legitimacy of orthodoxy of this or that faction and so determine its legal rights to protection and support by the state. Thus Constantius tried to secure subscription to a symbol agreed upon by delegates from the twin councils of Rimini and Seleucia and to make it a legal badge of official orthodoxy. Pope Damasus was said haughtily to require word-for-word subscription to the Roman symbol to identify religious legitimacy. Such compliance was a matter of no mean importance since the Emperors Gratian, Valentinian II, and Theodosius in their famous edict *Cunctos Populos* of 380 defined as official the Nicene religion of Damasus and Peter of Alexandria and consequently declared all other conventicles subject to whatever punishment imperial "clemency" saw fit to extend. In 381 the Nicene Creed itself was declared the religious law of the land.

Finally, there is the emerging legal concept of the Church itself. While Augustine in his *City of God* echoed Paul's concept of the Church as a mystical body unrestricted by institutionalization, he, as a bishop, could not escape the realization of his age that the Church was *de facto* a Roman corporation exercising a *plenitudo potestatis*, an imperium inherited from a new set of greater spiritual ancestors, the apostles. Its fundamental scriptural law, stated in formal creeds, was implemented by a corpus of conciliar canons expressed in due legal phraseology and by official pronouncements or decretals of a new Pontifex Maximus. With its own graduated professional full-time clergy monopolizing a sacramental system claiming ex opere operato efficaciousness and its corps of professionalized theologians elucidating dogma drawing validity from a closed Scriptural canon, the Church became more and more a law to itself, empowered and justified as a legal body, according to Rufinus and other Fathers, to transform its own growing tradition into articles of faith. Ambrose so impressed Augustine with the imperium and magisterium of the Church that the great African father accepted its *auctoritas* as final and authoritative; only it, in the last analysis, could guarantee the integrity of the Scriptures and interpret the new law of Christianity. While pulled out of context, Augustine's famous remark: *"Roma locuta est, causa finita est"* had considerable truth in it. Whether Jesus intended all this probably will be debated forever.

CHAPTER 5

THE ARISTOCRATIC

THE CLASSICAL ARISTOCRATIC TRADITION
"The Best Men Rule" . . . Aelius Aristides

Realizing that all human affairs have to be operated by some elite and that every elite must claim some virtue, Greeks debated throughout their history what excellence, or what arete, entitled one to be thought virtuous and therefore fit to be an "aristocrat." Their philosophical thoughts and their experiences concerning the matter had a lasting influence on the wider Classical world and eventually on Christianity itself.

Early Greeks equated arete with physical prowess in many fields, even love-making, but especially in the martial arts, which, by their very nature, were reserved for those who enjoyed the subsidy of a fixed landed estate. Distinguished with a badge of noble lineage and courtly manner, heroic worthies indulged, with great gusto, in valorous exploits of loyalty and revenge, relishing the power to assist friends and harm foes with impunity. Homer's Achilles remained so much the heroic ideal that even Alexander slept on a copy of the *Iliad* for inspiration. Upholding his honor against all challengers, Achilles bowed only to the will of the immortal aristocrats of the Pantheon whose lifestyles were tailored to justify the righteousness of human courtly privilege. Aristocracy and polytheism fit well together. The *Iliad*, singing of heroic men and deeds, makes place for only one commoner deliberately presented as misshapen, uncontrolled of speech, and as the "ugliest man who came to Ilium." In the poem men are equal only in respect to the undesirable vicissitudes of life such as sickness, old age and death. If the *Odyssey* is an anti-aristocratic statement, as some have tried to make it,[1] it had little effect on the heroic scene at large; nor would Hesiod's later *Works and Days*. Heroic arete would for ages to come be the theme of glorious western epics celebrating, as hallmarks of one's importance, one's courage and stamina in requiting both ally and enemy. Even when, in time, glorification of sports tended to sublimate the martial arts, only those

---

[1] See S. G. Farron, "The Odyssey as an Anti-aristocratic Statement," *Studies in Antiquity* 1 (1979–80):59–101.

economically subsidized could compete; consequently when the Theban poet Pindar glorifies the athletic prowess of Olympic victors, he simultaneously lauds the landed ancestry and heroic traditions of noble families whose members alone are able to indulge in such pastime.

Since the emerging polis did not compensate its personnel financially, the political establishment necessarily became identified with the corporate body of landed nobility who alone were economically free to serve the community. Since only landed endowments could subsidize the ownership of weapons and provide the leisure to fight, especially on horse back, both logic and practicality demanded that the extent of one's martial contribution to the commonwealth should determine his civic position. As a result, the early Classical polis became an expression of the egoistic interests of a privileged class that completely ignored the concerns and culture of the peasantry. Such aristocratic dispositions found blatant expression in Sparta where they were extolled by the noble poet Tyrtaeus who proclaimed warrior feats in service of the polis the true arete which would win the nobleman heroic immortality.

When non-noble classes, those of non-landed incomes, arose and became in turn able to subsidize themselves militarily, they began to share in the arete of state service. Such were the hoplites or heavily-armed infantry which, largely due to Greek topography, became the major contingent of the Greek military even, somewhat paradoxically, in highly aristocratic Sparta. In Athens, even when Solon, and more so Cleisthenes, included all freeborn citizens in the assemblies, boules, and juries the lower classes continued to be excluded from high magistracies because they could contribute little or nothing in the way of military service.[2] However, the Persian Wars by forcing Athens in the early fifth century to rely heavily on state-subsidized non-noble naval service, seriously weakened the traditional Athenian aristocratic ideal so well represented by contemporary worthies like Aristides and Cimon. It was indicative of the future that the latter, as a member of the aristocratic cavalry, patriotically hung up his bridle for less honorable service on shipboard. One non-noble, the great Themistocles, actually broke into the circle of leadership during the war years by sponsoring the levelling naval bill; admittedly his non-noble mother and his uncourtly inability to sing and play the lyre so made him the butt of ridicule in the circle of the "400" that he had to wait one hundred fifty years for Aristotle to recognize his unparalleled service to the commonwealth during the war. Pericles, hailed as the patron saint of democracy, was the scion of two prominent Athenian families; as such he conceived of democracy as an

[2] An informative set of notes recording source materials as well as notices of modern research on Spartan and early Athenian constitutional history can be found in J. B. Bury and R. Meiggs, *A History of Greece*, 4th ed. (New York: St. Martin's Press, 1975) pp. 523–29.

enlarged oligarchy rather than a movement aiming to enfranchise slaves and foreigners. But the Periclean age might be seen as the last great noble era in Athens. The Peloponnesian war discredited great aristocrats like the incompetent Nicias, the untrustworthy Thucydides, and the mercurial Alcibiades; simultaneously it fostered the rise of low-brow demagogues like Cleon and Cleophon, and enabled democratic leaders to overthrow the treacherous revolution of aristocrats in 411.

To some extent a new generation was rising. Sophocles won renown even though he was the son of an armor maker; Euripides was the heir of a middle-class landowner; Socrates, the son of a stone cutter. Aristocrats obviously were disturbed; the pro-noble Aristophanes lampooned, among others, the democratic leaders who had unheroically bungled the last years of the Peloponnesian war and the Old Oligarch bitterly bewailed his day for allowing the better classes, the cream of society, to be exploited by the poor masses, the riffraff, the baser folk, unable to contribute anything to the cultivation of higher tastes.

Good breeding did not determine culture only as it was expressed in terms of prowess in warfare, sports and citizenship. Already in the *Odyssey* the nobility of the well-bred hero is considered advanced by his cunning ability to give sage counsel in assembly and to use the apt word and devise the clever plan. Alertness of mind enhanced activity in deed. The Sophists, however, by teaching that nothing was sacred in itself, cleared the air of all kinds of out-worn assumptions including noble claims to a monopoly on culture. In actuality they accelerated a revolutionary levelling movement by asserting that anyone could acquire through education an intellectual arete of knowledge and skill to operate critical intellectual processes necessary to inquire into the nature of man, politics, and ethics. The idea that cultivation of such an excellence could be inculcated by self-appointed professional educators was a logical step for a secular society like Greece to take, since truth depended not on faith in an objective revelation but on subjective competitive human judgment. To keep contention over values to a minimum, the Greek world by necessity would have to look to a trained intellectual elite for some degree of leadership: the scientist and the philosopher instead of the priest and the outmoded noble whether as warrior, athlete, or dilettante statesman. Sophists like Protagoras, Gorgias, and Prodicus merely asked: if the true warrior and athlete could be trained and the ideal human physical figure could be carved, could not the model intellectual be fashioned through philosophy and rhetoric? By the mid-fifth century the search for the ideal possessor of intellectual arete was on. Audiences heard Euripides' characters argue and analyze at length man's warring elements; devotees of symposia dissected human nature enthusiastically while they drank and watched dancing girls for inspiration.

Philosophy, knowledge, and rhetoric became the hallmark of the new man.[3] If once Simonides, the aristocratic poet of the early fifth century, portrayed intellectual arete as a goddess approachable by only a few, she would, as the fifth century wore on, give her favor to a host of scientists and philosophers. For the moment, one type of scientist especially respected for his knowledge was the physician because the art combined scientific observation with Empedoclean philosophical speculation. Already Pythagoras had assigned the highest order of existence in transmigration to physicians; now Hippocrates assured them that they belonged to a true elite fortunate enough to be initiated into esoteric mysteries of gnosis. Of the immediate philosophers none was more important than Socrates. Remaining free from the value subjectivism of the proverbial Sophist, he became not only the teacher par excellence of the later fifth century but the model intellectual of all time. He assured his disciples that knowledge emerged from the awakening of the rational animated logos within them, that anyone could rediscover knowledge, equivalent to virtue, within himself through a regimen of dialectics and spiritual vision.

Plato's *Republic* tried to associate the new intellectual arete available through education with the older arete of birth. Prospective governors, Plato insisted, had to be selected from among the "best" candidates who, after being scientifically bred, were almost miraculously safeguarded from contamination by the external environment during their youth. Education for the governors was to begin when they were seven. Ten years of instruction followed in gymnastics, martial arts, music and poetry which, including Homer, was to be censored to muffle appeals to passion and emotion. Between the ages of seventeen and twenty, military training weeded out the unfit so that the final selectees could study mathematics and dialectics between twenty and thirty. The next five years would cull out the final few through the study of philosophy which, by teaching them to rise above sensible concerns and to contemplate eternal Absolutes, would make them fit to pilot the community for fifteen years when they were between thirty-five and fifty. During their administrative term they were to avoid the crowd lest their dedication to contemplation of basic reality be distracted and weakened, and lest their ability to exercise undisturbed the reasoning part of their souls be lost. At the same time the governors must deprive themselves of other amenities of life such as property and wives. To perpetuate their kind

---

[3] The lack of universal education in the Greek Enlightenment made the "divorce between beliefs of the few and beliefs of the many absolute, to the injury of both. Plato is almost the last Greek intellectual who seems to have real social roots." Epicurus: "The things which I know, the multitude disapproves, and of what the multitude approves, I know nothing." So Dodds, *The Irrational*, pp. 192, 241.

they were to be bred to state-appointed partners who were between the ages of twenty and forty. After fifty governors were to retire, still holding themselves available for further service. Because the governors were able through selection and training to spurn the appeal of the appetitive part of their souls which sought only profit and honor, they were distinguished as different from the inferior class of workers and soldiers. Admittedly, Plato thought better of much of this after his failure to implement the ideas of the *Republic* in Syracuse. His revised political thinking in the *Laws* is less optimistic about human potential.

In a way, the whole story of Greek arete culminates in Aristotle. While he is the arbiter of intellectual virtue as no other, he, too, could not quite ignore the old aristocraticism of birth. Although willing to accept an arete of "general righteousness" for the outmoded noble military code, Aristotle held the old heroic virtue of courage in high esteem. Moreover, he insisted that, since the capacity for noble deeds and happiness necessitated material means, those sprung from proven ancestors were likely to be better men; for him, owners of landed wealth were naturally citizens in the truest sense and therefore could best excel in political excellence, the proper badge of honor for man as a political animal. Like Plato, he saw no exalted place as citizens of the polis for husbandmen, artisans, and merchants. In fact, work constituted a hindrance for the proper exercise of political arete and was, therefore, a ban to virtue. Working people were akin to slaves: the former slaved for the public while the latter slaved for an individual,[4] but both were alike in being unable to requite insult or to cultivate virtue by practice and free exercise of the will, because their time and wills were not their own. The very lack of ability to protect and avenge one's honor was a mark of servility.[5] But above all, the highest excellence to which man could aspire was intellectual, the exercise of reason.

If Greeks sublimated the primitive personal martial arete to include political expertise and finally intellectual excellence, they seem not to have put a compelling value on economic elitism. Admittedly, soon after the introduction of coinage into Athens Solon found mortgage holders and creditors already in a position to exploit and even to enslave the populace. Fortunately his precocious legislation forbidding one to sell

---

[4] Greek historians have a deep distrust of democracy if it includes the participation of commoners. Herodotus exhibits his feelings through the mouths of Darius and Persian nobles, while Thucydides pictures the Athenian assembly as fickle, unreasonable, and brutish. Philosophers think similarily. See, e.g., Aristotle, *Pol.* 1.1260a10–15, 3.1279b10–1280a35, 7.1329b–1330a.

[5] The idea of vengeance is so basic to Classical heroic arete that Christians will be chided for lacking it. See Aeschylus, *Prometheus Bound* 1066; Plato, *Rep.* 1.331–332; Aristotle, *Rhet.* 2.2,2–7 and *Nich. Ethics* 5.5. The idea continues on in Cicero, *De off.* 3.19,76, *De re pub.* 3.11; Quintilian, *Orat.* 7.4,6; Juvenal, *Sat.* 13.

himself into servitude and his allocation of funds to redeem Athenians already sold into slavery assured Athens a future free citizenry. Certainly Solon's laws and his adoption of a new coinage had in mind the economic betterment of the commonwealth through encouragement of trade. Clearly, too, geographical expansion and colonization in the sixth and fifth centuries encouraged the rise of a "bourgeoisie" and a subsequent surge of economic dislocations which fomented throughout Greece revolutions under tyrants or dictators: Theagenes, supporting the peasantry, fought the noble wool barons of Megara; Polycrates supported the shipping interests of Samos; Pittacus arranged class compromise in Lesbos; Peisistratus, championing the Athenian "Hill," tried to merge commercial and peasant interests. Polycrates' wealth was said to rival even that of Croesus. Cleisthenes' new constitution reveals the deep levelling inroads liquid wealth was making in late sixth-century Athens, when it enjoins aristocrats of the "Plain" to share representation in the Boule or Council with merchants of the "Coast" and even hill-billies of the "Ridge." There is no question that income from the state silver mines at Laurium as well as the tribute from the empire brought welcome wealth to Athens. In the fourth century the city enjoyed growing economic returns from mining, quarry, and pottery works together with increased revenues from its navigation acts regulating Black Sea trade. Occasionally we hear of wealthy individuals. The fifth-century Athenian Nicias of Peloponnesian-war infamy was able to rent out a thousand slaves to a mining concession at a profit of ten talents a year; a certain Pasion supposedly ran a bank of fifty talents,[6] and Demosthenes' father manufactured munitions, furniture and cutlery with a factory force of up to fifty slaves. Indeed, we even hear of the Spartan Gylippus who despite his "communist" training, was harboring a cache of Attic owls under his eaves.

Yet on the whole the capitalistic ethos—dedication to constant reinvestment for greater production and profit—remained foreign to the Greek mind. Despite the growth of liquid wealth, land remained the mark of gentility and distinction. If commercial wealth was sought, it appears used more to subsidize one's landed status, to protect one from working for a living, than to provide capital for reinvestment. Even with increased economic well-being sizes of estates in Attica seem to have remained moderate in not exceeding one hundred and twenty-five acres. The revolutions by tyrants wracking Greece between 650 and 500 seem to arise from normal peasant unrest almost as much as from excessive "bourgeois" ambition, and the upheavals appear to end up quite often as compromises rather than clear-cut triumphs of plutocratic factions. Trade, in places like Athens, was generally left to metics or half-citizens and to foreigners. The income from Athenian mines at Laurium was more likely to be distributed to the populace than invested and even the great income from the Athenian empire seems to have benefited primarily the lower classes; there is no evidence, for instance, that it created new societal strata of bankers or entrepreneurs. Even in Athens' liberal and somewhat prosperous period between 404–337, when the state mercantile system was paying dividends, upper-class officials showed no tendency to establish a plutocracy such as that of Carthage. Precocious in most fields, Greeks never developed a notable banking system and displayed little or no scientific interest in investigating economic principles, capitalist or otherwise; nor do we see great commercial cities like Corinth and Syracuse passing on any appreciable economic expertise either theoretical or practical to the later Classical world. Indeed, the enterprise of their traders was not sufficient to drive merchants beyond the Pillars of Hercules.

The fact that Hellenic literature does not vehemently indict wealth suggests that it was not regarded seriously as a dangerous obsession. Those who do rail against wealth, landed or otherwise, are apt often to be prompted by vested interests rather than principle. The sixth-century poet Theognis naturally condemned the peasant revolutionaries who had confiscated his Magaran estates. For the same reason, the dour Demosthenes later inveighed mightily against the self-indulgence of the rich, meaning the kind of men who had cheated him of his inheritance. In the same questionable vein, political opponents blamed new wealth for making Cleon and Cleophon demagogues, ill-bred flatters, inexperienced upstarts ignorant of their own incompetence. More honestly, the pious Aeschylus, in the tragedy of his day, had condemned wealth for its insolence; and Plato, philosophically true to his other-worldliness, declared it vulgar to equate the ability to make money with arete; was virtue not despised where money was prized?[7] Aristotle sought moderation: economic independence was indeed necessary for the good life but old money was preferable because it could transmit old values; the life of the trader and business man was tolerable only so far as it served the community.

True, Hellenistic times nourished Greek economic interests as never before. The growth of liquid capital in the post-Alexandrian period was so phenomenal that ambitious Greeks deserted the homeland in great numbers to exploit the economic opportunities of the East. The Ptolemies turned Egypt into a vast financial venture, making all eco-

---

[7] Plato, *Rep.* 8.550–551a. See Jaeger, *Paideia*, 2:330–35. Aristotle *Pol.* 1.1256a12–1257b40, *Nich. Ethics* 1.1096a5–7. The art of money-making to acquire surpluses is contrary to the nature of money as a necessary device to be used only for good household management and for exchange of goods.

nomic life, industry, and commerce a royal concession; Alexandria's wealth became known throughout the world. Critics rose against this new Hellenistic economic extravagance with interesting proposals—utopias which would limit or outlaw all wealth. While Hecataeus of Miletus seems to have started this genre already in the mid-sixth century by advocating mildly that landed property be equally held, now Zeno, the Stoic, pressed for a world of communal equality which does away with temples, money, commerce, fashions, and conventions. A pupil of Aristotle even urged a return to the world of the noble savage where one could live gratuitously on fruits. Euhemerus of Messana advocated communal land to be worked by all; finally, the unrealistic Sun State of the visionary neo-Platonist Iamblicus envisioned a tropical communistic paradise of sun worshippers all equal in wisdom, wealth, and ignorance.

By the time Rome came seriously in contact with the Greek East (c. 200 B.C.)—a land hitherto regarded strange and perfidious—old Classical Hellas, as we saw, had long debated what arete made one virtuous and therefore entitled to be considered an aristocrat. Now the Hellenistic East was the heir and arbiter of Greek values. Here, unlike in Greece proper, new economic opportunities encouraged an aristocracy of wealth, a commitment, as we saw, not held especially eminent by Hellenic standards. Yet Magna Graecia had a better legacy to impart—the importance of an intellectual elite. While Aristotle almost alone represented scholarship in Athens, a Hellenistic galaxy of scientists, philosophers, and artists, already sufficiently spoken of, burst from cities of Pergamum, Pontus, Rhodes, Cyprus, Samos, and Greek cities of Italy such as Tarentum and Syracuse. But no intellectual center would compare with Alexandria, the gem city of ancient learning graced by its great library and Serapaeum. It would take Rome some time to digest this tempting Hellenistic fare.

Romans, like most peoples in the early stages of their histories, were ruled by an aristocracy of birth but one not quite as heroic as that of Homer's world. Roman nobles like the legendary Cincinnatus would seem uncouth to Greeks. Did they not stoop to plow their own small estates? Best to say nothing of their inability to speak Greek when even parrots could do it. The martial arts, of course, were held in high esteem allowing Romans of future ages to marvel at the bravery of Horatius at the bridge in the Etruscan wars, the exploits of Camillus against the Gauls, and the steadfastness of the old blind Appius Claudius against Pyrrhus. The great amount of gold rings retrieved from the bodies of Roman nobles killed at the battle of Cannae attested to the valor and devotion of the early nobility, an inspiration that would swell the hearts of young Roman boys far into the future.

Noble heroism and dedication to honor were sorely tried after 200 B.C. when the Punic wars introduced Roman nobility to alluring temptations offered by overseas imperialism. Patricians, those who had fathers important enough for history to remember, began to view the constitution of the Roman republic as a Magna Carta entitling them to take turns at elective office to exploit the new provinces by misgoverning them. Unfortunately for the old guard, these opportunities did not escape the notice of wealthy plebeians. These non-nobles had long given patricians trouble, but up to the mid-third century nobles had ingeniously managed to devise all sorts of devious constitutional devices to placate them and frustrate their persistent clamors for political equality. By inventing the plebeian tribunate (c. 494) patricians hoped, as we saw, to diffuse contemporary unrest by giving plebeians a limited negative voice in government; by setting up the tribal assembly and later concocting the consular tribunate (c. 445), the nobility chose to risk the danger of a confused double-track system of government rather than admit commoners to the traditional consulship with its coveted prerogative to stage heroic triumphs for its incumbents.

Even after 250, when all offices of the Republic were thrown open to plebeians and intermarriage with patricians was allowed, few non-nobles managed to reach the highest office in government. Some twenty noble families, tightly intermarried, formed virtually a closed corporation to control elections in the assemblies and pass around offices among themselves entitling them to rape provincials economically. Nevertheless, the future lay with ambitious plebeians bent on substituting an arete of wealth for the patrician excellence of birth. They were called Equestrians or Knights because originally as wealthy peasants or local nobles of allied Italian cities—but not nobles in Rome—they could provide costly military service on horseback. They were quick to reap the economic harvest nourished by imperialism in the wake of the Punic and eastern wars, serving as tax farmers, bankers, and owners of shipping companies especially after 218 B.C. when patricians supported a law preventing themselves from demeaning their nobility by engaging in trade. Noble provincial governors found it increasingly galling, but expedient, to swallow their pride and use state troops to enforce the ruinous contracts and extortionary loans being exacted by rapacious equestrian financiers. For noble governors, refusal to cooperate meant indictment for extortion before a hostile equestrian-controlled court. In the first century B.C. the equestrians had advanced so far that they were officially incorporated as a separate order of citizens distinguished for their possession of 400,000 sesterces—roughly 20,000 dollars in mid-twentieth-century terms—and were entitled to the distinction of wearing a toga with a narrow purple stripe. Wealth had ennobled itself. The old nobility, of course, had not yielded graciously to the successful rise of these upstart capitalists. Patrician henchmen murdered the plebeian Gracchi between 133–123 B.C. because they championed popular reforms; in turn, the equestrian Marius was killed after having wrought murderous havoc on the state and its economy by teaching soldiers to demand their share of the economic spoils. Too late, the patrician Sulla with great slaughter tried to prop up the old aristocracy. Cicero, after crushing Catiline's share-the-wealth revolutionaries, would pay with his life trying to reconcile these two classes warring for the right to exploit the wealth of empire.

Finally, decimation of the old nobility in the wars and proscriptions of the Roman Revolution,[8] as well as Caesar's tendency to open state service to talented individuals regardless of class, served to advance further the fortunes of the equestrian order. Octavian, clinching the revolution, depended on the new *nobiles* for consultants as well as personnel for his recently installed track of procuratorships which controlled the powerful praetorian guard, the corn supply, and the governorship of Egypt. So politically and socially acceptable were these new capitalist politicians that one late republican equestrian, Titus Pomponius, who took the cognomen Atticus, might have successfully intruded his descendants into the Julio-Claudian imperial line had not his great grandson Drusus been poisoned in 23 A.D. After 70 A.D., the old nobility no longer monopolized the emperorship. Under the Antonines the bureaucracy was dominated by equestrians. Hadrian, for example, established regular grades, salaries, and titles for their services as tax-collectors, curators of the post, and as legates extraordinary. Such a professionalization of the bureaucracy adroitly took advantage of the fact that the equestrian order was not hereditary—unlike the "Nobility of the Robe" of French history. Since admission to and distinction within the order—as *Eminentissi, Spectabilies* or *Illustres*—generally depended on appointment to a specific state office by the emperor on the basis of talent or influence, the equestrians would not resemble the modern corps of honorary nobles knighted in England. It is revealing of the new arete of wealth that equestrians, collectively distinguished as *Egregii* (outstanding ones), preferred to designate themselves as *Sexagenarii, Centenarii,* or *Ducenarii,* parading the fact that they earned salaries of 60,000, 100,000, or 200,000 sesterces. *Perfectissimi* earned 300,000. Diocletian put equestrians in charge of all provincial troops, posts which once were cherished reserves for the old aristocracy. After A.D. 200, the few remaining old nobles sat as senators in a Rome no longer the capital enjoying their honorary title of *Clarissimi* (most eminent ones) while nostalgically recounting their emasculated pedigrees reaching back dubiously to such as the republican Cornelii or Sempronii. A few honors

---

[8] The Roman revolution, besides ending the republic and destroying the old aristocracy, left an indelible imprint on Roman psychology. See the classic work of R. Syme, *The Roman Revolution* (Oxford: Oxford University Press, 1982), esp. chaps. 14, 31, 32. Syme (p. 507) calls the period from Tiberius to the end of Nero's reign "The Decline and Fall of the Roman Aristocracy."

came their way but only the ancient, but now attenuated, republican office of consul offered them some measure of immortality since the year was designated by the names of consular incumbents. Even the senatorial title of *Clarissimi* degenerated in time so as to be held by even the lowest office holders.[9] So far had social mobility triumphed that Constantius' new senate could be made up of all kinds of people.

Thus, in Rome of the Christian era, the leveling pseudo-arete of wealth was, for all purposes, completely triumphant over the snobbish one of birth. With slaves available in great numbers since the mid-second century B.C. to work immense latifundia and operate commercial enterprises, the time was long past when a Cincinnatus would plow his own fields or when an equestrian Atticus would personally run his great financial conglomerates. Gone were the days when Rome forbade its major officers to trade or when a venerable Cato, censor in 184, would declare loaning of money, while profitable, not honorable, or when such as Dentatus, the victor over Pyrrhus, would refuse a state bonus of land because he already owned seven acres. Gone, too, were the days when Rome would relinquish economic leadership to a rival such as Puteoli, once called the "lesser Delos" of Italy, or would allow Rhodes to be the financial center of the eastern Mediterranean. In the last days of the Republic, Rome displaced even Alexandria as the undisputed economic arbiter of the Classical world. Octavian, temporarily reining in the radical ideology of soldiers and openly advancing the interests of the equestrian class, made the Roman world safe for capitalism; his defeat of Antony even assured it a vast new subdued East to exploit.[10]

But for his idealism, his conservative devotion to the Republic, Cicero would have been able to see that a new day of social mobility had triumphed, that he himself was part of a revolutionary era. As an equestrian, born of a wealthy contractor of Arpinum and as a strong supporter of capitalist convictions, he maintained that wisdom commanded a man to increase his fortune, albeit honestly, that economic prosperity was sufficient justification for Rome's imperialism, and that government might well be properly dedicated first and foremost to the protection of private property. He was just one of many late republicans like a Clodius, Lucullus, Scaurus, Pompeius, Antonius, Metellus, and Atticus who were millionaires able to pay 25,000 dollars for a table, to maintain many mansions, summer houses with fishpools, retinues of

[9] Jones, *Later Empire,* 1:134–36 suggests that the dwindling Roman aristocracy probably found personal service to the eastern emperors "beneath their dignity" and that they eschewed military posts in the face of an influx of barbarian generals. The fact that the Constantinian dynasty recruited talent for promotion to high office from the curial class, which composed city councils, suggests that the emperors were seeking some conciliar experience in their appointees. If so, the policy would help explain imperial endorsement of conciliar forms in ecclesiastical government.

[10] An observation well made by Syme, *Revolution,* pp. 351, 290.

retainers and slaves, as well as extensive art collections. Crassus, the richest of them all, seems one of the few satisfied with one estate. Caesar paid a few hundred thousand dollars for the pearl he gave his mistress, Servilia; eventually he owed Crassus a millionaire's fortune. Cicero thought it worthwhile, in defending a client friend, to point out that as a young man Caelius was not already head-over-heels in profligate debt.

The scramble for wealth became so scandalous that many Romans raised their voices against the degeneracy of the day. The historian Sallust, friend of Caesar, decried the bribery, greed, and excessive profit-taking of the political-economic oligarchy; yet powerless to suggest a remedy he retired from politics to write history, assuring himself that virtue departed when money became a badge of honor and an easy avenue to fame, military position, and political power. Catullus, Horace, and Virgil, also without answers, began to extol the simple life of the country with the hope that Octavian as savior somehow would be able to restore sanity in a new golden age. The Stoic Seneca judged the soul at its best when it craved no wealth; how could riches, he asked, be considered a good when they could fall to the lot of any man base or not, including even panderers and trainers of gladiators. Citing the Stoic Posidonius, he declared that since riches generally resulted from sacrilege and theft they naturally goaded men to evil. Yet while stalwartly maintaining that it was base to make the happy life depend on silver and gold, he himself could not summon enough moral courage voluntarily to give away his own millions. Epictetus, more honest, praised the Cynic who practiced virtue for virtue's sake and traveled penniless and propertyless throughout the empire to preach the brotherhood of man under the fatherhood of God. Cynics, however, neglected to extoll the glorious side of Roman wealth illustrated by the prodigious philanthropy of an Herodes Atticus in Greece or of a Pliny at Como and Tibernum in Italy, or of a Petronius Felix at Thuburbo Majus in north Africa; nor did they laud the growing concern of the state to expend monies for social welfare and free education. Everywhere towering aqueducts, arched bridges, paved roads, exalted temples, the blooming of new African cities as well as the plethora of expensive mausolea and funereal monuments the world over, all eloquently extolled the glories of Rome's materialistic capitalistic mentality. Aelius Aristides, who felt the need for psychiatry in the midst of this exciting world of enlightened self-interest, put it all very well in his speech of 154 praising Rome as a world state where the best men ruled: the well-to-do Roman citizen now drawn from all quarters of the empire.[11]

---

[11] Plutarch, *De fort. Rom.* had earlier made the same point: Roman success in empire was due not only to Fortune but to the lofty character of individual Romans. When Virgil said much the same earlier he was speaking about the old heroic nobility.

As a practical, spiritually uninventive people happy with the pursuit of material things, Romans were far less inclined than Greeks to create an intellectual elite interested in discovering and propagating virtue. The arena and the gladiator early smothered the theatre and tragic actor. Yet it is important to recall that Romans had the good sense to recognize their intellectual betters. Already by the latter half of the third century B.C. Romans could learn about Greek heroic ideals in a Latin translation of the Odyssey; native Italians like Naevius and Ennius were writing tragedies, translating some of Sophocles and Euripides, and composing an epic on the story of Rome in heroic verse. Throughout Roman history distinguished pockets of intellectuals gathered anxious to hand on the intellectual arete Greeks had labored so long to acquire. In the mid-second century B.C. a famous salon centered around Aemilius Paulus—the same who transferred Perseus' whole library to Rome—and around Scipio Aemilianus hosting Greek luminaries like the historian Polybius and the Stoic Panaetius of Rhodes. The Gracchi, raised in the new Stoic atmosphere by their learned mother, Cornelia, tried to carry their lofty convictions into politics, with tragic results. Cicero apologized for writing in Latin. Trained by the Stoic Posidonius of Apamaea and by the Academics Philo of Larissa and Antiochus of Ascalon, this "noblest Roman of them all" did much to keep alive an interest in philosophy. Handicapped, however, by his eclecticism, by the panic of the Roman Revolution, and by his own belated dedication to professional philosophy, he never managed to create a school of followers. As the Christian era drew near, Epicurean-Stoic illustrious *urbani* like Horace, Virgil, and Ovid gathered in learned circles around intellectuals such as the bibliophile Asinius Pollio or the sober-minded Maecenas, friend of Augustus. The period of the second-century Antonines, the so-called Second Sophistic, created such an active revival of Greek-Roman authorship in both philosophy and literature that Christianity could grow up in an unusual intellectual age. There were Sceptics such as Lucian and Galen, Stoics like Epictetus and Marcus Aurelius, Middle Platonists like Plutarch, Celsus, Numenius of Apamaea, Albinus, Ammonius Saccas, and Maximus of Tyre all forerunners of the neo-Platonists Plotinus and Porphyry. In addition there were more or less contemporary literati like Quintilian, Juvenal, Josephus, Pliny, Suetonius, Arrian, Appian and Pausanias, as well as the scientists Galen and Ptolemy. Such men assured the kind of learned atmosphere necessary if Christian Fathers like Justin, Clement of Alexandria, the Latin Hippolytus, and Origen were to direct Christianity into intellectual channels and institute the development of a Christian corps of intellectual elite, a new type of philosopher—the theologian. It is not particularly surprising to learn that Origen was invited to visit the learned circle attending the court of the Severi.

Considered in a left-handed sort of way, it may have been fortunate

for Christianity that much Classical scholarship in the first two centuries
of the Christian era grew progressively more resigned and pessimistic in
tone revealing misgivings about the future on the part of the literati of
the day. There is little doubt that the great republican revolution had left
its sinister mark. Strangely, it inspired no creative treatise on political
science, even though the great upheaval truly had many lessons to teach.
Since, unlike our French Revolution, the Roman civil war was not followed by a great diversion like the Industrial Revolution capable of
absorbing interests and redirecting energies, it drove Romans into a
profound quiescence, doubt, and despair. Horace eloquently asked why
Rome had merited the pangs of such a great civil war: was it to suffer the
fate of Troy because it was stained by the blood of Remus at the hands of
Romulus so long ago? No Aristotle came forward to encourage man as
master of his own destiny. Although a few scholars, such as Galen and
Ptolemy, were able to enhance man's intellectual standing for centuries
to come, only one author, Virgil—beloved above all Classical writers by
Christians—seems to express a message of hope in a bright future. In
this sense his *Fourth Eclogue* has become a classic. His *Georgics* aptly has
been described as a glorious "hymn to Italy, the rich mother of fruits and
men"; yet it has its pessimistic overtones, lauding as the good life Epicurean withdrawal from society and retirement in an idyllic countryside.
One must remember that the great poet was influenced by Lucretius not
only stylistically but also philosophically. Even Virgil's magnificent
Aeneid, while celebrating Rome's heroic mission to civilize the world
through peace and law, has its melancholy message: history is a necessary
tragedy, though one not without hope if only future generations will be
as virtuous as Rome's heroes of old.

Many of the disillusioned sought assurances of well-being by trying
to detach themselves from earthly concerns. While Stoics and Epicureans joined hands in recommending tranquility of mind as the greatest good even at the price of withdrawal from society, others sought a
mystic escape in an attractive new Platonism. Still others, not so lofty-
minded, dispelled their disappointments by exhausting their energies in
physical love, made respectable so artistically by Catullus, Propertius,
and Ovid. Tacitus found the new empire of Tiberius, Nero, and Domitian not a day of promise but one of disillusionment, one foreign to
virtue. Suetonius reported the carnival of Caligula; Petronius "seized the
day" by acting as an exquisite arbiter of vice for high society. Others
expended their intellectual energy seeking relief in gnostic neo-
Pythagoreanism with its religious fervor, Orphic and Dionysiac secret
rights, mystic experiences, arcane theurgy, and astrology. As a pseudo-
intellectual corollary of Fate, astrology will grow, as we shall see, so
popular that the Christian Fathers felt they had to meet it head on with
the best contemporary scholarship. It had come to Rome already in the

second century B.C. and though banned by the senate in 139 it gained great support in high places after Cicero's friend, Nigidius Figulus, professed to have predicted by horoscope the future greatness of Augustus on the day of his birth in 63 B.C. Stoic approval helped astrology win the support of all classes, even imperial circles, despite periodic expulsion of astrologers from Rome. Augustus, Tiberius, Claudius, Nero, and the Flavians all had astrologers at their elbows. Under the "Greekling" Hadrian, Vettius Valens flourished. One of the most learned astrologers of all times, he practically perfected the art of horoscopy. The philosopher prince Marcus Aurelius kept practitioners in his entourage during his many unpleasant wars. Even Christian emperors were to succumb.

Imperial Rome's intellectual elite seems to be speaking, albeit learnedly and beautifully, for a world which had forgotten creative thought and politics and opted instead for quiescent, mystic, and fatalistic philosophies which, to many, seemed only to drive away ancient self-reliant virtue.[12] Indeed Christianity found much in the contemporary Roman elitist scene to contaminate its Master's commitment to the virtues of love, poverty, and intellectual simplicity. Then, too, the Church would have to be on guard lest its momentous monopoly on the saving "good news" lure it to transform itself into a new elite at the expense of pristine pentecostal virtue.

THE CHRISTIAN EXPERIENCE WITH ELITISM

"The First shall be Last" . . . Luke

Far from being confronted by a rigorous caste system, young Christianity was not faced by even the vested interests of an entrenched nobility of birth. As we saw, Roman imperialism after 150 B.C. had fostered the rise of a new corps of non-hereditary capitalist equestrians who exploited money and talent, rather than kinright, to justify their claim to importance. In addition, the battle casualties and proscriptions of the ensuing Roman civil wars between 80–30 B.C. so effectively decimated the ranks of the old Roman republican aristocracy that equestrians could capture the emperors' new prefectures and consistories, and even the imperial office itself. The social mobility of the early Christian era would be construed by partisans as a godsend for the young Church.

Conversions among the few proud patrician remnants clustering, for the most part, about the city of Rome did not prosper; indeed, illustrious pagans remained in control of the Roman senate and local

---

[12] Momigliano, *Conflict*, p. 85 maintains that the liquid social situation was so great that the new leading class after the third century had difficulty in knowing the simple facts of Roman history.

prefectures well into the fifth century. In contrast, the prospering middle class, whether engaged as new *nobiles* in politics or as private business men, seems to have been much more prominent in the early Church than is generally asserted in biased reports of pagan writers like Celsus who would have us believe that Christianity accepted only commoners, women, children, and slaves, all nobodies who subverted Classical courage and wisdom with peasant traits of timidity and ignorance. Paul, it is true, reports in his very early days that not many Christians were wise in the worldly sense, nor influential, nor well born. Even so, the last section of his Epistle to the Romans, even if possibly misplaced, by saluting some twenty-five prominent Christians in one locality, provides valuable evidence that all early Christians were not upstart simpletons, strangers to any talent or reputation;[13] moreover, Paul was able to collect sizeable sums to help the church of Jerusalem. Again, a contemporary of his, a certain Pomponia Graecina, was distinguished enough, as the wife of Aulus Plautius the conqueror of Britain, to get her name in the pages of Tacitus because she was accused in the early sixties of espousing a "foreign superstition," very probably Christianity. A few years later we hear that a Manlius Acilius Glabrio,[14] consul in A.D. 91, was ordered by Domitian to fight in the arena and was later executed along with a Flavius Clemens, a Christian first cousin of the emperor himself. Indeed, Clemens had two sons who were actually Domitian's heirs and was married to a Domitilla whose grandmother and mother were respectively the wife and daughter of Vespasian. Clement, bishop of Rome c. 95, is probably a wealthy freedman of the distinguished family of Titus Flavius Clemens. A Christian, Aurelia Petronilla, was the daughter of an uncle of Vespasian.

After the first century evidences of high social position and wealth among Christians became plentiful. Several prominent heretics were wealthy. Marcion (c. 135) was a ship owner able to donate a fortune to the Roman church which, in turn, was sufficiently well off to return his gift; one Theodotus was a rich leather merchant, another was a banker. It seems obvious that the cultivated Artemonites were persons of means. The Epistle of James (c. 100?) warns against according the wealthy special attention in church; Clement of Alexandria wrote his *Quis Dives Salvetur?* for the benefit of the wealthy. Origen, in turn, boasted that Christian congregations were equal or superior to city assemblies. An Apollonius, probably a senator, was executed under the Antonines, and Valerian's persecution assigned special penalties for senators and equestrian officials who had converted to Christianity. Even a few Christians

---

[13] See W. A. Meeks, *The First Urban Christians* (New Haven: Yale University Press, 1983), pp. 51–73. For the fourth century see A. H. M. Jones, "Social Background of the Struggle between Paganism and Christianity" in Momigliano, *Conflict*, chap. 2, pp. 17–37.

[14] Cassius Dio, *Hist.* 67.14. Glabrio is condemned for atheism of the "Jewish persuasion."

were buried in the wealthy pagan cemetery under St. Peter's. Diocletian, the great persecutor of the Church, had to dissuade his own wife and daughter from being catechumens. By Constantine's time, then, the stage had long been set for the many conversions of upper class families anxious to climb on the imperial dais. Free from class restraints, the Christian emperor could appoint the prominent or the unknown to his new senatorial class in Constantinople. These appointees included even sons of a sausage maker and of a cloakroom attendant. We have already spoken of the influx of lawyers into church service and of Ambrose's distinguished background. From the mid-fifth century on it became more and more expedient to draw bishops from wealthy families who could subsidize the defense of cities from the growing disorder of the day. Such was Sidonius, elected bishop of Clermont, a classically educated "aristocrat" of Lyons who had earlier married into imperial circles and had been honored with a public statue for his services to the community.

With respect to elitism, it should once again be kept in mind that the prevailing wide social mobility in the Classical world contemporary with the rise of Christianity would cause the Church little anxiety about the need to adjust to an inherited aristocracy of birth. Under such conditions, the creation of an hereditary priestly caste within Christendom was quite unthinkable. Later adoption of celibacy or of restricted rules of clerical marriage readily forced recruitment of ecclesiastical personnel on the basis of acquired qualifications rather than of birth, and at the same time prevented priestly inheritance of church property, a problem that was left to vex Pope Gregory VII later.

More pressing for the moment was the problem of the wealthy. Wealthy converts naturally sought an imprimatur for their riches from the Church, even though its founder strove to make poverty a virtue. Rather than lay up perishable treasures, his followers were advised to give away their possessions if they would be perfect. But how many among rich converts could relish the prospect of going through the eye of a needle or envision themselves in the dim predicament of Dives in contrast to Lazarus? Did not Jesus' remark that the poor would always be at hand indicate in retrospect that he had planned no radical communistic economy to eradicate poverty or to indict private property? Would not much of the alms-giving he enjoined have to be forthcoming from the wealthy? Seemingly, the Master's economic program was none other than one which charity could implement. Whatever Jesus' economic message truly was, many Christians from the start interpreted it in such a way that it would do no violence to the prevailing Classical capitalistic ethos of the day.[15] Paul, while collecting for the Christian poor of

---

[15] C. G. A. Schmidt, *The Social Results of Early Christianity* trans. Thorpe (London: Isbister, 1889) contains one of the most comprehensive, yet compact, list of references dealing with Christians' attitudes toward wealth.

Jerusalem, explicitly urged that alms be given according to one's means and not begrudgingly or from compulsion. The "communism" of Acts is voluntary. The *Didache* absolved one from giving alms to those able to work; those who would not work should not eat. For the *Second Epistle* of Clement to offer remission of sin as a bonus for alms, it had to hold charity voluntary. Tertullian's *Apology* stated specifically that almsgiving must be voluntary, never compelled.

However, it was Clement of Alexandria's *Quis Dives Salvetur?* which directly addressed itself to the problem of wealth and voiced the attitude, quite Stoic, that the Church would generally adopt. As a homily on Mark 10: 17–21, it averred that wealth in itself was not a bar to heaven, that beggars were not necessarily the best of the faithful since poverty did not automatically make a man holy. What good did it do to renounce wealth if one continued to coddle his vices? Mark, according to Clement, meant to exhort Christians not to become obsessed with wealth. Since wealth in itself did not condemn, the attitude toward wealth was the issue, not its possession. The poor in spirit, not necessarily the poor in material possessions, were to gain heaven. Seneca would have approved. Nonetheless, many Christians gave away their wealth—Origen and Cyprian for example—even while maintaining that poverty was not to be a test of virtue and the arbiter of one's eternal status. Cyprian repeated the theme that voluntary almsgiving, as a principal good work, reduced the flames of hell; Ambrose, restating Clement's views, put the matter quite classically: it was not the census but the quality of soul that revealed the rich blessed man.[16]

At times patristic literature speaks out rather emphatically against the evils and dangers of wealth in a way that mimicked the dour Cynics. Barnabas disturbingly hinted that the "communistic" availability of spiritual and eternal blessings ought to be mirrored in temporal things. Origen contemptuously stamped money with the seal of the devil; it was something a virtuous Christian better not possess. Did not Jesus reveal his disdain for it by getting the coin of the tribute to Caesar from a fish, a source outside himself? In fact, Origen gave qualified approval to taxes only as a way to relieve oneself of filthy lucre.[17] Ambrose condemned the unequal distribution of wealth as a result of violence, greed, and pride; John Chrysostom, dismayed that one half of the population of Constantinople was subsisting at the poverty level, railed unmercifully against the selfish rich who flaunted their wealth. Usury was denounced

[16] Cyprian, *De opere et eleem.*; Ambrose, *Epis.* 63.89, *De off. minis.* 1.28; Lactantius, *Instit.* 4.16; See Theodoret, *Orat.* 6 (*PG* 83:1861), John Chrysostom, *Hom. in Act.* 7 and 11.

[17] Origen, *Hom. in Luc.* 23 (*PG* 13:1861), 35 (*PG* 13:1892–4), 39 (*PG* 13:1899–1900), *Comm. in Matt.* 13.10 (*PG* 13:1119), 17.27–28 (*PG* 13:1558), *Hom. in Ezech.* 13.2 (*PG* 13.761), *Comm. in Rom.* 9.25 (*PG* 14:1226).

as a double sin: as it created miseries for the poor, it fed the greed of the wealthy; Cyprian, Basil, Ambrose, Gregory of Nyssa, John Chrysostom, and Augustine all inveighed against collecting interest in ways that an old virtuous Roman like Cato would understand.

Yet despite such harsh words, the indictment of wealth was always qualified: its rejection was declared commendable but not imperative. In fact, Ambrose, Jerome, Paulinus, and Augustine all spoke out directly against the condemnation of riches per se. Private property was to be acceptable if acquired justly and used properly. In fact, wealth conveniently was declared a virtual loan from God which, as such, should not be questioned. As a loan, however, it entailed the dangerous and burdensome obligation to use it as the divine donor intended—for the needy. Freely given out of love, it would benefit the giver spiritually, fulfill the command of Jesus, and at the same time soften the inequities of the poor. In a way, the poor man, far from being shunned as unimportant, became an arbiter determining which rich Christian would be saved, a gauge by which he would be judged at the end of time. It was all a new concept for the Classical world, as Lactantius noted: what pagan philosopher, he asked, had ever given precepts about beneficence or really practiced it? Ambrose, probably with pagan philanthropy in mind, pointed out the vanity of giving to the poor for the sake of honor and applause. Augustine, after claiming that charity alone could justify Christian accommodation to the Classical arete of wealth, drew the startling conclusion that since charity was the most excellent of virtues, the faithful actually were the only ones who could possess wealth justly and honorably since they alone would make proper use of it.[18] New, too, was the idea that everyone was obligated to practice charity, not only the wealthy who could give from their abundance but also the less fortunate who might have to tax the necessities in their larders.

Everywhere the command for charity went out in tireless letters and homilies by such as Polycarp, Cyprian, Origen, Athanasius, Basil, the Gregories, John Chrysostom, Cyril of Alexandria, and Augustine. Ambrose spared not even the Church: could not the sacraments be celebrated without gold and silver which could better serve the needy? Bishops were supposed to be protectors of the poor, their houses and tables available to the needy. Deacons probably were originally instituted to distribute charitable funds collected for widows, orphans, captives, the sick, and the leper, especially during crises such as the plague in Carthage c. 250. About this time, Pope Cornelius supported fifteen hundred poor in Rome and the bishop of Antioch three hundred. Even Christian hospitals arose in the fourth century, like Basil's at Caesarea, Chrysostom's at Antioch, and those at Ostia and Porto near Rome.

---

[18] Augustine, *Epis.* 153.26 (*PL* 33:665), *Ser.* 239.4 (*PL* 38:1128).

Fabiola, of the wealthy Fabian gens, became famous evermore in Christian lore for her hospital charity.

There were many, of course, who found charity difficult to cherish. Paul had to reprove those who shamed the needy at the eucharistic service. That the clergy had to be warned frequently against avarice is attested to in literature from Cyprian to Salvian. By the time of Pope Damasus, bishops of Rome were setting a table worthy of Roman emperors; as the "ladies' ear-tickler" Damacus went legacy hunting among wealthy Roman matrons, a practice which had to come under an imperial ban. Ammianus Marcellinus reported that many Christians advanced their piety by enriching themselves with the spoils of pagan temples. Churches vied with each other to obtain state subsidies. To protect their wealth Christians of the curial class often had themselves ordained to escape their state fiscal obligations, another practice that earned imperial displeasure. By the mid-fourth century those who would be perfect gave up on the world to seek solace and virtue in monasteries.

If the Classical endorsement of wealth, which the Romans turned into a pseudo-arete, received at best a restrained approval from Christianity—leaving the poor actually in something of an enviable spiritual position—other allurements threatened to create their own kinds of elitism within the Body of Christ. One particularly troublesome threat came from its doctrine of grace, a teaching which had implications for both the Christian community as a whole and the individuals within it.

The idea that the Church itself was a divinely elected elite struck pagans as an unbelievable assumption irrationally elevating the weak, the sinful, and the ignorant to a place of privilege. Tacitus, we recall, labeled Christians haters of the human race, presumptuous better-than-thous; Celsus chafed at the arrogance which led Christians to believe that at this late point in history the whole world had been made for them. Lucian denigrated them as poor wretches deluded with the idea that they would be immortal. Indeed, Christian pronouncements about their election as a superior group were not self-effacing. I Peter borrowing Jewish expressions, said it best: Christians were a people set apart, a holy nation, a purchased race, a royal priesthood. Irenaeus spoke of Christians as temples of God; Clement of Alexandria approved calling Baptism "Perfection" because by it Christians were adopted as children of God, sons of the Highest. Cyprian praised Baptism as a second birth which made its recipients new beings of marvelous enlightenment. Others saw it as a unique grace which could free Christians from an unclean world to make them temples of the Holy Spirit, friends of God, masterpieces of God. To the Cappadocians Christian grace "deified" mortals by making them participants of the divine life of God. Thus Gregory of Nyssa envisaged Christian grace lifting up men from their own mortal nature while Basil reminded his flock that grace gave Christians the right to call

God Father. John Chrysostom saw it metaphorically transform man as a leper to a graceful youth surpassing all humankind in beauty and wisdom, bright of countenance, clothed in purple and a diadem of royalty. To pagans this new grace seemed dispensed irrationally and ineffectively, creating at best a deluded "elite" not classically heroic, wealthy, or wise.

Early converted gentile Christians, despite any euphoria over their group election as a "holy people," had to struggle with their former allegiance to the classical philosophical consensus that humanity as a whole was capable of rational thought about the divine and able to devise reasonable ways to curry divine favor through appropriate action without being members of a splinter ecclesiastical elite elected by grace. Was it true that such personal ends as spiritual fulfillment and ultimate salvation promised by the new Christian movement were obtainable only by a few through a gratuitous inclusion in some sort of spiritual "racism"?

Any tendency of the early Church to appoint itself an arrogant aristocracy of grace or to encourage its members to think of themselves as individual aristocrats of grace seems to have been kept in check quite successfully. For one thing, Paul's message that only some would become saints and that salvation depended on a direct call by God—that God had mercy on whom he would and that he hardened whom he pleased—fell largely upon barren ground until Augustine, along with Ambrose, made stark predestination an issue albeit with limited immediate success. But however predestinarian they might be, Paul, Ambrose, and Augustine did not have the temerity to boast of personal election. In fact, Paul clearly warned against such self elation: even though he was called to be an apostle and set apart for the gospel of God, boasting was out of order. Let no one rate one's self more than one ought but only according to the apportionment of faith given by God, a gift for which one could take no credit. One should more properly boast of one's weakness and infirmity. John Chrysostom saw that if one praised and marveled at the grace displayed toward him he should be all the more devoted and sober. Augustine, the first to treat grace analytically, kept Christians on pins and needles about their election. However righteous one might be, it was well to think of what was blameworthy within one's self. It was well to remember, too, that the grace of final perseverance was a gift. Who really knew ultimately whether he belonged to the City of God?

Were not those, though, who gave evidence of charismatic gifts members of the elect, an elite able to demonstrate their election among those not so favored? Apparently Paul quickly sensed the danger of dividing Christians into approved and unapproved factions. Although he spoke of divinely inspired charismatic individuals, those who possessed wisdom, knowledge, powers of healing, prophesy, tongues and so on, his Jewish background made him suspicious of individuals who pointed to these gifts as evidence of a familiarity and favor with God. Charismatic abilities must be contained to serve the group; were not, he asked, all such gifts and their working manifestations of the same spirit given to different persons in different degrees? Were tongues not worthless unless they could be interpreted for the edification of the entire body?[19] Acts, of course, reports that charismata such as clairvoyance, miracle working, and glossolalia were so sought for that Simon Magus earned permanent notoriety by trying to buy them. The *Shepherd of Hermas* still prized prophesy, but as expectancy of the Parousia wound down institutionalized clergy more and more crowded out any lingering charismatic witnesses such as apostles, prophets, and teachers spoken of in the *Didache*. Since the Spirit seemed ever less inclined to inspire extemporaneous prayer, standardized liturgies had to develop. Indeed, by 200 any apocalyptic movement like Montanism, with its ecstatic prophetesses Prisca and Maximilla, was apt to find itself relegated to the fringes of the Church as a schism. Tales of isolated famous charismatic wonder-workers, of course, continued to appear from time to time such as those of Gregory Thaumaturgus, pupil of Origen, or of later monks like the famous Antony of Egypt. But by 300 the pagan Porphyry could make a joke of Christian charismatic gifts by suggesting that all episcopal candidates should qualify for consecration by first drinking poison and sustaining snake bites; had not the Scriptures promised them immunity?

If predestinarianism did not catch on in the early Church to justify a spiritual elitism and if charismatic prowess was too limited and sporadic to mount any true leadership, another spiritual "aristocraticism" did emerge claiming arete in the performance of good works, which, rightly or wrongly, was generally considered, as we shall later see, meritorious to salvation rather than mere evidence of prior election.

During the Decian persecution, some confessors were so pleased with their good works that they offered to share their superfluity of merits, along with those of the martyrs, to shorten the terms of canonical penance for those who had not as courageously acknowledged their faith in the face of danger. Cyprian thought the threat of such presumptuous prima donnas dangerous enough to justify censure and the establishment of more controlled ecclesiastical penitential machinery to reinstate the lapsed.[20] Gregory of Nazianzus alludes to the same kind of elitism manifested in his day by some of his contemporaries who, he says, were

---

[19] I Cor. 12:30, 14:6–12. Meeks, *Urban Christians*, p. 149, believes, on the strength of modern studies dealing with glossolalia, that ancient speaking-in-tongues became highly structured as part of early ritual.

[20] Shotwell-Loomis, *See of Peter*, pp. 332 n.107, 340–41, 345 n.126. Cyprian, *Epis.* 21.22 also *Epis.* 27 as well as 13 and 14.2–3, *De unit. eccles. cath.* 20–22.

so proud of their deeds that they attributed all of their success to themselves and nothing to God. Monks, of course, notoriously overstepped the line by promoting themselves as stalwart doers of good works; they will prove, as we shall see, the most vocal opponents of Augustine's predestinarianism through grace. But such elitism was rebuked by the Church's indictment of Pelagians who, as overzealous humanists, judged themselves able to handle their own salvation virtually unassisted by Church or sacrament. Against such a bold elite only a declaration of heresy could prevail.

One spiritually elitist movement based on works managed to stay within the confines of the Church—monasticism. Many incentives—political, economic, and psychological—impelled thousands of Christian men and women from the third century on to withdraw as hermits or cenobites into the deserts of Egypt or to secluded areas of Mesopotamia, Palestine, and Syria. Certainly the overriding impetus of the movement was spiritual: determination to seek the kind of perfection recommended by Jesus to the rich ruler involving renunciation of the world and its wealth. Followers of a Pachomius, Basil of Caesarea, Martin of Tours, Jerome, Cassian, and finally Benedict, all honored, as athletes of God, a spiritual arete of merit based on good works, a position firmly defended by Jerome against Jovinianus. Individual ascetics and encratites there always had been, but organized monasticism now introduced into the body of Christ a dual sort of citizenship: those who would be perfect and those who chose to compromise with the Church's progressive relaxation of moral discipline in a dirty world. The movement received high praise. The Cappadocians and John Chrysostom hailed the pursuit of Christian perfection in monasticism as the true "philosophy" developing the perfect interior life through contemplation of holy things, and facilitating the acquisition and practice of self-control. Monks would now truly achieve the tranquility or *apatheia* that Stoics had longed for. Sitting, as it were, at the helm safe in harbor the new Christian Cynics could eschew the sinful worldly temptation of the market place and the city; according to another metaphor they could go about, like old roving Scythians, pitching their tents wherever they would war against the devil. Trained to pursue only pleasures that were both necessary and natural, monks were hoplites in the army of the Church relegating ordinary Christians to the rear guard. Angels, John Chrysostom said, lodged in the huts of monks; no delicacies distracted their diet of bread and water; no political or social banter disturbed their elevated discussion; unlike the rank and file of men who, as wild beasts, spent concern on their bodies, monks were citizens of heaven. Many, including Ambrose and Jerome, eulogized the pursuit of virginity; Isodore of Pelusium valued it far above the married state, a view harking back to Paul and Tertullian. Augustine praised monks' communistic ideals. Popular deference to monks was common; awed by the new heroic arete of asceticism, the faithful recounted and elaborated upon all new evidences of monachal charismata especially miracle-working and discernment of spirits. Such gifts were attested to by Athanasius in his famous *Life of St. Antony*. Sozomen noted that in the East Christians commonly deferred to the opinions of monks because they were valued for their virtue and the philosophical tenor of their lives.

The new monastic *perfecti*, mostly laymen, assigned themselves a unique status quite apart from the control of the episcopal hierarchy. Sozomen records that Eustathius' monks in Armenia, Paphlagonia, and Pontus despised married presbyters; Cassian actually admonished monks to avoid bishops along with women since both distracted their pure eyes and disrupted their contemplation of sacred things. Gregory of Nazianzus refers to monks as the over zealous part of the Church, a reputation they seemed to relish. Theophilus of Alexandria found such to be the case when the three hundred recalcitrant monks he had driven out of Egypt requited him by tattling on him to John Chrysostom, the primate of Constantinople, to bring about the farce known as the Synod of the Oak. Augustine found his monks at Hadrumentum in an uproar against his predestinarian views. The monk Eutyches provoked such theological dissension that it brought on the "Robber Council" of Ephesus where monks so robustly manhandled Flavian, patriarch of Constantinople "of blessed memory," that he died from the attack. Monks upset even emperors. Julian called them the Cynics of the Christian world, an apt designation considering Epictetus' description of the simplistic arrogance of pagan Cynics and their flaunted disregard for the normal decorums of life. The emperor Theodosius professed mild puzzlement over monkish fanaticism.

It is not at all surprising that monastic rules constantly emphasized the need for humility. Among the eight capital sins discovered by monks—later reduced to seven—vainglory and pride ranked especially high because it caused those monks who had made greater progress toward perfection than others to rely too much on their own strength and too little on grace. It seems appropriate that a lay monk should be the father of Pelagianism.

Nor is it surprising that the ecclesiastical establishment strove to bring this new self-appointed aristocracy of works under control. By recording that the bishop of Rome, Soter, forbade monks to touch the altar and offer incense in church the late *Liber Pontificalis* anachronistically antedates later clerics' traditional mistrust of monks back to 175! Basil tried to inject some ecclesiastical discipline into monasticism by requiring that original professions of monkish candidates take place before a bishop. Pope Siricius attempted to siphon off monks of high reputation, and doubtless of sterling trouble-making capacity, into the ranks of the clergy; if they were under thirty they were to pass through all the lower ranks of ordination. The third Council of Arles (455) in the West and of Chalcedon in the East began to regulate monasteries closely by the mid-fifth century by putting them under some episcopal restraint. The highly institutionalized Roman church appropriately fought off monastic establishments in Rome itself until the late fifth century.

Among the elite groups seeking recognition in the Church probably the most interesting and dangerous were those professing an arete of knowledge in the style of Greek philosophers. Unlike the Greek philosopher, however, who operated within no official hierarchical organization, the Christian theologian was in a position to intrude himself into key positions of a formal church establishment. In such a role he could readily influence dogma by establishing a specific school of theology such as that of Alexandria or of Antioch. Followers of an Origen or an Augustine were able to split the Church intellectually for centuries. As we have already seen, Origen, Basil, and Jerome, as well as others, considered themselves somewhat set apart to refine the rule of faith and to explain the content of Scripture. Others, such as Gregory of Nazianzus and Augustine, clearly felt that the ability to "theologize" was given only to a few elite capable of unusual learning and piety.[21] Fortunately for the Church, many of the intellectual elite were successfully contained within the "orthodox" system and were willing to submit themselves to the traditional rule of faith expressed in creeds, to the canon of Scripture, conciliar decisions, and even papal decretals. Power in the Church, as in most institutions, never coincided with intellectual leadership; the western popes were nondescript as scholars and eastern patriarchs did not often compete in learning with such as the Cappadocians. Indeed, those intellectuals who created schools at variance with the traditional rule of faith or disturbing to established leadership in the Church generally found themselves dismissed as heretics and their followers branded as brazen innovators. Innovation was treason in pagan Rome; heresy in the Church. Among the outcasts were the adoptionist Artemonites, an elite group if there ever was one, devoted to Classical science more than revelation. They, along with others who tried to

---

[21] Expressions praising intellectual elitism are many. Gregory of Nazianzus, *Orat.* 27.3 avers that philosophizing about God is "not so cheap" a profession that everyone is entitled to practice it. According to Origen (*De prin.* preface 3) the apostles kept silent on some matters so "the more zealous of their successors who would be lovers of wisdom" might have subjects on which they can display the fruit of their talents. *C.C.* 7.11 speaks of only those "wise in the faith of Christ" as entitled to explain Scripture. Augustine, *De util. cred.* 7.17 (*CSEL* 25.21) and 17.35 (*CSEL* 25.44–46) compares theologians to experts such as Asper, Cornutus, and Donatus who are needed to read Terentianus Maurus, and lists them among other proofs of faith. See also *Cyril of Jerusalem and Nemesius of Emesa*, trans. Telfer, *LCC* #4 (Philadelphia, Westminster Press, 1955) p. 353 n.1.

fathom the mysteries of the Trinity or of Christology, were among some thirty-five or more major splinter groups before 450. Especially threatening were the logically attractive "unitarians" or Sabellians, the "monophysite" Apollinarians, and the "Christokosian" Nestorians.

But by far the most threatening movement toward elitism in the early Church was that posed by the famous and baffling Christian gnostic sects described so seriously by Irenaeus.[22] Especially active in the second and third centuries, gnostic schools were particularly divisive because they existed within the body of the Church itself while orthodoxy gradually was emerging. The gnostic *Apocalypse of Peter* (3rd. cent.?) even complains of "separated" Christian brethren who call themselves bishops and deacons "as if they have received their authority from God."[23] Hippolytus early recognized the Christian gnostic systems as heretical patchworks which disfigured revelation with alterations by Greek philosophers: thus Heraclitus corrupted Simon Magus, Pythagoras and Plato affected Valentinus, Aristotle confused Basilides, and Empedocles did the same for Marcion. The Christian gnostic movement was, in actuality, a more complicated development; rather than a new arrival, it represented a sophisticated culmination of an age-old and persistent quest to escape evil by discovering some saving secret gnostic talisman.[24] Gnosis could express itself in awareness and use of simple spells, magical names, passwords, secret liturgies involving purifications, astrological calculations, transmigrational experiences or mystic visions. Ancient mystery cultism is a mild manifestation of the movement. Like all gnostics, Christian devotees claimed an arete of saving knowledge, secret information about the divine nature and economy derived from inspired insights, private revelations, assorted pagan lore and even esoteric instruction by Jesus after the Resurrection.

Behind the emergence of the radical Christian gnostic sects, then, lies a long pre-Christian syncretism of common gnostic tenets like those preserved, for instance, in the Greek and Latin philosophical gnostic corpus attributed to Hermes Trismegistus compiled between 100–200 A.D. The first treatise in the pagan Hermetic writings, called Poi-

---

[22] Irenaeus, *Adv. haer. 1 and 2;* Hippolytus, *Philos.* 1–7. E. R. Dodds, *Pagan and Christian in an Age of Anxiety* (Cambridge: Cambridge University Press, 1965) p. 18 n.2 is helpful in alerting one to the difficulties surrounding the terms gnosticism and gnosis.

[23] *The Nag Hammadi Library,* trans. by members of the Coptic Gnostic Library project of the Institute for Antiquity and Christianity. Ed. J. W. Robinson (San Francisco: Harper & Row, 1977) p. 343.

[24] The readable study by R. M. Wilson, *The Gnostic Problem* (London: Mowbray, 1958), pp. 64–75 treats the subject as a vast syncretism finding room for every type of thought from the highest philosophy of mysticism to the lowest forms of magic. Wendland, *Kultur,* pp. 54–56 stresses gnosticism's pre-Christian origins as a reaction against the fatal power of star gods of the East in order to break astral bonds and provide a way to freedom.

mandres, seems however to have some passing acquaintance with the New Testament and the Septuagint. Some sections in the lately-discovered Nag Hammadi library show how cleverly Christians adapted existing gnostic tracts to suit their purpose.[25] Although the thorny questions of the nature, provenance and significance of gnosticism will occupy scholars for a long time, they tend to agree that certain basic assumptions emerged in time to create something of a recognizable gnostic system holding 1) that the world of material and darkness is evil; 2) that as a result it cannot be the product of a good providential god; 3) that the basically divine nature of human beings in some way became trapped in the quagmire of matter; and 4) that individuals must, therefore, somehow be extricated from their plight and return to their proper world of the divine and thus bring to an end the travail existing in the present monstrous cosmos of intermingled but irreconcilable spirit and matter.

The first assumption, that the visible cosmos was evil and was separated by a fatal and defying chasm from a divine pleroma of true Being, finds expression in some degree or form in many areas: Babylonian astronomy-astrology, Persian and Parmenidean-Platonic dualism, Egyptian neo-Pythagoreanism, neo-Platonic mysticism, and even in disillusioned Hellenistic Jewish thought featuring Essene Wisdom literature, and Philo's work. In fact, the pessimistic assumption that the world is evil and opposed to the spiritual abode of Good is so commonplace that it has been explained as the unconscious psychological projection of human perplexity and frustration, which continually confounds any quest for truth and security. The disillusionment already present in the Orphic assumption of a "fall," in Hesiod's projection of declining ages, and in Plato's doctrine of pre-existent souls entrapped in bodies, found more concrete expression in the pessimism of Romans bewildered by the cost of human history which seemed forever plagued by some evil mysteriously embedded in human nature or environment. We have already noted that the Roman republican revolution confirmed the consternation of its contemporaries who pined for the past golden age when gods walked among men and decency meant something. All human efforts seemed benighted, the cost of some earlier tragedy. Only the Stoics seemed able to envisage a cosmic regeneration; only Cynics, if Epictetus' picture of them can be trusted, seemed disposed to work on the assumption that human perfection was within grasp. Yet Marcus Aurelius ends the Stoic era disillusioned and sad.

[25] For editions and studies of the Hermetic writings see *Oxford Dictionary of the Christian Church*, ed. Cross (London: Oxford University Press, 1963), p. 631. For a Christianized pagan gnostic text see "Eugnostos and the Blessed and the Sophia of Jesus Christ" in *Nag Hammadi Library*, pp. 206–28.

The second assumption of gnostics seemed logical: that a world in which baleful darkness, matter, and evil prevailed had to be the product of some monstrous mistake, some misfortune, some offense, some accident or even a plot. It may be the result of a fallen divine power or a faulty world soul such as Plato hinted at in the *Timaeus*, or the product of a sinister plan wrought by a personal evil principle acting as a baleful demiurge through a succession of lower powers or intermediary divine emanations bridging the gap between the Abyss or One on one hand and the worldy matter outside the pleroma on the other.[26]

The third stage in the gnostic process pictured man generally as a being created by an evil demiurge who was himself the product of an errant, inquisitive, or proud eon; as a blighted product man found himself a monstrous creature whose divine spark was entrapped in matter and barred by the seven planetary heavens from its rightful abode. Cosmic travail ensues until this unnatural mixture can be resolved by the escape of man's divine element from material bondage. Return to the pleroma, which often proceeds progressively through the concentric realms of the seven planets, is made possible only by secret gnosis, saving knowledge given a few through some esoteric enlightenment which in most cases strained or transcended rational understanding.

By the advent of Christianity the general Hellenistic religious syncretism had sufficiently enough outlined the gnostic process for Christian thinkers to feel they could supply true knowledge of the agent destined to carry through the last phase of the gnostic system: redemption of humanity from the matter and evil to which Yahweh as the evil demiurge had condemned it. The Christian idea of a Logos, Christos, temporarily entering fleshy matter in the docetic form of the historical Jesus, was an attractive arrangement for the task at hand. Bizarre sects resulted. One, that of the Ophites, which definitely incorporated pre-Christian and Christian gnostic ingredients, featured an errant female eon, Sophia or Wisdom, who begot Ialdabaoth as Yahweh, the demiurge who created man. The eon Christos provided redemption for members

---

[26] Due to pessimism engendered by the Babylonian captivity and the later desecration of the temple in Maccabean times even Judaism did not escape the idea of emanations from God so common in gnosticism. The tendency to regard God as more and more aloof and transcendental led to the need for intermediaries whether angels or such emanations as the Word of God or his Wisdom. Sophia became hypostasized and personified as the divine agent in creation and thus provided the Jew with an intermediary corresponding to the Logos. See Wilson, *Gnostic Problem*, pp. 196–99. Wolfson, *Church Fathers*, pp. 498, 501–3, takes a narrow interpretation of the term gnosticism and sees it as a Christian development with a minimum of Jewish influences since Jews found it difficult to claim any knowledge in depth about God. M. Hengel, *Judaism and Hellenism*, 2 vols. (Philadelphia: Fortress Press, 1981) finds gnostic penetration of Judaism slight except possibly among Essenes. See pp. 229, 241.

of the sect scattered over Asia Minor, Palestine, Egypt, and Mesopotamia. The system of Basilides, which flourished in the first half of the
second century, featured some three hundred fifty eon-heavens topped
by an Ogdoad built around a Persian-like struggle of Light and
Darkness. The gnosis involved was so esoteric that Basilides reportedly
thought it best not discussed since only one person in one thousand and
two in ten thousand could comprehend it. To find warrant for his true
gnosis he is reported to have altered the Christian gospels.

By the mid-second century gnostic leaders were waxing bold within
the Church. Valentinus presented a complicated pleroma incorporating
different sets of male and female eons stemming from Intellect and
Truth descending in a complicated way through hypostasized attributes
of God, concepts of Man and Church, earthly archetypes, and Platonic
Ideas. The errant Sophia and her spouse Jesus, who respectively provided the material aspects of the visible world and redemption for man
through Christos, resided in their own heaven; below it existed the
sevenfold planetary cosmos ruled by the demiurge, then the world of
human beings, ruled by the devil, and finally a sunken world of unar-
ranged matter. Valentinus is reported to have written an apocryphal
gospel to help explain his system somewhat. The semi-gnostic Marcionites, supported by their own canon of Scripture and ecclesiastical
organization, became one of the greatest threat to the Church. Without
intermediary eons, this school supplied a simple system in which two
gods operated: one the true God, the other the demiurge or Yahweh.
Manicheans, flourishing in the late third century, attracted a large following including, for nine years, the great St. Augustine. As an organized
church with a simple ritual it spread throughout Rome's empire; despite
opposition from Constantine and Justinian, it persisted in some form
into the Middle Ages. Manichean manuscripts have been unearthed
even in the twentieth century in Turkestan and Egypt. In this system, the
struggle between Light and Darkness allowed Satan to make man a
pawn. Light became contaminated trying to rescue him from Darkness.
Reincarnation was declared necessary for those without sufficient gnosis
to achieve immediate salvation. Manicheanism, like most gnostic sects,
divided its adherents into subgroups, often three, distinguished by their
declining possession of gnosis; the perfect enjoyed full gnosis while
those at the bottom were lost because of a lack of it. Thus Valentinus
spoke of the pneumatics who would be given the full gnosis and be
chosen to enter the pleroma, the psychics who were destined to dwell
only in the region of the demiurge, and the hylics who were hopelessly
engrossed in matter and declared lost.

Gnostic sects poured forth a host of apocryphal "hidden" books:
gospels, apocalypses, and acts which, Jerome attests, many took seriously
as canonical Christian works. Thus appeared the *Gospel of the Egyptians*

possibly of gnostic origins, the *Gospel of Thomas* of disputed Manichean provenance, the gospels of Andrew and of Philip, and even that of Judas which was supposedly prized by the Cainites in the same way as the *Gospel of Eve* was dear to the Ophites.

After 200, when a line could be drawn between heresy and orthodoxy, the reaction against gnosticism was in full swing. There was much in its bizarre theology for Christians to attack. Its popular assumption that fate rather than sin caused man's entrapment in evil was roundly condemned as was its identification of evil with matter against the teachings of Genesis. Furthermore, to weaken the association of the divine eon Christos with matter, gnosticism assigned a docetic interpretation to Jesus' flesh making him an impassible phantom. Such teaching by Cerinthus, who is held by some early writers to be the author of John's Revelation, and by the Manicheans brought up fresh problems in soteriology and at the same time ignored the question of grace, an aid supposedly given to man, as an essential means of salvation, through an historical redemption accomplished by a Logos who willingly assumed true flesh without contamination. In addition, the various gnostic systems led to wild excesses of asceticism on one hand and of antinomianism on the other. Saturninus taught that only rigorous asceticism would make one invulnerable to Satan; the Marcionites ascetically rejected marriage, alcohol, and sex; the latter activity, they said, served to expand human entrapment while celibacy broke it. On the opposite side, the Cainites, with their apocryphal *Gospel of Judas,* interpreted perfect gnosis as including experience of all sins. The Carpocratians systematized immorality insisting that compliance with traditional ethics served only to support the baleful cosmic condition while disobedience weakened the evil forces' sway. To the left of the gnostic movement, they held a communism of property and women. For such gnostic views as well as for others like vicarious baptism of the dead and the employment of women as ministers, Irenaeus' *Against the Heresies* could find no authority in the tradition preserved by apostolic churches.

To condemn was not sufficient. The very popularity of the gnostic systems revealed a need for constructive thought. Marcion's scripture had to be offset by an authoritative canon, Jesus' humanity had to be protected in credal statements, and ecclesiastical authority fixed in the tradition of apostolic churches. In addition a basic epistemological problem was at stake. Even though gnosticism with its reliance on the power of arcane knowledge alienated many, such as Plotinus, because it did violence to Greek rational philosophical thought, it attracted Christians, especially those deeply impressed with the time-tested, essential Classical conviction that knowledge was power; simple faith and grace had yet to prove themselves. Christianity would have to face the question how it could enlist knowledge into the service of faith without vitiating it. If knowledge was declared desirable or even necessary for perfect faith, would not Christianity itself foster an intellectual elitism and become another philosophy for the few?

In a way, Paul had already raised the issue. In something of a gnostic way he spoke of God as mysterious, hidden, foreordained and unknown even to the rulers of the world. The significance of Christ's death and resurrection was to him a mysterion revealed to Christians alone, and even among them not all would profit from this esoteric knowledge.[27] Yet, for Paul it is faith and not knowledge which saves. Moreover, to the Apostle human bondage to the evil powers of death, the flesh, and the law is due not to some cosmic fate but to sin, and the predicament can be escaped only through grace made available by the soteriological action of Christ.

Most early Christian writers had little to say about a role for knowledge in salvation. True, Justin called Christianity the "true philosophy," but he did so more to emphasize the superiority of Christianity over pagan thought than to suggest that *scientia* was a means of salvation. Irenaeus and Miltiades, the apologist, writing against the gnostic sects suggested no way to recruit rational Classical reliance on the power of knowledge into the service of Christ. Although Tatian was disposed to see little efficacy for Christians in Classical *scientia*, he nonetheless subscribed to the idea that true spiritual knowledge could be power. Consequently, he lost himself in a group of Christian gnostics, encratites who were so intent on asceticism that they spurned marriage and even wine in the Eucharist. As we saw, Tertullian, in depreciating the value of Classical thought, proclaimed that Christianity was a revelation not a school of learning; if knowledge were desirable let it be that of the simple man of the street undisturbed by the vain belchings of Greek philosophy.

It was largely Clement of Alexandria who found a moderate way to welcome an arete of knowledge into the Christian system of revelationary faith.[28] Just as a beggar, in respect to the arete of wealth, was not necessarily the best Christian, neither in Clement's mind was the ignoramus automatically a better Christian than a philosopher. Would one not be ignorant of the power of God without study of the Scriptures? Should not one be able to judge the holy books written to try men? Did Jesus not distinctly ordain that Christians should be "experienced bankers" able to separate the spurious from the genuine? The true Christian gnostic must be not only an erudite person but also one who loves the Lord in faith. The true Christian gnosis could clearly not be that of the

---

[27] Some see a Pauline gnosticism in I Cor. 2:1–3, 2.6–10, Col. 1:25–28.

[28] *Strom.* 1.5.28, 2.4; 2.17, 6.1 See H. Chadwick, *Early Christian Thought and the Classical Tradition* (New York: Oxford University Press, 1966), pp. 53–54, and Wolfson, *Philosophy*, pp. 576–77.

Artemonites who used knowledge to judge faith, or that of the radical gnostics who made knowledge esoteric and largely irrational. Clement's knowledge would include that of the rational Greek philosophical schools, which he deemed an actual part of divine revelation to prepare men to accept the faith and then to deepen their insight into it. Knowledge, then, wherever it is well expressed in philosophy—be it Stoic, Platonic, and even Aristotelian, all *scientia* inciting to righteousness and piety—should be welcome. Clement consequently had strong words of condemnation for the gnostics who assumed that orthodox faith and knowledge were irreconcilable.

Clement's pupil Origen followed his master's moderate position.[29] Christianity was to be neither an intellectual exercise for the few nor a blind faith for all. All who believed, even the ignorant with no philosophical understanding of faith, received sufficient knowledge from the teachings of Christ to meet their needs for salvation. Origen tells Celsus that Christian conversion, which had a power far superior to any pagan learning experience, was intended for all, the ignorant and the intellectually well endowed. Until the day of utopia arrived when all Christians would become philosophers through the words of the Scriptures, there would exist a sort of triple track to salvation. Was it not implied in *Mark* that, in one way or another, the disciples alone were given direct knowledge of the mysteries of the kingdom of heaven while the multitude was not and had to rely on parables? There were, indeed, different ranks of Christian elite: those capable of nothing more than faith, those capable of limited knowledge, and those who needed to be approached through demonstration by means of "questions and answers" and dialectics. Simple Christians were saved through simple faith, others through some knowledge and faith, and others again through a sublime wisdom engulfing faith. This message he hoped to spread through his famous school at Alexandria where no branch of knowledge was taboo. Thus although Origen retained the triple division of believers common in heretical gnosticism, he made room for universal salvation; all ascended, as it were, a mountain to God. The dualism of Plato is thus, in a sense, unified: the world of true knowledge native to the pre-existent soul was opened by revelation to all who lived in the sensible world.

---

[29] Origen, *Comm. in Matt.* 2.4 (*PG* 13:911-914), *C.C.* 6.13.14.

CHAPTER 6

THE HUMANISTIC

THE CLASSICAL QUEST FOR HUMANISM

"Man is the Measure of all Things" . . . Protagoras

It is manifestly improper to impose a modern term such as "humanism" on the Classical world. Yet ancient man's obvious awareness of the human plight over the centuries prompted him to ponder the same kind of issues that the modern word suggests. Humanism, of course, is an elusive concept because it is relative to a society's changing social strata and to a culture's intellectual sophistication. Human capabilities and worth are conceived differently in an aristocratic or democratic structure, in a cosmopolitan or parochial environment, or even in an urban or rural setting. Then, too, revelation and observation, reason and mysticism constantly vie for supremacy as intellectual tools of truth and consequently present man in different lights. Arbitrary decrees of gods in time often give way to deterministic rules of cosmic logic or to inexorable axioms of science. Science, in turn, forges its own new ontological absolutes unless it is kept in bounds by being relegated to the status of a mere methodological tool; depending on how it is used it can either dwarf or exalt humankind.

In trying to arrive at a workable definition of historical humanism it would seem useful to begin with Protagoras' famous remark that "man is the measure of all things." Immediately, however, the seemingly clear statement becomes controversial. Did Protagoras mean to say that every one was free to establish his or her own subjective truth since it was obvious to him that there were no gods or at least that it was a waste of time to try to discover them? Or did he want to teach that man in the generic sense was the final arbiter of values since as yet the existence of a higher supernatural order was not proven? In any event, both Protagorean interpretations would not allow humanism freedom to postulate religious or philosophical absolutes and would make man, singly or collectively, arbiter of what is true in an agnostic or atheistic setting. An alternative would be a Socratic type of humanism which would honor aspirations and desires of the entire human psyche including not only those issuing from the soul's rational faculty but also those arising from its emotional intuitive instincts and spiritual insights which put man in touch with god. A Socratic type of humanism would make room for Augustine's "credo ut intelligam" which asserts that faith lies at the basis of all intellectual activity both religious and secular; it would grant the human being freedom to discover and embrace religion especially if it is defined as a rational human means employed to alter the environment whether spiritual or material, individual or corporate. If, in a Socratic fashion, man does accept some absolute above himself—be it an uncontrollable Fate, Necessity, Nature, Zeus, or Providence which circumscribes his Protagorean freedom—can the demands of humanism still be satisfied if the arrangement assures some human dignity under the unalterable? These are the issues the Classical world pondered for a thousand years without benefit of our term "humanism." Everything considered, it might serve to define historical humanism as "an intellectual commitment extolling human freedom, dignity, and urbanity" in that order.

Since Greeks too often are sweepingly characterized as intellectual anarchists free from all constraints, it might be well to note that intellectual freedom was earned somewhat laboriously even in the Classical world. In reality the Greek thinker, too, was a person of good will generally pious in religious predispositions and traditions. He was, however, quite disposed to think about them and to sit in judgment over them. In doing so, the Greek philosopher automatically pondered human nature, its assets and potentialities, its limitations and constraints. Such questions lie at the heart of humanism. Obligated more to perform perfunctory traditional religious rituals than to subscribe to definite tenets, Classical man lived relatively free from crushing divine moral or intellectual imperatives. Recipients of no revelation of the Jewish kind, which settled once and for all the efficient and final causes of things, Greeks were generally inclined to honor only those theoretical absolutes they could rationally endorse; if they chose to create absolutes at all they were, as human inventions, subject to alteration and dismissal. No final creed, infallible church, or closed canon of truth restrained Greeks from lampooning their own myths and taboos or from developing a natural religion to provide some intellection of the universe and to buttress pragmatic moral principles. Moreover, to curious and inventive Greeks polytheism with its fickle gods provided attractive loopholes in causality, where either some degree of human influence could be inserted or some extraneous remorseless erratic Chance or Fortune imagined.

From prehistoric times vicissitudes of weather and season had overawed man with unexplainable physical forces and strange rhythms of biological compulsions. Homeric aristocracy naturally marshalled a hierarchy of divine powers to explain seemingly arbitrary physical and psychic phenomena. The very concept of aristocracy itself suggested that Chance or Destiny was in charge; was not noble birth itself, as Pindar opined, the crown of all gifts from heaven, an arbitrary arrangement of Nature or *Physis*? Once Hesiod made an audacious effort in the *Theogony* to impose some rational order on the gods under Zeus as a strong monarch, impassioned philosophical effort followed to search for some rational arrangement in the visible cosmos as well and eventually to establish some order in society through imposition of positive law. But Greeks continued to ask whether Zeus was actually in charge of Olympus and was a proper model for order on earth. Was the great god himself arbitrary or was he subject to Fate, some compulsion or Necessity existing in the makeup of Nature and exercised in its cosmic laws?

As time went on, Greek colonization of the Mediterranean, especially in the sixth and fifth centuries, and the accompanying intellectual enlightenment created such wide interest in anthropology and cosmology that philosophers and tragedians vied with each other to expose the nature of man and his universe. In the later individualistic and cosmopolitan Hellenistic environment the advance of science would bolster confidence in human reason to such a degree that Aristotle felt sufficiently secure and free to slight Fate and abandon its accompanying pessimism. Neither philosophy nor science, however, succeeded in allaying man's wonderment and dismay over his own imperfections and weakness in the face of forces overwhelming and often sinister; at the very twilight of the Classical age most pagan thinkers, overcome by what has been called a "loss of nerve," felt constrained to resort to a religiously passive acceptance of some form of providential determinism. At this point in history Christian thinkers were at hand to take up the persistent riddle of man's plight; Augustine truly stands on a familiar stage.

The Classical witnesses in the debate over humanism are of all sorts. Poets, philosophers, historians, rhetoricians, and artists were all anxious in one way or another to comment upon the mystery of human nature and the ability of human thought to deal with the bewildering and seemingly overwhelming universe. At one podium stood the human soul and its potential; at the other stood man's Lot or Destiny dictated by Fate, Zeus, Necessity, Providence, Reason, or Nature accompanied by lesser attendants, Fortune or Chance.

That few Greek thinkers spared colleagues their thoughts on the human soul seems evident from the many references to such authors in works as far apart as Cicero's *Tusculan Disputations* and Nemesius' *On the Nature of Man* (c. A.D. 400). The long story might well begin when the Cyclops, Polyphemus of Homeric fame, dashed out the brains of Odysseus' mates. In doing so he acted not only robustly but scientifically since "soul" at times was identified with the brain fluid which supposedly drained through the spinal cord to provide life and the liquid of procreation. Sudden puzzling human psychic experiences, including dreams, were ascribed by Homer to divine agencies outside the body.

Sometimes the soul was identified as the spirited life of the body, warm and vaporous, generally located in the heart or breast. If the religious trouble-shooter Epimenides, who visited Athens c. 630, did not already view man's soul as a detachable entity capable of reincarnation, certainly Pythagoras did a century later. By the beginning of the Greek enlightenment c. 500 the Classical age had inherited, as Dodds sums up in his *The Greeks and the Irrational*, a hodgepodge of conflicting views of the soul.[1] It could be a corpse living in a tomb, a phantom in Hades, a transcendent breath, a transmigrating semi-divine entity. In such uncertainty, troublesome uncontrollable psychic impulses and drives such as love, anger, courage, forgetfulness, and ecstasy continued on as divine visitations. The poets Theognis and Pindar, the latter one of the first to think of the soul as truly divine, made psychic experiences more personal by attributing them to beneficent daimons assigned to individuals. Plato, much later, still valued his daimon's inspirational activity which he was careful, nonetheless, to subject to the dictates of reason.

The sixth-century enlightenment, introduced by religious reformers like Xenophanes, complicated anthropology by tending to discount divine intervention and inspiration, leaving man more puzzled with himself than before. The physician Alamaeon of Croton probably did not realize his contribution to the eventual conceptualization of an independent human psyche when he removed emotions from the breast and located them in the head, where the soul was at that time thought to reside.[2] The time was now ripe for Protagoras and Socrates, but especially Plato, to emphasize the full potential of the human soul and to dissect it as a complex agent, preeminently as the seat of reason and discernment.

Plato, of course, had much to say about the soul. He did not always agree with his revered teacher Socrates on the matter nor was he himself always consistent, but he never doubted Socrates' contention that man was a unique rational being exalted above all creation as the possessor of an entity sharing in a divine nature. In the *Phaedo* the soul is an eternal, transmigratory, pre-existent simplex. In its earlier pure existence it dwelt in the realm of the Absolutes, of the Ideas, of true Being or Reality where eternal Beauty, Justice, and Piety dwelt. Though antithetical to matter, the individual soul unfortunately was destined to become entrapped, even incarcerated, in a material body which, as a hostile environment, forced it to suffer debilitating consequences. Its vision

---

[1] Dodds, *Irrational*, pp. 178–180.

[2] W. C. Greene, *Moira* (New York: Harper & Row 1963), p. 289 n. 64, and R. B. Onians, *Origins of European Thought* (Cambridge: Cambridge University Press, 1954), p. 115, deal with the importance of Alcmaeon. Dodds, *Irrational*, pp. 138–40, attempts to deal with the early development of the independent psyche.

became blurred, its potential enfeebled. In the *Sophist* the soul is pictured somewhat diseased or maimed, "fallen"[3] as it were, reminiscent of Orphic lore which condemned divinity and matter to exist in a monstrous mixture thanks to the "original sin" of the ancestors of the human race, the Titans, who ate the divine flesh of Dionysos. At times, Plato speaks of man as a dual combination joining body, marred by passions and appetites operated by an animal soul, with a human soul, spirit or nous, as the seat of intelligence and reason. In the *Republic* he suggests that the soul might be divided into three parts: the desirous or appetitive, the courageous or spirited as the seat of feeling and willing, and the rational part, which is immortal. In this case passions are quite intimately associated with the soul's activity and can be directly monitored and sublimated, elevated so to speak, through the sensory to, the intellective level. Whatever the exact composition of Plato's soul, its rational part makes man man.

Aristotle thought it worthwhile to write an entire work *On the Soul*. Somewhat like Plato, he distinguishes three types of souls: plant, animal, and human. The first type concerns itself with nutrition and reproduction, the second with sense perception and in most cases with locomotion; the third, the human soul or the mind, deals with the intellective, the rational. Since the three types of soul cannot exist apart, transmigration is impossible. The human soul, of course, is the seat of the intellectual virtues spoken of in the *Nichomachean Ethics* a work greatly interested in man's rational and irrational composition. Unique in having his animal soul and human soul interconnected, the human being exists as both an emotional and a rational being. Mindful of the dual physical aspect of form and matter and the psychic duality of potentiality and actuality, Aristotle divides the human soul into two parts: one is the reasoning power itself, the form, that which makes the soul what it is; the second is that which the soul becomes as it incorporates the knowledge gained through its own activity.[4]

As deterministic, mechanistic materialists, Epicureans declare the soul to be, like all matter, a combination of atoms. To Lucretius, the Roman Epicurean, the human mind or intellect, the *animus*, located in the breast, is a part of the human being in the same sense as his foot is. In an unclear manner, Lucretius interconnects with the mind a vital spirit,

---

[3] Plato's shift from considering evil a non-reality, the absence of good, arising largely out of human ignorance, to accepting it as a force stemming out of an imperfect world soul, is of momentous importance both to orthodox Christianity and gnosticism. Dodds, *Irrational*, p. 213, finds evidence of the change in the *Sophist* (227D–228E), in the *Phaedrus* (237D–238B), and in *Laws* (863A–864B). Consider also *Laws* 957A and *Rep.* 410A.

[4] W. D. Ross in choosing significant passages for his *Aristotle: Selections* (New York: Scribner, 1938) cites *De anima* 408a34–408b31 to describe the soul as an instrument, and 412a3–415a13 to reveal the soul as partly a product of its own activity.

anima, made up of atoms of breath or air and of heat which are subtly
diffused throughout the body but not in alternate blocks alongside body
atoms, as Democritus had claimed. To Lucretius, it seemed obvious that
both mind and spirit had to be material since they responded to material
stimuli. Mind atoms are small and spherical to facilitate quick motion;
spirit atoms comprise such a tiny mass that their combined weight is so
negligible as to prove immeasurable at death. Another unnamed component added to the composition of the soul and made up of the most
rarified kinds of atoms imaginable, provides the "sensory motions
throughout the body," electrical impulses we might say, to stir the heat
and breath atoms into motion. At any rate, since all components of the
soul are atomic, the soul is mortal. Unable to exist in its intricate composition apart from body atoms, it dissolves at death, dispersing its
different atoms into the general mass of like particles in the universe.[5]

The fourth book of Cicero's *Tusculan Disputations,* given over to a
discussion of the soul, records many different views held on the subject
by ancient writers, including even those few philosophers like Di-
caearchus and the Aristotelian Aristoxenus who denied its existence.
Cicero himself, in true Sceptic fashion, does not contribute any definite
personal convictions to the larger discussion on the soul's prospects for
immortality. He seems anxious, however, because of the death of his
beloved daughter Tullia, to have us believe in a detachable soul capable
of afterlife.

Stoicism, originally a monistic materialistic pantheism, held that the
soul was part of the divine fiery aether of the cosmos. As part of cosmic
Reason the soul was pronounced unique, compared to the rudimentary
principle of natural cohesion which supposedly bound together inani-
mate objects, or compared to the primitive living principle in plants and
animals. Centered in the breast, the soul operated on the physical level
by sending out connectives to the proper organs of the five senses as well
as to those of speech and reproduction. A *tabula rasa* at birth, it received
its intellectual content via impressions through stages of perception,
recollection and conception.[6] Even though divine and rational, the Stoic
soul enjoyed no personal immortality; at death it dissolved, either immediately or ultimately, into the universal Soul as Reason, Zeus, or Providence.

Later Stoicism, more dualistic, led philosophers like Seneca to hope

---

[5] Trying to fit rationality and free will into a mechanical system forces Lucretius into a
most complicated and controversial description of soul. *De rerum nat.* 3. 95–180 and 231–
90.

[6] Tertullian in *De anima* 14 says Panaetius divided the soul into five or six parts while
Posidonius mentioned fourteen. As Aristotle saw, the divisions are basically powers or
faculties. For old Stoicism, especially Chrysippus, consult E. Bréhier, *Chrysippe et L'ancien
Stoïcisme* (Paris: University of France, 1951), pp. 157–81.

for the soul's liberation from the body as a separate part of the immortal divine cosmos. Seneca chose to follow Posidonius in distinguishing three functions in the soul—instinctive, sensory, and rational. Thus he would make the soul a more personalized entity composed of an irrational and a rational part; the latter, as the supreme divine element, would reflect the will of Providence. Epictetus, in turn, says little in any analytical way, about the soul. Although quite dualistic in his views, he entertains few prospects for personal immortality. Marcus Aurelius, in a very Platonic dualistic fashion, views the soul as an aerial, fiery substance overpowered in the body. If sometimes he speaks of man as constituted of body, breath or life, and intellect or mind, he always deems the last component alone worthy of concern in its own right as something of a benevolent daimon or god within him. At times, the great Stoic emperor seems to distinguish two rational souls. One is capable of mere expertise in some craft or art but not equipped to partake in the rational Soul of the universe; the other is equipped with Reason, common to man and gods, fitting it to participate in the life of the divine. Although divine in origin, nature, and destiny, the rational soul might enjoy at best only a temporary individual return to god after death. Nonetheless, the soul as intellective Reason is man's crowning glory since it alone can take cognizance of its environment and even of the divinity within itself.

Like the Stoics, neo-Platonists connect the soul directly with divine essence. But in this case it is an extension of a Plotinian trinity of the One, the Nous, and the World Soul. One's individual soul, a distinct but not separate part of the universal Soul, is capable of descending into the material world where body can share it. Yet its descent does not entirely detach its higher aspect or nous from the spiritual world. The soul merely projects itself into the body as a logos of its own intellective level which continues in touch with the Trinitarian Nous. Nonetheless, the soul is hampered to a degree by sharing in the life of the body and does suffer a sort of "fall" since it cannot operate freely but only in respect to its particular body. Discovery of its true self comes when it returns to the Nous temporarily through contemplation and rejection of body; full self-realization, attainable by only a few aspirants, is experienced through illumination allowing their souls to reach to the wholly transcendent One itself. The soul of the neo-Platonist has three levels, so to speak: one looking toward the Nous, one toward the body and a third intermediary section which can direct itself either upward or downward. The spirituality of each soul depends on the degree to which it indulges in or rejects concerns of its particular body.[7] In the last analysis, as with St. Augustine, man's soul cannot rest in peace until it rests in God.

---

[7] Selections in A. H. Armstrong, *Plotinus* (New York: Collier, 1962), pp. 84–112, provide a brief but workable introduction to Plotinus' concept of soul.

Such, briefly, was the resource—a soul equipped with Reason generally thought divine—that Classical man gave himself to challenge Fate in hopes of winning some measure of freedom or at least some degree of dignity. By whatever name it was called the soul's adversary seemed invincible: Fate by nature was arbitrary and overpowering; as Necessity rooted in a cosmic deficiency, it was compelling. Both Fate and Necessity, as unconscious powers, knew no pacification. Even as a conscious Zeus, or Providence, Reason or Nature, the adversary was relentless because by its very constitution it was unable to abdicate its control. The fickleness of Fortune, Chance, and Accident put even these lesser forces beyond human wits.

Homer's day, too unsophisticated to conceive of awe-filled impersonalized forces, attributed happenings to the will of heaven marshalled under Zeus. But his leadership appeared at times to be so arbitrary, puzzlingly irrational, and possibly malevolent that often it became difficult to distinguish it from unconcerned Fate. Humans, it appeared, could simply decide some things and not others; to the sinister situation one must be resigned; for those helpful, gratis visitations of psychic grace, as Dodds describes them, those mysterious impulses to courage and energy which saved one's life in battle, one must be thankful. Metaphors of binding and weaving are common; individuals simply are forced to do what they are "bound" to do. Under Zeus' pragmatic realpolitik the three Moirai or Fates operate in Hesiod's *Theogony* as daughters of Night spinning and cutting the threads of Destiny under the names of Klotho, Lachesis, and Atropos. In Hesiod's *Works and Days* a conscious Zeus visits increased hardships on humankind through successively deteriorating ages because of his anger over Prometheus' affront. Man's progressive anxiety and pessimism over his portion, which never seemed to allow conditions to meet expectations, spawned even the idea that the gods were touchy about their dues and actually vindictive, jealous enough of human prosperity to lead men deliberately into temptation or put them to the test, an idea still found in the Lord's Prayer. The oracle at Delphi so confounded Cylon that his attempted coup in seventh-century Athens ended in his sacrilegious murder which, by violating divine taboos, conjured up so great a paralyzing fear that the Cretan wizard Epimenides was imported to allay it by ritualistic purification. Croesus' unfortunate interpretation of the oracle's double-talk led him into a classic disaster. Divine jealousy lured the opulent sixth-century Polycrates, despite his show of good will and repentance, to such an unusual doom as punishment for hybris that Herodotus shrinks from describing it. Pythagoras, following in Orphic fashion, somewhat exonerated the gods by associating man's consignment to suffering with the original sin of the Titans; quite conversely, the poet Theognis somewhat blasphemously began to chide Zeus for arbitrarily punishing the innocent and pampering the wicked. Would it have been better for mortals never to have been born? Simonides, while poetically conceding that all came from the gods, seems to wonder whether their actions were not somehow constrained by Necessity. Pindar, too, touches on the unpredictable ways of the gods who arbitrarily predestined not only one's birth and rank in society, but sealed even the lot of individual Olympic victors.

While each Greek tragedian handles his materials in his own unique complex way, Greek tragedy in general exploits the theme that some external force inflicts men with inherited curses, uncontrollable passions, ineptitudes, unexplained folly or blindness—all of which drive them to some predetermined doom. Aeschylus, piously absolving the gods of jealousy and the desire to tempt men, would hold the Immortals only mildly responsible for the human plight in so far as the gods possibly afforded man an original opportunity to sin on his own. But he prefers to assign any compulsion to some residue or substratum of evil in the universe which circumscribes even Zeus in his "necessary" struggle to fulfill his own destiny as the ultimate paragon of justice. For humankind, though, Zeus' will is irresistible but well intentioned.[8] Sophocles, less interested than Aeschylus in analyzing and evaluating divine justice, simply accepts the human lot as divinely ordained by gods who, though still jealous in nature, are basically just. Euripides bereft of any trust in divine concern in an iconoclastic age, often permits his characters to succumb in modern fashion to their own inner psychic compulsion and thus, in a way, experience a new kind of psychological necessity rooted in a human nature beyond their control.

Even early historians are not immune to asking philosophically why things happen. Herodotus relied on a dramatic theistic determinism to explain Greece's astounding victory over Persia. Did not Persian armies and navies gather in vain at the Hellespont since they were doomed by offended and unforgiving gods? Once having sacrilegiously whipped Poseidon with chains and constrained him with a bridge, Xerxes could no more escape divine retribution than Polycrates before him. Should not Croesus, too, have realized that only that human being is happy who dies before a reversal of his fortune?

In a sense, Herodotus is the last of the old theistic determinists who pictured anthropomorphic gods controlling human affairs jealousy, or irrationally, or with limited concern. Thinkers of the fifth century, especially rising philosophers, preferred to turn their attention to more secular, human matters and to minimize Fate, certainly to discount it as the will of a primitive anthropomorphic Zeus. In the strange charismatic

[8] Aeschylus' view of Zeus' relation to Fate is discussed by Greene in *Moira*, pp. 107–08. Zeus is made subject to his moral nature emphasizing justice so that he is not unlike the Christian God who cannot violate his own nature of goodness.

Empedocles religion is still blended with physics and medicine. But in his contemporary Anaxagoras, as well as in the atomist Democritus—both significantly interested in medicine—little or no room is found for gods who would direct human affairs. The proto-Sophist Protagoras helped pave the way for later Sophists like Prodicus who were interested in dethroning theology and even traditional philosophy in favor of more pragmatic concerns about man's immediate freedom. In daily life should he be restrained by nature *(physis)*, or by law *(nomos)*, or by both? In the face of such matters Fate to the Sophist became a meaningless insoluble matter better ignored.

To Plato all such Sophistic subjectivism was disquieting. Socrates, he thought, rightly sought an ultimate rational objectivity in the universe which the gods directed toward an established good. By assigning Reality only to a world of eternal and unchangeable Forms or Ideas, Plato created an absolute world over man culminating in the highest Idea of the Good, virtually god, a world which negated both the subjectivism of the Sophists and the materialism of the followers of such as Anaxagoras and Democritus. Plato's providential arrangement supervises in a benign way not only the operation of the cosmos as a whole but also, to some extent, the occurrence of single earthly happenings. The highest Good controls the world of Ideas, subsidiary astral deities direct organic processes, daimons oversee particular acts and functions. Chance, Fortune, or Accident are also divine rational agents even though man doesn't know it. In Plato's sharp cosmic dualism, matter became the realm of non-Being harboring a certain "evil," better described as "resistance," which the demiurge of the *Timaeus* encountered by "necessity" when he tried to order and arrange pre-existing matter by imposing upon it the Forms or archetypes of the real world. "Necessity", as the irrational, the deviant, the resistant, the unordered in matter, becomes a negative compulsion or causality which Providence handles in an intelligent way. In the *Laws*, however, Plato located a stronger concept of "evil" in the World Soul itself which the demiurge created imperfectly as the source of original motion. In this view, the World Soul, if not actually to be understood as a dual entity of good and evil,[9] is at least made capable of acting rationally and irrationally. The human being in this case is buffeted by a force stronger than "Necessity"; the basic weakness is located in the human soul itself as a reflection of the fatal imperfection in the cosmic World Soul.

Aristotle, a practical man, is not concerned about Fate. His famous discussion of tragedy proves to be more interested in the psychological aspects of the art-form than the determinism which lies behind it. To

---

[9] Plutarch's interpretation (*De Isid. et Osir.* 369a–d) of Plato's World Soul as dual natured, capable of good and evil, was an influential one.

him matter is a hypothetical basis of everything or, put in another way, the unintelligible residue left when all that is intelligible is extracted. As such it is not evil in itself, even if its potentiality is hampered by a certain natural "necessity" which interferes with its own becoming and therefore disrupts indirectly the rational plans of men as well. In fact, "necessity" impedes all objects from attaining their proper perfection in the unfolding of nature's own imbedded rational teleology, which seeks the realization of its own best potential under the operation of the good, but unprovidential, unmoved Mover. Fate at most is, then, nothing but an offal of the cosmic operation. Chance or Accident, Aristotle declares in his *Physics*, is a minor force since by its very nature it cannot be prior to the essential; because it is accidental in relation to a greater given, it is largely an indifferent concern, unworthy to account for human history even though at times it might prove beneficial.

If Cicero on the Roman scene, as an eclectic Academic with a strong strain of Scepticism, found it difficult to fully endorse Providence in his *On the Nature of the Gods,* he was even less inclined to be tolerant of determinism in his partly extant work *On Fate* which was based on a similar study by Posidonius the Stoic. Cicero reveals a good deal of contempt for the idea because of its superstitious connection with the word *Fatum* (spoken word or prediction); to believe that a word unleashed a mysterious power into the universe which can effect causality required childish credulity. All happenings, Cicero thought, could be understood if scientific knowledge were up to it. Devotees of divination, astrology, and Chance should see that they are dealing with meaningless commitments if Fate determines all things.

Cicero's contemporary, the Epicurean Lucretius, probably did more in his eloquent persuasive work *On the Nature of Things* to reinforce the crass fatalism of earlier atomists such as Leucippus and Democritus than he might have intended. Any effort on his part to soften the blow of Fate is easily lost sight of in the overall description of a mechanistic world in which nature moved in obedience to set patterns bereft of gods or a providential force.

Despite two centuries of good times in the early Roman imperial era, a sense of resignation to the will of an overpowering Providence became more and more evident. A growing concern for a providential religion, whether a product of a "loss of nerve" or not, is quite in evidence since the days when Augustus recognized the revival of the old time religion of the pantheon taking place at the opening of the Christian era. The emperor's patriotic religious restoration, however anachronistic it may have been in the long run, became immortalized in Virgil's *Aeneid* which did much to restore the gods' reputations as providential powers. Once the gods had decreed that defeated Troy should be reborn, Aeneas, as Venus' son, dutifully accepted his lot in the enterprise so that the pre-

existent future heroes of Rome already waiting in Hades could be born
to assume their destined roles in the unfolding of Rome's greatness.
Virgil's renewed commitment of Rome to a divine providential destiny
was kept alive by emperors who claimed, as we saw, to host within their
persons the living goddess *Roma* herself. Plutarch hailed *Fortuna* as
propitious to Rome and strove to keep the old gods in charge of its
history, along with their oracles. Finally, Julian the Apostate in Christian
times assigned the pagan gods providential care over the empire's different races and peoples under the general management of Helios as
cosmic king. Although in some instances late neo-Platonism became
imbued with Aristotelean studies, it found ways to stress Providence
under such leaders as Hierocles of Alexandria. Proclus, the learned
Platonic "priest" composed, in a scholastic manner, a final and influential
summa theologica of the past teachings of his school, to the last defending Providence as the only rational foil to evil in the world.

Nowhere does a pagan Providence play a larger role than in Stoicism
which replaced Fate with an immanent, pantheistic, divine force conscious and benevolent, a view somewhat anticipated c. 500 B.C. by
Heraclitus who first identified Fate as the Logos, a cosmic spiritual
energy. Stoics came to call it by various names—Zeus, Providence, Reason, Nature, Logos. In this pantheistic system divine Reason constituted
or permeated the entire universe so remorselessly that an endless chain
of cause and effect resulted in a rigid logical determinism which entangled man, as well as everything else, in a relentless, yet benign order.
In the Stoic pantheistic world everything was so minutely associated that
every cause through its effect is linked to another cause so that nothing
happens which was not bound to happen. Nor was anything to happen
except that which could trace every efficient cause of its happening to
Nature. Cleanthes' famous third-century *Hymn to Zeus* paid moving
tribute to the great god who rules all as Reason, to whose dispensation all
must capitulate as an object of religious worship. Eternally bearing sway,
Zeus allows nothing in the entire universe to be done by men or other
agencies. Chrysippus, in turn, allows god's foreknowledge uncontrolled
sway over every detail of existence; it leads the willing, pulls along the
objecting.[10] Panaetius of Rhodes temporarily chose to tone down
Stoicism's cosmological determinism in favor of a practical ethic to suit
Roman temperaments. But Posidonius, whom Cicero heard in 78,
quickly returned to traditional themes maintaining in his *On Fate* that
Reason as Zeus permeated all substances and arranged everything by a

[10] The literature on Stoic fatalism, especially that of Chrysippus, is enormous. J. M.
Rist, *Stoic Philosophy* (Cambridge, Cambridge University Press, 1969), chap. 7, pp. 112–132,
and E. Bréhier, *Chrysippe*, should be consulted. A short, pointed statement can be found in
the editors' introduction to "Plutarch's" *De fato* in the Loeb edition of the *Moralia* 7:303–
309.

divine wisdom. Later Stoics in the imperial period, less anxious to stress the theoretical, preached abject obedience to the wise force in and around men; only then would human beings live rationally and have peace of mind. Epictetus, for one, so religiously submitted to the divine governance of the universe that he urged his readers not only to accept but to encourage any terminal disease Providence had arranged for them. Later Stoics also were particularly anxious to disassociate old Fate as blind Necessity from the will of Zeus of Providence. Seneca thought both forces demanded willing compliance from men. Marcus Aurelius, like Seneca apparently unsure of the true cosmic dispensation, fatalistically asked: if Necessity exists, why try to resist? If Providence exists why not make oneself worthy of it? Astrology became more and more popular in the empire thanks much to the Stoics' assumption that it provided a rataional way to discern the true intentions of cosmic nature so one could surrender to them intelligently.

Like Stoicism, the last great school of Classical philosophy, neo-Platonism, could find meaning only in a providential dispensation. So called middle-Platonists like Plutarch, Albinus, and Numenius provided an easy second-century transition to the neo-Platonism of Plotinus and Proclus. All were highly religious philosophers zealously committed to explaining "creation's" relationship to the Absolute by postulating a trinity of emanations generally known as the One, the Nous, and the World Soul. Plutarch, sincere pagan priest and moralist, somewhat pessimistically interpreted Plato as teaching the existence of an evil World Soul. Bound up in pre-existent matter from the beginning, this Soul, despite its orderly transformation at "creation" by the demiurge into the divine Soul of the universe, still remained a repository of evil which daimons helped dispense among men. The work *On Fate,* wrongly attributed to Plutarch but quite compatible with middle-Platonic thought, tried ingeniously to subordinate Fate to god in a trinitarian system: Providence or god ordained Fate as his law to his offspring gods whose wills constituted a second level of Providence. The wills of daimons, who tended the doings of men, made up a third kind of Providence all existing in a descending, or ascending, whole.[11] Albinus and Numenius, supporting a trinity of the One, the Demiurge, and the World Soul, also like Plutarch tended to make the last emanation evil because of its combination with matter where daimons lurked. The great Plotinus preferred to declare matter not evil but faulty or lacking because of its inertness and final remoteness from the One. Even though matter was essentially non-being without quality, it yet entertained a certain Necessity as its inescapable lot incurred by being the last extention from the highest quality, the One. Body, as part of matter, limited man's soul by

[11] Plutarch, *De fato* 572F–574D.

forcing it to associate with Necessity. Neo-Platonism, in the last analysis, presented man with a final Absolute so transcendental that one could not describe it, so compelling that he could not escape it, so alluring that he would not wish to. Of the prevalence of astral determination we will speak later.

The debate is now ready. Man with his soul is at one podium; blind Fate, compelling Necessity, domineering Providence is at the other. In the ensuing historical debate man is intent, somewhat pathetically, on asserting some freedom or at least some dignity for himself. Perhaps Fate will have a lapse of attention, or man will conjure up an ingenious argument, or possibly a god will enter the fray to settle it.

In archaic Greek thought, which was devoid of ethical definitions, moral attitudes were vague, unsophisticated, and situational to the extent that acts of violence, for instance, were blameworthy against friends but legitimate against enemies. Even such rudimentary ethics, however, entailed some sense of responsibility and freedom to act with limited dignity within the context of Fate. Since human potential for self-fulfillment was somehow limited by lot, arete demanded that one accept his allotted portion without challenge and not try to overstep it. The early Greek evidently enjoyed enough freedom to act well when he fulfilled his limited potential, or to act badly when he failed to know himself and thus failed to realize his selfhood. Failure to "think thoughts appropriate to mortals who must die" and folly to pursue goals to excess were chief evils. Both the *Iliad* and the *Odyssey* by implying that mortals may exceed by their own folly the measure of evil and woe to which they were fated, certainly attributed to men the dubious freedom to co-sponsor evil.[12] Later, as the gods progressively came to be considered authors of only good—god is blameless Plato will say, and the Stoics will make deity benignly providential—man had to take more and more responsibility for evil; he, in turn, sought something of a scapegoat in blind Fate or Necessity, in external forces, as Aristotle remarked in commenting on ethics. Yet such formidable forces must not be overwhelming lest mortals lose the freedom and incentive to make what they will, for good or evil, of the opportunities assigned them. Sometimes man asks whether in his lot certain areas exist which are not necessarily bound by the threads of Fate, that are free, as it were, from close supervision by Zeus. In such enclaves humans could hope for freedom to create their own opportunities for good as well as for evil. Was such an area discovered by Hesiod in the world of the peasant, an unheroic sphere of activity disdained by Zeus, where physical labor was allowed to create an en-

---

[12] Onians, *Thought* pp. 390–92 considers the idea that not everything is bound, in so far as men can exceed their own folly, an important step in the development of human autonomy. Also M. P. Nilsson, *A History of Greek Religion* (New York: Norton, 1964), p. 168.

vironment where man enjoyed the possibility to create good? Since Solon, as a practical lawgiver in early sixth-century Athens, naturally had to hold citizens responsible more for the evil they committed than the good they did, it was easy for him to conclude that the gods could not be held responsible for human offences and troubles, which obviously resulted from man's own pride and material greed. Simonides, court poet in Athens under the Pisistratids, seems motivated as much or more by self interest than by piety in his assessment of divine determination. Subsidized by the court to sing of the divine sanction supposedly given to the Thessalian tyrant Scopas, he cleverly avowed that only that man could be just—as his patron obviously was—whom the gods favored, and therefore if one failed in the struggle for virtue there should be no blame but rather admiration for expended efforts. Theognis, though angry and puzzled by events, held the gods blameless for the kind of justice which allowed the violence and greed of peasants to confiscate his Megaran estates. Evil was clearly man's doing; whatever good came his way came from the gods.

Up to this point mortals seem pathetically willing to accept responsibility for some evil in exchange for the freedom to commit it; at the same time they seem dubious about how much capacity for good they should assume. Pythagoras in the sixth century appears to be one of the first sound Classical historical figures who, while recognizing human responsibility for evil, sought opportunities for individuals to act more positively and thus somewhat to loosen the bonds of Fate. His doctrine of reincarnation served not only to explain present injustices and unmerited evil as curses for prior transgressions in former existences, but at the time it lent opportunities for man to act positively in atoning not only for the original Titan offense but also for any pollution later contracted through choice. In addition, Pythagorean gnosis of sundry effective ascetic practices, ritualistic initiations, and mystic unions, like the cultism of later mystery cults, guaranteed man the ability to obviate disabilities incurred by his own choice. Of course, charlatans like those mentioned in Plato's *Republic,* and found in later neo-Pythagorean circles, always arose to overdo and misdirect this kind of positive thinking by claiming a sacrilegious gnosis which could order even the gods not only to bind victims with evil fortune but also to release a treasure of "grace" to free men from their bonds. Pindar expressed in a few poems to his patrons an interesting hope that through the Eleusinian mysteries individuals could somewhat determine the state of their souls after death to compensate for their lack of control over their earthly lot.

Even if Greek tragedy by nature is basically fatalistic, portraying victims suffering severely for some flaw in their character, individual tragedians could not deny themselves some humanistic nuances in dealing with the freedom, or at least with the dignity, of their characters.

Aeschylus, for example, basically seems to allow men the opportunity to have made the original mistake from which their subsequent sufferings flow. Although his characters are not free to alter the contemporary tragic action, they deliberately choose to struggle with honor against what they cannot change. This is all the more true for Sophocles' characters who elect to bear allotted suffering with unusual dignity. And here, too, evil in the plot can be taken as the result of earlier free choice. Finally, human suffering is meritorious in that it can be sublimated as educative, enlightening, and possibly contributory to the eventual triumph of cosmic Justice. Euripides, always controversial, has been held the most humanistic of the tragedians in the sense that his sophistic characters largely determine the dramatic action by their own human, albeit often irrational, behavior.[13] Euripides' use of the *deus ex machina* can be interpreted as a device the poet deliberately uses to disrupt Fate and bring matters to an unexpected conclusion. Even the Christian Eusebius thinks that Euripides, in dealing with Oedipus, wants to allow man to break through and disrupt the chain of Fate. Finally, another humanistic interpretation of Euripides may be reflected in Menander's suggestion that the gods grant sufficient "grace," as it were, to allow individuals to control their fate by injecting human decisions about which the gods are largely unconcerned.

Protagoras and the Sophists approach the outlook secular humanists applaud. Since certain knowledge of the gods was not at hand and too elusive to pursue, Protagoras, as we saw, declared that human judgment, by default, would have to be the arbiter of truth. As a result philosophy yielded to rhetoric, a tool calculated to enhance one's freedom by minimizing one's danger of falling into the intellectual power of an adversary. To men like Gorgias and Isocrates oral persuasion became almost a divine art since verbal articulation could, in a way, create and recreate human nature at will and at the same time transmit, through a new utilitarian paideia, a relativity of values which the creative pace of contemporary society demanded. Such a disposition made a Sophist little inclined to worry about being engulfed in any objective cosmic context such as Fate; all must be taken hypothetically, as temporary, reversible, and subject to emendation.

Reacting against Sophistic relativism, Plato put himself in an inconsistent and dubious humanistic position. On the one hand, he was proud of the human potential evinced in the fifty-century enlightenment; on

---

[13] The non-fatalistic aspects of Greek tragedy, especially of Aeschylus but also Sophocles, are explored by Greene, *Moira,* p. 91. Even Aeschylus' Prometheus (266) says "by my free will I have sinned; in aiding humanity I wrought my own suffering." Telfer, *Cyril and Nemesius,* p. 436 n.2, calls attention to the fact that Menander, a devoted imitator and interpreter of Euripides, maintained that the gods have given to each one a character that fits him to be master of his fate.

the other, afraid of anarchy, he was driven to advocate a reactionary spiritual outlook reminiscent of early Greek religion. To modern admirers like Jaeger, Plato, following Socrates, seemed to elevate humanity in dignity by giving it a higher spiritual meaning and so afford humanism a foundation in philosophy. To Plato's adverse critics, such as Schiller, the great philosopher fastened an incomprehensible, irreversible Absolutism or Providentialism on man so compelling that it imprisoned him in a valueless world of non-reality where freedom and dignity can't exist and where only death is a welcome boon. At any rate, Plato would mold man through infallible institutions and censored education so that proper knowledge would make him order priorities suitably. Only then could he strive for an end outside himself, a vague identification with the essence of the Good. By it all, man is put in something of a conflicting position; on one hand, he is important to Plato as a creative agent and a necessary one since the cosmic universe cannot fully realize itself without man, who shares part of its World Soul; on the other hand, man is subjected to the disabilities of an earthly confinement precisely because he is part of the World Soul—an imperfect one. Yet, hopefully through education, transmigration, and purification mortals would eventually have a place with the gods.

Plato is not always consistent about the nature of the freedom or dignity he wants to give humankind. In the *Phaedrus* the charioteer driving two steeds of opposite temperament allegorizes the soul torn between good and evil struggling to give rein to the better force. Similarly in the *Republic* the divine rational third of the soul is expected to control the appetitive and spirited parts. Book X thus assumes that man can develop his character through free choice within the context of the fated lot he has chosen earlier from among those offered him at random by Lachesis. In the *Myth of Er* Plato more or less ignores Fate and asserts man's liberty by putting his place in the afterlife squarely on his human shoulders; the blame is his who chooses. God is blameless. Human misfortunes and ill choices are, in a humanistic way, declared redeemable by being made educative in the afterlife where transmigration offers opportunities for purification. The *Timaeus* equates a soul's welfare proportionately with its triumphs over all kinds of weaknesses including those inherent in its own nature, those induced by bad habits, and those incited by external stimuli. Yet in the *Laws* Plato makes humankind god's outright property, his puppet to jerk around; here god is the measure of all things and the proper end of all education. If human law is to work, the demiurge, as well as his children gods and the daimons guarding mortals, cannot be held blameworthy for human actions. Consequently man should honorably recognize his responsibility for evil and the deeds that emanate from his blighted soul. Yet, on the whole, Plato comforts his readers with the assurance that evil is only the absence of

Good rather than a positive sinister force and that no one deliberately chooses it but succumbs to it from ignorance or delusion, both remediable by education. Furthermore, the gods promise never to forsake those who try to be just, and beneficent daimons are at hand to guide them. Fate, made Providence, aids man with divine Chance, a sort of undeserved "grace" to help save him at times from his own folly and just deserts. All in all, Plato proves no more effective in harmonizing freedom of will with his world of unchangeable Absolutes as he is in connecting his abstract Forms with matter. In a baffling way man is put in a formidable context, admittedly benevolent, within which he is held responsible for his bad actions whether they are due to an evil imbedded in his blighted nature or to a remedial unsubstantial evil resulting from human ignorance rather than ill will. But even so, the Platonic arrangement is such that man enjoys a type of both tragic freedom and dignity which would have troubled Protagoras. While human beings have the capacity for self realization through rational communion with transcendent Truth and Goodness they rarely realize it.

Aristotle, breathing less ethereal air, axiomatically assumes that man enjoys virtually unlimited freedom of will and responsibility for his actions. Yet one must remember that Aristotle is speaking only of aristocrats who were economically free to think virtuous thoughts and to cultivate virtuous habits. Unlike Plato and the Stoics, he divorced ethics from theology and the larger cosmic condition. Neither an evil nor providential principle operates in the universe and even its "necessary" existing lack of perfection, which creates environmental conditions hampering human fulfillment, can be used as an asset or liability. Happiness, man's greatest good, is a humanistic product, neither a theistic gift nor a fortuitous happening. To Aristotle it would be entirely unworthy of one to attribute his greatest good to any source other than his own activity of soul in accord with virtue which, in turn, is a product of his volition and deliberately cultivated habits. The importance of voluntary and deliberate acts is so important to Aristotle that he directs much of Book III of his *Nichomachean Ethics* to praise man's reason for modifying and controlling desire through deliberation and reflection. Since good and evil do not depend on the gods or on changes of Fortune, it was absurd for one to blame his wrongdoings on external causes while claiming praise for his noble acts.

The later Peripatetics, by remaining loyal to Aristotle's views on the human condition, provided most of the strong free-will arguments against the growing fatalism in the late Classical world. Typical is Alexander of Aphrodisias whose work *On Fate* (c. A.D. 200) attacked Fate by arguing that its blind nature could never allow it to be a final cause; furthermore, it defended human freedom by proposing that acts due to man's reason existed as contingencies alongside those influenced by some Necessity in nature. In typical Aristotelian fashion, the work emphasized practice and habit to strengthen human ability to resist irrational impulses, and declared that reward and punishment, virtue and vice, were irrationally distinguished if no free human will existed. Was not postulation of fatalism or some supposed divine foreknowledge nothing but a moral evasion?[14] Well into the Christian era a commentary by an Ammonius continued Aristotle's line of argument against Fate in its general discussion of providence, divine foreknowledge, and free will.

Carneades of the new Platonic-Sceptic academy, who taught in Rome c. 150 B.C., probably proved to be the most quoted antagonist of Fate in the Classical world. Unlike Aristotle, who more or less slighted the subject, Carneades, although writing nothing, provided ten or more cogent arguments against Fate which writers both pagan and Christian saw fit to repeat. They fell into two categories: one line of argument stressed inherent difficulties within Chrysippus' assertions of cosmic sympathy stemming from his failure to adequately distinguish necessary from contingent causes; the other more practical argument emphasized the disastrous effects of Fate on human law and institutions.[15]

History generally hails Cicero as Rome's outstanding humanist. An illustrious lawyer and statesman, Cicero naturally found it difficult to understand how ethical responsibility and political stability could be safeguarded without granting human choice and responsibility. Part Sceptic, he preferred to assume, like Carneades, that human freedom was an indisputable datum of experience and human judgment; part Stoic, he could better understand a providential arrangement in the world than a blind mechanical Fate or *Fatum*. His *On Fate*, reflecting Posidonius, defends the honor and freedom of humanity against the strong fatalistic position of the Stoic Chrysippus whose cause-and-effect rigid determinism could offer man only an illusory freedom of will while actually enslaving him. For Cicero events caused by a supposed "nature" or "accident" were simply results of a normal cause-effect relationship unrecognized or imperfectly understood. Although he thought luck and fortune worthy of some recognition, his *De officiis* declared that ultimate success and failure depended largely on one's own doing. In *De divinatione* he castigated the folly of such activity.

Cicero's studied commitment to human freedom and dignity led him to add a new optimistic dimension to the concept of humanism; in

[14] For Alexander of Aphrodisias, as yet untranslated, see Greene, *Moira*, p. 374, also Telfer, *Cyril and Nemesius*, commentary on p. 313, but especially Eusebius, *Praeparatio Evangelica* 6.9.

[15] Carneades' influence and his five main arguments against Fate are well treated in D. Amand, *Fatalisme et Liberté dans L'antiquité Grecque* (Louvain: Bibliotheque de l'universite, 1945), pp. 71–88 and 571–86.

addition to coining the term *Humanitas*, he included urbanity as a necessary adjunct to human dignity. Should not man's value reflect itself in a
certain humaneness, civility, social polish, wit, eloquence, and politeness?
And should not a measure of economic comfort be sought to afford
opportunities for a cultural appreciation of the arts and to provide
means to support a paideia based on both philosophy and rhetoric which
would liberate man from any sordid limitations unworthy of him? His *De
officiis*, popular among Christians later, humanely emphasized that only
through concern for one's fellow man could one ideally honor *Humanitas*
and express his nature in the highest degree.

Man's eternal quest for freedom finds a brief but telling expression
in the Roman Epicurean Lucretius, a contemporary of Cicero. He
sought to find in even his deterministic atomic system a loophole to
"snap the bonds of Fate" as he put it. Finding Democritus too fatalistic,
he followed in the spirit of Epicurus who said wise men laugh at Destiny
and that man could determine events even if some resulted from Chance
or Necessity. Like Epicurus, Lucretius postulated a mechanically unpredictable swerve in the movement of atoms to break a deterministic
sequence of cause and effect and to allow room for the action of free will.
Did not a human being originate the movement of the fine atoms that
trickle through his limbs to snatch the will from mechanical compulsion
and enable it, by free actions, to put within one's grasp earthly pleasure
and the happiness of tranquility? Through a robust use of observation
and reason man would be able to discern and discredit religion, superstition, and fear of death which brought so much misery into human
history.[16]

One might readily interpret Virgil's *Aeneid* simultaneously as a
glorification of man's predestined role in the unfolding of Rome's destiny and as an assessment of his tragic entrapment in the project. Aeneas'
lot in the predetermined enterprise demands his assent, but as a son of
Venus he has to be honorably persuaded rather than forced to cooperate
even though, as a semi-divinity, he is scarcely free to act unheroically by
refusing to obey. At times Virgil seems overwhelmed by the tragic
human cost of the fated drama: "Oh what trouble it was to found the
Roman people." Then, despite the effort spent on the arduous project
Fate seems to ordain a frustrated result: though Rome was destined to
civilize others, it could not civilize itself, a fate the poet seems to bewail in
the final pages of the *Aeneid* when the pious Aeneas slays the suppliant
Turnus. Both a demi-god and men seem caught up in a situation at once

---

[16] Lucretius' anxiety to snap the "bonds of Fate" and preserve free will in his mechanistic system seems one of the most desperate and laudible attempts in ancient literature.
De rerum nat. 2.240–60. Greene, *Moira*, p. 423.

glorious but blighted; tragically, government is a burden that commits the bearer to surrender personal happiness in choosing the claims of justice over mercy. In the less propagandistic *Georgics*, Virgil, somewhat like Hesiod, judges human achievements accomplished in struggle with nature too glorious and joyful not to be a product of man's own exertion.

As we saw Stoic anthropology, by making human reason part of divine cosmic Reason, involved man in a system of logical determinism. Yet even Stoics worked hard to find some room for human freedom, moral responsibility, and the practice of virtue in this cosmic fatalism. While the founder of the system, Zeno, did little beyond giving mortals the usual freedom to sin, and to be responsible for the crimes of their passions, Cleanthes in his famous *Hymn to Zeus* tried to make the doctrine of inevitability more palatable by differentiating between Fate and Providence, a separation all Stoics want to maintain. Yet, the assertion that Providence may be Fate but that not everything fated was providential did little but restate Providence's non-responsibility for evil. The hymn at best hopes that the great god of Reason as Providence will use his good intentions to save man from his own misdirections and turn them into good. Chrysippus, the most fatalistic of Stoics, declared Fate, as we noted, such an inexorable chain of cause and effect that it led the willing but dragged along the unwilling. Yet in his diffuse writings even Chrysippus tried to avoid an out-and-out fatalism. Eusebius praised him for his positive efforts although Cicero, Plutarch, Origen, and Nemesius thought that he failed to extricate human freedom from the Stoic fatalistic, albeit providential, arrangement. Troubled that human incentive would be crippled by an inexorable Fate and that evil could not be educative if man did not have the ability to withhold assent to some of the concepts he formed from sensation, Chrysippus sought to pin moral responsibility on the character one developed in his youth. To find a way for this character to exert itself, he suggested that Fate might direct only the nature of things without necessarily directing the will of the agent acting upon them. He tried to distinguish complete or principal causes from aiding or consequent causes which required an antecedent condition. The latter he declared the realm of Fate which was restricted to binding or drawing together events each of which represented only one possibility. Complete or principal causes expressed the spontaneity of human agents who introduced contingencies. An act was "co-fated"; Fate did not determine, for instance, that the sick patient would recover whether or not a physician was called; the calling of the physician was the co-fated. Both Fate and co-fate could not exist separately. Chrysippus' fatalism, then, would remain a rigorous system but one of conjoint contingent possibilities; events were destined to produce themselves only if others produced themselves conjointly with them. Critics retorted that by postulating a limited competency for Fate Stoics destroyed the complete sway necessary to it by its very nature; Fate could not be half-fate.[17]

The so-called Middle Stoa was principally the work of Panaetius of Rhodes, who spent considerable time in Rome during the second century B.C. He seems satisfied merely to assert, without much profundity, that the human will was able to effect some moral progress within a fated structure. Posidonius, thinking in terms of a continuous ascending cosmos, portrayed man balanced between the divine universe of the intelligible and the sublunar world of the perishable and phenomenal. Man, so positioned, Posidonius judged capable of going either way since the creator had given him proper power to fulfill every aspiration proper to his being. Posidonius declared the rational part of man's Platonic-like soul of three faculties free to offset evil by controlling the soul's lower emotional, irrational inclinations. With that said, Posidonius would leave the matter stand and in a very Roman way content himself with stressing punctilious performance of duty as the essence of Stoic doctrine. Why discuss unprofitably the eternal dilemma whether one was meaningfully free to assent to the ordained when in the last analysis one was forced to conform to it anyway?

Late Roman Stoicism grew increasingly resigned to Fate in the guise of Providence. It asserted that moral progress, an advance in virtue, could come only by living in harmony with divine Nature's intentions and it promised only a sterile tranquility of mind achieved by not fighting the compulsive ordinances of providential Reason. As a result Stoicism rested content in the assumption that even if one could claim no freedom to change things external to himself, one had dignity as a part of god.

One who shared such views was Seneca, one-time tutor to Nero. His rather stilted writings constantly admonish his tri-part soul to strive for moral progress with the help of god within it. Through philosophy the emotions would be mastered, human beings would become independent and even contemptuous of external circumstances, and wisdom would constitute the only true freedom. The ex-slave Epictetus piously extolled the human endowment of divine Reason as a gift of the gods; but upon scrutiny it appears a gift that does little more than set man above all creatures in his ability to be cognizant of himself and therefore able to

---

[17] The reaction to Chrysippus' fatalism is wide spread. Cicero (*De fato* 20 and 31) uses Carneades to attack Chrysippus' determinism even though the Stoic tries to concede that human actions have an impact on what happens. Plutarch, *De fato,* while not disdaining Chrysippus' "contingency" concessions, prefers a middle-Platonic way to minimize Fate by postulating a triple level of Providence (572F–574E). See also his *De Stoic repug.* Eusebius, *Praep. Evang.* 6.8, in quoting Diogenianus' answer to Chrysippus, clearly approves Chrysippus' own efforts to make some reservations about Fate in the second book of his work, *De fato.*

realize that he must agree with the decrees of Providence which he cannot change. To avoid evil—basically a misjudgment or intellectual lapse—and to deal intelligently with his impressions or data experience so that he could properly decide to act or not, man must come to learn that the gods, seemingly restrained by Zeus or Providence, did not put man's body or earthly matters completely in his power. Far from being annoyed with the ordinance which Zeus laid down in conjunction with the Fates who were present at every one's birth and continued to spin the entire thread of his life, everyone must strive to cooperate fully with that which lies outside himself. Marcus Aurelius, the last of the great Stoics, was distressed by his troublesome imperial duties and frustrated by his zeal to transform humanity. His solace? Let the Stoic conviction suffice that man could bear any suffering, that the soul was subject only to its own movement, that external things could not control it. Misfortune could not change human nature nor compulsion alter man's true being. Virtue resulted from the free will's decision to love that which happens to one, that which is spun with the thread of Destiny. Within the given dispensation, rational intelligence must, of course, always dominate human appetites and so interpret sense impressions properly that it remained the ruling faculty doing nothing it does not choose to do. The emperor piously blamed himself for even non-intentional acts because they resulted from his failure to train himself to make proper judgments.

Middle Platonism is well represented by such as Plutarch and Albinus. Plutarch, far from being discouraged by "Plato's" evil World Soul which blighted human freedom, attributes all the glorious and evil deeds in history to those who rationally did or did not exercise self-control over their actions. The work On Fate by pseudo-Plutarch is a desperate attempt to reconcile Fate and Providence and then to harmonize Fate with free will. To achieve the first objective, the work simply asserts the primacy of Providence by making Fate god's rule of law. Fate, like law, the work next argues, legislates only within general terms leaving specific antecedents of action undetermined, open to the operation of Chance or contingent upon man's will and power. Fate merely arranges or binds together consequences of actions which it has no power to provoke or prevent.[18] Consequently no inexorable unbroken chain of logical sequences operated such as that which constrained Chrysippus when he posited immediately preceding logical effects as the antecedents or causes of subsequent results. Albinus, like Plutarch, rejected fatalism, convinced that free choice was necessary to uphold ethics and to absolve god from responsibility for man's evil.

Although the great neo-Platonist Plotinus objected to the overall

---

[18] Plutarch, De fato 573C–E, 569E–570, 571B–C.

fatalism of the Stoics, he scarcely did better than they since he, too, allowed humans freedom to act responsibly only within the framework of an Absolute. He did, however, offer mortals some opportunity to alter their position in the cosmic arrangement so that they could eventually lose themselves in the One. While each one's soul necessarily had to descend into a body, its higher part or nous, as we saw, never descended entirely but partly lingered on in touch with the universal Nous. Thus, even though involved in body, the soul's partial attachment to cosmic Intelligence permitted it to remain its own cause able rationally to decide which bodily desires to satisfy or not. Admittedly human efforts to achieve good could be frustrated but the frustration brought about more of an educative disorder than some fated evil because evil was a mere lack of quality, meaningless because of its remoteness from the One. Man could be said to act evilly and enslave himself in Necessity natural to matter only when he failed to assert his freedom to escape his hampered condition by not trying to soar to the One through an ascent of mystical experience.[19]

Even early man must have realized that being given freedom to commit evil was a hollow victory. In seeking to strengthen man's own capacity to effect good, to cheat the power of Fate or of Necessity which impedes human ability to do good, and thus to come to share more fully in the beneficent nature of the gods, Classical thinkers, especially Platonists and Stoics, contrived a master stroke which ingeniously superseded Fate and jealous gods with a higher benevolent rational force or Providence which could absorb Fate merely as its cosmic law. Now man was supercharged to think good thoughts and perform good deeds inspired, directed or even aided by the providential Father above them. Development of Providence in the pagan world was in itself a long and arduous struggle. As we saw, Fate early became blurred with a concerned but limited Zeus who meted out prosperity to good and bad as he willed. By the mid-seventh century Archilochus poetically described a gracious Zeus watching over even the beasts; Solon declared that the eyes of the god were on everything. Sixth–century Zeus, now master of gods and cosmos, became more and more benevolent, providential, and foreseeing. Consequently, Theognis so naturally expected Zeus to act rationally and justly that he was disturbed by the god's apparent mismanagement of justice leaving the poet puzzled how to please divinity. Pindar, too, asked why Zeus gave no sign to mortals who were buffeted by the wind of Destiny. It was up to the Socratic school, however, first to develop the idea that a benevolent god created or ordered the universe. Cleanthes'

---

[19] Relevant citations in the *Enneads* would be 3.2,9, 3.1,8, 4.3,12–13, 6.8,15. See Greene, *Moira*, pp. 378–84.

sacred *Hymn to Zeus* reveals how early the great god became metaphorically a loving father for Stoics. By identifying Zeus with all-pervading
Reason as the Logos, Stoics hoped to defeat Fate at the hands of Providence; by making man part of Providence they achieved the ultimate for
him in dignity as a vicarious source of good even if Providence threatened to rob him anew of his freedom.

Since under a providential governance "free" choice could now be
extended to include doing good if one opted to live according to Providence's proper nature, it is quite in order to ask whether providential
deity initiated or aided human beings to make good choices and do good
deeds with grants of "grace." No doubt those early Homeric psychic
visitations quickly became something to pray for. Who—unless he were
an agnostic Protagoras, an "atheistic" Lucretius, or a hide-bound fatalist
like the second-century A.D. Vettius Valens who declared all prayer,
sacrifice, and temples a waste of time—could doubt that heaven once
having ceased to be jealous, would not honor the pleas of men, especially
those of Stoics, which were uttered by the divine nature itself encapsu-
lated in them? Consequently, poets asked for the grace of inspiration;
others sought the largesses of the Graces or Charites who theoretically
dispensed all favor. Cleanthes piously asked Zeus not for earthly aid but
for the grace of a virtuous mind. Plato in the *Laws* depicts god providing
human beings with the possibility of moral growth through a granting of
grace; in the *Republic*, too, he asserts that he who is willing and eager to
be righteous will never be neglected by god. And could the pious Marcus
Aurelius ever doubt that his ardent prayers for a tranquil mind or the
grace of perseverence in his lot were in vain?

Indeed, the opportunity for transmigration and trial regeneration
was an especially gracious gift of some gods providing aid to ultimate
salvation. Certainly Pythagoreans appreciated it. Pindar rejoiced that
three virtuous reincarnations, with rewards and punishments meted out
in between, assured the grace of final reception into the Isles of the
Blessed. Plato, too, promised his readers in the *Phraedrus* that, depending on their trial behavior during their transmigrations, god would give
them a better or worse final portion.

To those who desired assurances of more immediate and tangible
aid, the mystery cults were at hand to provide the grace of conversion
and salvation. Claiming that they were masters even of the stars and
Destiny, Isis, Serapis, Mithra, Cybele, and Asclepius extended the grace
of election to aspirant devotees through dreams, visions and enthusiastic
frenzy. So lavish, indeed, were savior gods' graces that some commentators were disturbed by the prospect that a converted thief might enjoy
a lot after death more blessed than that of an uninitiated great hero like
Epaminondas. Plato reports that some charlatans waxed bold enough to

claim power, through spells, to compel gods to release their treasures of grace so that not only the sins of the living but even the evils besetting the dead might be erased.

So the Classical debate went: man's rational soul versus Fate or Providence. Finally, Providence seemed to beckon with a gracious and assuring countenance. Nemesius, learned Christian writer (c. 400), praised the Stoics for having taken a step forward in espousing Providence. They realized it was folly to argue that some free choice was left man under Fate by claiming that it neglected to control certain areas of Destiny or farmed them out to limited daimons to exploit, or that man could somehow operate contingently in the system. The Stoics, then, were to be commended in substituting Providence for Fate, even though inevitability was not lessened by virtue of being directed by a conscious, benevolent force. Man still remained part of divine Nature's teleology. The trouble was, Nemesius adds, that Stoics did not know they were dealing with the wrong Providence.

THE CHRISTIAN ENGAGEMENT WITH THE HUMANISTIC

"All are under Sin" . . . Paul

The ancient question of human freedom and dignity in a way became more acute once the Logos became flesh and dwelt among men. Interest in anthropology among Christians would have to develop in order to cope with their new Providence towering over mankind as not only a monotheistic force but also an omnipotent and loving one as well. To study the relationship of the human soul, the new Christian personality, to old Classical Fate and to the new challenge of Providence, the Fathers drew almost exclusively on Classical sources since neither revelation nor Jewish apocalyptic thought provided much scholarly analytical background material to guide them. About the only pagan views totally rejected were Epicurean.

Already Irenaeus, for example, saw the Christian man in familiar Platonic terms as a tripart being of body, animal soul, and spirit or rational soul even though he might make the soul corporeal. The Roman theologian Hippolytus preferred an Empedoclean interpretation that declared human beings a combination of fire, water, earth, and spirit or soul.[20] The soul permeated the body in a somewhat Epicurean manner via passages in every joint and limb, a view which makes understandable

---

[20] This interesting attempt to combine Greek medical philosophy and Christian anthropology occurs in a lost work, *On the Universe,* attributed to Hippolytus. For a discussion of its authenticity consult Quasten, *Patrology* 2:195. Compare Nemesius, *On the Nature of Man* 24 in Telfer, *Cyril and Nemesius,* pp. 307–13.

Cyril of Jerusalem's later explanation that the Eucharist, as a refreshment of the soul, entered all the members of a communicant. Tertullian, the first Christian to write a serious tract *On the Soul,* while berating pagan views as of dubious or harmful value in view of revelation, loudly called upon the Stoics to support his conception of the soul as an evanescent material substance. In addition, his erudition allowed him to comment on views of the soul held by Pythagoras, Empedocles, Plato, Aristotle, Panaetius, Posidonius, Lucretius, Heraclitus, Democritus and pagan medical writers. Origen, always Platonic, apparently saw some value in Empedocles' and Pythagoras' ideas as well. All Christian writers responded with enthusiasm to the pagan consensus that the soul was rational and therefore was automatically something divine, an entity distinct from all others. A common agreement by pagans and Christians on the soul's unique character and essential qualities made it possible for Tertullian, Gregory of Nyssa, and Nemesius to adapt to Christian theology the common Stoic figure used by Posidonius, Chrysippus, and Seneca which depicted man as a microcosm reflecting the harmony and rationality of God's macrocosm. Again, common pagan and Christian concepts of the soul as a spiritual entity readily encouraged Nemesius to put in a Christian light Posidonius' concept of man as a being poised between the mortal and the immortal, linking the two worlds of the phenomenal and the intellective so that everything in the sensible world looked to him as the final creation while he himself alone looked to the divine. The long list of Classical comments on the soul cited by Christians reached something of a climax in *On the Nature of Man* by Nemesius, Bishop of Emesa c. 400. His combined theological and medical interests led him to emphasize the relationship of man's soul to his body, and thus become the first important Christian anthropologist. Throughout the tract he called upon Democritus, Plato, Aristotle, Epicurus, many Stoics, Galen, Ammonius, Plotinus, Porphyry and even Iamblicus to add what they could to his endeavor.

In fact, Christians found Classical views of the soul so attractive that it became difficult to eradicate some questionable pagan interpretations. One such eventual heretical view, based on Pythagoras and Plato, supported transmigration which in Christian hands, however, always restricted reincarnation hosts to rational beings. The view was held not only by strange Gnostic heretics such as Simon Magus and Carpocrates but also possibly by Clement of Alexandria and probably by Origen.[21]

---

[21] Origen's idea of pre-existence of souls in itself approaches metempsychosis. See *Comm. in Matt.* 13.1 but especially *De oratore,* 27.8, trans. J. O'Meara in *ACW* (Westminster, Maryland: Newman, 1954), 19:97–98. O'Meara's notes 394, 617, 454 and 529 are significant. Nemesius, *Nature of Man* 18 believes all Greeks who say the soul is immortal believe in transmigration. See also Telfer's commentary on Nemesius 24 n. 14, p. 312 in *Cyril of Jerusalem and Nemesius.*

Suspect, too, was the Platonic notion of the pre-existence of souls which appealed especially to Origen, who found it a convenient way to explain the unequal endowments of souls on earth by declaring their differences commensurate with the souls' deserts earned in their previous existences.[22] He found illustrious supporters throughout the Christian era, including Didymus the Blind, the honored Platonic director of the catechetical school at Alexandria, the independent-minded Synesius of Cyrene, and probably Nemesius. Origen, as well as others including to some extent even Augustine, found creationism close to blasphemy since it commanded God to cooperate with whims of human lust practiced even by adulterers and rapists. Tertullian, Gregory of Nyssa, Peter Bishop of Alexandria, and Methodius Bishop of Philippi, preferred to support, in some measure, Stoic conceptions of the soul; consequently they advocated traducianism, maintaining that souls, as material substances, were imparted through human copulation. Arnobius, overly influenced by Plato's *Timaeus*, was inclined even to advocate the proposition that the human soul, because it was so fickle and prone to evil, was created not by God but by inferior beings intermediate between the mortal and immortal. Only Irenaeus, it seems, maintained that immortality was not an indigenous quality of the soul, as Plato taught, but that it was acquired through moral development of will and meritorious act. Whatever the Christian preferences about the soul, they put such a high price on its Classical rationality that they would not allow Apollinarius to substitute even the Logos for a human soul in the person of Jesus.

Naturally Christians felt that, however discerning Classical thought might be in extolling the soul as rational and divine, pagans could not know its true nature because they did not know the true nature of the divine itself. When theologians from Barnabas on—Irenaeus, Clement, Origen to Theodore of Mopsuestia—celebrated the Christian's soul they were referring to an entity far more lofty than that could be which was a part of the maimed Platonic World Soul produced by a limited demiurge who was merely one god among many. When they spoke of the soul as an image of God they had in mind a divinity far more personal than the general pantheistic Reason of the Stoics. Rather the human soul was an image of the only God, created individually by the omnipotent creator of the universe. Because man possessed such a soul, Gregory of Nyssa glorified humankind as the greatest wonder of the world since nothing

---

[22]Origen on pre-existence: *De prin.* 2.9,37, 4.23 and *C.C.* 1.32. Didymus, head of the catechetical school of Alexandria as Athanasius' appointee, agreed with Origen per Jerome *Con. Ruf.* 1.6 (*PL* 23:419) and 2.5 (*PL* 23:458). Also Synesius, *Epis.* 105 (*PG* 66:1487). On sins committed in pre–existent state: Origen, *De prin.* 1.7,4, *Comm. in Matt.* 15.35 and 20.6.7.

else was made in such an exalted image able to know God and experience
a mystical vision of the divine when human reason failed.

Just as Christian writers readily recruited Classical views of the soul,
they anxiously enlisted pagan arguments against Fate or Necessity into
the new order and tried to correct Platonic and Stoic conceptions of
Providence. Christian attacks on Classical determinism are constant,
motivated not only by respect for the new true Providence but also by
concern for the faithful at large who, according to Origen and John
Chrysostom, were generously duped by an attraction for Destiny and
astrology.[23] The denunciations draw heavily on appropriate Platonic
sources, Aristotelian writers, and the Sceptic Carneades. Justin early
inveighed against Fate because he was disturbed by the practical observation that it destroyed the validity of praise and blame. Soon after, we are
informed, Minucius Felix contemplated a tract *On Fate* which, however,
may never have been written or is lost. Definitely no longer extant is
Tertullian's work on the same subject dealing with the incompatibility of
Necessity and free will. Origen's *Commentary on Genesis* tried to obviate
the popularity of astrological fatalism among Christians by pointing out,
as does Plotinus later, the difference between stars as signs and causes.
He objected to the casting of horoscopes because the free will of the
individual was destroyed by the very belief in the efficacy of astrological
prediction. Common sense drove Origen to admit that certain things
occurred which were not in human power but he denied, against the
Stoics, that an inexorable chain of events follows from them because man
could interfere. Using some of Carneades' arguments, as well as some
new Christian ones, he pointed out that Fate not only invalidated common-sense punishment and reward but rendered Christian faith,
prayer, the Church, and even Christ himself vain; worst of all, it made
God the author of evil.[24] Did not Plato speak truly in saying "the blame is
his who chooses, that god is blameless"?

Methodius, Bishop of Philippi, kept that attack going, followed
swiftly by the historian Eusebius who reports that even Constantine felt
compelled to speak against Fate in one of his sermons. Platonist at heart,
Eusebius devoted the sixth book of his *Praeparatio Evangelica* to discounting fatalistic views of such as Archelaus, Euripides, Cleanthes, Democritus, and Porphyry. In doing so he relies on both pagan and Christian
authors quoting extensively from Origen and the late-Aristotelian Alexander of Aphrodisias while reminding his readers at the same time that
Homer, even Chrysippus and Euripides, tried to circumscribe Fate. Like

---

[23] Six orations on Fate and Providence (*PG* 50:749–774) attributed to John
Chrysostom are apocryphal.

[24] Amand, *Fatalisme*, pp. 318–25 deals with Origen's use of Carneades.

Carneades, Eusebius saw that Fate made a mockery of philosophy, prayer, religion, virtue itself, merit, and even law. In familiar pagan terms Eusebius averred that Fate, far from being an independent logical chain of causes associated with the course of the stars, was actually a law under the sway of the true Christian Providence who controlled any and all would-be Fates and their spindles. Should it not be apparent to Christians that pagan Fate had been forced to deny itself in the face of the victorious Christian religion? If some things happen contrary to human purpose due to habit, impulse, contingencies, and the like, should not Christians realize that such events are the price of man's bodily existence arranged by God?

The barrage against Fate continued. Unfortunately, the eight-book work *Against Astronomy, Astrology, and Fate* by the scholarly Diodorus of Tarsus exists only in fragments. All the Cappadocians entered the fray. Basil attacked astrology and Fate in a Carneadean way in his sixth *Homily on the Hexameron*, while Gregory of Nazianzus chose to turn an honored Classical medium against fatalism by writing poetry in favor of Christian Providence. Too little is made of the small cogent work *Against Fate* by Gregory of Nyssa, Platonic scholar and mystic. The tract, a theoretical discussion between Gregory and an anonymous philosopher, in trying to confound Posidonian assertions of universal cosmic sympathy, presents some twenty interesting arguments revealing the internal, logical, and observable inconsistencies of Destiny and astrology both in theory and practice. At least two arguments are drawn from Carneades; they exploit the dilemmas presented to astrology by catastrophic collective deaths and the diversity of barbaric customs. Another of Gregory's arguments, the assertion that unpredictable daimonic manipulation of events destroys astral predictability and credibility, attests to the persistent credulity of the fourth century even among Christian theologians.[25] Deserving of more attention in the light of the contemporary Augustinian controversy is the attack on determinism by Nemesius of Emesa, who devotes three chapters to Destiny in his anthropological study *On the Nature of Man*. In attacking Fate both theoretically and practically, especially as it supposedly manifests itself in astrology, Nemesius, like Origen and others, reiterated arguments that Fate and astrology negated law and prayer and made God the cause of abominable crimes. Apparently using pseudo-Plutarch's *On Fate*, Nemesius maintains that Chrysippus had failed to reconcile Stoic cosmology and ethics, Stoic rational determinism and human responsibility. Chrysippus' arguments, Nemesius maintains, were not sound enough when he suggested that some human impulses might possibly be outside the realm of Fate or that

---

[25] Gregory of Nyssa, *De fato* (PG 45:146–74). See col. 171 for daimons. Amand, *Fatalisme*, pp. 432–35 describes the influence of Carneades on Gregory.

the unbroken chain of cause and effect operated only to determine the outcome of what human beings did. To Nemesius Stoic Fate by definition had to exercise complete, not partial sway and therefore left no place for human interference.[26]

Such was the Christian onslaught against Classical Fate. In quite a different vein Christian theologians readily cited Classical scholarship in support of Providence. When Athanasius observed that no sparrow fell to the ground or that no blade of grass or strand of hair went unnoticed by God, he said nothing that pagans had not said before. From the start Christian authors like the writer of the *Clementines*, Aristides, and Minucius Felix repeated common Stoic arguments based on the harmony of the universe; Gregory of Nazianzus extolled the beneficence of Providence in Classical poetry. In order to emphasize Providence's important role in sustaining differentiation in the cosmos after creation, Nemesius adapted Aristotle's unmoved Mover to Christian theology by transferring to Providence its task of directing things to their proper development in the most favorable way.[27] Confounded by the awareness that this control involved almost infinite complex particulars, Nemesius declared Providence unfathomable. His medical interests led him to extend Stoic arguments of cosmic harmony by pointing to that concord exhibited in the composition and inter-operation of the human body and soul. In his *Discourses on Providence* Theodoret of Cyrus added Classical proofs from the moral and social order as well.

But just as Classical thought could not appreciate the exalted position of the human soul, so it could not, Christians thought, understand the depth of compassion and love the new Providence entertained for his human creatures. Indeed, the new Providence was itself incomprehensible to the Classical mind because it rose superior to the logical limitations and contradictions of philosophy. Did not Christian Providence confound Parmenidean Being and Becoming, Platonic Reality and matter, Stoic pantheism and human personality? The new Providence had by its incarnation and redemptive work honored the human race as never before; it shared not only its Reason with man but condescended to share even human flesh—an idea impossible and repulsive to Platonists—and even promised to glorify fleshy matter through a resurrection to immortal incorruptibility. Such lavish gifts gave entirely new meaning to anthropology and human history. Nemesius pointed out that only the Christian Providence was able to grant humans freedom from fatalistic compulsion since, he was not himself stymied, as Plato's creator,

[26] Nemesius, *Nature of Man* 53 asserts no half-fate can exist. Man cannot be given choice of action while Fate is given control over the outcome of the actions.

[27] Nemesius, *Nature* 63. Aristotle's agnostic unmoved Mover fulfills itself by "instinct" while God does so by thought and design and consequently is able himself to attend to the continued operation of particulars in the functioning of the cosmos.

by any resistance of Necessity. Astounded by God's enhancement of
man's dignity far beyond the imagination of Classical rhetoricians,
Nemesius exclaims:

> How can we exaggerate the dignity of his [man's] place in crea-
> tion? In his own person, man joins mortal creatures with the immor-
> tals, and brings the rational beings into contact with the irrational
> . . . and is therefore rightly called 'the world in little.' He is the
> creature whom God thought worthy of such special providence that,
> for his sake, all creatures have their being . . . He is the creature for
> whose sake God became man, so that his creature might attain
> incorruption and escape corruption, might reign on high, being
> made after the image and likeness of God, dwelling with Christ as a
> child of God, and might be throned above all rule and all authority.
> Who, then, can fully express the pre-eminence of so singular a
> creature?[28]

Let us grant that what has been said fairly well represents what
Christians held regarding the human soul, Fate, and Providence. Now
that Christians have inherited the eternal dilemma of human freedom
and dignity, they have to face the old Stoic quandary: To what extent is
the soul rendered helpless before Providence especially now that Providence has become concerned, lovingly and eternally, with each human
personality. A brief discussion of early Christian views on such topics as
Original Sin, free will, meritorious works, and grace should provide
some insight into the matter. At the same time, the discussion should
raise the question whether Christianity's other-worldly message was just
another ideological manifestation of the debilitating loss of humanistic
nerve besetting the Classical world after A.D. 250.

In Christian eyes, Classical awareness of the soul's handicaps were
thoughtful but wrongly arrived at. To ascribe the soul's inadequacies, a
defect inherent in the very nature of the soul as part of an evil Platonic
World Soul, was just as misguided as to blame them on the soul's unhappy association with corruptible matter due either to some ridiculous
dietary sin of the Titans, or to some fall of a blasphemous gnostic eon.
That there was, indeed, a "fall" of some sort all Christian writers agreed,
except the Pelagians and a few other theologians such as the learned
Theodore of Mopsuestia, student of the great pagan Libanius.[29] In

---

[28] Nemesius, *Nature* 10.

[29] Patristic statements dealing with Original Sin are too overwhelming, both in
number and complexity, to be quoted here. For a fuller treatment refer to the respected,
quite unbiased, study by E. Jauncey, *The Doctrine of Grace up to the end of the Pelagian
controversy* (London: SPCK, 1925). A collection of translated excerpts in J. R. Willis, ed., *The
Teachings of the Church Fathers* (Montreal: Palm, 1966) is useful, esp. pp. 265–334.

general, early Christianity developed such a vague and mild conception
of Original Sin that very often it is difficult to discover whether a definite
sin itself is thought transmitted to mankind or whether only its consequences are handed down; and generally, the consequences themselves are considered more physical than spiritual. Because Scripture is
explicit, all the Fathers are constrained to accept man's doom to physical
death as the inevitable result of Adam's transgression. Only Theodore of
Mopsuestia might be unwilling to do so; some interpretations of his
largely lost writing against Augustine claim that he denied not only
Original Sin itself but all its supposed consequences, as well, including
even physical death since man, in his mind, was created mortal in the
first place.[30] Justin Martyr and Tatian view Original Sin, in a commonly
held fashion, as merely a prototype of individual sin but nonetheless the
true cause of physical death. Irenaeus, fascinated by his recapitulation
theory, entertained more definite, and somewhat harsher, ideas about
man's fall. He declares that the human race was clearly involved
vicariously in the event—"we have offended in the first Adam"—and,
having lost the "robe of sanctity," we share in a general source of sinfulness severe enough to put us in such a resisting and hindering
position in respect to effecting good, that only total submission to God's
will can accomplish anything. Human disabilities, of course, were offset
by recapitulation effected by the second Adam.

Generally, though, the early understanding of Original Sin was less
harsh than that of Irenaeus. Theophilus of Antioch thought of Original
Sin in physical terms alone; he labeled Adam's Fall the source of labor,
pain, grief, and death. Clement of Alexandria's strong Platonic concept
of evil forced him to declare that sin was foreign to original human
nature since it was basically negative, a lack of knowledge which only the
teaching of the divine Instructor could cure. Adam's sin was at most a
bad example which was not transferable to new souls and therefore did
not stain children. Origen allegorized away the entire fall in paradise,
making the story a mere type of man's later condition. Far from help-
lessly inheriting sin from Adam, souls, in Origen's system, more robustly
would fall of their own volition already in their Platonic pre-existent
state, leaving children in need of Baptism for only personal transgressions. Methodius of Olympus believes only physical death is the consequence of Original Sin. Athanasius, close in time to Augustine, speaks
of "sin reaching to all men." Yet in his *On the Incarnation of the Word* he
seems to blame hankering after personal sins—such as idolatry, homo-
sexuality, and adultery—more than an inheritance of Original Sin as the
chief cause of the dulled image of God in man. Ephraem is content
merely to say that Adam set an example for sin. Cyril of Jerusalem in his

---

[30] For a discussion of the views of Theodore, refer to Quasten, *Patrology* 3:419.

Catechetical Lectures avers that Adam put man under divine wrath which God clearly displayed by visiting death on the world. But he does not elaborate on the matter for the benefit of his catechumens.

On the whole the eastern Fathers are not clear on Original Sin. The Cappadocians employ such vague expressions as "stain," "corruption," "curse," and "debt" in dealing with the subject that it is impossible to decide whether a specific sin is meant or its consequences. Of the Cappadocians, Gregory of Nyssa seems the least interested in the subject; Original Sin for him involves at best an inheritance of a bias toward sin rather than a sin itself. Significantly, he is silent on the subject when he writes about children who die prematurely. Basil treats Original Sin mostly as a prototype. However, his colleague, Gregory of Nazianzus, in a less benign way, declares Original Sin "our first sin," one able not only to cause impairment of will but actually to condemn a newborn to limbo. John Chyrsostom spoke of Original Sin as depriving Adam and Eve of immortality and wisdom. Although Augustine quotes him as favoring infant Baptism, Chrysostom himself nowhere in extant writings explicitly attributes Original Sin to children; they were to be baptized, nonetheless, to give them holiness and to introduce them to God.

In short, it appears that if there be a line in the early Church leading to Augustine's stance on Original Sin, it could be discovered in the writings of Tertullian, then Cyprian, and Ambrose. Yet even Tertullian is somewhat equivocal about the subject. He maintains that Adam's sin reeked havoc on the human will but not so overwhelmingly as to destroy its freedom. He also holds that everyone died in Adam "as a bodily substance," that men were given over to death, and that the whole human race was infected by Adam's seed to become a transmitter of condemnation. Consequently, he deems grace necessary for any saving act. Yet his *On Baptism,* seemingly in maintaining innocence of the newborn, opposed infant Baptism and even his *On the Soul,* written in his semi-Montanist period, chose to deal with Classical views of the soul rather than with any exposition of the nature or effects of Original Sin. Cyprian, an admirer of Tertullian living in evil days of persecution, is more prone to see Original Sin as a fatal depravity condemning man to constant struggle and necessitating the need of infant Baptism. This ministration, he claims, would staunch the contagion of spiritual death, the loss of grace which the newborn contracts simply by being conceived after the flesh. Didymus the Blind, in turn, was, like Turtullian, inclined to think that Original Sin was transmitted through sex. Finally, Ambrose, who did much to influence Augustine's views of sin and evil pronounced Original Sin a completely injurious calamity defiling man with universal guilt. But, on the whole, considering the light attention given Original Sin in the early Church, it is not surprising that its existence never became an article of faith in creeds which were so anxious to stress soteriology, and that Pelagians accused Augustine of inventing the doctrine.

We have seen in the protracted Classical involvement with free will beginning already with Homer, that the traditional gods, as the time went on, tended at worst only to handicap man's power to do well and prosper; late benign Stoic Providence was not so detached because in its anxiety to lead the willing it dragged along the unwilling in the course of fulfilling its own divine nature. Aware that the long Classical humanistic quest for freedom had not proven entirely productive, gentile Christianity, in its first impulse, declared itself a liberating movement critical of Classical explanations for the deficient and blighted nature of the human soul; as we saw, it was critical, too, of Fate, and even of pagan Providence. To account for the soul's limitations Christianity offered a vague sense of Original Sin; Fate it desperately would try to destroy; Providence it approved in more a neo-Platonic than Stoic form but then only if the concept underwent serious transformation.

Only a few early Christian thinkers coming out of the humanistically inclined Classical environment comprehended the novel, awe-filled, and deep complications which the Christian view of personal immortality and the postulation of a sole omniscient God presented for free will. Most early Fathers simply assumed and asserted it; they defended it, when necessary, with familiar Classical arguments stressing particularly that it was an obvious and indispensable corollary of human reason and was necessary to law, art, and virtue. How could one conceive of God creating man in his rational image and then negating the work by crippling the human will. The new Providence could not be a throw-back to compelling Classical Fate or to a totally commanding causal cosmic Stoic Reason.

Beginning with Justin, Irenaeus, and even the astral-minded deviant Bardesanes of remote Edessa, the roll call of free will advocates runs steadily on with few exceptions to Augustine.[31] Tertullian, as a lawyer conditioned to believe that human responsibility was essential to law and order, upheld free will strenuously against the gnostic Valentinus. Both he and his disciple Cyprian saw in the Christian dispensation not an annulment but only an impairment of man's will, nor did they sense in the "fall" any compulsion by an arbitrary Providence. Clement of Alexandria, eclectic Platonist and admirer of Musonius Rufus' robust Stoic moralism, could do no other than make salvation obtainable by free choice alone; only personal sins due to free will stained the soul and

---

[31] Again, brevity precludes full citation from the Fathers on free will. Besdies Jauncey, *Grace*, and Willis, *Teachings*, one can profitably consult Amand, *Fatalisme*, which treats views of Christian writers from Justin to Nemesius on free will in connection with the problem of Fate.

demanded accountability. Origen, called the "illiberal humanist" by Chadwich, would have it no other way. Even the Scriptures would have to yield. Verses speaking of "hardening" of hearts would have to be taken figuratively or understood as explanations of judgments and punishments meted out for sins opted in a pre-existent state. Did not the Church, along with common sense, call upon human beings to practice virtue? Were they not capable of forming habits, of conversion, of heresy? His *De principiis* insists that every rational soul possesses free will at all times even though the price human nature paid for this freedom was high. If people were everywhere in chains, they were of their own making, the price of their own liberty. Origen's wide influence shows in Fathers like Methodius who, although critical of Origen's Platonic excesses, agrees with him that of all creatures only man had the power to obey what he pleased without constraint.

Fourth-century writers continue on in much the same vein. Eusebius, too, follows Origen and quotes him extensively in his *Praeparatio Evangelica* along with the Aristotelian Alexander of Aphrodisias for their free will stance. He himself concluded that free will could overcome all difficulties which hamper free choice, even those due to the disabilities of old age, pain, and natural or societal environments. The Christian alone was truly free because only the worshipper of the true God, free from Fate, could follow without hindrance the divine plan of salvation. Eusebius should be given more credit for his psychological insights claiming that humans are aware by natural law that they have consciences which instinctively tell them that they have an operative free will. Why should men not realize that they are actually using their free will while they call it Fate? Cyril of Alexandria puts the matter bluntly: the devil has no power over man except by consent of his free will; one does not fornicate by chance nor blame sin on the stars. God's fairest work was to endow humankind with free will so each could do what he chooses. Jerome, in turn, saw one's ability to choose a merciful gift of God, a gift he left free; while its origin belonged to God, its operation did not.[32] Of the Cappadocians, Gregory of Nyssa is very vocal on the subject. Agreeing with Origen that the history of the world is quite tragic because of free will, he declared it, nontheless, a faculty indispensable to man as an image of God. As a protagonist against Apollinarius who would deprive Jesus of a human will, Gregory taught in his *Great Catechism* that everyone was capable of perfection and immortality precisely because his will

---

[32] Despite his sometimes stormy relationship with Augustine, Jerome agrees with him that "it is ours to be able to wish and reject but that, without the mercy of God, it is not ours." His *Dialogue against the Pelagians* (*PL* 23:518–618) connected Pelagius' beliefs with Origen and caused his monastery to be sacked and his life threatened. Even so, Jerome is often seen as semi-Pelagian.

could not be enslaved. God does not force men to yield; where otherwise would their free wills be? Only irrational creatures are persuaded by the will of another. Conversely, man must assume responsibility for his sins as Plato had suggested long ago.[33] Two writers, Epiphanius of Salamis and John Chrysostom, seemingly prefer to base their subscription to free will more on Christian needs than on the Classical consensus. Epiphanius argued that it was needed negatively to explain sin and heresy; John Chrysostom, such an outright free will advocate that the Pelagians cited him, also concluded that the very presence of sin proved that man was free. Theologians like Theodore of Mopsuestia and Nemesius of Emesa are no less supporters of the Classical humanistic quest for freedom because they are contemporaries of Augustine.

Nemesius, great admirer of Origen and Aristotle, exalts human freedom and dignity, qualities due men as the privileged recipients of reason and its conjoined free will. One senses that he would have liked to have wished success to "the wisest of the Greeks," presumably Stoics, in their effort to harmonize free will and Fate. He himself treats the problem of free will in an uncommonly orderly manner asking first if human beings truly enjoy self determination, then what acts are in their power, and finally why they have a free will. In logical fashion reminiscent of Basil, he first eliminates God, Necessity, Fate, Nature, Fortune, and Accident as possible authors of human actions, thus leaving every one standing alone as responsible. Man has to enjoy free will because he is rational and changeable. Did not Aristotle rightly see that free choice involving voluntary and involuntary actions was a concomitant of reason? Did he not wisely say "things we have to do, we learn to do by doing them"? Dealing with the second consideration, Nemesius declares that one's innate conscience tells him what is in his power and what not; common sense tells one, too, that choices always relate to contingencies where contrary possibilities existed. Finally, without free will who could take council, contemplate, deliberate? Why scriptural admonitions and prohibitions, laws, art, and virtue? What, in effect, would happen to Classical *paideia*?

Granted free will, the question remains: Is there any purpose in man's choosing; does any merit flow from human choices? For such questions Stoics really had no satisfactory answers because for them human choices affected in no way the ultimate intentions of Providence.

The practical and humanist bent of the Classical mind made it

---

[33] In contrast to Gregory of Nyssa, Gregory of Nazianzus holds a rather equivocal position. Augustine appeals to him quite frequently among eastern theologians. Yet even he, while holding the soul depraved by sin, considers the will, on its own, not totally impotent. His intermediate stand seems expressed in his view that new born children, if unbaptized, go to "limbo."

difficult, if not impossible, for early gentile Christian converts to understand Paul's disparagement of man's native ability to perform meritorious works.[34] It is to be expected that virtually no one paid attention to the Apostle's view. The early Fathers simply assume that if rationality, as part of the image of God, presupposes free will, free will, in turn presumes that meaningful results flow from its use. Without the ability to perform effective salutary works, free will could be logically a travesty of God's image in human beings. All the Fathers, of course, do not assume that works can force divinity to compensate them—even pagans knew that—but they do assume that deity could be depended upon, after respectful nagging, to exercise its goodness by rewarding the choices of human good will to perform works which deity itself had commanded. Early Fathers like Clement of Rome were much too close to the Classical legal and humanist scene not to imagine that fulfilling God's commands earned forgiveness of sins or for the writer of *II Clement* not to assume that freely-given alms worked to the same end. Nor did Polycarp's followers find it unreasonable to hear, without stress on grace, that one deserves praise for his good works. Barnabas, in turn, assumes that every one can, and must, work for ransom of sins. Justin, always a good Hellenist, could never doubt that logic demanded punishment and reward be rendered in relation to deeds. We have learned, he says, also from the prophets that rewards follow the merits of one's actions. Theophilus of Antioch, somewhat later, likewise assumed what seemed obvious: that God honored the righteous choice by rendering rewards to each person; would not those who acted well consistently be given life everlasting? Irenaeus advises one to struggle if he would acquire the crown; only goodness arising from free choice had any value. Tertullian as usual stated his legal mind robustly: a good deed made God a man's debtor. If penitential discipline helped justify the living, would not prayers aid even the suffering dead? Hippolytus, characteristically Roman, naturally takes for granted that God rewards each one according to his actions; those who act well secure eternal bliss.

The list of free will supporters goes on without interruptions. Cyprian, while objecting to vicarious atonement via the surplus merits of confessors, yet professed that one merited God by one's own character and good works. Origen, as an ascetic and uncompromising advocate of free will, could not believe otherwise. Methodius of Olympus maintained in a practical way that the fruit of obedience created a debt which one could reclaim from the creator; a merited salary is earned by free

[34] Again, statements regarding merit are too numerous to list. Chadwick, *Christian Thought*, p. 119, sums up the problem of merit by maintaining that when the question of predestination arises in the early Church it is always viewed in relation to foreseen merits. Again, Jauncey, *Grace*, will be of assistance in what seems a well balanced account.

obedience to the will of God. Was it not a great prospect that man could
be recompensed with eternal incorruptibility for observance of precept?
Even younger contemporaries of Augustine say nothing different. One
such was Ephraem of Edessa, friend of Basil. Hilary of Poitiers proclaimed that human beings had the liberty to work righteousness to keep
the commandments, to earn the Holy Spirit; Cyril of Jerusalem considered expectation of reward a legitimate incentive for the soul to perform
good works. Did not every laborer hope for recompense? Does one tire
one's self for nothing? Gregory of Nazianzus testifies to the popular trust
in human spiritual potential when he complains that some Christians too
robustly attributed all their success to themselves and nothing to God;
such, he thought, were responding too vigorously to the teaching that at
the end of time Christ would judge human beings with equity according
to their merits. Gregory of Nyssa, like so many, considers it obvious that
virtuous merits follow from possession of free will. Others, like John
Chrysostom and Nemesius, contemporaries of Augustine, were so convinced that their actions could attract grace that they have been associated with Pelagian tendencies.

By 400, though, a few western theologians seem to respond to the
general feelings of insecurity and impotence by reflecting the "loss-of-
nerve" psychology gripping western thought as the Roman empire began to collapse internally and externally. Serious forebodings of predestination by Optatus of Milevis and Ambrose of Milan appear to
anticipate Augustine, whose views, in turn, caused scholars like Pelagius,
Celestius, and the learned Julian of Eclanum to react and take up
cudgels for what was left of Classical Socratic and Aristotelian humanism.

Besides consistent endorsement of meritorious works by early theologians, two developments in the Church attest to the belief that one
can to a degree earn one's own way; both readily show how Roman
legalism served to reinforce Classical humanism. The idea that works
could justify as well as condemn, that good deeds could satisfy for evil
ones, gave rise to the penitential system already mentioned. Clement of
Rome was the first of many to believe that good deeds could cancel
punishment for bad ones. Soon the organized graduated penitential
discipline designed to satisfy for sins spread in East and West supported
by Tertullian, Cyprian and Basil, as well as by synodal canons. By the
time of Augustine the assumption was common, too, that if one wished
to be perfect, monasticism could provide a propitious environment for
good works and ascetical satisfaction. More interesting, however, is the
notion that sin can be atoned for vicariously through an accumulated
treasury of merits. Ignatius of Antioch is probably the first to advocate
the idea that works can be banked, as it were, to be drawn on later by
their depositors as accrued capital to be applied to themselves; says

Ignatius, "let your works be deposits so you may secure the sum due you." The *Shepherd of Hermas* repeats the theme, in an interesting way, by holding that Christians can do things beyond the command of God and thus acquire greater glory and favor than they were supposed to have. The idea of superabundant works continued to find supporters in Tertullian, the confessors who handed out "indulgences" during the Decian persecution, and even in Augustine's contemporary, John Chrysostom, who spoke of accumulating works to provide a store for man's journey to his native land.

So far we have seen that the freedom of the Christian had fared well in the hands of early theologians in so far as they generally declare man hampered by only a vague Original Sin, possessed of free will and the potential for meritorious action. Yet Christians faced one more hurdle if they would continue the long Classical trek to freedom and dignity: a workable interpretation of the rather novel and paradoxical character of Christian grace. Even after redeeming the individual's soul and dignifying his flesh through his historical incarnation, the new Providence chose to intervene constantly on man's behalf by a largess of grace so infinitely lavish as to overindulge his creatures and so powerful as possibly to contort divine concern into control. Moreover, this new Providence was not only more personally active, omniscient, and omnipotent than paganism had known but was also almost extravagant with his love. The question arose whether anyone, confronted with such love and concern, could be free.

Like pious pagans throughout the ages, Christians were aware that God's image was clouded within them; they were, therefore, quite ready to welcome divine aid, or grace, to fight the good fight and obtain the crown.[35] That grace was necessary no Father of the Church seriously questioned before Pelagius. Clement of Alexandria saw it as an illumination of the mind; to Ignatius, Cyprian, and John Chrysostom it was an inspiration of the will; to Cyril of Jerusalem an "internal motion." Irenaeus considered it as indispensable as rain from above, and necessary for man to persevere in sanctity. Cyprian averred that no one was strong in himself; Gregory of Nyssa held the favor of grace necessary for virginity. Gregory of Nazianzus maintained that even to wish well one needed the help of God. Even the strong advocate of free will, John Chrysostom, said that without an impulse from above all was of no purpose. But probably Origen put it best: grace made possible what was impossible for human nature. But since clarification, promulgation, and defense of the "good news" so thoroughly occupied the attention of the

---

[35] For a bibliography of studies on grace see *The Oxford Dictionary of the Christian Church*. Among the books recommended is the study by the Anglican E. Jauncey already recommended here in connection with free will and Original Sin.

early Church, many serious theological issues received little or no analytical treatment. Consequently, no systematic tract on grace appeared
before Augustine to plumb the profound implications of God's favor on
human freedom and dignity. Much simply was taken for granted, accepted in the light of Greek reason and Roman practicality. The question
whether grace was so coercive that it could not be resisted received little,
if any, consideration[36] because such a stance would be considered irrational and undignified, both to God and man. Yet Tertullian, the first to
look into grace in his work *On the Soul*, does say, seemingly alone and
rather reluctantly, that grace is so strong that it subjects even the free will
which generally he held to be master of itself. To most it was apparent
that humans had always been accorded freedom to choose badly and
commit evil. And did not the gods always appear to enjoy punishing
them for it? How could virtue be virtue under restraint, Gregory of
Nyssa asked; how could it continue to be that adornment without which
life was not sufficiently dignified to endure?

A second set of related perplexing questions also received slight
consideration before Augustine. Could each person count on grace by
virtue of being a man or was it dispensed arbitrarily by Providence? Were
individual destinies doled out in some inscrutable fashion known only to
an omniscient God? Did God wish to elect some and assist them toward
salvation while abandoning others to the inevitable consequences of sin?
Such a prospect seemed too irrational to contemplate seriously; if grace
were arbitrarily bestowed would it not be coercive and also too fright-
eningly unjust for reason to accept? If hell, as has been said, is itself a
savage prospect, deliberate divine abandonment of man to it would be
unthinkable. Consequently, the Fathers almost completely ignored Paul's
views of arbitrary election brought up in Romans and Ephesians which
declared that God had mercy on whom he would and that whomever he
would he hardened. Greek humanism in general found such Pharisaic
predestinarian speculations quite foreign. Even the heretic Marcion,
Paul's admirer, might have had difficulties with such predestinarian
views. Did not such "arbitrary" determinations better suit his sinister
Jewish demiurge? In brief, the views of Clement of Rome, Justin, and
Origen in the early Church and of John Chrysostom, Jerome, Hilary of
Poitiers in the later period may be taken as representative of the wide
belief that grace was given to all. Arnobius put it colorfully: the fountain
of life was open for all to drink.

A third consideration concerning grace, one in a sense embracing all

---

[36] Augustine, however, does say in one instance (*De corrept. et gratia* 14.5) that it cannot
be doubted that man's will cannot withstand the will of God. None of the elected and
predestined can perish for "if any one of these perished, God is mistaken; but none of
them perishes because God is not mistaken."

others, would become a *cause célèbre*. If grace was not denied some, if
God willed all to be saved, was grace, as the very word suggests, given
totally gratuitously or was its distribution determined by a divine judgment contingent on human conduct? Was the tacit humanistic assumption that man's deeds were meritorious, as a simple corollary of free will,
reverent enough of God's prerogatives? How could human action determine the output of grace since the Christian Providence was at once
omniscient Creator and timeless Sustainer? How could divine
foreknowledge not ordain unless God were able and willing to suspend
or even thwart his original will that all men be saved by introducing a
time sequence into his Being allowing human action to determine a
divine verdict? In short, could God ignore his foreknowledge? Then,
too, if somehow man's deeds were contributory to the distribution of
grace was the human role limited only to initiating a release of grace or
was it able to effect a continuous flow of divine aid as well?

Again, such questions were asked only rarely before Augustine. It
would seem that such was the case not because the issues were too
sophisticated for early Christian theologians to contemplate; after all,
Greek philosophers constantly and freely discussed similar problems in
dealing with Zeus, Fate, or Providence. Rather, the early Fathers, because
they considered Christianity a liberating movement from pagan fatalistic
entrapments, quite understandably interpreted predestination in terms
of divinely foreseen human merits; simply put, it was the Classical,
humanistic thing to do. Since the concept of free will and grace as
contenders did not become a major issue until the fourth century, an
early rational compromise sufficed: grace was declared a cooperative
venture, a joint operation of God and man. Early Fathers such as Origen
and Cyprian, as well as later ones like Gregory of Nyssa[37] and John
Chrysostom, would agree that it was necessary, on one hand, for men to
be their own masters but, on the other, that salvation was obviously from
God. Writers before Origen are quite likely merely to make assertions on
the matter than to analyze it. Justin, for example, though a trained
philosopher, only partly saw the problem and simply asserted that God's
foreknowledge left intact man's will; grace was given to all who willed to
repent. However, Ignatius of Antioch, always somewhat Pauline, seems
dimly to have anticipated prevenient grace as a necessary preparation for
fruitful good works; Irenaeus, in turn, rather enigmatically says, if one
delivers up to Him which is one's own—faith and subjection—one will
receive His handiwork;[38] Clement of Alexandria thought it necessary to
remark that one gets grace by deserving it.

---

[37] Jaeger, *Early Christianity*, pp. 87–100, records Gregory of Nyssa's efforts to follow in
the best tradition of Greek *paideia* by trying to preserve in his *De instit. Christ.* (*PG* 46:287–
306) the efficacy of human effort in the face of Christian grace.

[38] Irenaeus, well representative of the usual view that God's foreknowledge is of man's

Origen, usually precocious, was the first theologian to seriously sense the difficulties presented by God's prescience and human free will. As a violent foe of Fate and supporter of free will, he maintains that God's foreknowledge does not ordain; just as an observer of a pedestrian on a slippery pavement does not cause his fall, so God did not ordain Judas' betrayal. For Origen the future event causes God's foreknowledge of it; he knows what acts will follow from man's own wickedness committed through his own fault. For his view that freedom precedes while grace follows and supports, Origen has been called the Father of Pelagianism. Not only does divine favor attend human choice but such favor, or grace, will be given to all who deserve it; in fact all will eventually earn it even if the trauma of reincarnation is necessary so that all rational creatures can be saved. Origen skillfully resorts to Platonic pre-existence of souls to rationalize Providence's unequal distribution of grace by tying it to the measure of sin committed freely by the soul in its pre-earthly state. Eusebius has no reservations about endorsing Origen's interpretation of foreknowledge along with his views of free will.

The list of those who explain predestination through God's foreknowledge of human acts continues to grow. Cyril of Jerusalem almost adopts what will become a later heretical stance in his *Catechetical Lectures*. Stated simply: God gives grace to those worthy of it; yet, let no one presume upon it. Divine grace—in this case that given in Baptism— meets up with human faith; where God finds the disposition good, he grants the saving seal of baptismal favor. Hilary of Poitiers holds that one must earn the Holy Spirit. Optatus of Milevis, to whom Augustine is somewhat indebted for reinforcement of Paul's doctrine of faith over works, says God gives grace to those who do what they can. Gregory of Nyssa refutes the objections of those who say that grace has not been accorded to all; has it not even been proclaimed in all languages? In addition, Gregory maintains that man not only wills to use the grace afforded him but increases the amount of divine assistance in proportion as he expands effort. Indeed, Gregory would make the inculcation of grace-producing attitudes and habits almost a task of Christian paideia. If God leaves something to human initiative should not the proper dispositions leading to grace be cultivated through education? Gregory of Nazianzus, in a different vein, insists that man required a gratis infusion of both prevenient and assisting grace since God's favor is the beginning and end of all good; Augustine praised him for his views. Quite opposed is John Chrysostom. In many ways quite Pelagian, he teaches that God gives grace to all after waiting for them to take the initiative. Grace is subsidiary to the human will; it must first choose the good, and God then leads it on, completing rather than initiating. In no

---

response, prefers (*Adv. haer.* 4.29,2) to have humans prejudged on their willingness or unwillingness to believe rather than upon their actions.

way could divinity anticipate man's choice without outraging free will. The Spirit fell upon Cornelius of Acts because he first fulfilled his part by contributing faith. It is our own to choose and work; God completes. His drawing us does not take away free will even though divine assistance is necessary. To enlighten the problem of foreknoweldge which he declared non-constraining, Chrysostom distinguishes between that divine will which later came to be called God's antecedent or first will by which he desires all rational creatures to be saved, and that which will come to be known as God's subsequent or second will by which he limits his intent by the free choice he gave mankind. Finally, Nemesius, a contemporary of Augustine, would vigorously have opposed the great African Father had he heard of him. In the best tradition of Classical humanism, Nemesius holds that once given free will by God, human beings can be good as well as bad regardless of circumstances. It is man, then, who determines God's favor. Caesarius of Arles promised that God never deserts a person unless he first deserts Him.

It is ironic that before closing forever the doors on its glorious history, the African church should contribute one of Christianity's greatest thinkers in the person of Augustine. That he should present the greatest Christian challenge to Classical humanism is understandable; he lived in an age dismayed by the troubles of the Roman world collapsing under Christian leadership. Augustine would have the establishment, operation, and fulfillment of all human values and history turn so completely about God's disposition in respect to sin and grace that, for many, he left little, if any, room for human spiritual potential and even for concern over the advancement of secular affairs. God will control content, ends, and means in his *City of God;* everything touching on the meaning of life, on human destiny and salvation belongs to God. In some twenty-five major works dealing with Original Sin, freedom, merits, and predestination, Augustine extolled the goodness and mercy of God toward helpless humanity after its fall. Many are works of his later life in rebuttal of Pelagius, a British or Irish lay monk, and his colleagues who, about 411, began to expound in Africa a robust Classical-Christian humanistic doctrine, conceivably of Roman origins, claiming that it was possible for one to be perfect by his own natural forces, that one could attain salvation without supernatural grace. Augustine's responses, sometimes heated and confusing, comprise the first serious analytical treatment of the nature, operation and kinds of grace. In his works the great African theologian would exhaust, to many in an anti-humanistic fashion, the old Classical—as well as Hebrew—dilemma of the interaction of divine and human forces. To many he seemed to inject ancient would-be "fatalistic" themes into the new Christian context, introducing insights into anthropology penetrating but disturbing. The *Enchiridion,* often considered the most seasoned and succinct manual of Augustine's predestinarian thoughts, reveals clearly enough, along with his other late works, that the learned African Father is reciting familiar themes on a stage hallowed over the ages by Protagoras, Socrates, Platonists, and Stoics. In a way, it might be said he represents more the end of an era than the beginning of a new one.

With a lethal Original Sin inherited from Adam's fall, man, to Augustine, became a mass of damnation which included even unbaptized children. Having lost the original capacity not to sin, man was now not able not to sin. A benevolent Providence, in an inscrutable but not unjust way, chose to elect a relatively few for salvation graciously saving them from their just damnation by providing prevenient, actual, sanctifying and persevering graces. Following Paul, the selection of the elect is made not in consideration of any intrinsic merit of human works but according to God's own unfathomable purpose.

Man's acts are to have no value in themselves but only as God chooses to make them meritorious; the just will have their merits but no previous merits make them just. As Augustine explained it in Epistle 194 to Pope Sixtus: when God crowns human efforts he crowns nothing other than his own gifts. Foreknowledge becomes not prescience of man's meritorious acts but foreknowledge of the gifts of grace God knows he himself will grant to the elect. Put another way, it becomes foreknowledge of the extent to which individuals will avail themselves of their freedom to use the grace preordained for them.

In *Grace and Free Will* Augustine maintained that free will could be harmonized with God's favor; in fact, he argued that to exercise free will in any situation without grace was futile since only grace allowed the free will to operate. Without grace one could choose only sin. In the case of the elect, actions are truly theirs; they are by nature free to cooperate with or reject grace so that their acts, made meritorious by divine prearrangement, truly determine their salvation. Yet even among the elect the free will is not strong enough to desire the good or perform good works unassisted. Grace is necessary throughout even in an initial way to prepare in the would-be elect proper dispositions for conversion involving a conviction of sin and a desire for good. Then, grace constantly had to assist the will once set in operation by making its freely chosen acts meritorious and by providing the gift of final perseverence. The elect can choose, but they will the good effectively and meritoriously only when God permits it through grace. For the non-elect the implications are quite stark. Those from whom God withholds grace, those who are "hardened," have no effective free will at all since they are productive only in sinning; even their good actions serve no meaningful purpose since they are deprived of meritoriousness.

Why does God deny aid to the crippled will of some of his creatures? Does he not wish the salvation of all so that his Son dies for only a few?

Augustine explains at one point that God indeed wished salvation to all but substituted his original will antecedent to the Fall which planned for a universal salvation, with a subsequent will made necessary by man's exercise of free will which caused his Fall with its mortal consequences. Sometimes in a casuistic way he seems to interpret "all" as meaning "all the elect." But in the last analysis, Augustine's humility forced him to declare the paradoxical matter insoluble, an unspeakable mystery. In the *Grace of Perseverence* he tries to comfort the faithful with the advice to keep running, knowing that by the very fact of their running they have been predestined to run successfully. But only death will reveal the true situation, an observation not dissimilar to a common Greek injunction never to consider oneself fortunate until one is dead.

Augustine was, indeed, standing on a familiar stage acting out a familiar plot, but his dialogue was paradoxical and disturbing to the shades of those who had fought the long Classical fight for liberty and dignity. The Aristotelian Nemesius in far off Emesa, who apparently never heard of Augustine, would have seen him entrapped in the discarded Classical view that divinity could be capricious or even jealous, and caught up as well in the old Stoic dilemma of trying to support freedom under a Providence that ultimately dragged men where it would. Were not Christians, certainly the non-elect, like Stoics willing vainly and ineffectively, choosing non-meritoriously to modify nothing? Nemesius might well have directed against Augustine one of his succinct summations against Fate: if Providence arranges "that some men should be worshippers of the divine and others not, it will be found that we are back once more to all things being fated."[39]

Many, unlike Nemesius, did know Augustine and objected so strenuously to his views that a long and acrimonius struggle ensued. Pelagius, of course, gave his name to the humanist, anti-Augustinian faction maintaining, as we saw, that divine grace, even that of Baptism, was unnecessary since human beings could be virtuous and save themselves by their own innate liberty unimpaired by a fictitious Original Sin.[40] Semi-Pelagianism, a term invented in modern times, is used to refer to those who held out for some measure of human sovereignty by insisting that at least the beginning of faith, the first impulse toward conversion, as well as the power of perseverence were within human power. Pelagius found an early supporter in a fellow Briton, Celestius, and in John, the Bishop of Jerusalem. It was, indeed, reported that many good Christians

[39] Nemesius, *Nature of Man* 52.

[40] Pelagius' large corpus of writings has mostly disappeared except for a commentary on Paul's epistles preserved in an edited form by Jerome (*PL* 30:645–902). Consequently, Pelagian teaching is transmitted by hostile witnesses such as Paulinus, a deacon of Milan, who charged Pelagius, at the synod of Carthage in 412, with seven specific heretical stances largely recorded in Augustine's *De pecc. orig.* 2.3,12 and *De gest. Pel.* 23.

were astounded at Pelagius' condemnation by African councils. Eighteen bishops in Italy refused to submit to censure for supporting Pelagianism among them the learned, aggressive Aristotelian humanist, Julian of Eclanum, who claimed Augustine invented Original Sin. Augustine was generously reviled by his enemies and his doctrines turned into travesties. Monks, supposing that their merits counted, were stirred up especially in Africa and Gaul; councils fulminated. Popes became involved including the ambitious Innocent I, the wavering Zosimus, the ineffective Celestine, and even the future Leo the Great. Finally Boniface II approved a solution arrived at by a few western bishops assembled in Synod at Orange in Gaul.

Theologians took up the dialogue from the wings. Jerome shrewdly attacked Pelagianism as a survival of paganism. Prosper of Aquitaine, a layman friend of Leo the Great, objected to Augustine's implied predestination to evil and damnation but nonetheless decided to support him actively. So did Fulgentius, bishop in North Africa. Caesarius, Bishop of Arles, originally a monk at Lerins, was largely responsible for a "settlement" at the second Council of Orange in 529 that quieted the matter mainly in Augustine's favor.

Augustine's chief opponents centered, reasonably enough, in monasteries, especially those of southern Gaul. Perhaps the most outspoken was Cassian, founder of St. Victor's at Marseilles, who might be called the author of Semi-Pelagianism some ten years before Augustine's death. Hilary, Bishop of Arles, originally from the monastery on the island of Lerins south of Cannes, was less openly involved. Faustus of Riez in Provence, also from Lerins and still revered today as a saint in Southern France, was far more critical in his *On Grace,* which received approval from a council of Arles, c. 473. In general, Provence teaching, while freely admitting the need of grace for supernatural good and complete faith, held that individuals could take the initiative in releasing grace, that grace did not precede meritorious acts but accompanied and amplified them, that grace was given to all, and that the grace of perseverence was in human power. Predestination was postulated on God's foreknowledge of an individual's meritorious acts.

The second Council of Orange, meeting largely at the initiative of Caesarius, used as a basis of discussion his agenda of twenty-five articles. The synod, composed of only fourteen bishops, issued eight canons vindicating Augustine's position that Original Sin dealt out spiritual death and helplessness, that grace came initially before justification, and that it was a prerequisite for all salutary acts leading to salvation including all pious dispositions and prayer. Seventeen propositions or *Sententiae* reinforced the canons. They affirmed the powerlessness of free will for good when left to its own resources and declared that "man has nothing of his own except falsehood and sin," and that even the good works which one might do naturally were somewhat sinful.[41] But the shades of Aristotle, Cicero, and Origen did not turn over completely in their graves because a profession of faith appended to the council's document, probably Caesarius' more liberal contribution, somewhat sabotaged the council's work by declaring, "we believe the baptized, Christ helping and cooperating, can and must implement what concerns salvation of the soul, if they have chosen to apply themselves diligently." This addendum, while a blow against Pelagius' denial of Original Sin and consequent need of baptismal grace, left considerable room to circumvent strict Augustinianism. In addition to rejecting predestination to evil, the council left other matters in the dark, including Augustine's *massa damnata,* the damnation of unbaptized children, comments on the extent that God wills the salvation of all, and a precise definition of foreknowledge.[42]

The decision of Orange approved by Pope Boniface II in January 531 can readily be viewed in the light of subsequent history more as a temporary and theoretical settlement than an effective solution, a resolution needed to quiet theological disruption in the Church already strained physically by Arian barbarians. Leo the Great seems to express what may have been the general sentiment of the day: it is unwise to seek for what has been declared, to retract what has been perfected, to tear up what has been defined. Classical humanism, which long sought freedom or at least dignity for humanity, was only temporarily overwhelmed by the "loss of nerve" besetting the perishing Roman world. Not entirely defeated, it rose again in the flourishing of monasticism wedded to meritorious acts, in Gregory the Great's endorsement of a vulgar catholicism that emasculated Augustinianism, and in the growing sacramentalism of the Church which dispensed ex opere operato grace in a legalistic way upon application—an arrangement which Augustine himself did much to popularize.

[41] "Solution" of the Pelagian controversy by fourteen regional Gallic bishops in synod is such an anti-climax that certain questions seem inevitable in retrospect. Were the issues overdrawn in the first place by a few protagonists largely from the western empire suffering from a "loss of nerve"? Was the power of the papacy so decisive that its recognition of Orange's deliberations could "settle" the matter? Was the settlement made more out of ennui than inspiration?

[42] Text of the synod's definitions comprising eight canons, seventeen propositions, and a profession of faith can be found in J. Mansi, *Sacrorum Conciliorum Nova et Amplissima Collectio,* 31 vols., 1758–98 (reprinted: Paris, 1901) under Concilium Arausicanum II, Capitula xxv, 8:712–720. Also in *CSEL Concilia Galliae* 138:55–76. Translation in C. J. Hefele, *History of the Ecclesiastical Councils,* trans. W. R. Clark (Edinburgh: Clark, 1895) 4:152–165. The controversial passage reads: "*Credimus quod omnes baptizati, Christo auxiliante et cooperante, quae ad salutem animae pertinent, possint et debeant, si fideliter laborare voluerint, adimplere.*" Mansi, column 717.

In the East, too, rugged Augustinianism gave way. Here the definitive John of Damascus (c. 275), by choosing to emphasize the antecedent
will of God desiring universal salvation for men, did much to lay Augustinian predestinarianism at rest in favor of the views of the "illiberal
humanist" Origen, and indirectly of Aristotle and Cicero.

EPILOGUE

Such is the story of the intellectual give and take between Athens and Jerusalem during the first four and one half centuries when Jewish-Christian convictions encountered the commitments of the honored but aging Greek and Roman Classical world. On the whole, it would appear that Christianity was quite selective in its rejections, compromises, and endorsements of Classical values. It was fortunate that such was the case because the choices were momentous ones destined to have an incalculable impact on emerging western thought arising out of the synthesis of the two cultures, a synthesis so profound that it would reach its apex only in the thirteenth century and would suffer serious dissolution only in the Enlightenment of the eighteenth century.

It was probably fortunate that expectations of the Parousia taught the early Church to be unsolicitous about its corporate image. Its convert members, unlike citizens of the Classical commonwealth, were encouraged to seek fulfillment not in a collective good but in their own personal welfare. As a service agency for the individual, the "Body of Christ" had, except possibly in Origen's mind, no utopian message even for its own society as a collective group. Admittedly, the developing ecclesiastical organization encouraged the Church to concern itself with its own self preservation as the Ark of Salvation; but the "good news" itself was never stripped of its basic message: the individual's eternal salvation, a welfare that would outlive the Church itself. The revealed tidings assured the faithful that each individual was a divine creation personally redeemed to enjoy hopes of eternal life effected through grace distributed on a one-to-one basis, and to entertain even prospects of individual bodily resurrection from the dead. Such promises, which made Christians strikingly aware of their individual consciousness and selfhood stood in sharp contrast to most Classical views which considered humans, merely links, specimens necessarily occurring in the on-going endless process of preserving the type which had already largely spent its potential. To the Christian, however, each person was something of a unique co-actor in the cosmic economy of a providential God unfolding his will in a straight historical line leading to a grand eschatological assize in which every individual would be involved at the end of time. Classical views of anthropology and history, in contrast, can be said actually to resist formation of any fixed conception of selfhood, to depersonalize the self, by liquidating human existence at death or by involving it in seemingly endless repetitious cycles or by consigning it to arbitrary reincarnations even in irrational hosts.

If the so-called Edict of Milan, which reactivated Gallienus' earlier edict of toleration, is rightly considered momentous because it lifted the persecution against Christians, it is more deserving of comment in the long run as the final recognition by the Classical polity that its "totalitarian" power, that is, its control over the total human being, should henceforth be removed from certain legitimate areas of human activity. The edict is, in actuality, a prototype of all later bills of rights. Thereafter under such early Christian leaders as Hosius, Athanasius, Ambrose, and Gelasius, as well as their successors, the West was schooled in the belief that that governance was best which was limited by competing and balancing sovereignties so that State and Church, each zealous in vying for man's allegiance, would strive to protect human rights against a monopoly by the other. If in the new Christian-Classical world the Church seemed early on to cow the state, the situation was not permanent; as all western historians know, it tended to swing to and fro. The breach in total control was to remain final, however: no pope was to be emperor; no emperor pope. The king, from Theodosius to Henry II of Germany and even the great Sun-King himself, was to learn that he, too, was under fundamental moral law, that it was dangerous to invite ecclesiastical censure. Under the dual arrangement it was as difficult for the Church to erect a theocracy as it was for the state, short of destroying the Church, to raise its "totalitarian" stance again.

If Christianity did not look for "salvation" in the corporate and rejected the "totalitarian" competence of the Classical commonwealth, it readily espoused the rational mentality so long praised in Hellenism. First and foremost, God's revealed word must be constrained to make sense by subjecting itself to every skilled Greek device of textual criticism and literary interpretation; Revelation and Mysticism must welcome Reason and Observation as intellectual tools. However theologically desirable or undesirable later history may see it, the rather brash triumph of rationalism in Christianity was almost a necessity, as early theologians like Justin and Clement readily saw. They could scarcely imagine, much less help induce, the unthinkable intellectual cataclysm which would have ensued if the Classical world's rational heritage of philosophy, science, and literature had been rejected. Such a disastrous hiatus separating the world of Plato, Aristotle, Virgil, and Cicero from that of Christ would have destroyed a thousand-year historical continuity and denied Christianity the opportunity to have a learned clergy, the hallmark of all great world religions. What would the dark ages of barbarian invasions have been like without available Christian scholars capable of reeducating Europe?

As in the case of rationalism, Christianity's endorsement of Classical legalism and institutionalism was complete and spontaneous. The defeat of Paul's anti-legal stand, the development of ex opere operato sacramentalism, the emergence of creeds, Scriptual canon, development of hierarchy and especially of the papacy—while decried by some as entrenchments of a formalism which would imperil spontaneous personal piety—all seem in retrospect understandable expressions of a contagious contemporary Classical legal-institutional commitment. It was a commitment necessary for Christianity to adopt once it had forced a division of sovereignty on the ancient world. Made aware by Classical experience that religion and law were indispensible twin pillars of civilization, it was incumbent, now that the Church was a co-sovereignty, for it too, to clothe itself in the mantle of a familiar workable legalism if it would operate effectively along with the new limited state in carrying out a mission in the world. Was it not obvious to the converted gentile that only dedication to rational law and institutions could guarantee a consistent theological message free as much as possible from the irrational, the bizarre, the arbitrary, the confusing, the anarchistic? Could everyone be invited to be infallible in an already disoriented world?

With the aristocratic nature of the Classical world Christianity made something of a subtle, yet momentous, compromise. Since the leveling process was already under way in the early Christian era, the Church was scarcely confronted by an old Classical heroic nobility of birth, even though its dying ethic lingered on. Its experience with such nobility was yet to come when a new martial, landed aristocracy would arise and overwhelm her later in feudal Europe. In dealing with the blatant Roman aristocracy of wealth Christianity found need to qualify the Master's message and humble example. Yet neither to the wealthy, nor to any privileged group did it offer a monopoly on salvation. Repudiation of a divinely elected charismatic aristocracy of grace, containment of monastic exclusiveness, supervision of the theologically elite, divorcement from philosophical circles, all displayed Christianity's determination to avoid becoming itself an aristocracy of one sort or another, especially an intellectual one which would consider the Gospels a new philosophy meant only for the mentally gifted. Even celibacy, in its own way, made it impossible for an hereditary clerical caste to arise and monopolize administrative arete progressively more and more prized as the Christian body expanded and became more complexly organized as a Church. Even more than late Roman Stoicism, Christianity startled the Classical world with the message that all men were created equal in being even though, in the temporality of the present world, superficial inequalities existed. No two heavens, no different sets of sacraments, creeds, or basic ethics were promulgated to divide the noble, the plutocrat, or the sage from the commoner so that even slaves like Callistus, and peasants like Gregory VII, could become popes. Any clerical abuse of spiritual equality became all the more glaring because the ideal was clear; any temporal abuses of equality—socially, economically, and politically— were made tolerable in the light of an eternal equalization after death.

The long Classical quest for humanism was scarcely interrupted by the Christian movement. As have seen, Paul's early threat of pre-destinarianism and his disparagement of human works as meritorious found little if any, support in the early Christian centuries. It was roundly assumed that everyone eventually got what he or she personally bargained for. Original Sin, largely undiscovered before Augustine, did not yet overpower man so that he could, in some measure, perform meritoriously to earn, or at least to initiate divine assistance to offset his potential and freedom to defy God. If human beings enjoyed an individualism and even a perverse sense of dignity in sinning, they had the capability to make God, in some measure, their debtor. If Christian freedom could not be the absolute type Protagoras would want because it was limited by a Providence and grace, a Socratic type of humanism, which envisioned human dignity under a godhead was, as Nemesius saw, possible in Christianity as never before. The early Classically-minded Christians, who readily considered themselves as much recipients of divine Reason as of grace, apparently found it difficult in the long run, despite seeming official recognition by the Church, to accept Augustine's exaggerated Pauline predestination which seemed to offer persons little, if any, dignified initiative in their own salvation and dragged them, much as Fate had, where it would.

History, of course, cannot deal in conjecture. Yet it is tempting to ponder whether western political science could have exerted concern for the sacredness of the person as evinced in the development of enlightened despotism, bills of rights, and constitutions were it not for the early Christian encounter with the corporate and the "totalitarian." Could the medieval university—where theology and philosophy were queens—and even later western science have arisen if Christianity had not long taught scholars to worship at the shrine of reason and generally—with only temporary, limited and rare exceptions—encouraged them in a Greek way, to use all the intellectual tools available to them? Could barbarians have been civilized without church law and institutions or could the philosophes of the Enlightenment and the French Revolution have secularized the basic Christian concept of spiritual equality if the early Church had fallen completely prey to aristocraticism? Finally, how much secular progress could the western world have made if Augustine, in an unqualified way, had had his anti-humanistic way prone to view man as a *massa damnationis* and all pursuit of human excellence mere vanity? Would not Protagoras, Aristotle, and Cicero have lived largely in vain?

BIBLIOGRAPHY

Major Sources and Reference Works

Ancient Christian Writers. Edited by J. Quasten and J. Plumpe. 44 vols. Westminster, Maryland: Newman, 1946–.

L'Année Philologique: Bibliographic, Critique, et Analytique de L'antiquité Greco-latine. Paris: Société d'édition "Les belles-lettres," 1928–.

The Ante-Nicene Christian Library. Edited by A. Roberts and J. Donaldson. 24 vols. Grand Rapids: Eerdman's, 1951.

The Cambridge Ancient History. Edited by J. B. Bury and others. Vols. V–XII. New York: Macmillan, 1923–1939.

Cayré, F. *Manual of Patrology*. 2 vols. Paris: Desclée & Co., 1935.

Corpus scriptorum ecclesiasticorum latinorum. Edited by Academy of Vienna. 70 vols. Vienna: Academy Press, 1866–.

Dictionary of Christian Biography. Edited by A. Smith and H. Wace. London: Murray, 1877.

Dictionnaire d'archéologie chrétienne et de liturge. Edited by F. Cabrol and H. Leclercq. 30 vols. Paris: Letouzey et Ané, 1924–1952.

Die griechischen christlichen Schriftsteller der ersten drei Jahrhunderte. Edited by Academy of Berlin, 41 vols. Berlin: Academy Press, 1897–.

The Loeb Classical Library. Edited by T. E. Page and others. 428 vols. Cambridge: Harvard University Press, 1912–1967.

Patrologiae cursus completus, Series Graeca. Edited by J. P. Migne. 161 vols. Paris: Garnier, 1857–1866.

Patrologiae cursus completus, Series Latina. Edited by J. P. Migne. 221 vols. Paris: Garnier, 1844–1855.

Oxford Classical Dictionary. Edited by M. Cary. Oxford: Clarendon, 1949.

The Oxford Dictionary of the Christian Church. Edited by F. L. Cross. London: Oxford University Press, 1958.

Paulys Realencyclopädie der classischen Altertunswissenschaft. Edited by G. Wissowa and W. Kroll. 71 vols. with supplements, Stuttgart: Metzler, 1894–.

Quasten, J. *Patrology*. 3 vols. Westminster, Maryland: Newman, 1962.

A Select Library of Nicene and Post-Nicene Fathers of the Christian Church. Edited by P. Schaff and H. Wace. 28 vols. Grand Rapids: Eerdman's, 1952.

Select short general histories of Greece and Rome.

Bury, J. B. and Meiggs, R. *A History of Greece*. New York: St. Martin's. 1972.

Cary, M. *History of the Greek World, 323–146 B.C.* London: Methuen, 1951.

Downey, G. *The Late Roman Empire*. New York: Holt, Rinehart & Winston, 1969.

Jones, A. H. M. *The Later Roman Empire*. 2 vols. Norman: University of Oklahoma Press, 1964.

Laistner, M. L. W. *History of the Greek World 479–323*. London: Methuen, 1947.

Marsh. F. B. *A History of the Roman World from 146 B.C. to 30 B.C.* London: Methuen, 1935.

Parker, H. M. D. *A History of the Roman World from A.D. 138 to 337*. London: Methuen, 1935.

Salmon, E. T. *A History of the Roman World from 30 B.C. to A.D. 138.* London: 1966.

Swain, J. W. *The Ancient World.* 2 vols. New York: Harper & Row, 1950.

Tarn, W. W. *Hellenistic Civilization.* Cleveland: Meridian, 1967.

Trever, A. A. *History of Ancient Civilization.* 2 vols. New York: Harcourt, Brace, 1939.

Select Short Studies of Classical Religion

Bailey, C. *Phases in the Religion of Ancient Rome.* Sather Classical Lectures. Berkeley: University of California Press, 1932.

Cornford, F. M. *Greek Religious Thought.* Boston: Beacon, 1950.

Fowler, W. W. *The Religious Experience of the Roman People.* London: Macmillan, 1911.

Glover, T. R. *The Conflict of Religions in the Early Roman Empire.* Boston: Beacon, 1960.

Guthrie, W. K. C. *The Greeks and their Gods.* Boston: Beacon, 1956.

Legge, F. *Forerunners and Rivals of Christianity.* Cambridge: Cambridge University Press, 1915.

Murray, G. *Five Stages of Greek Religion.* Garden City: Doubleday, 1951.

Nilsson, M. P. *A History of Greek Religion.* New York: Norton, 1952.

Studies of Early Christianity

Bainton, R. H. *Early Christianity.* New York: Van Nostrand Reinhold, 1960.

Bigg, C. *The Church's Task under the Roman Empire.* Oxford: Clarendon, 1905.

Chadwick, H. *The Early Church.* Harmondsworth: Penguin, 1967.

Coleman-Norton, P. R. *The Roman State and the Christian Church: A Collection of Legal Documents to A.D. 535.* London: SPCK, 1966.

Duchesne, L. M. O. *Early History of the Christian Church from its Foundation to the End of the fifth Century.* Trans. J. Murray. London: Murray, 1957.

Foakes-Jackson, F. J. *The History of the Christian Church to A.D. 461.* New York: Doran, 1924.

Frend, W. H. C. *The Early Church.* Philadelphia: Fortress, 1982.

Goodenough, E. R. *The Church in the Roman Empire.* New York: Holt, 1931.

Guignebert, C. *The Early History of Christianity.* New York: Twayne, 1927.

Jalland, T. G. *The Origin and Evolution of the Christian Church.* New York: Hutchinson, 1948.

Lebreton, J. and Zeiller, J. *The History of the Primitive Church.* 4 vols. New York: Macmillan, 1949.

Lietzmann, H. *A History of the Early Church.* 4 vols. Trans. B. L. Woolf. London: Lutterworth, 1949.

Lightfoot, J. B. *The Apostolic Fathers.* London: Macmillan, 1891.

McGiffert, A. C. *A History of Christianity in the Apostolic Age.* New York: Scribner, 1912.

Markus, R. A. *Christianity in the Roman World.* New York: Scribner, 1974.

Mattingly, H. *Christianity in the Roman Empire.* New York: Norton, 1967.

Piganiol, A. *L'Empire Chrétien.* Paris: Presses Universitaires de France, 1947.

Ramsay, W. M. *The Church in the Roman Empire.* London: Hodder & Stoughton, 1907.

Young, F. M. *From Nicaea to Chalcedon: A Guide to the Literature and its Background.* Philadelphia: Fortress, 1983.

Volz, C. A. *Faith and Practice in the Early Church.* Minneapolis: Augsburg, 1983.

General Bibliography

Most works of Classical and Christian writers cited in the various chapters of the book can be found in the *Loeb Classical Library* or in *The Ante-Nicene Christian Library* and *A Select Library of Nicene and Post-Nicene Fathers of the Christian Church*, Series 1 and 2. Ancient authors whose works are dealt with repeatedly or at some length will have their texts specifically identified in the bibliography only if they are not available in the corpora mentioned above or if another text is preferred. Texts and translations of the Fathers can be found readily in the patrologies of Cayré and Quasten mentioned under Major Sources and Reference Works.

Adkins, A. W. H. *Merit and Responsibility.* Oxford: Clarendon Press, 1960.

Alexander of Aphrodisias, *In Metaphysica Commentaria.* ed. by M. Hayduck. Vol 1 of *Commentaria in Aristotelem graeca.* 23 vols. Berlin: Academy of Letters, Reimeri, 1891.

Amand, D. *Fatalisme et Liberté dans L'antiquité Grecque.* Louvain: Bibliotheque de l'université, 1945.

Angus, S. *The Mystery Religions and Christianity.* New York: Scribner, 1928.

Armstrong, A. H. ed *Cambridge History of Later Greek and Early Medieval Philosophy* Chapters 1–29. London: Cambridge University Press, 1967.

————— and Markus, R. A. *Christian Faith and Greek Philosophy.* London: Longman and Todd, 1960.

Arnim, J. *Stoicorum Veterum Fragmenta.* 3 vols. Lipsiae: Teubner, 1921.

Bailey, C. *The Legacy of Rome.* Oxford: Clarendon, 1923.

Baker, G. P. *Constantine the Great and the Christian Revolution.* London: Nash and Grayson, 1931.

Barker, E. *Greek Political Theory.* London: Methuen, 1960.

————— *The Politics of Aristotle.* Oxford: Clarendon, 1946.

Bauer, W. *Orthodoxy and Heresy in Earliest Christianity.* Translated by the Philadephia Seminar on Christian Origins. Philadelphia: Fortress, 1971.

Baynes, N. H. *Constantine the Great and the Christian Church.* London: Melford, 1930.

Beardslee, W. *Literary Criticism of the New Testament.* Philadelphia: Fortress, 1970.

Bevan, E. *Hellenism and Christianity.* London: Allen and Unwin, 1930.

Bigg, C. *The Christian Platonists of Alexandria.* Oxford: Clarendon, 1913.

Boas, G. *Rationalism in Greek Philosophy.* Baltimore: Johns Hopkins University Press, 1961.

Boissier, G. *La Fin du Paganisme.* 2 vols. Paris: Librairie Hachette, 1909.

Boman, T. *Hebrew Thought Compared with Greek.* London: SCM, 1960.

Bonner, R. J. *Lawyers and Litigants in Ancient Athens.* Chicago: University of Chicago Press, 1927.

Bonner, S. F. *Education in Ancient Rome.* Berkeley: University of California Press, 1977.

Bonner, W. A. "Origen and the Tradition of Natural Law Concepts." In *Dumbarton Oaks Papers* No. 8, pp. 51–82. Cambridge: Harvard University Press, 1954.

Boren, H. C. *Roman Society.* Lexington, Massachusetts: Heath, 1977.

Botsford, G. W. and Sihler, E. G. *Hellenic Civilization.* New York: Columbia University Press, 1915.

Bowra, C. M. *The Greek Experience.* London: Weidenfeld and Nicolson, 1957.

Boyd, W. K. "The Ecclesiastical Edicts of the Theodosian Code." In *Studies in*

History, Economics, and Public Law. 24 #2, 1905. New York: Columbia University Press, 1905.

Breen, Q. *Christianity and Humanism.* Grand Rapids: Eerdmans, 1968.

Bréhier, E. *Chrysippe et L'ancien Stoicïsme.* Paris: University of France, 1951.

Brown, P. *The Cult of the Saints: Its Rise and Function in Latin Christianity.* Chicago: University of Chicago Press, 1980.

Brown, P. L. *Augustine of Hippo: A Biography.* Berkeley: University of California Press, 1967.

———— *Religion and Society in the Age of St. Augustine.* New York: Harper and Row, 1972.

Bubacz, B. *St. Augustine's Theory of Knowledge.* New York: Mellen, 1984.

Burn-Murdoch, H. *The Development of the Papacy.* New York: Praeger, 1954.

Cadoux, C. J. *The Early Church and the World: A History of the Christian Attitude to Pagan Society and the State down to the Time of Constantius.* Edinburgh: Clark, 1955.

Caesarius of Arles. *Homilies and Letters.* Patrologiae Series Latina 67:1041–166.

Carlyle, A. J. *A History of Medieval Political Theory in the West.* London: Blackwood, 1903.

Case, S. J. *Social Triumph of the Ancient Church.* London: Allen and Unwin, 1934.

Caspar, E. *Geschichte des Papsttums.* Vol. 1. Tübingen: Mohr, 1930.

Chadwick, H. *Early Christian Thought and the Classical Tradition.* New York: Oxford University Press, 1966.

———— and von Campenhausen, H. *Jerusalem and Rome: The Problems of Authority in the Early Church.* Philadelphia: Fortress, 1966.

Clark, E. C. *A History of Roman Private Law.* New York: Tannen, 1965.

Clarke, M. L. *The Roman Mind.* New York: Norton, 1968.

Cochrane, C. *Christianity and Classical Culture.* New York: Oxford University Press, 1957.

Conrad, C. "Stoic Conception of Natural Law." In *Great Events from History.* 1:388–92. Edited by F. Magill. Englewood Cliffs, New Jersey: Salem, 1972.

Cornford, F. M. *From Religion to Philosophy: A Study on the Origins of Western Speculation.* London: Arnold, 1912.

———— *Greek Religious Thought from Homer to the Age of Alexander.* New York: Dutton, 1923.

———— *Plato and Parmenides.* London: Paul, Trench and Trubner, 1939.

Croiset, M. *Hellenic Civilization.* New York: Knopf, 1925.

Cumont, F. *The Oriental Religions in Roman Paganism.* Chicago: Open Court Publishing Co., 1911.

Cyprian, *On the Unity of the Catholic Church.* Trans. M. Bénevot. *Ancient Christian Writers.* Vol. 25. Westminster, Maryland: Newman, 1957.

Danielou, J. *Theology of Jewish Christianity.* Translated by J. Baker. London: Darton, Longman & Todd, 1964.

Davies, J. G. *Daily Life in the Early Church.* London: Lutterworth, 1952.

Davies, S. L. *The Revolt of the Widows: The Social World of the Apocryphal Acts.* Carbondale, Illinois: Southern Illinois University Press, 1980.

Dawson, C. *The Making of Europe: An Introduction to the History of European Unity.* New York: Sheed and Ward, 1945.

———— *Religion and Culture.* New York: Sheed and Ward, 1948.

———— *Understanding Europe.* New York: Sheed and Ward, 1952.

DeLabriolle, P. *La Réaction Paienne: Etude sur la Polemique antichrétienne de Ier au VIe Siècle.* Paris: L'Artisan du Livre, 1948.

Dill, S. *Roman Society in the Last Century of the Western Empire.* London: Macmillan, 1910.

―――― *Roman Society from Nero to Marcus Aurelius.* Cleveland: Meridian, 1956.

Dillon, J. *The Middle Platonists.* Ithaca: Cornell University Press, 1977.

Dodds, E. R. *The Greeks and the Irrational.* Berkeley: University of California Press, 1964.

―――― *Pagan and Christian in an Age of Anxiety.* Cambridge: Cambridge University Press, 1965.

Doresse, J. *The Secret Books of the Egyptian Gnostics.* New York: Viking, 1960.

Dvornik, F. *Byzantium and the Roman Primacy.* New York: Fordam University Press, 1966.

―――― *Early Christian and Byzantine Political Philosophy.* 2 vols. Dumbarton Oaks Studies No. 9. Washington: Harvard University Press, 1966.

Ehrenberg, V. *The Greek State.* New York: Barnes and Noble, 1960.

Ehrhardt, A. *The Apostolic Succession in the First Two Centuries of the Church.* London: Lutterworth, 1953.

Ellspermann, G. L. *The Attitude of the Early Christian Writers toward Pagan Literature and Learning.* Washington: Catholic University Press, 1949.

Eno, R. B. *Teaching Authority in the Early Church: Message of the Fathers of the Church.* Wilmington, Pennsylvania: Glazier, 1984.

Eusebius Pamphili. *Evangelicae Praeparationes.* 4 vols. Trans. E. Gifford. London: Clarendon Press, 1903.

Evans, G. R. *Augustine on Evil.* New York: Cambridge University Press, 1983.

Fairweather, W. *Origen and Greek Patristic Theology.* Edinburgh: Clark, 1901.

Farnell, L. R. *The Works of Pindar.* London: Macmillan, 1930.

Faustus of Riez. *On Grace and Sermons.* Ed. A. Engelbrecht. *Corpus Scriptorum Ecclesiasticorum Latinorum.* Vol. 21. Vienna: Academy of Vienna, 1891.

Ferguson, J. *Pelagius: A Historical and Theological Study.* Cambridge: Heffer, 1956.

Festugiere, A. *La Révelation d'Hermes Trismegiste.* Paris: Lecoffre, 1954.

Finley, M. I. *Economy and Society in Ancient Greece.* New York: Penguin, 1983.

Fisher, G. P. *The History of Doctrines.* New York: Scribner, 1901.

Fox, R. G. *Pagans and Christians.* New York: Knopf, 1987.

Freeman, K. *Ancilla to the Presocratic Philosophers.* Oxford: Basil Blackwell, 1952.

Fuchs, E. *Das urchristliche Sakramentsverständnis.* Bad Cannstatt: Mullerschön, 1958.

Fustel de Coulanges. *The Ancient City.* Garden City: Doubleday, no date.

Gilson, E. *The Christian Philosophy of St. Augustine.* New York: Random House, 1960.

―――― *Reason and Revelation in the Middle Ages.* New York: Scribners, 1938.

Grant, R. M. *Gnosticism: A Source Book of Heretical Writings from the Early Christian Period.* New York: Harper, 1961.

―――― *Gnosticism and Early Christianity.* 2d. ed. New York: Columbia University Press, 1966.

Greene, W. C. *Moira: Fate, Good and Evil in Greek Thought.* New York: Harper & Row, 1963.

Greenslade, S. L. *Church and State from Constantine to Theodosius.* London: SCM, 1954.

Gregg, R. C. and Groh, D. E. *Early Arianism,* Philadelphia: Fortress, 1981.

Gregory of Nyssa. *Against Fate. Patrologiae, Series Graeca.* 45:146–71.

Guthrie, W. K. C. *In the Beginning: Some Greek Views on the Origins of Life and the Early State of Man.* Ithaca: Cornell University Press, 1957.

―――― *The Greek Philosophers.* New York: Harper and Row, 1960.

Hadas, M. *Hellenistic Culture.* New York: Columbia University Press, 1959.

Hagendahl, H. *Latin Fathers and the Classics.* Göteborg: Göteborg University Press, 1958.

Halliday, W. R. *The Pagan Background to Christianity.* Liverpool: Liverpool University Press, 1925.

Hanson, R. P. C. *Allegory and Event: A Study of the Sources and Significance of Origen in Interpreting of Scripture.* London: SCM, 1959.

Hardy, E. G. *Christianity and the Roman Government.* New York: Macmillan, 1925.

Harnack, A. *The Mission and Expansion of Christianity in the First Three Centuries.* 2 vols. Trans. J. Moffatt. New York: Putnam, 1908.

Hasebroek, J. *Trade and Politics in Ancient Greece.* New York: Biblio & Tannen, 1945.

Hatch, E. *The Influence of Greek Ideas on Christianity.* New York: Harper, 1957.

——— *The Organization of the Early Christian Churches.* London: Longmans Green, 1918.

Hawkins, D. J. B. *Being and Becoming.* New York: Sheed and Ward, 1954.

Hefele, C. J. *History of the Christian Councils.* 2d ed. 4 vols. Translated by W. R. Clark. Edinburgh: Clark, 1894.

Heitland, W. E. *Roman Fate.* Cambridge: Cambridge University Press, 1922.

Hengel, M. *Jews, Greeks and Barbarians: Aspects of the Hellenization of Judaism in the Pre-Christian Period.* Trans. J. Bowden. Philadelphia: Fortress, 1980.

——— *Judaism and Hellenism.* 2 vols. Trans. J. Bowden. Philadelphia: Fortress, 1974.

Henry, P. *Plotin et L'occident.* Louvain: Spicelegium Sacrum, 1934.

Hess, H. *The Canons of Sardica.* Oxford: Clarendon, 1958.

Highet, G. *The Classical Tradition.* Oxford: Clarendon, 1949.

Huttmann, M. A. *The Establishment of Christianity and the Proscription of Paganism.* New York: Columbia University Press, 1914.

Jaeger, W. *Early Christianity and Greek Paideia.* Cambridge, Mass.: Harvard University Press, 1961.

——— *Piadeia: the Ideals of Greek Culture.* 3 vols. New York: Oxford University Press, 1945.

——— *The Theology of the Early Greek Philosophers.* Oxford: Clarendon, 1948.

Jalland, G. G. *The Church and the Papacy.* London: Morehouse, 1944.

Jauncey, E. *The Doctrine of Grace.* London: SPCK, 1925.

Jeremias, J. *Infant Baptism in the First Four Centuries.* Trans. D. Cairns. London: SCM, 1960.

Jones, J. W. *The Law and Legal Theory of the Greeks.* Oxford: Clarendon, 1956.

Judge, E. A. *The Social Pattern of Christian Groups in the First Century.* London: Tyndale, 1960.

Kelly, J. N. D. *Early Christian Creeds.* London: Longsman, Green, 1952.

——— *Early Christian Doctrines.* 5th. ed. London: Adam & Black, 1977.

Kirschbaum, E. *The Tombs of Sts. Peter and Paul.* Translated by J. Murray. London: Secker and Warburg, 1959.

Kunkel, W. *An Introduction to Roman Legal and Constitutional History.* Oxford: Clarendon, 1966.

Laistner, M. L. W. *Christianity and Pagan Culture.* Ithaca: Cornell University Press, 1951.

——— *Greek Economics.* New York: Dutton, 1923.

——— *The Intellectual Heritage of the Early Middle Ages.* Ithaca: Cornell University Press, 1957.

Leclercq, J. *Aspects of Monasticism.* Translated by M. Dodd. Kalamazoo: Cistercian Publishing Co., 1978.

Leonard, W. E. *Fragments of Empedocles.* Chicago: Open Court, 1908.

Lietzmann, H. *From Constantine to Julian.* Translated by B. Woolf. New York: Scribner, 1950.

Loenen, D. *Protagoras and the Greek Community*. Amsterdam: Nord-Hollandsche Uitgevers, Maatschappij, 1941.

Lot, F. *The End of the Ancient World and the Beginnings of the Middle Ages*. Translated by P. Leon and M. Leon. New York: Knopf, 1931.

Marrou, H. *History of Education in Antiquity*. Translated by G. Lamb. New York: Sheed and Ward, 1956.

—————— *Saint Augustine and his Influence throughout the Ages*. Translated by E. Hill. New York: Harper, 1962.

—————— *Saint Augustine et La Fin de la Culture Antique*. Paris: DeBoccard, 1958.

McFayden, D. *Understanding the Apostles' Creed*. New York: Macmillan, 1927.

McGiffert, A. C. *A History of Christian Thought*. 2 vols. New York: Scribner, 1933.

McIlwain, C. H. *The Growth of Political Thought in the West*. New York: Macmillan, 1932.

MacMullen, R. *Christianizing the Roman Empire*. New Haven: Yale University Press, 1984.

Maritain, J. *True Humanism*. New York: Scribner, 1938.

Mattingly, H. *Roman Imperial Civilization*. Garden City: Doubleday, 1959.

Means, S. *St. Paul and the Ante-Nicene Church*. London: Black, 1903.

Meeks, W. A. *The First Urban Christians: the Social World of the Apostle Paul*. New Haven: Yale University Press, 1983.

Meyendorff, J. *Byzantine Theology*. New York: Fordam University Press, 1974.

Momigliano, A. *The Acts of the Pagan Martyrs*. Oxford: Clarendon Press, 1954.

—————— *The Conflict of Paganism and Christianity in the Fourth Century*. Oxford: Clarendon, 1963.

Morrison, K. F. "Rome and the City of God: an Essay on the Constitutional Relationships of Empire and Church in the Fourth Century." *Transactions of the Philosophical Society*. 54 (1964): 1–55.

Muntz, W. S. *Rome, St. Paul & the Early Church: The Influence of Roman Law on St. Paul's Teaching and Phraseology and on the Development of the Church*. Milwaukee: Young Churchman, 1913.

Murray, G. *Stoic, Christian and Humanist*. Boston: Beacon, 1950.

—————— *The Stoic Philosophy*. London: Watts, 1915.

The Nag Hammadi Library in English. Translated by Coptic Gnostic Library. Edited by J. W. Robinson. New York: Harper and Row, 1977.

Nemesius of Emesa. *On the Nature of Man*. Translated by W. Telfer. *Library of Christian Classics*. Vol. 4. Philadelphia: Fortress Press, 1955.

The New Testament in the Apostolic Fathers. By A Committee of the Oxford Society of Historical Theology. Oxford: Clarendon, 1905.

Nock, A. D. *Conversion: The Old and the New in Religion from Alexander the Great to Augustine of Hippo*. London: Oxford University Press, 1933.

—————— *Early Gentile Christianity and its Hellenistic Background*. New York: Harper and Row, 1964.

—————— *St. Paul*. New York: Harper, 1937.

Oates, W. J. *The Stoics and the Epicurean Philosophers*. New York: Random House, 1940.

O'Leary, J. S. *Questioning Back: The Overcoming of Metaphysics in Christian Tradition*. Minneapolis: Winston-Seabury Press, 1985.

Onians, R. B. *The Origins of European Thought*. London: Cambridge University Press, 1954.

Origen *Contra Celsum*. Translated by H. Chadwick. Cambridge: Cambridge University Press, 1965.

Palmer, P. F. *Sacraments and Forgiveness*. Westminster, Maryland: Newman, 1960.

Pelikan, J. *Development of Christian Doctrine.* 4 vols. New Haven and Chicago: Yale University and University of Chicago Presses, 1969–1984.

———— *The Christian Tradition.* Vols. 1 and 2. Chicago: University of Chicago Press, 1971.

Proclus Diadochus. *The Elements of Theology.* Translated by E. R. Dodds. Oxford: Clarendon Press, 1963.

Prosper of Aquitaine. *Defense of St. Augustine.* Trans. P. deLetter. *Ancient Christian Writers.* Vol. 32. Westminster, Maryland: Newman, 1963.

Rist, J. M. *The Stoic Philosophers.* Cambridge: Cambridge University Press, 1969.

Rist, M. "God of Abraham, Isaac, and Jacob." *Journal of Biblical Literature* 57 (1938): 289–303.

Ross, W. D. *Aristotle.* Oxford: Clarendon, 1926.

Runciman, S. *The Eastern Schism.* Oxford: Clarendon, 1955.

Sanders, E. P. *The Tendencies of the Synoptic Tradition.* London: Cambridge University Press, 1969.

Sayers, D. L. *The Emperor Constantine.* Grand Rapids: Eerdmans, 1976.

Schaff, P. *The Creeds of Christendom.* New York: Harper, 1919.

Schiller, F. C. S. *Studies in Humanism.* London: Macmillan, 1907.

Schmidt, C. G. A. *The Social Results of Early Christianity.* 2d. ed. Translated by Mrs. Thorpe. London: Isbister, 1889.

Schulz, F. *History of Roman Legal Science.* Oxford: Clarendon, 1953.

Seeberg, R. *History of Doctrine in the Ancient Church.* Vol. 1 of *Textbook of the History of Doctrines.* 2 vols. Trans. C. Hay. Philadelphia: Lutheran Publishing Co., 1905.

Setton, K. M. *Christian Attitude toward the Emperor in the Fourth Century.* New York: Columbia University Press, 1941.

Sherrard, P. *The Greek East and the Latin West: A Study in the Christian Tradition.* London: Oxford University Press, 1959.

Shorey, P. *What Plato Said.* Chicago: University of Chicago Press, 1933.

Shotwell, J. and Loomis, L. *The See of Peter.* New York: Columbia University Press, 1927.

Smith, T. V. ed. *From Aristotle to Plotinus.* Chicago: University of Chicago Press, 1959.

———— ed. *From Thales to Plato.* Chicago: University of Chicago, 1957.

Snell, B. *The Discovery of the Mind: The Greek Origins of European Thought.* Oxford: Blackwell, 1953.

Sokolowski, R. *The God of Faith and Reason: Foundations of Christian Theology.* Notre Dame, Indiana: University of Notre Dame Press, 1982.

Swift, E. *The Roman Sources of Christian Art.* New York: Columbia University Press, 1951.

Syme, R. *The Roman Revolution.* Oxford: Oxford University Press, 1982.

Symonds, H. *The Church Universal and the See of Rome.* New York: Macmillan, 1939.

Taylor, H. O. *Ancient Ideals.* 2 vols. New York: Macmillan, 1913.

———— *The Classical Heritage of the Middle Ages.* New York: Columbia University Press, 1903.

Theodoret of Cyrus. *Ten Discourses on Providence. Patrologiae. Series Graeca* 83:555–774.

Tillard, J. M. R. *The Bishop of Rome.* Wilmington, Delaware: Glazier, 1983.

Toffanin, G. *History of Humanism.* New York: Las Americas, 1954.

Trevor-Roper, H. *The Rise of Christian Europe.* New York: Harcort and Brace, 1965.

Trigg, J. W. *Origen: The Bible and Philosophy in the Third-century Church.* Atlanta: John Knox, 1983.

Troeltsch, E. *The Social Teaching of the Christian Churches.* New York: Macmillan, 1956.

Urquhart, W. P. *Humanism and Christianity.* Edinburgh: Clark, 1945.

von Balthasar, H. U. *Origen: Spirit and Fire.* Washington: Catholic University Press, 1984.

von Campenhausen, H. *The Fathers of the Greek Church.* New York: Pantheon, 1959.

—— *Formation of the Christian Bible.* Philadelphia: Fortress, 1972.

—— *Men Who Shaped the Western Church.* New York: Harper and Row, 1964.

Watkins, O. D. *History of Penance.* New York: B. Franklin, 1961.

Walsh, M. *The Triumph of the Meek.* San Francisco: Harper and Row, 1986.

Watson, A. *Rome of the Twelve Tables.* Princeton: Princeton University Press, 1975.

Weltin, E. G. *The Ancient Popes.* Westminster, Maryland: Newman, 1964.

—— "The Concept of Ex-opere-operato Efficacy in the Fathers as an Evidence of Magic in Early Christianity." *Greek, Roman, & Byzantine Studies* 3 (1960): 74–100.

—— "The Effect of Christianity on Civil Society as Envisaged by Origen." *The New Christianity* 17 (1951): 85–94.

Wendland, P. *Die Hellenistische-Römische Kultur in Ihren Beziehungen zu Judentum und Christentum.* Tübingen: Mohr, 1912.

Whittaker, T. *The Neo-Platonists: A Study in the History of Hellenism.* 2d. ed. with a supplement on the commentaries of Proclus. Cambridge: Cambridge University Press, 1918.

Wikenhauser, A. *Pauline Mysticism.* New York: Herder, 1960.

Wilkinson, L. F. *The Roman Experience.* New York: Knopf, 1974.

Williams, N. P. *Ideas of the Fall and of Original Sin.* London: Longmans Green, 1929.

Willis, J. R. ed. *The Teachings of the Church Fathers.* Montreal: Palm, 1966.

Wilson, R. M. *The Gnostic Problem.* London: Mowbray, 1958.

Winter, M. *St. Peter and the Popes.* Baltimore: Helicon, 1960.

Wright, W. R. *Empedocles: The Extant Fragments.* New Haven: Yale University Press, 1981.

Wolff, H. J. *Roman Law.* Norman, Oklahoma: University of Oklahoma Press, 1951.

Wolfson, H. A. *The Philosophy of the Church Fathers.* Cambridge: Harvard University Press, 1956.

Zeller, E. *The Stoics, Epicureans and Sceptics.* Translated by O. Reichel. London: Longmans Green, 1892.

—— *Outlines of the History of Greek Philosophy.* Cleveland: World Publishing, 1950.

Zimmern, A. *The Greek Commonwealth: Politics and Economics in Fifth-century Athens.* Oxford: Clarendon, 1931.

INDEX

Abortion, 46.

Actium, battle 31 B.C., 122.

Aeschylus, dramatist (524–456 B.C.), educational influence, 36; on wealth, 157; on fate, 191, 198.

Albinus, middle-Platonist (*f.* 150), 195, 205.

Alcmaeon, physician (*f.* 480 B.C.), 186.

Alexander, bishop of Alexandria (313–328), 135.

Alexander of Aphrodisias, Peripatetic philosopher (*f.* 200), on fate, 200, 201; 211, 218.

Alexander of Macedon (*f.* 336–324 B.C.), 29, 38, 151.

Allegory, 93–5.

Almsgiving, 168–70.

Ambrose, bishop of Milan (374–397), educational background, 12; and Classical culture, 15, 16, 19; on penance, 48; and the state, 56–7; on Scripture, 83, 90, 94; on saints, 100; *De officiis,* 104, 106; on miracles, 111; on sacraments, 135, 149, 167; on wealth, 168–9; 171; on original sin, 216; on works, 221.

Ammianus Marcellinus, historian (330–400), 11, 20, 170.

Ammonius Saccas, neo-Platonist (*d.* 242), 8, 102, 163, 209.

Anaxagoras, Ionian philosopher (*c.* 500–428 B.C.), 37, 61, 67, 71, 192.

Anaximander, Milesian philosopher (*c.* 610–547 B.C.), 74.

Anaximines, Milesian philosopher (585–525 B.C.), 64.

Antiochus of Ascalon, Academic philosopher (*d.* 68 B.C.), 8, 163.

Antiochus Epiphanes, Seleucid king (176–163 B.C.), 29.

Antisthenes, Cynic philosopher (445–365 B.C.), 27.

Antony, Roman triumvir (*f.* 43–30 B.C.), 26, 122, 161.

Antony, priest of Fussala (*f.* 420), 148.

Antony, Egyptian hermit (*c.* 251–356), 108.

Apiarius, priest of Sicca (*f.* 420), 148.

Apollinarius, bishop of Laodicea (*c.* 360–*c.* 390), and Apollinarianism, 47, 85, 176, 210, 218.

Apollonius of Tyana, neo-Pythagorean saint (*f.* 70), 8, 47, 73.

Apostolic Succession, 144, 145.

Appian, Greek historian (96–*c.* 165), 163.

Appius Claudius, Roman censor (*f.* 300 B.C.), 39, 117, 159

Aquila, Old Testament translator (*f.* 120–140), 92.

Archelaus of Athens, proto Sophist (*f.* 450 B.C.), 30, 39, 211.

Aristarchus of Samos, astronomer (310–230 B.C.), 63.

Aristides, Christian apologist (*f.* 175), on society, 50; 99, 104, 213.

Aristides, pagan scholar (*f.* 175), 7, 162.

Aristo of Pella, Christian apologist (*f.* 140), 77.

Aristobulus, Jewish philosopher, (*f.* 180 B.C.), 5, 95, 105.

Aristophanes, comedian (*c.* 450–*c.* 380 B.C.), educational influence, 13, 17, 36, 61; on gods, 73; 153.

Aristotle, Greek philosopher (384–322 B.C.), educational influence, 8; and heresy, 15, 84, 93, 98, 106, 176; 21, 23, 30; *Politics,* 24, 115; *Nichomachaean Ethics,* 24, 68, 187, 200; on law, 31, 114, 118; *Economics,* 33; and education, 36; on soul 43, 187; 62; *Organon,* 63; 70; *Metaphysics,* 74; *Constitution of Athens,* 116; 152, 155; on wealth, 157; 158, 182, 185; and fate, 192–93; *Physics,* 193; 196; humanism, 200, 201; 209; unmoved mover, 213; 219, 230, 231.

Aristotelianism (Peripatetic School), 65, 100, 103; and Christianity, 104–05; 200.

Aristoxenus, Aristotelian music theorist (*f.* 400 B.C.), 188.

Arius, heresiarch (*c.* 250–*c.* 336), and Arianism, 53, 54, 58, 84, 141, 145.